The Complete Guide to HUMAN RESOURCES and the LAW

Dana Shilling

2002 SUPPLEMENT

PRENTICE HALL

Library of Congress Cataloging-in-Publication Data

(Revised for Suppl.)
Shilling, Dana.
Complete guide to human resources and the law / Dana Shilling.
p. cm.
Includes index.
ISBN 0-13-092652-3
1. Labor laws and legislation—United States. 2. Personnel management—United States. I. Title.
KF3455.S55 1998 98-5107
344.7301—dc21 CIP

This publication is designed to provide accurate and authoritative information in regard to the subject matter covered. It is sold with the understanding that the publisher is not engaged in rendering legal, accounting, or other professional service. If legal advice or other expert assistance is required, the services of a competent professional should be sought.

—From a Declaration of Principles jointly adopted by a Committee of the American Bar Association and a Committee of Publishers and Associations.

Printed in the United States of America

10 9 8 7 6 5 4 3 2 1

ISBN 0-13-092652-3

PRENTICE HALL
Paramus, NJ 07652

On the World Wide Web at http://www.phdirect.com

Contents

Chapter 18 Labor Law—201

Chapter 19 Unemployment Insurance—213

Chapter 20 Worker's Compensation—217

Chapter 21 OSHA—227

Chapter 25 Family and Medical Leave Act (FMLA)—299

Chapter 26 The Age Discrimination in Employment Act—309

Chapter 27 Procedure for Discrimination Suits—319

Chapter 28 Wrongful Termination—335

Chapter 29 Corporate Communications—347

Chapter 30 Insurance Coverage for Claims Against the Employer—351

Chapter 31 Effect of Corporate Transitions on Liability—357

Chapter 32 Forms—373

Index—387

Introduction

The main volume of this work was published in 1998, by and large covering the events up to 1997. This is the third cumulative supplement, dealing in large part with 1998–2000 events, with a few detours for late 1997 developments and news from the first quarter of 2001.

Added to the main volume is Chapter 31, covering potential areas of employer liability if the corporation merges, is acquired, or otherwise goes through transition. There are also new sections and subsections through the supplement.

What trends emerged between publication of the main volume and the supplement? More Supreme Court involvement, for one thing; a surprising number of cases from the High Court are discussed here, although many involve public employers and not private enterprises. Of course, the lower courts continued to issue decisions, and administrative agencies such as the Internal Revenue Service (IRS) and National Labor Relations Board (NLRB) continued to issue rules. OSHA issued a highly controversial ergonomics rule.

The emerging areas of discussion and litigation include the Americans With Disabilities Act and Family and Medical Leave Act, especially in the disputed territory where the two statutes interact (and affect other areas of law, such as Worker's Compensation and wrongful termination). Retaliation cases became one of the leading subjects for antidiscrimination suits. The Supreme Court made it more likely that employers will be liable when quid pro quo sexual harassment occurs, thus making it more important than ever to maintain a meaningful program for preventing, detecting, and punishing harassment.

The "traditional" pension—the defined benefit plan—is no longer the "conventional" pension. Employers are showing much more interest in market-oriented plans such as the 401(k) and, especially, the cash-balance plan. Such plans shift much of the risk from employer to employee. Health plan trends also show greater employee copayment responsibilities, as well as a continuing shift from indemnity to managed care. However, it has become far more likely than before that managed care plans will be required to answer state-law claims and will not be held entitled to ERISA preemption. A brand-new form 5500 has been drafted, revolutionizing routine plan reporting.

One trend that emerged is the ever-increasing dominance of HR software, and especially the (public) Internet and corporate intranets in administering payroll and benefits and communicating with employees. Even companies that have no plans to engage in e-commerce are likely to find that many back office functions can be performed more efficiently and less expensively online.

You'll also note that many references and citations are made to online rather than print sources, because a few mouse clicks can bring you powerful information (often at no cost).

The year 2000 was a very unusual one in electoral politics. After all, whether or not you are pleased by the result, it's usually easy to tell shortly after a Presidential election who has been elected!

The transition from a Democratic to a Republic administration was not a particularly smooth or harmonious one. In particular, the last weeks of the Clinton Administration were marked by very intensive issuance of regulations, dealing with significant topics such as claims in health plans, SPDs and other notices, and privacy in employee health records.

Shortly after his inauguration, President Bush's Chief of Staff, Andrew Card, circulated a memorandum to the heads and acting heads of executive departments and agencies: see 66 FR 7701 (1/24/01). The department and agency heads were instructed not to send any final or proposed regulations to the Office of the Federal Register until the rules have been approved by the department head who will serve under the Bush administration. The agencies were also told to withdraw all regulations that had been sent to the Office of the Federal Register but had not yet been published.

The effective date of regulations that had been published but were not yet effective was postponed for 60 days, with an exception for emergency and urgent situations relating to health and safety and regulations that were promulgated pursuant to statutory or judicial deadlines.

According to Hewitt Associates ["Washington Status Reports—January 26, 2001," http://was.hewitt.com/hewitt/resource/wsr/20001-01-26-01/htm; no www.] the effective date was delayed on certain important regulations, such as IRS' minimum distribution rule, the joint IRS/DOL/HHS rules on applying the HIPAA nondiscrimination rules, and the regulations on qualified medical child support orders (QMCSOs).

However, certain regulations were not affected by the moratorium, because their effective date occurred while President Clinton was still in office. Regulations in this group include IRS Regs. on COBRA and cafeteria plans, the new rules on claims procedures and plan disclosures via SPDs and, perhaps the most controversial of all, OSHA's ergonomics final rule—but this rule did not take effect: See ¶21.8.

Once again, the purpose of this book is to communicate in plain English with nonattorney HR professionals, and to place developments in the legal system in the context of the practical issues faced by your counterparts throughout the United States.

Preface: EGTRA! EGTRA! Read All About It!

After the type for this Supplement had been set, Congress convened at a highly unusual Saturday session just before Memorial Day, 2001, in order to pass sweeping tax legislation, the Economic Growth and Tax Relief Reconciliation Act of 2001 (EGTRA), P.L. 107–16. This Preface summarizes the EGTRA provisions relating to employee benefits. The Second Edition of this book, scheduled for 2002, will incorporate a full discussion of pensions and benefits in the post-EGTRA environment.

There are also significant income tax provisions (including cuts in tax brackets and 2001 tax rebates) and estate tax provisions (gradual reduction in estate tax, leading to repeal in 2010) in the bill. However, all EGTRA provisions are somewhat temporary, because the entire statute sunsets in 2011 unless Congress chooses to renew it. That is, on January 1, 2011, all of the EGTRA provisions vanish as if they had never been enacted, and the Internal Revenue Code and ERISA go back to their pre-EGTRA status quo.

Many EGTRA provisions follow the same pattern: starting in a particular year (often 2002), a plan limit is increased. Further increases are scheduled for succeeding years, until a terminal year. After the terminal year, the amount in question is indexed (i.e., increased to reflect inflation)—but only if and when the indexing amount reaches a threshold such as $500 or $1000. Indexing will occur only in increments of that amount. Therefore, if the amount is $1,000, and the rate of inflation would otherwise call for an increase of $1,139, the amount will be increased by only $1,000.

It should also be noted that, although these issues are beyond the scope of this book, EGTRA makes major changes in the taxation of IRA accounts (including significantly increased contribution limits; a tax credit, over and above the tax deduction, for low-income IRA owners; effective for 2003 and later years, qualified plans are allowed to "facilitate" IRA contributions by employees) and 403(b) (non-profit organization/governmental) plans. The rules for the "top-heavy" plans often sponsored by small businesses have also been liberalized from the employer's point of view.

In this discussion, reference to, e.g., "E §611" means §611 of EGTRA; "Code" means the Internal Revenue Code.

PLAN LIMITS

Starting in 2002, the amount of compensation that can be taken into account in calculating plan benefits (E §611; Code §401(a)(17)) goes up to $200,000. In later years, it will be indexed in increments of $5,000.

The amount of elective deferrals (e.g., under 401(k) plans)) goes up to $11,000 in 2002 (under prior law, the limit was $10,500). For 2003, the amount is $12,000; for 2004; it's $13,000, for 2005; it's $14,000; and for 2006, it's $15,000, at which time it will be indexed in increments of $500.

For plan years that end after 12/31/01, the Code §415(b) limit on annual benefits that can be provided under a defined benefit plan goes up to $160,000, which will be indexed in increments of $5,000. Furthermore, it is no longer necessary to impose an actuarial reduction on the maximum benefit when a person retires between age 62 and age 65. The maximum annual contribution under a defined contribution plan goes up to $40,000 (it was $35,000 under prior law); it is indexed in increments of $1,000.

The total annual contribution to a defined contribution plan can be as high as $40,000 a year—and, furthermore, is no longer limited to 25% of compensation, as long as it does not exceed 100% of the employee's compensation. This provision is effective for years that begin (not years that end) after 12/31/01.

The contribution limit under a profit-sharing plan is increased to 25% of the employee's aggregate compensation. All money-purchase plans are subject to this limitation because, for this purpose, they are considered profit-sharing or stock bonus plans (E §616).

When the sponsoring corporation's tax deduction for a pension plan is being calculated, "compensation" includes elective deferrals made by the employee, e.g., to 401(k) plans.

The rule has always been that employees are always 100% vested in their own elective contributions to a pension plan. EGTRA §633 changes the vesting schedule for the employer's matching contributions that respond to the employee's elective contribution. Vesting must occur either on a three-year cliff schedule, or a six-year graded schedule, beginning with 20% vesting in the second year of the employee's service.

As ¶15.1.1 of this Supplement shows, the IRS proposed Regulations simplifying and liberalizing the rules for required minimum distributions from qualified plans (and IRAs) in January, 2001. EGTRA does not address this issue directly, but EGTRA §634 does mandate that the Treasury update its life expectancy tables to take into account increases in life expectancy.

401(k) CHANGES

EGTRA makes several quite significant changes to the 401(k) plan rules, probably because these plans are becoming more popular (and thus more significant in the overall picture of employees' retirement security) as employers seek to reduce their involvement in paying for pension and benefit plans. This is clearly a positive development for employers although it may reduce access to post-retirement income for employees who are not disciplined enough to engage in a long-term savings program via expanded IRAs and 401(k) plans, or whose current expenses make saving unfeasible.

Starting in 2006 (i.e., an even longer phase-in period than most of the EGTRA provisions), participants in 401(k) plans can treat the plans like Roth IRAs. See E §617, which adds a new §402A to the Code. That is, employees will be allowed to make contributions to the 401(k) plan, in the form of elective deferrals of part of their salary, that will be taxable income when they are made (unlike ordinary 401(k) elective deferrals) but will not be taxed when they are withdrawn.

This technique is referred to as a "qualified plus contribution program." To qualify for this tax relief, the employees must leave the elective-deferral contributions in the account for at least five years after they were contributed, and tax-free distributions can only be made after the plan participant reaches age 59 1/2 or becomes disabled (or to the participant's estate after his or her death).

The tax credit for low-income contributors is available for 401(k) plans as well as IRAs: see E §618. This is a non-refundable credit (i.e., the Treasury does not issue a refund check if the effect of the credit is to reduce tax liability below $0), with a maximum amount of $1,000 (50% of a $2,000 contribution).

The credit is set at 50% of the first $2,000 contributed to the 401(k) plan by a joint return filer whose income is under $30,000, phasing down to 10% of the first $2,000 contributed for joint return filers with income between $32,500 and $50,000. For single persons, the income limits are half those for joint return filers. The tax credit is available for tax years beginning after 12/31/01 and before 1/1/07.

Under EGTRA §636, employees who get hardship distributions from their 401(k) plans are not allowed to make elective deferrals or contributions to the plan within 6 months after getting a hardship distribution, and they are not allowed to roll over hardship distributions to another plan. In other words, hardship distributions must be treated as genuine emergency measures, not a way to enhance investment results.

In the pension context (as distinct from general employment law, where it usually refers to issues such as race and age) "discrimination testing" means the highly technical process of analyzing a plan to see if it provides too high a percentage of its benefits to "highly compensated employees" (HCEs) instead of to the rank-and-file workers. The Tax Reform Act of 1986 added a special definition of HCE to be used only for 401(k) plans. But EGTRA §663 repeals the special definition, so for plan years beginning after 12/31/01, HCEs are defined the same way for 401(k) plans as for ordinary qualified plans: as a 5% owner of the company, or a person who earned more than $85,000 in the previous year. Employers are allowed to elect a modification of the definition, restricting HCEs to people who not only earned $85,000 the year before, but were in the top 20% of employee compensation.

EGTRA §666 slightly simplifies the process of testing a 401(k) plan for discrimination, but it is such a technical provision that you should discuss it with your legal advisor or actuary.

ROLLOVERS BETWEEN PLANS

Another EGTRA objective, in response to an increasingly mobile work force, is to give employees additional flexibility to roll over amounts between plans. EGTRA §641 permits rollovers from qualified plans, 403(b) plans, and 457 (governmental) plans; IRA distributions can be rolled over into any one of these plans. However, to allow capital gains and income averaging, distributions from a qualified plan must be rolled over to a "conduit IRA" before being rolled over into a qualified plan, rather than just rolled over to the second qualified plan. Employees' after-tax contributions to 401(k) plans can be rolled over to a qualified plan or to an IRA. These provisions are effective for distributions made after 12/31/01.

Pre-EGTRA law required rollovers to occur within 60 days of receipt of funds from the first plan. EGTRA §644 does not abolish this rule, but does allow the IRS to extend the time limit if a casualty or disaster prevents the employee from carrying out the rollover within the 60-day limit.

Employers gain some flexibility under the EGTRA §631 rule that says that, if all employees who have reached age 50 are allowed to make catch-up contributions to 401(k) plans (the maximum catch-up contribution allowed for 2002 is $1,000, rising to $2,000 in 2003 and up to $5,000 in 2006, after which time the amounts will be indexed in increments of $500), the amount of the catch-up contributions will not be considered in calculating limits on contributions. Nor will the catch-up amounts be used in the calculations that determine whether or not the employer's plan discriminates in favor of highly compensated employees. This provision takes effect for taxable years beginning after 12/31/01.

In general, employers cannot force employees to accept a lump-sum distribution from the plan if the employees prefer an annuity or other distribution form offered by the plan. The exception, under Code §411(a)(11), is the small balance (under $5,000) that would be too burdensome for employers to administer. EGTRA §648 provides that the employer can exclude rollovers to the plan, and earnings on the rollovers, when determining whether the employee's plan balance is more or less than $5,000. Also see EGTRA §657 for rules about rolling over the de minimis amounts distributed when employees are "cashed out" of a plan.

EMPLOYER'S DEDUCTION

One of the most powerful incentives for a company to maintain pension and other deferred compensation plans is the availability of an income tax deduction for the costs associated with the plan. Therefore, increases in the size of the available deduction tend to be pro-employer.

Before EGTRA, Code §404 provided that the employer's deduction for a defined benefit plan is the plan's minimum funding cost for the year; for plans with 100 or more participants, the deduction would be at least equal to the plan's unfunded current liabilities. For profit-sharing and stock bonus plans, the §404 deduction equaled 15% of the compensation for the year of the employees covered by the plan. The deduction was limited when the employer sponsored both a defined benefit and a defined contribution plan (or multiple defined contribution plans, including at least one money purchase plan).

Furthermore, elective deferrals by employees (generally, under 401(k) plans) were treated as employer contributions, thus reducing the amount that the employer could deduct. This was especially critical because a 10% excise tax was imposed on non-deductible (i.e., excessive) contributions to the plan.

However, because of EGTRA §614, for years beginning after 12/31/01, employees' elective deferral contributions to plans are not considered when the deduction limits are calculated—i.e., they do not reduce the amount that the employer can deduct. EGTRA §616(b) provides that the employee's "compensation" includes these elective deferrals, so they may increase the amount that the employer contributes on the employee's behalf, even though the employee does not have taxable income on account of the salary reductions.

FUNDING LIMITATION

An important objective of the Internal Revenue Code and ERISA provisions about defined benefit plans, backed up by PBGC insurance, is making sure that the plans have enough assets to satisfy the plan's obligations to pay benefits. (This is not an issue for defined contribution plans, because there is a separate account for each employee, and the retiree's pension entitlement depends on the investment results of the account.)

Pre-EGTRA law included a definition of "full funding limitation"—i.e., the amount that the employer was required to contribute in order to keep the plan sound—consisting of two components. Before EGTRA, this was defined as the plan's accrued liability, or 160% of its current liability (whichever is smaller) minus its assets. EGTRA §651 increases the current liability full funding limit to 165% of current liability for plan years that begin in 2002, and to 170% for plan years that begin in 2003—but repeals the current liability full funding limit for plan years that begin between 2004 and 2010. (Remember, all of the provisions of EGTRA sunset at the end of 2010.) Therefore, for plan years between 2004 and 2010, the full funding limit is simply the difference between the plan's accrued liability and the value of its assets.

ERISA RULES ELIMINATED

EGTRA eliminates two ERISA rules that employers often found burdensome. The anti-cutback rule (incorporated in ERISA §204(h)) required that, when benefits are transferred to a new plan (e.g., in conjunction with a corporate transition), all the prior forms of distribution had to be made available under the new plan. But EGTRA §645 provides that, if the employee elects to transfer the benefits, and the participant could have elected a lump-sum payout, then optional benefit forms can be eliminated from the successor plan. EGTRA also streamlines plan administration by permitting elimination of certain optional benefit forms, as long as lump sums are still available, and the rights of participants are not adversely affected. The Department of the Treasury is ordered to issue final regulations by 12/31/03 to carry out these new rules.

Also see EGTRA §659, which adds a new Section 4980F to the Code, imposing a penalty of $100 a day for failure to provide adequate notice to participants of significant reductions in the rate of future benefit accruals. That is, employers retain the right to modify their plans (unless they are scofflaws about notice requirements) but will be penalized for failure to give employees the appropriate notice.

The "same desk" rule provides that distributions cannot be made to a terminated employee who has been re-hired and continues to perform the same job functions for a successor employer. For distributions after 12/31/01, EGTRA §646 repeals this rule for 401(k), 403(b), and 457 plans (but NOT for conventional employer-sponsored qualified plans). Note that repeal refers to the date that the distribution was made, not the date when the individual stopped working for the initial employer.

RETIREMENT ADVICE

The Code includes a long list of fringe benefits that can be provided by the employer without generating taxable income for the employee. EGTRA §665 adds another one: "qualified retirement planning services" (retirement planning advice and information) provided to employees and spouses under an employer-sponsored plan that does not discriminate in favor of HCEs. But tax preparation, accounting, legal, and brokerage services don't qualify. This section is effective for plan years that begin after 12/31/01.

Chapter 1

THE HIRING PROCESS

1.5 RECRUITING IN A COMPETITIVE ENVIRONMENT

In a competitive environment within a mobile society, it's not only a challenge to recruit a good workforce, it can be tough to retain employees. Another job offer, the need to move to accompany a spouse, or simple dissatisfaction can trigger high turnover.

Not every employee is a paragon, of course, and it may seem easier to allow employees to drift away than to fire them (and worry about potential liability). But even an employee who earns only $30,000 a year in straight salary costs the company close to $40,000 a year (once taxes and benefits are taken into account), plus recruitment and training costs and the initial period of diminished productivity as the new hire gains expertise. So reducing turnover even of unexceptional employees is helpful.

Companies can improve recruitment and retention by adopting a more structured approach. As new jobs are created, or jobs open up, the manager who will supervise the new hire should complete a formal requisition:

- Job title
- Why it has to be filled
- Why the job is required at all—could the functions be delegated among existing employees, outsourced, or assigned to part-timers or temporary employees?
- Hiring date
- Degree of priority for hiring
- Special qualifications required
- Formal job description, or changes in the existing description

Job descriptions and interview questions should be reviewed for compliance with the American with Disabilities Act (ADA) and other antidiscrimination laws. Before the offer is extended, at least a basic background check should be done, such as checking references provided by the candidate and consulting objective sources of information. (These suggestions come from James T. Ryan, "Avoid Hit-or-Miss Hiring," *HR Magazine*, "Focus," 11/98, p. 23.)

➠ TIP

Remember that, to the extent that credit-related information is investigated, the provisions of the Fair Credit Reporting Act must be obeyed (see ¶1.11 in the main volume).

In 1997, only 30% of companies offered signing bonuses. By 1999, with unemployment very low and competition for managerial and technical talent very fierce, 44% of managers responding to an American Management Association survey provided such bonuses in 1999. In fact, bonuses were paid at all levels of the organization, not just the top. A one-time bonus can work better than a higher pay level, because it is an incentive during the negotiating process. Best of all, it doesn't inflate the new hire's compensation package in the long run, and doesn't raise the salary and benefits for the new hire's entire pay grade.

Probably the best incentive is obtained by paying the bonus in a lump sum, rather than in installments, although if the objective is to prevent turnover, it makes sense to pay part of the bonus after a certain number of months of satisfactory work. A common tactic is to have the employee sign an agreement that makes the bonus repayable to the company if the employee leaves in less than 12 months (perhaps two years for executives who receive five-figure bonuses).

Bonuses are taxable compensation income, but some companies accept the burden of paying the taxes themselves, fearing that the goodwill effect would be lost if the employee saw part of the bonus disappear in the form of withheld taxes. (See Andrea C. Poe, "Signing Bonuses: A Sign of the Times," *HR Magazine*, 9/99, p. 104.)

As more people gain Web access, at home, at the office, or in public places such as libraries and airports, Internet recruiting becomes a greater factor. A truly nationwide (and even worldwide) pool can be accessed.

Many of the costs of recruiting, such as Help Wanted advertising, can be reduced or eliminated. Now that thousands of people have posted their resumes online, the HR department can do a rapid screening of resumes and target the best candidates, without offending anyone or hurting anyone's feelings. In-house recruitment departments can adopt some tactics usually used by headhunters.

Although it might be considered unethical to make an effort to recruit employees from a competitor, there is no ethical problem if the employees have already voluntarily posted their resumes to a job site on the World Wide Web. Sherry Kuczynski makes this point in "You've Got Job Offers," *HR Magazine,* 3/99, p. 51. (Resume posters have taken at least a small affirmative step toward getting a new job, so it is easier to scan the resume database and find a good match than to publish a Help Wanted ad and hope that the right person will read it.)

In fact, an automated voice mail system, known as IVR (for interactive voice response), can mechanize the early stages of the recruitment process. Applicants call a toll-free telephone number and answer a series of questions to indicate whether they have the basic qualifications for the job. If they fit the profile, the system can direct them to send in a resume or schedule an in-person job interview. (See Ruth E. Thaler-Carter, "Reach Out and Hire Someone," *HR Magazine,* 5/99, p. 8.) Applicants like the flexibility of the system (and those who already have jobs can call from home, outside normal working hours!). The HR department will have to review the responses, and the phone time itself can be expensive: The average IVR call costs the employer about $4 (an eight-minute phone call at 50 cents a minute).

Users of Web recruiting tools say that the company's own Web page, listing job openings, is the best tool for this purpose, followed by sites that create a database by allowing candidates to post their resumes, links to the company's Web page, coordination with recruiters, and job listings in Web sites for job hunters. (Ruth E. Thaler-Carter, "Recruiting Through the Web: Better or Just Bigger?" *HR Magazine,* 11/98, p. 61.)

However, the availability of the Web doesn't eliminate the need for headhunters and search services, especially when a top job has to be filled and finding the right candidate is crucial. In those cases, it often makes sense to use the Web to communicate with the search service—and let the headhunters use their own Web tools to narrow down the candidate pool.

Unless you hire only immigrants newly arrived in this country (which carries with it its own set of problems!) or recent graduates with no work experience, at least some of your new hires will come from other businesses. Because you want relevant experience, the odds are that some of your new hires will previously have been employed by competitors, and some of them will have been actively recruited.

In a worst-case scenario, your competitor will charge you with wrongfully inducing employees to leave their jobs and come to work for you—perhaps in violation of covenants not to compete, or perhaps giving you access to confidential customer lists and trade secrets. Recently, for instance, Wal Mart accused amazon.com of luring away skilled merchandisers, and a department store sued an executive recruiter for interfering with employment contracts. (See Joseph E. Bachelder III, "Inducing an Executive to Change Jobs," *New York Law Journal,* 3/29/99, p. 3.)

In the worst part of the worst-case scenario, you might be forced to pay a competitor's lost profits as well as its costs of recruiting its own new executive. But that would require proof that you interfered improperly with an employment contract.

There is very little chance that an individual acting on behalf of his or her corporation would be subjected to personal liability for "luring away" a competitor's executive, but the hiring corporation itself might be liable.

> **TIP**
>
> An important part of any high-level interview (or the screening process performed by a recruiting firm you have retained) is to make sure that either there is no express or implied contract, or that hiring the candidate would not violate it.

Courts recognize the need to stay competitive by attracting top talent. Just make sure that you use accepted channels (including the Internet), not surreptitious targeting of competitors' executives. It's best if the position is open to a wide range of candidates, not the smaller fishpond of competitors' staffs! Make it clear that you are offering a position based on the individual's experience and transferable skills, not his or her potential for industrial espionage.

1.7 NONDISCRIMINATORY HIRING

A male social worker's sex discrimination claims, challenging the employer's subjective interview practices, failed in *Scott v. Parkview Memorial Hospital*, 67 LW 1720 (7th Cir. 4/23/99). The plaintiff claimed that the interview process unfairly favored women because it favored traditionally feminine qualities such as warmth and empathy. However, the Seventh Circuit viewed subjective interviews as a necessary part of professional recruitment and, furthermore, found that the qualities that were useful in the interview were also useful in performing the job, so the interview practice was valid and job-related.

In a March 1999 article ("Build a Legal Employment Application," *HR Magazine*, 3/99, p.129), Timothy S. Bland and Sue S. Stalcup suggest that it can be worthwhile to indicate on every job application form that the form will be rejected if the applicant includes extraneous information not requested on the application. That's because some applicants use the unwanted information tactically: They include it, then if they are not hired, they use the information as a premise for a discrimination charge. For instance, unsolicited information about union activism could be used against the company, if the inference is believed that the company refuses to hire union activists.

Some states (typically Southern states in which tobacco growing is a major economic activity) forbid employment discrimination on the basis of smoking, so outright asking applicants if they smoke could create legal problems. However, if your workplace is smoke free, or if smoking is restricted to designated smoking areas, it makes sense to disclose your policy and let applicants decide whether or not they can measure up.

1.9 IMMIGRATION AND HIRING PRACTICES

1.9.3 Employment Verification Documents

See 63 FR 5287 (2/2/98) for an Immigration and Naturalization Service (INS) Proposed Rule reducing from 29 to 13 the number of documents that will be accepted for verification of employment eligibility. In some circumstances, a newly hired individual can provide a receipt for a document rather than the original document itself.

Employers can complete the Form I-9 either at the time of hiring or before hiring (once a commitment to hire has been made). However, the form must be completed at the same point in the employment process for all employees.

The Proposed Rule includes a new Form I-9A, for reverification of employment eligibility that has already been established.

The full text of the Proposed Rule can also be found at http://www.ins.usdoj.gov.

1.9.4 H-1B Visas

The American Competitiveness and Workforce Improvement Act, P.L. 105-277, increased the number of visas that can be issued in fiscal year (FY) 1999–2001 to highly skilled immigrants undertaking temporary positions.

The H-1B visa is a nonimmigrant visa for temporary workers in "specialty occupations"—jobs that apply a highly specialized body of knowledge in both a theoretical and practical way. Most H-1B visa holders work in high-tech businesses, such as software development. The initial duration of an H-1B visa is three years, although it can be extended for three more years.

H-1B workers must have at least a bachelor's degree in their specialty or must have equivalent qualifications and expertise. If the job requires a state license, the H-1B visa holder must have the license.

H-1B workers must be paid either the salary the employer would otherwise pay for the job or the prevailing wage in the area. (Of course, this is required to deprive employees of an incentive to hire a foreign workers simply to lower wage costs.) Willful violation of this requirement or violation of the layoff requirement (see later in this chapter) can be penalized by a $35,000 fine and three years of debarment from federal contracts.

In practical terms, even the expanded number of these visas is less than the demand, so if you want to hire an H-1B worker, it makes sense to start early in the year. The quota is usually filled midway through the year, and visa processing takes several months. (The fiscal year begins in October, so applications can be made as of October 1 for the following year.)

The problem is that employers usually recruit workers from foreign students, who are in this country holding student visas and are about to graduate from a college or graduate program that gives them their specialized skills. But immigration law requires employers to wait until the student graduates before offering him or her a job. You can get around this problem by having the student get permission from the Immigration and Naturalization Services to add a year of PGPT (postgraduate practical training) to his or her student visa, so you can apply for the H-1B visa during this extra year.

Dan Hartsfield, Rodney A. Malpert, and Amanda Petersen's article "H-1B Visas for 'Specialty' Workers" (*National Law Journal*, 4/19/99, p. B5) explains these techniques. Also see "Labor Department Proposal Sets Out Employer Requirements Under the New H-1B Law," 67 LW 2391 (1/12/99).

People with student visas must leave the United States by July of the year in which they graduate, unless they have PGPT authorization. (Of course, many students remain and work in this country illegally, but this is not only unethical but a potential source of liability for the employer.)

ACWIA Regulations

The American Competitiveness and Workforce Improvement Act of 1998 (ACWIA), as amended in October 2000, modifies the H-1B visa process. On December 20, 2000, the DOL published interim final regulations implementing these changes: 65 FR 80109-80158 (12/20/00). [Also see the DOL OPA Press Release, 12/19/00, http://www.dol.gov/dol/esa/public/media/press/whd/opa 2000375.htm and Fact Sheet No. 042, Publication of Interim Final H-1B Regulations, http://www.dol.gov/esa/public/regs/compliance/whd/whdfs42. htm.]

The H-1B visa quota for the fiscal years 2001, 2002, and 2003 is set at 195,000 a year. Until October 1, 2003, "non-displacement" requirements are imposed on employers who are H-1B dependent or who have already violated the visa rules. An H-1B dependent employer is one that derives 15% or more of its work force from this source.

The non-displacement rule is that H-1B visa holders may not be hired until the employer has first attempted to recruit qualified U.S. workers, although a more qualified H-1B applicant can lawfully be hired instead of a less-qualified American. Employers are also forbidden to fire U.S. workers in order to replace them with H-1B workers, and temporary agencies and other suppliers of contingent workers are forbidden to make any placements of H-1B workers with a company that has displaced U.S. workers.

In addition to measures intended to protect the interests of U.S. workers, the December, 2000 rule includes protection for the foreign workers. They must be given benefits on the same basis as their U.S. counterparts. Whenever their employer places them in a non-productive category (e.g., a temporary lull in work), they must be kept at full salary. It is unlawful for employers to require H-1B workers to reimburse them for the cost of filing the employment petition, or to penalize workers for terminating their work assignment prematurely.

In order to encourage reporting of misconduct, protection is extended to applicants, employees, and ex-employees who assist the Departments of Labor and Justice in investigations. In fact, H-1B whistleblowers can be permitted to remain in the U.S. for up to six years.

The December, 2000 rule also makes procedural changes, such as phasing in a fax-back processing system for Form ETA 9035 labor condition applications. Employers with online access can download the new three-page form ETA 9035 and the ETA 9035CP, which includes instructions. The completed form should be faxed to (800) 395-0478. The employer attaches the official copy of the approved LCA to the Form I-129 (Petition for H-1B Non-immigrants) that is filed with the INS. Any rejected applications will be returned by the DOL, with an explanation of the reason for the denial.

NLRB Memo

On December 4, 1998, Fred Feinstein, the general counsel of the National Labor Relations Board, issued Memorandum GC 98-15, entitled "Reinstatement and Backpay Remedies for Discriminatees Who May be Undocumented Aliens in Light of Recent Board and Court Precedent." This Memorandum GC 98-15 can be found at http://www.nlrb.gov/gcmemo/gc98-15.html.

The purpose of the memo is to inform NLRB regional directors and their subordinates of current policy for dealing with discrimination charges filed by noncitizens who are not legally permitted to work in the United States. On the one hand, the NLRB is opposed to employment discrimination; on the other hand, the Immigration Reform and Control Act of 1986 makes it unlawful to hire or continue to employ an undocumented alien worker.

The NLRB's basic statement on this issue is *A.P.R.A. Fuel Oil Buyers Group*, 320 NLRB 408 (1995), enforced by 134 F.3d 50 (2nd Cir. 1997). The NLRB allowed undocumented aliens to bring charges of wrongful discharge on the basis of union activity, and awarded them back pay, but also conditioned their reinstatement on their proof of authorization to work in the United States. The NLRB memorandum advises its regional offices to seek an unconditional reinstatement order in similar cases. The exception is the situation in which the employer makes an affirmative showing that the complainant is not authorized to work in the United States. In such cases, it is the NLRB policy to seek conditional reinstatement.

A.P.R.A. did not resolve the situation in which the employer hired, then improperly fired, a person without knowledge of the fired person's employment status. The rule of *Hoffman Plastic Compounds, Inc.*, 326 NLRB No. 86 (9/23/98), is that the fired worker was not entitled to reinstatement (because, as it turned out, he was not authorized to work in the United States). Eligibility for back pay was tolled at the point that the employer discovered the worker's undocumented status.

However, undocumented status, while it reduces the remedies available to the discriminatee, does not exempt the employer from scrutiny of its conduct. According to Feinstein's memorandum, the employer's evidence about the complainant's immigration status is irrelevant to an unfair labor practice hearing and cannot be admitted. In a compliance proceeding, where the issue of reinstatement arises, the employer may be able to introduce evidence about work authorization status. This is permitted only if the employer has a reasonable basis, independent of the compliance proceeding, to claim that the discriminatee is not authorized to work in the United States. The NLRB "would object to the compliance proceeding being used as a fishing expedition to try to determine whether someone is unlawfully in the country." The NLRB's position is that questioning a complainant about immigration status violates IRCA's antidiscrimination provisions (8 USC §1324b(a)(6)).

EEOC, DOJ MOU

See 63 FR 5518 (2/3/98) for the Memorandum of Understanding (MOU) between the EEOC and the Department of Justice's Office of Special Counsel for Immigration Related Unfair Employment Practices. Under the MOU, each agency can act as the other's agents to receive complaints about immigration-related discrimination charges. The two agencies will coordinate to avoid duplication of effort.

In response to immigration-law changes, the two agencies will treat document abuse, intimidation, and retaliation as immigration-related unfair labor practices and will accept pattern or practice charges. The EEOC has agreed not to ask if the charging party is a U.S. citizen, national, or work-authorized alien as a condition for referring charges to the Department of Justice (DOJ). When wage and hour or Office of Federal Contract Compliance inspections are made, I-9 forms will not be inspected. The text of the MOU can be found at http://www.ins.doj.gov/public%5Faffairs/news%5Freleases/laborbg.htm.

> **TIP**
>
> It should be noted, however, that the full Fourth Circuit reversed its earlier three-judge panel decision and now holds that only a citizen, or an alien with a valid work visa, is a "qualified" employee. Therefore, an undocumented alien cannot make out a Title VII prima facie case: *Egbuna v. Time-Life Libraries Inc.*, 153 F.3d 184 (4th Cir. 1998).

Later, the EEOC placed its position on treatment of undocumented workers on record in "Enforcement Guidance on Remedies for Undocumented Workers Under Laws Prohibiting Employment Discrimination," No. 915.002 (10/26/99), available at www.eeoc.gov/docs/undoc.html. The EEOC position is that undocumented workers who suffer discrimination contrary to Title VII, the ADEA, ADA, or EPA can be entitled to back pay, hiring, and reinstatement, if this can be granted without direct conflict with IRCA and other immigration laws.

Therefore, for undocumented workers hired before the IRCA effective date, hiring and reinstatement remedies are available. Post-IRCA hires can be entitled to remedies unless the employer knew that they were not eligible for work in the U.S. If the employer did know, hiring and reinstatement remedies are available only for individuals who are now able to provide work documentation.

"Employers may no more discriminate against unauthorized workers than they may discriminate against any other employees" (Guidelines at p. 3.) The NLRB mentions *Egbuna* in a footnote, but simply says that it disagrees with the Fourth Circuit.

The EEOC's analysis is that the purpose of federal antidiscrimination remedies is to discourage employers from discriminating, and also to recompense workers for discrimination they have suffered. It's so important to create disincentives for discrimination that discrimination victims can get at least some remedies even if they themselves have been guilty of some kind of wrongdoing. On the other hand, the purpose of immigration laws is to deter illegal immigration, a purpose that can be served without exculpating employers who discriminate.

In the EEOC view, injunctions and other remedies forbidding future discrimination are compatible with immigration laws. Sometimes, however, awarding back pay and damages will not be proper because it will conflict with immigration laws. But otherwise, IRCA can be harmonized with Title VII and other employment laws by awarding remedies to workers who have been discriminated against. In this reading, the employer is liable for back pay, except for periods when the undocumented worker was outside the United States, or except for the situation in which the worker is either reinstated or unable to demonstrate work eligibility within a reasonable period of time after being offered a job or reinstatement.

However, remedies can be limited if the worker's undocumented status represented part of an employer's mixed motive, or if the worker's true status was after-acquired evidence for the employer. Only attorneys' fees and injunctive relief, not reinstatement, back pay, or damages, are available in mixed-motive cases.

The EEOC also takes the view that employers are never justified in using a worker's undocumented status as a rationale for discriminatory terms of employment or failure to promote, so back pay is appropriate in all such cases. Employers are also liable to retaliation damages if they reported, or threatened to report, undocumented workers to the INS to punish them for enforcing their rights as employees.

See *Granados v. Windson Development Corp.*, 257 Va. 103, 509 S.E.2d 290 (1999): an illegal alien is not an "employee" for Worker's Compensation purposes, and therefore cannot receive Comp benefits for an on-the-job injury.

1.10 ADA COMPLIANCE IN HIRING

Even if a job applicant is not disabled, he or she can bring suit under the ADA if employment is denied on the basis of the applicant's answers to pre-employment inquiries that are made improperly and in violation of the ADA: *Griffin v. Steeltek Inc.*, 160 F.3d 591 (10th Cir. 1998).

An EEOC opinion letter, dated January 31, 2000, tackles the situation in which it is decided to reassign a qualified disabled employee to a vacant job, in order to provide reasonable accommodation—and other candidates, including minority and female candidates, therefore are not offered the job. The company requesting the opinion letter asked if the manager or supervisor who interviewed the candidates can be informed of the reasonable accommodation motivation for selecting the disabled candidate. The EEOC said that the ADA's confidentiality requirements are not violated by "informing the manager/supervisor that an employee with a disability is to receive the position as a reassignment, regardless of whether the other candidate was equally or better qualified." However, the manager should be given only enough information to make sure that the disability is properly accommodated, and should be warned to keep that information confidential. ["EEOC Says Accommodation Takes Priority Over Affirmative Action,"http://www.lawnewsnetwork.com/practice/employmentlaw/news/A15911-2000Feb10.html.]

1.14 [NEW] REFERENCE CHECKS

Texas tort (negligence) law does not obligate an employer to report an employee's embezzlement to law enforcement authorities, or warn the new employer (even though the employee embezzled again in her new job). The theory of *San Benito Bank & Trust Co. v. Landair Travels*, 69 LW 1139 (Tex. App. 8/24/00) is that the first employer no longer controlled her actions, so there was no duty to prevent future crimes. In fact, even a current employer is not expected to prevent off-duty wrongdoing by employees.

Chapter 2

EMPLOYEE HANDBOOKS

2.2 LEGAL IMPLICATIONS OF THE HANDBOOK

A trend reported in 1998 was for unions to challenge the language of employee handbooks (as well as to challenge workplace rules)—and for NLRB regional offices to view these challenges favorably. The case of *Lafayette Park Hotel*, 326 NLRB No. 69 (1998), shows the way in which a union's challenge to one handbook provision can open the door to NLRB examination of the handbook as a whole. In this case, the handbook included a ban on false, vicious, profane, or malicious statements about the hotel or its employees. The NLRB struck down this rule, on the grounds that employees were not given adequate notice of what constituted improper conduct. But once it looked at that rule, the NLRB also invalidated another rule, requiring employees to leave the premises as soon as they finished their shift. This rule was unacceptable because it denied access to nonwork areas such as the parking lot.

An article by New Jersey attorney A. Michael Weber ("Unions Challenge Employee Handbook Language," *National Law Journal*, 2/8/99, p. S7) also discusses earlier NLRB cases in which the NLRB allowed employees to discuss wage and benefit information with the union during contract negotiations, despite a work rule prohibiting disclosure of confidential information; and a work rule banning "derogatory" statements could not be enforced to prevent the union from making truthful statements that questioned the medical care provided by the employer, a hospital.

Two Indiana workers were fired when a supervisor found them up on the plant roof—and there was a smell of marijuana in the attic through which the roof was reached. The employees said that they had been ordered up to the roof to clean the gutters (and were probably telling the truth). They sued the employer because the grievance procedures set out in the handbook were not observed before firing them. But they lost their case; it didn't even go to trial, because summary judgment was granted.

In Indiana, handbook provisions create a contract only if the employee provided some consideration other than merely taking the job. Anyway, the handbook didn't promise that the procedures would be followed in every case—in fact, it said that immediate dismissals could occur when necessary. [*Orr v. Westminster Village North, Inc.*, 1997 Westlaw 769409 (Indiana 1997)].

A Texas court took a very different view. A newly recruited employee was concerned about whether the job would be permanent. She was told that she could keep the job as long as she continued to perform well. Nevertheless, she was fired. A Texas court said that she had an oral contract permitting termination only for good cause. After her hiring, the employer issued a handbook informing all employees that they worked at will. To the court, this was not determinative, because the handbook itself said that handbook provisions did not have contractual status [*Doctors' Hospital of Laredo Limited Partnership v. Dromgoole*, 1998 Westlaw 75554 (Tex. App. 1998)].

In May 1999, an Arizona court decided that handbook provisions requiring good cause for termination became implied-in-fact contracts with the employees. Therefore, even though the handbook contained a provision stating that it did not constitute an employment contract, and even though the employer reserved the right to amend the handbook, the employer lost the power to alter the provisions unilaterally. Employees had to be notified, and to give their individual consent, for the changes to become operative: *Demasse v. ITT Corp.*, 67 LW 1725 (Ariz. 5/25/99).

A Washington court ruled that a handbook case was properly dismissed because it was brought too late. The employee claimed that the statute of limitations should have been six years, because the action was based on a written contract (i.e., the handbook itself). The court rejected this argument, because the employee handbook was a general document and did not relate to the specific facts of the employee's job with the company. The employee's next argument was that, because spoken (parol) evidence was needed to interpret the handbook, the statute of limitations should have been three years (the correct one for a partly written, partly oral contract). The court denied this argument too, because even if parol evidence can be introduced to interpret a contract (many contracts have an integration clause that rules out parol evidence), such testimony does not make the contract partly oral. The employee's claim was really one based on a promise of specific treatment in a specific situation. Reliance on a handbook provision is really a tort claim, not a contract claim, so contract concepts don't apply. The case is *DePhillips v. Zolt Construction Co.*, 136 Wash.2d 26, 959 P.2d 1104 (Wash. 1998).

Chapter 4

WORK–FAMILY ISSUES

4.1 INTRODUCTION

According to Faith Wohl, President of the Child Care Action Campaign, less than 10% of U.S. businesses offer any child care assistance to employees, and even companies that do take some role usually limit it to providing some discounts and information about child care programs. She says that the private sector pays only 1% of the overall costs of child care, with 49% coming from all levels of government and the rest paid by parents out-of-pocket.

The article where she is interviewed, "Seeking the Right Child Care Formula," (by Mary Williams Walsh; *NYT* 9/13/00 p. G1) reports that Marriott was unsuccessful in operating day care centers for its employees in Atlanta, because employees found it difficult to pay the $110-$135 weekly cost, and government subsidies involved too much paperwork. Marriott still operates day care centers, but now accepts that most of the children enrolled will not be the children of their own employees.

For a discussion of the corporate role in providing adoption assistance, see Gregory Weaver, "A Great Little Perk," *Indianapolis Star* 11/20/00, available at http://www.starnews.com/business/articles/adopt1120.html. The national average of such benefits, for the 31% of employers (according to a Hewitt Associates survey) who provide them, is $3,000. This is not an expensive benefit for the employer, because only about half of 1% of employees use it, but it creates a lot of good will.

A company that has every reason to be interested, Atlas Van Lines, performs an annual survey of corporate relocation policies. See http://www.atlasvanlines.com/survey. The 2000 survey shows that the strong majority of employees offered relocation accepted the offer, but 87% of rejections cited family reasons as a factor, and 65% mentioned the spouse's job. Sixty percent of relocations involved a spouse, and only 38% of companies in Atlas' survey offer employment assistance for trailing spouses.

IRS' revised Publication 503 for 2000 returns explains the application of the Code §21 tax credit and reimbursement under corporate dependent care assistance programs. Starting with 2000 returns, the dependent care credit can be used to offset the alternative minimum tax, not just ordinary income tax.

4.2 CHILD CARE OPTIONS AT WORK

In late 2000, the Census Bureau released its first survey showing that in 1998, a majority of families consisted of married couples, both of them employed for pay, and children (51% of families fit this pattern, versus 33% back in 1976). [Tamar Lewin, "Now a Majority: Families with 2 Parents Who Work," *NYT* 10/24/00 p. A20.]

According to the Census Bureau figures, 59% of mothers of children under one year old had paid jobs in 1998, versus 31% in 1976. Close to three-quarters of mothers of children over a year old had paid jobs, 52% of them full-time. More than half (55%) of the dual income couples had family income over $50,000, which was true of only 40% of couples where the husband had a paid job and the wife didn't.

In situations where it becomes impossible to reconcile work and family obligations, because of the birth or adoption of a child, the Department of Labor proposed, in December, 1999, that state agencies voluntarily make unemployment compensation (UC) payments available to new parents: "Birth and Adoption Unemployment Compensation," 64 FR 67972 (12/3/99), further discussed in ¶19.7.

For "The 100 Best Companies for Working Mothers," measured by criteria such as availability of parenting leave; flexibility; child care; work/life programs; and opportunities for women, see http://www.workingmother.com.

TIP

Your company can volunteer to participate as a mentor (if it already has a success story) or link up with a mentor; the Women's Bureau regional staff will help make the link-ups. Application forms can be obtained by telephone, (800-827-5335; by fax, 202-219-5529; or from the Women's Bureau Web site. See http://www.dol.gov/dol/wb/public/childcare/b2bintro.htm.) The National Partnership for Women and Families, (202) 986-2600, http://www.nationalpartnership.org, is another resource for the balance between work and family issues.

On April 23, 1998, the Department of Labor's (DOL's) Business-to-Business Mentoring Initiative on Child Care was launched. It will be run by the DOL's Women's Bureau. The Initiative intends to promote awareness of the importance of work-related child care and to link up employers that have already implemented successful child care programs with companies intending to do so. The experienced providers will serve as mentors for the novices. The Women's Bureau produces a resource kit, including standards and best practices and information about developing an effective child care program.

The 1998 BWLS reports on a sample of about 1000 companies and nonprofit organizations with 100+ employees. The survey's conclusions are not surprising: Better work–family support enhances job satisfaction, loyalty, and employee retention.

BWLS revealed that companies in the sample permitted eight flexible work arrangements. The most common (offered by 88%) was time off to attend family-related events. Eighty-one percent offered a gradual transition back to the workplace after birth or adoption leave. Basic flex-time arrangements were available in about two-thirds of these companies. Over half allow transitions between full- and part-time work, with occasional opportunities to work at home even for employees who are not engaged in a formal telecommuting arrangement. Almost half (46%) of survey respondents believed their work–family arrangements yielded a positive return on investment; about a third thought they were cost neutral; and only 18% thought that the cost of flexible work arrangements was greater than the benefits received.

The survey respondents were generally subject to the FMLA. Many companies provided more leave than the required 12 weeks. Eighty-one percent funded at least some pay for workers on maternity leave under their temporary disability plan. Thirteen percent offered at least some replacement pay for paternity leave, and 12.5% did this in connection with adoption leave. The FMLA requires granting leave to employees whose children are seriously ill; about half of the respondents also allowed time off (without loss of pay or vacation days) when children were mildly ill, for an average of 11 days per employee. One-quarter of employers said that the number of days off varied with the situation; 9% allowed employee parents to take as many days off as they needed to cope with minor childhood illness, and 5% provided care for mildly ill children (e.g., specialized day care centers).

Dependent care assistance plans (letting employees apply pretax dollars to pay for child care) were quite common, found in 50% of survey respondent companies. The only other common child care mechanism was information and referral. Less than 10% provided on-site child care, child care vouchers, reimbursement of employees' child care costs when they had to travel or work late, or other direct care mechanisms.

Paternity leave for men has never really caught on, perhaps because there is widespread perception, in many kinds of jobs, that paternity leave is not masculine and could impair the father's promotion possibilities if he is perceived as insufficiently competitive or dedicated to his career. A common pattern is to use vacation or personal days to avoid the stigma of paternity leave. [Melinda Ligos, "The Fear of Taking Paternity Leave," *NYT* 5/31/00 p. G1.]

Breast feeding for at least six months, and preferably a year, is the medical recommendation for newborn babies. So either new mothers must choose bottle feeding; delay their return to work until they are ready to stop breast feeding; or use a workplace lactation program that either allows them to feed their babies at the workplace or gives them an appropriate private place to pump and store breast milk. (See Kathryn Tyler, "Got Milk?" *HR Magazine*, 3/99 p. 69.)

Workplace lactation programs are extremely productive for employers because they aid employee retention. Furthermore, babies fed with breast milk are often healthier than formula-fed babies, so their parents need less time off to deal with babies' illnesses. The Los Angeles Department of Water and Power found that it got back between $3.50 and $5.00 for every dollar invested in the lactation program, cut absenteeism by 27%, and reduced health care costs by 35%.

The demands of a lactation program are modest. Breast-feeding employees need a private, reasonably quiet and pleasant place to express breast milk and a refrigerator or cooler to keep it cool, plus a sink to wash up. Some employers provide sophisticated, sanitary breast pumping equipment. Typically, employees will need about an hour a day to express milk (two 30-minute or three 20-minute breaks).

The conclusion drawn by "Breast-Feeding in the Workplace: What Should an Employer Do?" [WestGroup *Employment Alert* 3/16/00 p. 1] is that the PDA and the ADA do not cover breast-feeding. In general, federal and state courts hearing the cases have not required the employer to provide personal leave, modified schedules, or changes in job routines for employees who breast-feed after they return from maternity leave. In the courts' analysis, breast-feeding is a natural function, and is neither a pregnancy-related medical condition nor a disability.

However, some states have statutes governing breast-feeding at work. Hawaii, for instance, has enacted a law making it unlawful discrimination to refuse to hire, discharge, or discriminate against a lactating employee because she breast feeds or expresses milk in the workplace.

Various states (e.g., California, Florida, New York) have general statutes allowing mothers to breast-feed in public places where they are not trespassing, but these do not specifically cover workplace issues. Hawaii, Georgia, Minnesota, Oregon, and Tennessee have statutes that require or at least allow employers to provide unpaid break time so lactating employees can express breast milk. The employer also has to make reasonable efforts to provide a more suitable place than a toilet stall to do this.

Texas has a statute granting businesses a "mother-friendly" designation if they offer flexible work schedules, private spaces for breast-feeding and expressing milk, and hygienic storage for expressed breast milk.

However, in May 1999, MSNBC Cable won a case in the Southern District of New York. An ex-employee sued under Title VII and the ADA because she was not given access to a private place to express breast milk during the working day. The judge ruled that lactation is not a disability, so the ADA claim was invalid, and no evidence of sex discrimination was produced. (The plaintiff was not denied the opportunity to pump breast milk; the question was whether the locations in which she was permitted to do so were suitable.) The case of *Martinez v. NBC Inc*, #98 Civ.

4842 (S.D.N.Y. 5/19/99), is discussed in Deborah Pines's *New York Law Journal* article, "Discrimination Found in Lack of Privacy for Use of Breast Pump," available at http://www.lawnewsnetwork.com/practice/employmentlaw/news/A1598-1999May19.html.

4.4 CORPORATE ELDER CARE ACTIVITIES

As U.S. demographics shift, the need for elder care will expand, and therefore workplace implications will also increase. According to the Agency for Healthcare Research and Quality (AHRQ), there are about 9.4 million adults in the United States (about half of them senior citizens) who need help with basic daily activities like bathing, dressing, and eating.

In 1984, 35% of senior citizens had problems with three to six of these major activities; this was true of 43% of the senior citizen population in 1994. In 1984, 19% of senior citizens got both paid and informal care—a percentage that went up to 26% in 1994.

In 1984, 26% of all senior citizens were in institutions such as nursing homes, versus 30% in 1994. However, nursing home use is very much a function of age. In 1994, for instance, only 1% of the "young-old" (ages 65-69) lived in nursing homes, whereas 43% of the very old (95 and over) were nursing home residents.

The study estimates that 40% of elderly people who need long-term care get all their care informally (from friends and family), and two-thirds of the elderly get at least some informal care. In 1994, there were about 5.9 million informal caregivers taking care of 3.6 million elderly and disabled people. Some caregivers are retired themselves, but many of them are in the workforce. [William D. Spector et.al., "The Characteristics of Long-Term Care Users," available free from the AHRQ Publications Clearinghouse, PO Box 8547, Silver Spring, MD 20907, (800) 358-9295.]

The National Alliance for Caregiving and AARP's study, "Who Cares" (1999), based on their earlier study, reports that about one-quarter of caregivers take care of a person with Alzheimer's Disease or other dementing illness, and that there may be anywhere from 1.9 million to 4 million cases of Alzheimer's in the United States, affecting at least 2% of the senior citizen population, and perhaps as much as 12%.

Alzheimer's caregivers tend to be older than other caregivers and spend a lot more time on caregiving: more than a quarter of Alzheimer's caregivers spend more than 40 hours a week giving care. They are much more likely to be depressed and suffer physical and mental consequences from caregiving than other caregivers.

Therefore, if the employer can offer more supportive services for employees who have relatives with dementia, this is likely to pay off in terms of fewer employees quitting their jobs to become full-time caregivers, and in greater productivity while they are still employed. [GAO/HEHS-98-16, 'Alzheimer's Disease: Estimates of Prevalence in the United States," (January 1998); "Who Cares?" Alzheimer's Association/National Alliance for Caregiving (1999).]

Corporate awareness of the significant economic impact of elder care is increasing. In June 1997 the MetLife Mature Market Group and the National Alliance for Caregiving performed a major survey, releasing a report, "Family Caregiving in the U.S.: Findings from a National Survey."

TIP

Copies of the report can be obtained by telephoning (203) 221-6580.

According to MetLife's summary paper, "The MetLife Study of Employer Costs for Working Caregivers," in 1996 (when the telephone survey was done) close to one-fourth of all U.S. households (i.e., more than 22 million households) included at least one person with caregiving responsibilities. Almost two-thirds of those caregivers were employed, and over 50% worked full time. Therefore, there were 14.4 million Americans who combine caregiving and employment responsibility. Metlife's conclusion is that U.S. business loses productivity and encounters supervisory costs for resolving caregiving issues, to the tune of **$11.4 billion** per year (to replace employees; cope with absenteeism and partial absenteeism; deal with interruptions during the workday and the need for employed caregivers to drop their work and deal with family crises). The estimated average cost to business, per caregiver employee, was $1142 a year: $69 allocable to absenteeism, $85 to partial absenteeism, $657 for workday interruptions, $189 for crisis tasks, and $141 for supervisory involvement.

In addition, employers spent close to $5 billion a year to replace employees who had to quit their paid jobs because they were no longer able to balance caregiving and employment. Even in the employer's best-case scenario—when a person who wasn't doing a very good job even before caregiving began quits and is replaced by a better-skilled and more productive person—hiring and training someone new is time-consuming and expensive. The worst-case scenario for the employer is losing a superior employee, who is replaced by someone who has a lot less to offer the company.

More than 17% of caregivers at Levels III–V (moderate to fairly intensive caregiving) told the surveyors that they had to take early retirement or quit their jobs because of their caregiving responsibilities—estimated at 4% a year (given the approximately four-year duration of the caregiving obligation). The Conference Board thinks that the cost of recruiting a replacement and bringing him or her up to speed is about 75% of the salary of the replaced employee.

About 10% of the Level III–V caregivers spent six workdays a year or more absent from work for caregiving-related reasons. Fifty-nine percent of employed Level III–V caregivers engaged in partial absenteeism: not missing an entire day of work, but coming in late, leaving early, taking a long lunch break, etc. It has been estimated that at least an hour a week (50 hours a year) is lost this way, over and above what caregivers can make up by staying late on other days, restricting other breaks, etc. Level III–V caregivers were also estimated to lose an hour a week to interruptions during the day, such as receiving or making telephone calls related to the care needs of the elderly parent or in-law. Another three days a year were lost to coping with crises: the elderly relative's hospitalization or move to a nursing home, for instance.

MetLife stresses that the $11.4 billion figure is an extremely conservative estimate, because it takes into account only caregivers who are employed full time and who provide care at Levels III–V (i.e., moderate to very heavy levels of care). If the 8.7 million caregivers who work part time, or who provide Levels I and II of care (very light to light), are considered, the productivity impact could be over **$29 billion** a year.

Furthermore, caregivers add direct costs to the employer's health plan. Because caregiving is so stressful, caregivers are unusually heavy consumers of health and counseling services.

Women Caregivers

A May 1998 white paper, "Work and Elder Care: Facts for Caregivers and Their Employers," was issued by the Department of Labor's Women's Bureau and can be found at the DOL's Web site, http://www.dol.gov/dol/wb/public/wb_pubs/elderc.htm. This is a very useful, free, and public-domain resource; you're free to download it and reprint it for employees who need help with elder care. (It contains useful information about the various kinds of support services available to caregivers.) You can also place it on your HR Web site or intranet.

As the report says, "Women are more likely than men to be caregivers and to receive care, although an increasing number of men have parental responsibility. Many caregivers are caring for both children and elders. Caregiving impacts on work, causing caregivers to come in late, work fewer hours, and even give up work or retire early."

According to the Women's Bureau, 72% of caregivers are female. The typical caregiver is a 46-year-old woman; the typical care recipient is the caregiver's 77-year-old, chronically ill mother. Caregiving lasts an average of 4.5 years (until the person receiving the care dies, enters an institution, or—in rare cases—recovers enough not to need care).

The Women's Bureau notes that 41% of caregivers are responsible for children under 18 as well as for elderly persons. On the average, they provide eight hours a week of direct, hands-on physical personal care to the elder, plus 3.7 more hours of indirect care tasks such as shopping and cooking. Women caregivers spend an average of 19.9 hours a week on caregiving, versus an average of only 11.8 hours for male caregivers.

Juggling Act

A small, but suggestive, study was published in November, 1999. "The MetLife Juggling Act Study: Balancing Caregiving With Work and the Costs Involved" can be ordered from MetLife's Mature Market Institute, (203) 221-6580, MMI_MetLife @metlife.com.

This study goes back and looks at 55 participants in the 1996 survey, who provide an intensive level of care for a sick relative. The research identified key themes:

- It is common for caregivers to underestimate how hard it is to be a caregiver, or how much effort will be required over how long a time.
- In addition to informal work schedule adjustments, 84% of respondents made formal adjustments, such as leaving their jobs, taking early retirement, or using sick and vacation days.
- Caregivers lost access to promotions, transfers, training, and other avenues toward improving their career status.
- Close to two-thirds of caregivers lost income, and therefore lost the ability to invest and build wealth. The estimated median loss was $243,761; the estimated mean loss was $566,443.
- Caregivers' own retirement becomes precarious; if they work less, earn less, and save less, they are also entitled to smaller pensions from their employers and smaller Social Security benefits.
- Most caregivers help their relatives by providing financial assistance, too; on the average, they provided financial help over a period of two to six years, to the tune of an average of almost $20,000. This reduced their ability to invest in home improvements, and reduced their ability to make consumer expenditures (cars, vacations) and pay their children's college expenses.
- Many caregivers found that their own health deteriorated; 20% reported serious health problems related to caregiving.
- One-quarter of respondents found that their productivity at work declined because of caregiving; 10% felt it declined significantly for this reason.

What Employers Are Doing

It's not hard for corporate management to understand both the devastating impact of illness and frailty on a family (especially if the managers themselves are caregivers)—and of caregiving on corporate productivity. Although we don't have complete, current figures, it seems that approximately one-quarter to one-third of U.S. workers, at least in large companies, have access to some degree of employer assistance with caregiving. Providing intensive or comprehensive services is likely to exceed the pocketbook of nearly all employers, but there are many simple, cost-effective steps that an employer can do that will be extremely useful to caregiver-employees.

Information and referral (I&R) is the most popular employment-related caregiving service; 79% of employers offering elder care provided I&R, versus 25% providing long-term care insurance (usually on an employee-pay-all basis). Since much productivity is lost when employees have to do their own research into available elder care resources, providing complete, accurate information yields an immediate improvement in productivity. Other benefits offered by at least some employers include the following:

- Seminars about relevant topics (such as Medicare, Medicaid, and state- and charity-run programs available in the area). When the federal statute the Older Americans Act was re-authorized at the end of 2000, a new National Family Caregiver Support program was created and funded with $125 million nationwide. Be sure to work with your local Area Agency on Aging to participate in, and disseminate information about, caregiver support activities in your region.
- Support groups for caregivers
- Hotlines with elder care information
- Subsidized phone consultations with resource or elder care experts (including those in the parent's geographic area, if the caregiver child lives far away)
- Directories and other publications
- Caregiver fairs, with exhibits from the Social Security Administration and other public agencies as well as voluntary organizations and for-profit service vendors
- Counseling from a psychologist or clinical social worker
- Subsidies for adult day care for the parent
- Respite care
- Emergency care (including care in the home of the elderly person)
- Paratransit, such as wheelchair-compatible vans, to provide transportation to doctors' appointments and other trips that otherwise would require the employee's chauffeur services
- Subsidizing the cost of pagers that the parent can use to contact the employee in an emergency
- Case management—services of social workers or geriatric care manager (GCMs), who advise the employee about creating and managing a complete elder care plan for the parent's current and foreseeable future needs
- Adding elderly dependent parents to the coverage of dependent care accounts

In the unionized workplace, the AFL-CIO has prepared a worksheet titled "Bargaining for Eldercare," available from www.aflcio.com. It's worth a look so you can see the kinds of issues that are likely to be brought to the bargaining table.

Although it is quite costly for the employer to add LTCI as an employee benefit (especially if employees can get coverage for their parents), employee-pay-all LTCI coverage costs the employer little. There are many excellent free or low-cost elder care resources already available, and a basic I&R program can be created very inexpensively by collecting, indexing, and distributing these resources and working closely with local philanthropic and government organizations benefiting the elderly.

In June 1999, the International Federation of Employee Benefit Plans (IFEBP) published a research report, "Employer-Sponsored Long-Term Care Insurance: Did HIPAA Matter?" You can find this report at http://www.ifepb.org/relngtrm.html. The conclusion of the report is that only 15% of survey respondents offered group LTCI as an employee benefit, and among this small percentage, about three-quarters were very large companies with 1000 or more employees. In 80% of the plans, the employee paid the entire LTCI premium. Half of the plans were tax-qualified under HIPAA, half nonqualified.

Sixty percent of responding employers said that favorable tax treatment under HIPAA was a motivation for offering the benefit, whereas 76% said that they wanted to supplement their existing plan by offering an "emerging" benefit. However, LTCI was not very popular with employees: 71% of employers who offered group LTCI had participation rates below 10%, and most of those rates were below 5%. Seventy-five percent of respondents were not affected by HIPAA as to their attitudes toward group LTCI.

As for employers who did not offer group LTCI, 51% said they felt the benefit was still untested and had not proved itself, and about a third said employees don't know about or aren't interested in group LTCI. However, 48% said that HIPAA may inspire them to add a group LTCI benefit.

The small group of employers who did offer group plans usually made coverage available to the spouses, parents, and in-laws of employees: after all, if the employee pays the full premium, the employer doesn't stand to lose by liberal plan coverage. However, less than half covered retirees or retiree spouses under the LTCI plan.

What Employers Can Do

In a spring 1998 speech to the Northern Illinois Society for Human Resource Management and Northwest Human Resources Council, Joy Loverde suggested criteria for a compassionate, cost-effective corporate eldercare program. (See West Employment Alert, 5/14/98, p. 7.) An optimal program

- Educates employees
- Alerts employees to responsibility they can be taking for their parents' (or other recipients') elder care

- Teaches employees to share caregiving and create an informal network
- Motivates employees by focusing on caregivers' needs rather than elders' needs
- Provides employees with psychological tools for discussing sensitive matters with family members

As the main volume notes, employers can provide long-term care insurance. Even if employees pay the full premium cost themselves, this is a valued benefit—especially if the employees can get coverage for their parents under the same plan. Note that the amount of benefits that can be received tax-free under an LTCI policy increased from $175/day (for 1998) to $180/day (for 1999).

BWLS Results

The Business and Work Life Study also covered employers' elder care activities. I&R was the major corporate activity, provided by 23% of the survey respondents and under consideration by another 5%. Nine percent allowed coverage of family members in the LTCI plan, and another 12% were considering adding this. Only 5% offered direct financial support for local elder care programs, and only 2% were contemplating doing so in the future. Most respondents (60%) considered their elder care investment cost neutral; 19% thought costs outweighed benefits, and only 21% viewed the elder care investment as offering positive economic benefits.

Chapter 5

DIVERSITY IN THE WORKPLACE

5.4 ENGLISH-ONLY RULES

As of early 1999, almost half the statutes (most of them in the South or Northwest) had passed statutes declaring English to be the official language of the state. (This information comes from Alejandro Bodipo-Memba, "Wage Gap Widens in 'English Only' States," *WSJ* 2/25/99, p. A2.) Such laws were present in Alabama, Alaska, Arkansas, California, Colorado, Florida, Georgia, Hawaii, Illinois, Indiana, Kentucky, Louisiana, Massachusetts, Mississippi, Missouri, Montana, Nebraska, New Hampshire, North Carolina, South Carolina, North Dakota, South Dakota, Tennessee, Virginia, and Wyoming. The statutes usually include exemptions in certain situations, such as the criminal trial of a non-English-speaking person, or when promotion of health and safety requires communication in another language. About 40 municipalities also had similar laws of their own.

According to the Federal Reserve Bank of Atlanta, in states with English-only laws, men who were not fluent in English earned an average of 9.3% less than fluent English speakers (Hispanic males with limited English skills earned 10.3% less in states with English-only laws than in the other states). However, the wages of women who were not fluent in English did not differ significantly in the two groups of states (perhaps because many women for whom English is not a first language work in domestic or factory jobs where little communication with the public is required).

The Arizona Constitution forbids state officers and employees to use any language other than English in their jobs, but the Arizona Supreme Court struck this down as a violation of the First Amendment and of the Fourteenth Amendment's Equal Protection guarantee [*Ruiz v. Hull*, 66 LW 1683 (Az. Sup. 4/28/98)].

In September, 2000, the EEOC arranged a $192,500 settlement with an Illinois company that agreed to provide back pay for seven Hispanic workers who quit or were fired because of the company's English-only rule, plus punitive damages. [No by-line, "Employer's English-Only Policy Brings a Settlement of $192,500," *New York Times* 9/2/00 p. A12.]

The EEOC's rule on English-only policies, found at 29 CFR §1606.7, draws a distinction between blanket bans on other languages and partial English-only rules. (The Northern District of Texas has upheld the rule, on the grounds that it was within the EEOC's jurisdiction to adopt it: *EEOC v. Premier Operator Services, Inc.*, 75 F.Supp.2d 550 (N.D. Tex. 1999).)

Close scrutiny is applied to blanket bans, because they are presumed to stem from national-origin discrimination. [See "English-Only Policies," WestGroup *Employment Alert* 6/8/00 p. 3.] A partial ban can be justified by an employer who shows a business necessity and who tailors the ban to fit that necessity. For instance, requiring employees to speak English when they are in contact with public (but allowing other languages during meals and breaks), or when poor communication with other employees could be inefficient or dangerous.

According to *Roman v. Cornell University*, 53 F.Supp.2d 223 (N.D.N.Y. 1999), it's permissible for an employer to require bilingual employees to speak English based on complaints from non-Spanish-speaking employees that they felt excluded from conversations. Employers can impose tougher requirements on bilingual employees than on those who are not fluent in English. Not only must the rules be rational, they must be communicated clearly, and must cover all languages other than English instead of singling out one in particular. Furthermore, if the way the rule is applied shows hostility toward a particular nationality, it could constitute hostile environment discrimination. [*Velasquez v. Goldwater Memorial Hospital*, 88 F.Supp.2d 257 (S.D.N.Y. 2000); *Gotfryd v. Book Covers Inc.*, 1999 WL 20925 (N.D. Ill. 1999).]

5.5 PROMOTING DIVERSITY

The Society for Human Resource Management (SHRM) 1998 survey discussed in *Employment Alert* (8/20/98, p. 12) showed that 75% of the *Fortune* 500 had structured diversity programs, and only 36% of a general sample of companies did so. This is understandable—smaller or less-established companies have less money available for nonemergency, non-bottom-line projects. The survey costs $39.95 for non-SHRM members, $29.95 for members, and can be purchased from http://www.shrm.org/shrmstore or (800) 444-5006.

Three-quarters of survey respondents were satisfied with their diversity programs, but only about half of *Fortune* 500 companies, and about one-third of other companies, actually had metrics to gauge program success. Few companies (about a quarter of *Fortune* 500, a tenth of other companies) make success in promoting diversity a factor in top executives' compensation.

Ten percent of the *Fortune* 500 and 5% of other companies consider diversity skills in assessing performance, but not in setting compensation; 6% and 1%, respectively, consider diversity performance for compensation only; and 58% of the

Fortune 500, 79% of other companies, do not use diversity as a criterion for judging managers at all. (See Patricia Digh, "The Next Challenge: Holding People Accountable," *HR Magazine,* 10/98, p. 63.)

Nearly all firms with diversity programs considered employee diversity training an important component of the program. *Fortune* 500 and smaller firms provided about equal amounts of diversity training: an average of 8.63 hours a year for middle managers, 7.3 hours/year for top managers, and 5.3 annual hours for nonexecutive employees.

The good news is that commitment to diversity often translates into improved performance. A survey done by the American Management Association (AMA) and the Business and Professional Women's Foundation (BPW) showed that the average 1997 sales growth rate for companies led by white males was an impressive 13%. Does this mean that companies need a traditional Caucasian male leadership to succeed? No, because the average sales growth rate was 20.2% where senior management included African-, Asian- and Hispanic-Americans, and 22.9% in companies where the majority of top management was female. The survey can be ordered from AMA's Eric Rolfe Greenberg, (212) 903-8052, or Gail Shaffer (BPW), (202) 293-1100; the survey is discussed in Robert W. Thompson, "Executive Briefing," *HR Magazine,* 4/99, p. 10.

Korn/Ferry obtained somewhat similar results. (See Sherry Kuczynski's "If Diversity, Then Higher Profits?" *HR Magazine,* 12/99, p. 67.) However, diversity is not necessarily the direct cause of better returns; it could just be one sign of an effective company that attracts the best workers. Diversity within an organization leads to more creativity, but also more conflict.

The problem with diversity programs is that many of them stress fair treatment but don't make out a business case; or they target niche markets too much. Just hiring diversely doesn't bring out differences of experiences and viewpoints. Hiring women or minorities for niche marketing, and ghettoizing them within the company, doesn't help either.

Patricia Digh ("Getting People in the Pool: Diversity Recruitment that Works," *HR Magazine,* 10/99, p. 94) points out that *Fortune*'s 50 Best Companies for Asians, Blacks and Hispanics continue to outperform the S&P 500.

A Special Advertising Section in the *Wall Street Journal* [See Pepi Sappal, "Women and Minorities Continue to Take a Backseat in Business," *WSJ* 10/17/00 p. B22.] notes that only 4% of Fortune 500 companies have a minority-group member on their Board of Directors, and only 11% have one or more woman directors. The SHRM 1999 Barriers to Advancement Survey shows that over 90% of women, and 74% of members of minority groups, encounter some sort of barrier to career advancement.

On a scale of 1-5 (1 = no barrier, 5 = significant barrier), the SHRM survey reports that the greatest barrier perceived for women is that corporate culture favors men (4.01 rating), followed by stereotypes about women (3.85), lack of women on the company's Board of Directors to insist on opportunity for women

(3.69), lack of access to informal networks where information and power are shared (3.55) and management's perception that women will not be able to perform fully because of their family responsibilities (3.54).

A slightly different list of problems was cited for members of minority groups: stereotypes (4.02), lack of access to informal networks (3.91), shortage of mentors and role models (3.87 and 3.77, respectively) and a corporate culture that favors members of the dominant culture over minorities (3.64).

➠ TIPS

For a successful diversity program,

- Understand workforce demographics.
- Increase access and opportunities within your workforce.
- Maintain long-term relationships, not single projects, with minority organizations.
- Advertise in minority periodicals.
- Offer recruitment, internships, etc., at minority colleges and communities.
- When recruiting, check sites that post resumes of diverse individuals: www.diversityee.com; the National Diversity Newspaper Job Bank, www.newsjobs.com; Diversity Services, www.diversity-services.com; National Diversity Recruitment Services, www.HireDiversity.com.
- Don't just recruit, but retain, by promoting a minority-friendly corporate culture.
- Make sure employees understand the business case for diversity.

For a discussion of the potential divisive and contentious nature of diversity programs, see Simon J. Nadel, "Religion and Sexual Orientation at Work May Produce Combustible Combination," 68 LW 2163 (9/28/99). Employees may pose religious objections to diversity training that involves sexual orientation issues. One option is to allow employees to opt out of diversity training sessions that offend their religious beliefs. Make sure there are no references to "outdated" religious beliefs and point out that they don't have to change their beliefs about religiously appropriate sexual conduct; they just have to work with other employees, many of whom engage in conduct that religious employees consider immoral.

Chapter 6

The Role of the Computer in HR

6.1 INTRODUCTION

Large-scale enterprise resource planning (ERP) software can not only handle routine HR tasks, but can add immense power to interpret data about the corporation's workforce. At first, this power was available only in very expensive proprietary products, beyond the reach of all but the *Fortune* 500 and requiring extensive user training. Today, software vendors like SAP and PeopleSoft are not only offering smaller-scale, easier-to-use, more affordable packages—they are moving from proprietary standards to simple Web interfaces. So the products can be put to use right away, with little or no training cost. (See Jim Meade, "Adapting to the Shifting Software Market," *HR Magazine*, "Focus," 5/99, p. 3.)

See Chapter 1 for a discussion of the impact of the Internet on hiring practices, and the PBGC is expanding its efforts to use information technology to serve its constituents better. See PBGC Technical Update 01-1 (1/19/01), http://www.pbgc.gov/legal_info/tech_updates/tech01-1.htm.

In the interests of speed and economy, the IRS is seeking to phase out paper-based tax filing and move to an all-digital compliance and payment system. For "Q and A for Businesses Filing Taxes Electronically," see http://www.irs.gov/elec_svs/qa-bus.html, containing links to subjects such as Filing Form 941 with the Electronic Data Exchange (EDI) format, with a personal computer, a touch-tone telephone, or magnetic tape (including floppy disks). Form 940 can be filed online under the e-file and On-Line Filing programs, or on magnetic tape. A group of information returns (1042-S, 1098, 1099, 5498, 8027, W-2G) can be filed with the FIRE System.

6.2 DOING RESEARCH ON THE NET

Significant human resources/benefits information is available online. Most of it is free, although some sites include a members-only component, sell publications for which there is a charge, or require a paid subscription.

Nearly all federal agencies have at least one Website. To say the least, these vary in quality, attractiveness, and comprehensiveness. They also tend to be somewhat crash-prone, so be sure to close all your desktop files before pointing your browser at a government site. At least that way, you won't lose any data if you have to reboot your computer.

The best government sites (such as http://www.irs.ustreas.gov) are cornucopias of useful forms, explanations, and news summaries about, as well as the text of, new regulations. It's worth checking on a regular basis to see, for instance, if the Pension and Welfare Benefits Administration (PWBA) or Occupational Safety and Health Administration (OSHA) has proposed or implemented any new rules; if there will be hearings nearby at which you will want to testify; or if new forms and publications are available.

Also note that the National Labor Relations Board (NLRB) makes its forms for unfair labor practice charges and election petitions available at its Web site (http://www.nlrb.gov), so you may face additional charges or organization drives in light of the increased availability.

➠ TIP

There are many references throughout this book to law.com, which refers to the current and archived resources that can be found at http://www.law.com. There is an excellent free daily electronic newsletter, and reprints of articles from many law-related publications. The site includes a very full Employment Law Resource Center, although paid registration is required to use many of its features.

The following sites are worth looking into:

- Society for Human Resource Management (SHRM): http://www.shrm.org, SHRM Online.
- BNA Human Resources Library, part of http://www.bna.com.
- BenefitsLink. http://www.benefitslink.com/index.shtml.
- Employment Law Links. For information about sites dealing with various legal issues, see http://www.contilaw.com/links.html. Another "links list" is found at http://www.mtsu.edu/~rlhannah/employee_benefits.html.

- RIA InsideHR HR Wire (http://www.insidehr.com/HRwire/default/asp.
- Department of Labor eLaws, http://www.dol.gov/elaws/. eLaws stands for Employment Laws Assistance for Workers and Small Business; it's an interactive compliance assistance tool made up of chapters called "advisors."
- OSHA Expert Systems: http://www.osha.gov/oshasoft. OSHA furnishes free software to help employers identify hazards and estimate the cash benefits of implementing a sound safety program.
- Ross Runkel's Employment Law Page: http://www.rossrunkel.com.
- Work and Family from the *Wall Street Journal.* Jan Wilson hosts a radio talk show on Saturday morning, 10 A.M. to noon Eastern time (toll-free at 800-WSJ-TALK). The show is "Webcast" (broadcast on the Internet) at http://www.wsjradio.com/affils.html#family.
- www.hr-esource.com. A group of related sites, including HR Wire, EEO Advisor, Compensation & Benefits Advisor, and Human Resource Advisor.
- As its name suggest, Lawnewsnetwork is aimed at attorneys. However, its free daily e-mail newsletter and subscription-based employment law site are written clearly enough to offer the HR professional tremendous insights into the evolving law of the workplace. See http://www.lawnewsnet.com.

The company HR Direct, which sells personnel products such as paper forms for the HR department HR software training and motivational materials and HR software has a mail order catalog, (800) 346-1231, and a site at http://www.hrdirect.com.

Joyce Slayton's "HR Made Easy" [*The Industry Standard* 9/18/00 p. 298.] gives a rundown of HR tools available from more than 1000 HR vendors. In 1999, $2.6 billion in HR software and solutions was shipped, and the market is estimated to reach $3.7 billion in 2003. The trend is to use software to improve training, recruitment, and retention. These "third-generation" products are sophisticated enough to create a personalized analysis and alternative for every employee.

Popular HR applications include management of payroll and benefits, recruitment, training, dissemination of company policies, employee profiles, and performance reviews.

Towers Perrin's 2000 survey of HR service centers shows that just since 1999, the use of the Internet in HR has doubled or even tripled for tasks such as benefit enrollment, updated personal data, and changes in 401(k) deferrals. More than a third of respondents (39%) allowed online enrollment for benefits, 31% allowed changes in personal data to be entered online, and 19% used the Internet for initial enrollment of new hires in benefit plans. Most Internet users found that they could perform transactions on a more timely basis by substituting electronic for paper processing—but their workload didn't really decrease! ["News Briefs, More Companies Using the Internet for Human Resources," *Employment Alert* 10/12/00 p. 12.]

According to Baltimore's The Hunter Group, more than 90% of the major companies they surveyed (who have a total of over 6 million employees) rate their implementation of self-service benefits information on an intranet "successful" or "somewhat successful," and the system can provide a 100% return on investment in just a year. The average respondent in Hunter Group's survey spent about $1.5 million to install employee self-service benefit information systems, although costs varied wildly from $35 to $1,600 per employee depending on the size of the workforce and the complexity of the system.

Watson Wyatt found that 85% of large companies surveyed used an intranet in benefits management, 72% used the public Internet, 63% used an interactive voice response system (the familiar "for 401(k) information press 3 . . ." kind of system), and 43% used call centers. For small companies, the dominant electronic tools were intranets (used by 74%) and the Internet (68%). The current trend is to offer Web solutions, but also supplement them with access to operators in call centers. [Susan G. Wells, "Communicating Benefits Information Online," *HR Magazine* (February 2001), http://www.shrm.org/hrmagazine/articles/default.asp?page=0201wells.htm.]

6.4 CREATING AND MANAGING AN INTRANET

A large workforce, or even a smaller workforce disseminated among several work locations, can make it expensive to send communications by mail or memorandum. Employees don't always like getting a memo blizzard; they often prefer to have access to a centralized bank of information, then decide what to read. (Naturally, the employer must continue to deliver all legally mandated notices, whether or not any employee actually bothers to read them! For information about using electronic media to give plan participants notices or secure their consent to elections, see 63 FR 70071 [12/18/98]: IRS Notice of Proposed Rulemaking, "New Technologies in Retirement Plans.")

When Sedgwick Noble Lowndes talked to 327 midsized companies in the fall of 1998, the majority of them (60%) either already used an intranet for HR and benefit communications (including a comprehensive benefit statement disclosing all of the employee's benefit elections and costs) or anticipated doing so in the future. Only one-fifth planned to use a Web site for similar purposes—no doubt the disparity is due to the greater privacy and security available on an intranet. About a quarter (26%) used or wanted to use an intranet to instruct employees about benefit elections available to them. Twenty-four percent used or intended to use their intranet to collect personal data about employees and to distribute data to employees; the same percentage showed an interest in using an intranet to enroll employees in benefit programs. One-fifth used or intended to use an intranet for 401(k) and retirement information.

Of course, one limitation on the usefulness of a corporate intranet is limited access on the part of employees. In 41% of the surveyed firms, 80 to 100% of the workforce had access to the company's intranet or were expected to gain access within a year. In 9% of the respondent companies, 61 to 80% of the staff had access to the intranet. In 22% of the companies, intranet access was 20% or below. Note that there are mechanisms for giving employees access to intranet benefits information without putting a computer on every desktop.

TIP

Touch-screen kiosks, or a few dedicated computer terminals, can be placed in the HR office, the employee assistance program (EAP) office, or the cafeteria or breakroom, so that non-computer-using employees can use the intranet for this specific purpose.

Amoco handled its intranet implementation by splitting the intranet into an HR component (comprising HR publications, business unit information, benefits information, volunteer information, and ads posted by employees who wanted to sell personal items) and a benefits component (the employee benefits handbook; personnel policies; and links to relevant Internet sites, such as financial planning sites).

Motorola took a dramatic but risky step: It simply eliminated all paper forms and correspondence related to HR. The upshot was a saving of $1.5 million, but there were hard-to-estimate losses with respect to employees who needed additional technical support. This information comes from "Intranet Delivery of HR and Benefits Information," WestGroup Employment Alert, 2/19/98, p. 2; and "More Midsized Firms Communicate Benefits Information Through Intranets," *RIA Compensation & Benefits Update*, 10/7/98, p. 6. Sedgwick's site is http://www.sedgwick.com; the survey is called the 1998 Employee Benefits Minisurvey.

In April of 1998, the International Foundation of Employee Benefit Plans looked at the use of Internet and intranet technology to communicate about employee benefits. The Foundation got 433 respondents to its survey; 125 respondents were already employing Internet and/or intranet communications. Of that small group, only a quarter had been using the Internet/intranet for over one year; a third had been online for less than six months. Three-quarters of the users cited the speed of transmitting information and getting feedback as an advantage of Net communications; two-thirds favored the ability to reduce distribution of printed materials; and about half cited increased efficiency and ease of administration. The respondents were worried about some aspects of online benefits communications, though: for example, limited access by employees to computers, their lack of familiarity with the technology, and issues of privacy, security, and liability. Forty-three percent of users implemented more than one security measure; 185 used passwords, 10% had a firewall, 7% required PIN numbers, and only 1% used encryption; 15% had no security measures in place at all.

Twelve percent of Internet users said they were very satisfied with its performance; 32% were satisfied, 29% somewhat satisfied, and 115 neutral. Only 6% were "very dissatisfied" with the Internet communications experience.

The Net was frequently used in connection with both health benefits and pensions. Two-thirds of the Net users posted summary plan description (SPDs) for health plans on an intranet (but only 2% used the Internet for this purpose); 19% permitted intranet viewing of current benefit elections, versus only 3% using the Internet. One-fifth used the Internet to post directories of physicians participating in the health plan, and 12% used an intranet for this purpose. Understandably, Internet use is limited in an area that can involve both proprietary corporate information and employee privacy.

Pension plan SPDs were on view on 47% of the intranet sites (5% used the Internet for this purpose). Quarterly reports and fund balances could be seen on 14% of intranets and 19% of corporate Internet sites. Viewing Frequently Asked Questions could be done on 21% of intranet and 6% of Internet sites. Furthermore, 48% of the intranet sites posted the employee handbook.

Two-thirds of those not already online for employee benefits expressed a desire to do so in the future. For 23% of the nonusers, the limiting factor was employees' lack of Internet access; 10% were stymied by the cost of implementation, and 9% couldn't find the time for implementation. IFEBP's survey report, "Communicating Employee Benefits Via the Web," is available from the IFEBP, (414) 786-6700, www.ifepb.org.

One advantage of a corporate internet is that it can combine some of the advantages of the broader public Internet while limiting improper or nonproductive online use by employees. SurfWatch Software (Los Altos, California) reports that, based on data supplied by the CheckNet software program, which measures Internet use at work, almost 25% of the time that employees spend online is not work related. The top five nonwork areas are general news; sex; investment; entertainment; and sports. (See Bill Leonard, "Nearly a Quarter of Time Online is Nonwork Related," *HR Magazine*, 11/98, p. 26; SurfWatch's Web address is http://www.surfwatch.com.)

Chapter 7

Compensation Planning

7.1 INTRODUCTION

Until mid-2000, it was often assumed that stock prices follow one inevitable trend: upward. This is not, of course, a rational assumption. Stock options are awarded to all employees, or to especially valued employees, as an incentive, so that they can buy stock at an artificially low price and eventually earn a large capital gain profit by selling the stock.

This scenario won't work (and the incentive effect won't be present) if the options are "underwater": that is, the price at which the employee is permitted to buy stock is actually higher than the market price of the shares. Therefore, companies—especially companies that have to recruit crucial employees in a highly competitive market—have an incentive to reprice their options by canceling a grant of options and issuing a new grant that can be exercised profitably.

The big problem with repricing is that the company's stockholders usually oppose repricing, because it benefits corporate executives but not the stockholders themselves. In fact, it can harm stockholders directly, by sending a signal to the market that the company itself doesn't think its stock price is going to improve. Two major surveys, released in December 1998, showed that about 90% of companies would not reprice their options, even though most of them had at least some options that were above the market price. However, in a highly competitive industry, once one company decides to reprice, other companies may feel constrained to follow.

One way to balance stockholder against executive interests is to modify the stock option plan in connection with repricing: Executives could get a smaller number of lower-price options, or accept an extended vesting period (length of time between grant of the option and the date it can be exercised).

Option repricing is discussed in Stephenie Overman's article, "Stock Options: Reprice or Hold Fast?," *HR Magazine*, 4/99, p. 82.

7.2 DECISIONS IN SETTING COMPENSATION

On December 20, 2000, the EEOC issued a new section for its Compliance Manual dealing with compensation issues affected by various anti-discrimination statutes. According to the EEOC, the federal laws against discrimination apply to all aspects of compensation, including salary, overtime, bonuses, options, profit sharing, fringe benefits, and reimbursement for business expenses. The EEOC also directed employers to review any practices that have an indirect effect on compensation—for instance, work assignments, appraisals, and promotions—to make sure they are in compliance with anti-discrimination statutes. The EEOC position is that employers are **never** justified in taking race, color, sex, national origin, religion, age, or disability into account when setting compensation. [See http://www.eeoc.gov/epa/index.html for information about EEOC's equal pay initiatives.]

This supplements the EEOC's October revision of its Compliance Manual to tackle benefits issues (http://www.eeoc.gov/docs/benefits.html). The EEOC says that equal severance benefits are required for all similarly situated employees irrespective of age. Employers may not deny severance because the employee is eligible for a pension, although sometimes pension benefits can be offset against the severance pay. Denying recall rights to older workers operates as involuntary retirement. The cost of providing severance does not rise with the employees' age, so employers are not allowed to assert an equal cost defense.

However, retiree health benefits can legitimately be offset against severance if the retiree is eligible for an immediate pension; the retiree actually receives health benefit coverage; and retiree benefits are at least comparable to Medicare in type and value. If the retiree is over 65, benefits must be at least comparable to one-fourth of the value of Medicare benefits. The offset itself must be reduced by any percentage by which the pension is reduced for retirement before Normal Retirement Age (NRA), and any percentage of the premium that the retiree has to pay for retiree health coverage.

The Compliance Manual says that "If the employer provides additional pension benefits that are enough, or are higher than those necessary to bring an employee up to the level of an unreduced pension, the employer can offset the full amount of those benefits. On the other hand, if the employer offers benefits that are insufficient to raise the employee to an unreduced pension, the employer cannot claim any offset at all."

Another issue prominent in 2000 is whether employers can legitimately penalize employees for discussing what they earn with other employees, or with outsiders such as union personnel. In particular, feminist groups are opposed to pay confidentiality policies, claiming that they perpetuate situations in which women are paid less than comparable male workers.

Republican Senator James Jeffords of Vermont has introduced a bill making it unlawful for employers to impose pay confidentiality standards or fire workers for discussing their compensation, but the bill is still pending. There also have been

NLRB decisions stating that employees must be permitted to discuss their compensation, and employees fired for this reason are entitled to reinstatement. [Mary Williams Walsh, "The Biggest Company Secret: Workers Challenge Employer Policies on Pay Confidentiality," *New York Times* 7/28/00 p. C1.]

Hewitt Associates forecasts (see Bill Leonard, "HR Update," *HR Magazine,* 11/99, p. 32) that pay raises in the early twenty-first century will be much like those at the end of the 1990s. For 2000, the firm predicts an average increase of 4.2% for salaried exempt employees, 4.1% for nonexempts, and 4.4% for executives—figures that are closely in line with 1998 and 1999 trends. Although this is a low rate of increase, it still allows employees to benefit in real terms, because it still beats inflation. The Conference Board 1999 Salary Survey shows similar trends: see http://www.conference-board.org.

Hewitt expects the real growth to come in variable compensation plans; the company found that employers plan to spend 16% more on variable compensation in 2000 than in 1999. Because variable compensation plans depend on meeting goals, they are essentially self-funding. Seven hundred five of 1,133 employers surveyed have at least one variable compensation plan (47% more than in 1990 survey).

7.3 [NEW] MERIT INCREASES

The Court of Appeals, the highest state court of New York State, decided in October, 2000 that discretionary bonuses used by investment banks and law firms are not "wages" that are protected by state labor law. The bonus is not considered a wage, even if part of it is based on the firm's performance. The plaintiff in this case was a financial analyst who opted for a compensation plan that gave him a $40,000 salary plus participation in a bonus and profit-sharing pool involving both individual and firm performance components.

His share of the pool was determined to be $160,000, to be paid in four installments. He left after receiving one installment; the firm refused to pay the balance. The analyst sued, but lost, because the court excluded contingent compensation (especially discretionary amounts like this one) from the definition of wages, because the calculation involved the firm's success as well as the particular employee's individual performance. [John Caher, "Bonus Payments Not Protected, New York High Court Finds," *New York Law Journal* 10/18/00, available through law.com. The case is *Truelove v. Northeast Capital & Advisory Inc.*, No. 99 (N.Y. App.).]

7.4 INNOVATIVE PAY SYSTEMS

Almost three-quarters of U.S. companies have at least some variable pay element in their compensation system. A variable pay plan gives employees access to performance-based awards reflecting that year's performance but that do not get built into base pay. In 1990, companies devoted only 4.2% of total payroll to variable pay; the corresponding figure forecast for 1999 is 7.8%. Furthermore, in 1997, 85% of employees eligible to receive an award got one, so implementing a plan, or adding to the number of eligible employees, can be expected to have a significant impact on payroll. Variable pay is an important part of executive compensation, but many organizations allow variable pay for rank-and-filers.

However, only 22% of companies that offer such plans feel that they more than satisfied their business objective for implementing the plan. About half are neutral, and 28% report that the plan did not meet the business objectives that inspired it. The most successful measure (90% of companies offering it cited positive business results) was calculated on the basis of financial and operating results for the company, the employee's business unit, or his or her own results. Employers attributed positive results to cash variable pay plans 84% of the time—much better than stock options, which were considered to improve business results only 63% of the time.

Because the plans are supposed to create incentives for better work, communication is key. Formal annual review explaining how the award was calculated is useful in pinpointing areas in which employees succeeded and those in which more work is necessary. The most effective plans had "moderate stretch" (i.e., they asked employees to achieve targets that were not comfortably in view but were far from impossible).

The Hewitt survey is discussed in "Variable Compensation Plans Increasing and Improving, But Still Delivering Mixed Results," http://www.hewitt.com/news/pressrel/1998/10-07-98.htm, and "Variable Compensation Plans Often Miss the Mark," RIA *Compensation & Benefits Update*, 3/25/98, p. 6.

Speaking of bonuses, ECS/Watson Wyatt Data Services reported in 1998 that about two-thirds of a large (10,000+) sample of top managers got at least some of their compensation from bonus awards. The typical bonus award was about one-third of base pay. Over four-fifths of executives whose bonuses were premised on satisfying a target achieved the target and received a bonus award.

Just over half (51.6%) of respondents also provided deferred compensation plans for top management—and usually only top management were eligible for the deferred compensation plan.

To order the "1998/1999 ECS Survey of Top Management Compensation," contact ECS/Watson Wyatt Data Services at http://wyattconsult.com (no www) or (201) 843-1177; see "Bonuses, Deferred Compensation Typify Pay Plans for Top Management," *Compensation & Benefits Update*, 8/12/98, p. 5.

According to the Pay for Performance Report, September 1999 (http://www.ioma.com/nls/9909/pfp.shtml), despite attention to alternative pay techniques, annual bonuses are still the most popular and effective motivators, followed by one-time awards for outstanding performance, individual incentives, then long-term incentives for executives. In short, things haven't changed very much since 1997.

But plans that provide bonuses to special key contributors in advance (not tied to a particular exceptional achievement) are not very popular.

According to this survey, 64% of respondents had an annual bonus program in place. Fifteen percent considered this program highly effective; 41% said it was moderately effective; and 39% didn't rate the plan. This was by far the most common incentive plan. The next, one-time after-the-fact awards, was offered by only 41% of respondents. Fifteen percent said it was highly effective; 21%, moderately effective; and 60% wouldn't comment on effectiveness.

In 1999, 32% of top management were very happy with their company's pay system; 46% liked the plan but had reservations about it. In contrast, in 1999 only 8% of employees were very happy with the system; 41% liked it but had reservations, 23% were neutral, and 20% didn't like the system but accepted it.

The NBER Working Paper No. W7419 (11/99), "Output-based Pay: Incentives of Sorting?" (Edward P. Lazear) is available for $10 + shipping (paper) or $5 (electronic) from the National Bureau of Economic Research. Place orders at http://papers.nber.org/papers/W7419 (no www). The paper assesses the usefulness of variable pay (which fluctuates based on some measure of the company's economic health). The "selection" theory is that, because managers have inside information about the company's potential, variable pay makes them be more honest about the company, because their own pay reflects performance.

Only about a third of large U.S. companies currently offer Christmas or other holiday bonuses; in fact, more than half never offered such bonuses, and one-eighth used to but discontinued the practice. See "Holiday Bonuses Alive but Fading," http://www.hewitt.com/news/pressrel/1999/12-22-99.htm. Performance-based bonuses are far more popular because of their greater incentive effect. Among companies that do provide an end-year holiday bonus, 37% offer cash; 29% give a turkey, ham, or other food item; 24% offer gift certificates; and 26% have a Christmas party. (The numbers add up to more than 100% because of the possibility of multiple forms of holiday bonuses.)

Cash awards were by far the most expensive form of holiday bonus, averaging $767 per recipient. On the average, holiday parties cost $52 per employee; gift certificates, $35; and food gifts, $23.

Although variable compensation is often disappointing to the company offering the plan, broadbanding has been much more successful. A broadbanding plan eliminates finely tuned salary grades and groups several job titles into one pay band. The most common factor in setting compensation for each band is comparison with market salaries for similar work.

Eighty-seven percent of those surveyed by ACA/Hewitt were pleased with the outcome of broadbanding (although hardly any of the companies had a formal tracking procedure; they reported a subjective belief). Almost a third of respondents planned to expand the use of broadbanding for compensation. ACA/Hewitt noted that few companies have a formal training program to explain broadbanding, and its place within general career development, to employees. Whatever communications occurred tended to be via passive print materials, such as brochures, not face-to-face discussion. The study "Living With Broadbanding in 1998" is reported in RIA's *Compensation and Benefits Update,* 5/20/98, p. 10. Call the American Compensation Association (ACA), (602) 922-2020, for ordering information.

7.5 BENEFITS AS AN ELEMENT OF COMPENSATION

What differentiates the companies that *Fortune* anoints as the "100 Best Companies to Work For in America" from 100 other companies that came close but didn't make the cut? *Fortune* studies ten areas of HR practice, including worklife programs; financial incentives; how personnel are hired and trained; and how the organization's culture functions. The top companies get almost twice as many applications as next-level companies of comparable size, so they have a better talent pool to choose from. The top companies lose about one-eighth of their employees each year to voluntary quits, which sounds pretty bad until you realize that companies on the next level have a 26% turnover rate.

Two-thirds of the 100 Best companies are public companies, so corporate stock can be a potent motivator. (In the other third, perhaps a family atmosphere makes up for lack of access to stock market riches.) Sixty percent of the publicly traded 100 Best had broad-based stock options or grant programs—significantly more than the 43% of next-tier companies that had them. In half of the 100 Best companies, more than 80% of employees owned stock in the company (whether awarded or purchased on the open market).

The 100 Best companies provided a median of a full day more of training—40 versus 32 hours in the next-tier companies—and both administrative/support staff and managers had access to training on more equal terms than in the next tier of companies. The 100 Best were much more likely to provide career counseling, mentoring, and academic courses.

Above all, the 100 Best companies attract and retain employees with superior working conditions, including generous benefit packages. The report lists nine health and wellness benefits (e.g., health club discounts; workout facilities on site; stress reduction programs). All of them were much more commonly found in the 100 Best than in the next tier. The same was true of convenience and personal benefits, such as an in-plant cafeteria or meal subsidies; take-home meals; assistance with buying a home; and discounts on entertainment for those precious (and perhaps rare) off-duty hours. Fifty-six percent of the second-tier companies allowed casual dress every day—61% of the 100 Best companies did this. (This information comes from "Hewitt Associates Shows How the 100 Best Companies Get Their Edge," http://www.hewitt.com/news/pressrel/1998/12-28-98.htm.)

7.6 SEVERANCE PAY

Section 7001 of the IRS Restructuring and Reform Act of 1998, P.L. 105-206, provides that, when deciding whether money constitutes "deferred compensation" under Code §404(a), the money is not considered to be paid or received until it is actually received by the employee. Although the statute has its greatest applicability in the context of nonqualified deferred compensation plans for executives, the statute was passed to overturn *Schmidt Baking Co.*, 107 Tax Court 271, a case involving a company's accrued liabilities for severance and vacation pay.

A settlement award to a laid-off employee, reflecting his age, years of service, and earnings impairment, constituted "wages" for income and FICA tax purposes, according to the Eighth Circuit [*Mayberry v. U.S.*, 151 F.3d 855 (8th Cir. 1998)]. The court did not accept the employee's contention that the sum was a nontaxable personal injury award because it replaced wages and was not the product of settling tort claims.

Severance and Separation Benefits, published by Lee Hecht Harrison (Woodcliff Lake, N.J.), is a study designed to answer questions about severance policies and their competitive effects. Free copies are available from the company at (800) 611-4544; Lee Hecht Harrison's Web site is http://www.ihh.com. (See "How Does Your Severance Policy Stack Up?" *RIA Compensation & Benefits Update,* 2/10/99, p. 5.)

The most common allocation was one week of severance pay per year of service—a measure used for 70% of nonexempt employees, 66% of exempt employees, 57% of executives, and 51% of corporate officers. Next most common was two weeks per year of work, offered in about 20% of plans.

About a quarter of respondents allow appeals if employees feel their severance benefits have not been calculated correctly. To avoid future problems, about 70% of survey respondents condition severance payments on signing a release of employment-related claims. (But see ¶26.3 for a discussion of how to draft acceptable ADEA releases.)

In a 1999 survey, 200 companies disclosed their policies for severance of executives outside the context of changes in corporate control. Three-quarters of the respondents had a formal executive severance program (versus 61% in 1991), and 59% of respondents defined severance as a fixed percentage of pay. The others used more complex formulas, factoring in, for instance, salary level and length of tenure with the company. [Robert W. Thompson, "Executive Briefing," *HR Magazine,* 9/99, p.10; the study can be ordered for $200 from the Publications Desk, Hewitt Associates, 100 Half Day Road, Lincolnshire IL 60069, (847) 295-5000.]

Manchester, Inc., which is an outplacement firm, reports that severance practices have gotten less generous in some respects, but have improved in others. In 1992, for instance, the maximum severance pay offered to top executives was two full years' income replacement—which has plummeted to an average of 37 weeks as of 2000. For middle managers, the 1992 average was 52 weeks severance, declining to 29 weeks in 2000; non-managers got an average of 25 weeks' severance in both years. Over time, the gap between top management, middle management, and non-management severance policies has closed.

However, the company also reports that (for reasons of public relations, and/or to forestall lawsuits), companies have been getting more generous with the non-cash severance benefits available to laid-off non-managerial workers. Employer-paid health coverage was offered to 59% of this group in 1997, and 78% in 2000. Access to Employee Assistance Programs was available to 38% of displaced employees in 1997 and 51% in 2000, and outplacement services were offered half the time in 1997, 60% of the time in 2000. [Nia-Malika Henderson, "Getting Fired Isn't What It Used to Be, and That's Good and Bad," *NYT* 2/21/01 p. G1.]

Case Law on Severance Plans

A voluntary termination program that offered a one-time lump sum at severance, based either on compensation or years of service, was offered during a "window" period that could be extended at the discretion of the employer. The plaintiffs in *Rodowicz v. Mass. Mutual Life Ins. Co.*, 1999 WL 701724 (1st Cir. 1999) alleged that they were told that the benefit program would not change, but in fact a better package was offered after their retirement.

In the view of the First Circuit, the severance arrangement was not an ERISA plan, like the plan in *Fort Halifax*, in that only a single lump sum requiring limited administration was involved. Because there was no ERISA plan, the case was governed by state laws about estoppel and misrepresentation. Under Massachusetts common law, the test is not whether the revised plan was under "serious consideration." Instead, the question was whether it was more likely than not that a reasonable employee would have retired by relying on the misrepresentation.

Noorily v. Thomas & Betts Corp., 1999 WL 643363 (3rd Cir. 1999) holds that it was a valid business decision for an employer to deny severance benefits to engineers who refused to relocate after the company's acquisition. Although the District Court sided with the employee-plaintiffs, the Third Circuit upheld the characterization of the group of engineers as essential to the corporate business.

A 2001 Fourth Circuit case [*Friz v. J&H Marsh & McLennan, Inc.*, 2001 U.S. App. LEXIS 869 (4th Cir. 2001)] arose when an employee was terminated when his employer acquired another company. The employee's severance plan provided basic benefits of a lump sum of two weeks' base salary. Enhanced benefits based on seniority were available to some employees. The memo announcing the severance plan said that the enhanced benefits were conditional on signing a waiver and release, including an agreement not to solicit the company's existing accounts or its employees. An SPD adopted later did not mention the non-solicitation requirement, but did state that the enhanced benefits were conditional on signing a waiver and release form prepared by the company.

The plaintiff did not sign the form; did solicit clients of the ex-employer; and sued the ex-employer after being denied the enhanced benefits. The District Court, affirmed by the Fourth Circuit, held for the employer. The courts refused to disturb any reasonable decision made by an administrator of a plan that reserved discretion to determine eligibility and construe the terms of the plan.

TIP

The case would have been even clearer if the non-solicitation language had been repeated in the SPD.

Plan transitions, and administrator's discretion, were also involved in the case of *James v. General Motors* [#99-4078; 7th Cir. 2000. See http://www.spencernet.com/Archive/News111400.html.} The plaintiff worked for General Motors at a facility that was sold to Rolls Royce. The plaintiff was entitled to three years' worth of certain GM welfare benefits, including severance benefits if she was terminated without cause during the three-year period, but not if she quit her job. During the three-year period, the company was sold again, this time to a wholly-owned subsidiary of General Motors. The subsidiary offered her a job, which she refused.

The employer won in this case too. GM transition documents said that severance is not available to employees who refuse to take jobs offered by acquiring companies. The plan's standard of review was "arbitrary and capricious," and the court did not find it arbitrary or capricious to define the employee as having quit her job.

7.7 COMPENSATION DEDUCTION

When the Tax Court decided the case of *Exacto Spring Corp. v. CIR*, 68 LW 1316 (7th Cir. 11/16/99), it used a seven-factor test to determine the reasonableness (and hence deductibility) of executive compensation:

- The type and extent of services rendered by the individual
- The difficulty of finding qualified employees
- The particular employee's qualifications and earnings history
- His or her contributions to the business
- Compensation of comparable executives in other companies
- Characteristics of the particular business paying the compensation

Using these factors, the Tax Court decided that the CEO of a closely-held corporation had been paid about ten times as much as he should have been. However, the Seventh Circuit held that the seven-factor test was not valid because it didn't explain how to weight the various factors; some of the factors were vague; and some of the factors are irrelevant to the real objective of Code §162, which is to prevent dividends to employee-stockholders from being wrongly characterized as (deductible) compensation.

The Seventh Circuit ruled that the compensation ($1.1 million in one year, $1.3 million in another) was somewhat higher than reasonable, but most of the compensation was deductible because it rewarded the CEO for his unusually great success in increasing the investors' rate of return on their investment in the corporation.

Dexsil Corp., TC Memo 1999-155, involved the President and CEO of a closely-held company who owned close to two-thirds of the company's stock (his relatives owned another 21%). He raised corporate sales from $113,000 to $5 million in a seven-year period. The issue before the Tax Court was the reasonableness of his compensation in two years: 1989, when he earned $376,000, and 1990, when he earned $488,000. The Tax Court found the compensation unreasonably high.

On appeal, the Second Circuit said that the Tax Court should have used the test of whether a hypothetical independent investor in the company would have been willing to pay that much. Consideration should also have been given to whether comparable companies paid additional compensation to CEOs who took on other roles (here, the CEO was also the CFO and treasurer). When the case was remanded back to the Tax Court, it still said the compensation was too high because the hypothetical investor would be dissatisfied with the pay level, because it went up when corporate financial results declined, and because it was higher than normally paid to CEOs with multiple roles.

In contrast, the Sixth Circuit, in *Alpha Medical Inc.*, 83 AFTR2d ¶99-697 (6th Cir. 4/19/99) found that $4.4 million compensation paid to a drug company's president and sole shareholder in 1990 was all reasonable. The Sixth Circuit attributed much of the company's $7 million net income to his efforts, and felt that it was fair to compensate him highly when the company had funds, to make up for significant underpayment in years when the company was growing. Because the compensation was reasonable, it was deductible, and therefore the accuracy-related penalty that the IRS assessed against the company was void.

Chapter 8

Wage and Hour Issues

8.1 INTRODUCTION

According to the Bureau of Labor Statistics (BLS), wages and salaries were up 3.9% in 2000, versus a 5.6% increase in benefit costs (including paid leave, retirement, and insurance benefits) experienced by private industry. ["Benefit Costs Jump 5.6 Percent," http://www.cfo.com/printarticle/1,1883,0/83/AD/20212,00.html.]

In late 1999, the Third Circuit held that a bankrupt company remained liable for retroactive wage payments under a collective bargaining agreement, even though the collective bargaining agreement was supposedly assigned in conjunction with the sale of the company's assets. Under Bankruptcy Code §365(k), a debtor can avoid liability for contract obligations only if there has been a complete assignment of both rights and duties under those contracts. In this case, the purchaser specifically disavowed responsibility for those retroactive payments. The effect of the transaction was an attempt to unilaterally amend the collective bargaining agreement, which is forbidden by Bankruptcy Code §1133(f): *American Flint Glass Workers Union v. Anchor Resolution Corp.*, 68 LW 1324 (3rd Cir. 11/24/99).

In the view of the Seventh Circuit, an employee who has a good-faith belief that the employer committed wage-hour violations can bring suit under 29 USC §215(a)(3) [retaliation for filing an FLSA claim] even if, in fact, the employer fell below the FLSA's jurisdictional level of gross sales, and therefore is exempt from FLSA coverage: *Sapperstein v. Hager*, 188 F.3d 852 (7th Cir. 8/17/99).

The Fair Labor Standards Act (FLSA) allows the pay of hourly workers—but not salaried workers—to be docked for absenteeism. DOL Opinion Letter No. 89 (discussed in *Employment Alert*, 3/5/98, p. 11) says that making a deduction from a paycheck to reflect unpaid leave under the Family and Medical Leave Act does not convert an otherwise exempt person into a nonexempt wage worker. However, this relief provision is limited to FMLA leave, where both the worker and the employer firm are subject to the FMLA.

The Workers Economic Opportunity Act, P.L. 106-202 (5/18/00), amends the FLSA (29 USC §207) to make it clear that stock options are not part of the "regular rate of pay" for FLSA purposes. It explains the wage-and-hour treatment of stock option and stock appreciation rights plans.

8.2 MINIMUM WAGE

➠ TIP

If you require uniforms to be worn during working hours, and employees must supply their own, make sure that the cost of the uniforms doesn't drive their overall compensation below the minimum wage. This point comes from Simon J. Nadel, "Employers Relaxing Dress Standards But Potential Pitfalls Remain in Workplace," 67 LW 2195 (10/13/98).

8.4 THE CONTINGENT WORKFORCE

A government-issued report, "Contingent and Alternative Employment Arrangements, February 1999," published by the Bureau of Labor Statistics on December 21, 1999 at http://stats.bls.gov/newsrels.htm (no www), shows consistency in the size of the contingent workforce between February 1997 and February 1999. BLS statistics show that in February 1999, in a strong economy with growing employment, about 8.2 million people worked as independent contractors, 2.0 million worked on an on-call basis, and 1.2 million worked for temporary agencies. This report is valuable for the detailed charts it contains breaking down the different contingent and alternative working arrangements.

Several controversial interpretations have been made of the changes in the workforce. Labor groups say that workers have less access to traditional, career-level jobs with benefits, whereas employer groups point to the greater flexibility desired by workers themselves. According to the Employment Policy Federation, the number of traditional full-time jobs hasn't shrunk—instead, additional non-traditional ways of working have developed to accommodate greater productivity, and the integration of groups (such as women and minorities) not previously as heavily represented in the work force.

The BLS considers any worker (including a self-employed person or independent contractor) "contingent" if he or she expects the current job or assignment to end within the next year—even if it has already lasted for a year or more. By this definition, 4.3% of the workforce is contingent.

In 1999, according to the American Staffing Association and the BLS, the percentage of temporary workers had stabilized at about 2.2% of the non-farm work force (about twice as high as the 1990 level). On an average day, close to three million workers are supplied by staffing agencies. The ASA points out that more than 70% of temporary workers land permanent jobs within a year, and 29% of them are hired straight from a temporary assignment, which serves as a kind of audition for a permanent job.

However, by using a broader definition (freelancers, full-time temporary workers, consultants, independent contractors), Kelly Services reports that in 2000, 26% of the workforce was independent rather than holding conventional jobs. Kelly's survey showed that the median salary for workers employed by a company providing services under a contract was $756 a week, versus $640/week for independent contractors, $472 for on-call workers, and $342 for temporary agency workers.

The BLS, the ASA, and Economy.com report that from 1982 to 2000, the income of temporary workers remained fairly stable at about $20,000 a year (in 2000 dollars), whereas the income of non-farm workers as a whole went up from about $30,000 to nearly $40,000, also in 2000 dollars: the compensation increase was 14.8% for all non-farm workers between 1982-2000, whereas the inflation-adjusted income of temporary workers went up only 5.1% in the same interval

The same team reports that only 5.8% of workers for temporary agencies got pensions and 8.5% got health insurance, but benefit availability was much greater for on-call workers and workers from contract firms.

According to the BLS Employee Benefits Survey published in the autumn of 2000, 30% of part-time private-sector workers got paid holidays (far lower than the 83% of full-time employees entitled to this benefit)in the period 1996-1998. About one-third of part-timers (34%) got paid vacations, versus 87% of full-time workers. Sick leave was available to 15% of part-timers, 60% of full-time workers. [Yochi J. Dreazen, "Regulators Probe U.S. Reliance on Temporary Workers, *WSJ* 8/7/00 p. A2; Kathleen O'Brien, "Calling the Shots: Not Just Athletes Are Free Agents," *NYT* 10/16/00 p. G1; Dylan Loeb McClain, "Labor Puzzle as Need for Temporary Workers Soars, Pay Lags," *NYT* 12/27/00 p. G1; "Share of Full-Time Wage and Salary Jobs Unchanged from the 1950s," Employment Policy Federation Employment Trends, http://www.epf.org/etrend/2000/employmenttrends_Oct2000.pdf (10/24/00), *Compensation and Working Conditions* Fall 2000 p. 60.]

In August, 2000, the NLRB reversed its earlier decision, and allowed temporary workers to be included in the same collective bargaining unit as permanent employees, as long as the characteristics of the jobs are similar—and even if the agency supplying the workers, the company where services are performed, or both, refuse to consent to including the temporary workers in the bargaining unit: *M.B. Sturgis Inc.*, 331 NLRB No. 173, http://www.nlrb.gov/slip331.html (8/25/00).

In December, 1997 the EEOC published guidance on contingent workers as part of its internal compliance manual. (See http://www.eeoc.gov/press/12-8-97.html, discussed at 66 LW 2359.) Based on information from the National

Association of Temporary and Staffing Services showing that more than 2.3 million workers are employed by the temporary help industry, the EEOC stated that agencies and employers are both generally liable for civil rights violations committed in the placement of contingent workers.

If both the staffing firm and its client have control over the worker, then both are joint employers. The staffing agency has the burden of taking immediate and appropriate action (such as refusing to assign any more workers) if it finds that a client company has practiced discrimination against a temporary worker.

TIP

The guidance also notes that individuals in welfare-to-work programs are covered under federal antidiscrimination laws.

The important case of *Bronk v. Mountain States Telephone & Telegraph Inc.*, 140 F.3d 1335 (10th Cir. 1998), holds that, although ERISA forbids excluding employees from the plan once they have satisfied minimal age and service conditions, it is permissible to draft the plan to deny participation to leased employees, even if they are common-law employees. The Tenth Circuit's position (which is not exactly the same as that of the Ninth Circuit; see later) is that IRC §414(n)(1)(A) merely requires that leased employees be treated as employees—it does not require them to be offered plan participation. The decision quotes IRS Notice 84-11, Q&A 14, to support the permissibility of keeping leased employees out of the plan.

The Ninth Circuit reversed the trial court in *Burrey v. Pacific Gas & Electricity*, 159 F.3d 388 (9th Cir. 1998). According to the appeals court, people who had worked at Pacific Gas & Electricity (for 12 years!) through a temp agency were not §414(n) leased employees.

For FLSA purposes, a staffing company and its client companies do not become coemployers. The staffing company is the FLSA employer of temps provided to client companies, because the staffing company hires and controls the workers, assigns them to job sites, and controls their schedules [*Baystate Alternative Staffing Inc. v. Herman*, 163 F.3d 668 (1st Cir. 1998)].

In contrast, the Occupational Safety and Health Review Commission decided that an employee leasing company was *not* subject to the Occupational Safety and Health Act, because the workers were not their employees. In this reading, employees work in the employer's "business," and here the leased workers were assigned to a factory where the leasing company did not exercise significant control over them [*Sec'y of Labor v. Team America Corp.*, 1998 WL 733708 (OSHRC 1998)].

¶10.2 of the main volume discusses the *Vizcaino v. Microsoft* case. On May 12, 1999, the Ninth Circuit rendered another *Vizcaino* decision, #98-71388, 99-35013. Originally, in 97 F.3d 1187 (9th Cir. 1995), aff'd 120 F.3d 1006 (9th Cir. 1997), *cert. denied* 118 S.Ct. 899, the Ninth Circuit decided that members of the class action were really Microsoft employees, not independent contractors, and therefore entitled to participate in Microsoft's stock purchase plan. (For background on Microsoft's very large contingent workforce, see Steven Greenhouse, "Equal Work, Less-Equal Perks," *New York Times*, 3/30/98, p. D1.) The case was sent back to the District Court to sort out the rights of individual plaintiffs. The District Court narrowed down the plaintiff class to certain temp agency employees and workers reclassified as common-law employees by the IRS, and who worked at Microsoft between 1978 and 1990. Microsoft tried to narrow the class down even further, and plaintiffs and potential plaintiffs tried to widen it.

The May 1999 decision by the Ninth Circuit held that temp agency workers could still be common-law employees of Microsoft (and thus entitled to participate in the stock plan) if they also satisfy the common-law control tests. The Ninth Circuit remanded the case to the District Court *again* but required a broader class definition. Microsoft had to prove any reason why a particular person who either came from a temporary agency or was reclassified by the IRS should not have been allowed to participate in the stock purchase plan.

On January 9, 2000, the Supreme Court affirmed the Ninth Circuit without opinion (*cert.denied* #99-498), refusing once again to hear an appeal of the *Vizcaino* decision. In December, 2000, Microsoft agreed to pay $96.9 million to settle *Vizcaino* and another case, *Hughes v. Microsoft Corp.*, No. C98-1646C. The District Court for the Western District of Washington granted its preliminary approval of the settlement on December 12, 2000. The money will be placed in a fund to pay the claims of approximately 8,000-12,000 "permatemps" and to pay attorneys' fees. [See 69 LW 2363; the settlement agreement itself can be viewed at http://www.bs-s.com.]

The Microsoft case reminds us that there are special rules for computer professionals. FLSA §13(a) exempts computer systems analysts, programmers, and software engineers earning $27.63 or more per hour from the overtime rules. (This peculiar figure is derived from 29 CFR §541.303(c), which refers to six and a half times the minimum wage.) But some companies, especially overworked start-ups, do not pay overtime to computer workers who are not true professionals and therefore do not satisfy the §13(a) test. The exemption does not apply to entry-level workers and repair and maintenance technicians. States impose their own requirements too, such as California's overtime exemption, which is limited to highly skilled intellectual and/or creative work paying over $41 an hour. [Victoria Roberts, "Employers Must be Vigilant in Classifying Work of Computer Professionals Under FLSA," 69 LW 2355 (12/19/00).]

Also see *Wolf v. Coca-Cola Co.*, 68 LW 1437 (11th Cir. 1/18/00) finding that it is legitimate for a plan to be drafted to exclude certain categories of workers, so therefore leased employees can be excluded from participation even if they are common-law employees, because not every plan has to cover every common-law employee.

Herman v. Time Warner, 1999 WL 691904 (S.D.N.Y. 1999) permits the Department of Labor to seek equitable relief under ERISA §502(a)(5) for inappropriate classification of employees as project, supplementary, or temporary rather than permanent. The Southern District denied summary judgment, and allowed the DOL suit to continue, despite the availability of ERISA administrative procedures under which the beneficiaries themselves (rather than the federal agency) can enforce their rights to benefits.

An article by Frederick D. Baron, Carrie Battilega, and Mitch Danzig, "Workforce 2000: Alternative Staffing Arrangements," http://www.lawnewsnetwork.com/practice/employmentlaw/papers/lawfirm/A1487-1999May14.html, gives some practical suggestions for problem-free use of temporary workers:

- Have a written contract with the temp agency, clarifying the status of the workers.
- Don't train the temporary workers at your site; make sure that the temp agency provides any needed training.
- Check to make sure the temporary agency maintains appropriate Worker's Compensation coverage for its staff.
- If you ask your employees to sign confidentiality agreements, you can impose the same requirement on temps—but use a separate form that refers to their status as such.
- Want to hire a temp for your permanent workforce? Make it clear to the new hire that his or her start date is the date he or she became permanent (unless your counsel advises you that the new hire must be counted as an employee as of an earlier date).

Baron et al. discuss an emerging form of staffing: the Professional Employer Organization, or PEO. The PEO and its client are joint employers, and therefore have joint responsibility for the people who work under this arrangement. The PEO takes care of HR tasks, while the client trains, manages, and supervises the staffers referred by the PEO. (They are joint employers because each has meaningful employer-type responsibility, albeit in different roles.)

It's vital to make sure that you pay your appropriate share (e.g., of employment-related taxes and Worker's Compensation) and monitor compliance by the PEO of its obligations. In a 1996 bankruptcy case, the PEO client was considered responsible for payroll taxes, even though the contract with the PEO made the PEO responsible [*In re Earth Movers, Inc.*, 1996-2 USTC ¶50,549 (M.D. Fla. 1996)]. In short, a potential PEO arrangement should be scrutinized by your tax advisers, and any necessary adjustments should be made to your payroll system if you adopt the PEO as one of your staffing mechanisms.

Later Insights on Cohorts, Benefits

Hewitt Associates survey figures from October, 1999 ("Benefits for Part-Time Workers on the Rise," http://www.hewitt.com/news/pressrel/1999/10-14-99.htm)

show that, of a sample of about 350 large companies, the availability of medical and dental coverage, paid vacation and sick days, and flex scheduling for part-time workers is increasing. The majority of survey respondents provide benefits for part-timers putting in 30 or more hours a week.

Over three-quarters (78%) offer medical and dental coverage; 91% offer paid vacation and 77% pay for sick days for part-time workers, and nearly half offer flexible work schedules, including telecommuting options. Fifty-seven percent offer short- and long-term disability coverage for part-time workers. The full survey, "Part-Time Employee Benefits in 1999," can be ordered for $175 from Hewitt's publications office, 100 Half Day Road, Lincolnshire, IL 60069, (847) 295-5000.

The Department of Labor's Advisory Council on Employee Welfare and Pension Benefit Plans reported, on November 10, 1999, on its conclusions on the benefit implications of a growing contingent workforce, based on five hearings and the testimony of 15 witnesses. Scholars from EBRI, the Economy Policy Institute, and the Upjohn Institute reached very similar conclusions as to the size of the contingent workforce and their access to employer benefits. See http://www.dol.gov/dol/pwba/public/adcoun/contrpt.htm for this document. The Advisory Council was established under ERISA §512(a)(1) to provide data for the Secretary of Labor.

8.5 WORK SCHEDULING

Boeing required new hires to go through an unpaid orientation period. A class action in Washington State court accepted the plaintiffs' contention that the orientation period was really work. The lower court required payment at the minimum wage for the orientation period; the Washington Court of Appeals required pay at the normal contract rate for the job [*Seattle Professional Engineering Employees Association v. Boeing*, 963 P.2d 204 (Wash. App. 1998)].

In November, 2000, Hewitt Associates surveyed a thousand employers, finding that 57% offered flexible work schedules. According to BLS economist Thomas M. Beers, 25% of workers have access to a flexible schedule, but usually by informal arrangement; only 6% had a formal flextime plan. Women are more likely to have flextime schedules than men, and white workers more than minority workers. Flextime is more common in executive, administrative, managerial, and sales positions, less so in manufacturing, nursing, teaching, and police work and firefighting. [Carol Kleinman, "Many Flex Schedules Are Informal Arrangements," *Chicago Tribune* 11/1/00.]

The *Wall Street Journal*'s September 20, 2000 issue has several articles on page B1 about managing shift work and round-the-clock business schedules, including Sue Shellenbarger's "Some Employers Begin to Find What Helps Shiftworker Families," Kris Maher's "The New 24/7 Work Cycle," and Kemba J. Dunham's "Graveyard Shift Isn't Always a Dead-End Job."

8.5.3 Fewer Hours, Same Pay

Compensation and Benefits Update's 10/7/98 issue (p. 3) gives a thorough treatment of the pros and cons of the 9/80 work schedule, where each work week runs from noon on Friday to noon on the next Friday and includes 40 working hours.

Under California law, as long as the work week does not exceed eight hours, overtime pay is not required for the 9/80 schedule. A single shift can last up to 12 hours. However, the employer must hold a secret ballot and get consent of two-thirds of the workforce before changing the schedule.

8.6 TELECOMMUTING

The Department of Labor's extensive study, "Telework and the New Workplace of the 21st Century," can be found online at http://www.dol.gov/dol/as/public/telework/main.htm. Part I of the study deals with the evolution and economics of telework; Part II relates it to organizational behavior; and Part III examines the cultural and societal implications of working from remote locations with electronic tools.

The International Telework Association and Council says that approximately 24 million Americans telecommute regularly or at least occasionally. But the organization reports that companies are reducing the role of telecommuting (perhaps limiting it to established employees with a proven track record), because it can be hard for telecommuters to participate fully in the creative interactions of the office. Another issue is that broadband connections have not spread as fast as projected. [See Kemba J. Dunham, "Telecommuters' Lament," *WSJ* 10/31/00 p. B1.]

The Olsten Center for Workforce Strategies reports that half of the businesses in the United States and Canada have a pilot or permanent project that allows at least some telecommuting, but many programs are being scaled back for failure to achieve efficiency and cost savings. Employees working at home can get burned out. Just knowing how to use the necessary technology isn't enough for a productive telecommuting experience; employees also need to learn how to schedule and coordinate work.

Managers back at the office need to know how to measure telecommuters' productivity—and keep in-house employees from becoming jealous of what seems to be a sweet deal for the telecommuters.

➡ TIP

Some large companies have taken the pragmatic step of creating an in-house simulation lab to replicate telecommuting conditions. (Smaller companies can join forces to create a shared facility.) Some employees discover that they absolutely hate telecommuting conditions or can't be productive; it's best to find that out in advance, before disrupting everyone's schedule to allow and then phase out telecommuting for that person.

8.7 LEGAL ISSUES OF WORK SCHEDULING

Two recent cases involve police department policies requiring officers who are on sick leave or injury leave to remain at home at all times, except when they are getting medical treatment or have permission of their supervisors. *Aiken v. Memphis, Tennessee,* 190 F.3d 753 (6th Cir. 9/7/99) finds the policy compatible with the FLSA, and not intrusive enough to require the department to pay overtime to officers on leave.

Similarly, *DeBraska v. Milwaukee,* 189 F.3d 650 (7th Cir. 9/2/99) refuses to treat the at-home time as work hours subject to the FLSA. The hours are not "on-call" time (which requires compensation), because sick or injured police officers are not available for work.

8.8 OVERTIME AND OVERTIME PLANNING

In 1998, about one-quarter of the U.S. workforce (estimated at some 19–26 million workers) were exempt from overtime, because they came within one of the FLSA's exemptions (executive, administrative, or professional workers). The proportion of the U.S. workforce that is exempt continues to rise, for many reasons. The service sector is growing, and many service workers qualify for an exemption. Also, as the proportion of female workers in the workforce increases (42% in 1998 versus 33% in 1983) so does the number of white-collar workers entitled to exemption. The salary tests haven't kept pace with inflation, so many low-level workers are nonetheless exempt on this basis. Both employers and employees want clear tests that are easy to administer, although employers certainly have an interest in exemption, whereas employees often prefer to be eligible for overtime pay. (See Fair Labor Standards Act: White-Collar Exemptions in the Modern Work Place, GAO/HEHS-99-164.)

The Department of Labor's Wage and Hour Division handles about 40,000 complaints a year, and 70% of its investigations stem from employee complaints. In 1997, U.S. industry paid $63 million for back wages and penalties affecting over 125,000 employees. The DOL sued Iowa Beef Processors over 14 minutes of setup/cleanup work required of each employee each day. The suit resulted in an award of $7.1 million in back wages and interest. (See Carla Joinson, "Keeping Time," *HR Magazine,* 10/98, p. 120.)

In a similar case, the Tenth Circuit found that meat packers who were paid on "gang time," from the first animal part arriving at the workstation to the last, had to spend at least 10 minutes of compensable time before shift (to put on protective gear) and after shift (to clean up). Because this was not a trivial amount, and because the company was on notice because of other violations, the three-year statute of limitations for willful violations was applied, and the company had to pay $1.5 million in compensatory damages, plus pre- and postjudgment interest [*Reich v. Monfort, Inc.,* 144 F.3d 1329 (10th Cir. 1998)].

A refrigerator repairman who worked for a supermarket chain had the job of reporting to his scheduled first job of the day by 8 A.M., and covering repair sites in a three-state area. He was paid an hourly wage from 8 to 4:30 P.M. He sought overtime for the extensive (often 7-8 hours a day) of driving time, but lost his case. In the view of the Second Circuit, driving to the first job site, and home from the last job site, although admittedly extremely time-consuming, nevertheless fell within the definition of "normal travel" between home and work that is not compensable and not subject to overtime: *Kavanagh v. Grand Union Co.*, 68 LW 1204 (2nd Cir. 9/28/99).

The plaintiff in *Valerio v. Putnam Associates Inc.*, 1999 WL 188284 (1st Cir. 1999) was hired as a receptionist/administrative assistant, and was told that the job was exempt. Later, the District Court determined that the job was in fact nonexempt. When she asked for more research and administrative tasks (i.e., involving more discretion and professionalism) she was told that she was just a receptionist. She sent a letter to the employer, saying that in that case, she should receive overtime pay. She was fired; her final check included an amount representing overtime.

She brought suit under the FLSA for additional overtime payment and for retaliation damages. The First Circuit (like the Sixth, Eighth, Tenth, and Eleventh, but unlike the Second and Ninth) takes the position that an internal letter can constitute protected activity, retaliation for which is illegal. However, the Second and Ninth Circuits require litigation or a formal agency complaint to support a retaliation claim.

Several recent cases make a point that might seem obvious: the actual duties of the job, not the title, control whether overtime is payable. An auto dealer's office manager was held not to be an exempt "executive" (*Lott v. Howard Wilson Chrysler-Plymouth*, 203 F.3d 326 (5th Cir. 2000), but she did do office work such as payroll preparation, and supervised four other people, so she could properly be treated as an exempt "administrator."

Several class actions were brought in California in 2000 and 2001, alleging that ordinary hourly workers were being given meaningless "assistant manager" titles to get the employers off the hook for paying overtime. Cases have been brought against Taco Bell, Wal-Mart, U-Haul, Wendy's, and other large companies. [Shannon Lafferty, "Meaningless Titles Ploy to Avoid Overtime, Say California Workers," *The Recorder* 2/15/01 (law.com).] Mervyn's and Ross Dress for Less have already agreed to multi-million-dollar settlements about these practices.

Because their compensation was reduced for lack of work when business in the individual store was slow, Wal-Mart pharmacists were hourly rather than salaried employees, and thus qualified for overtime pay when business picked up and they had to work long hours: *Presley v. Wal-Mart Stores Inc.*, 1999 WL 591994 (D. Colo. 1999).

The employer in *Uphoff v. Elegant Bath, Ltd.*, 1999 WL 250849 (7th Cir. 1999) required a significant number of overtime hours, but paid only straight-time rates for this work. However, employees who worked overtime got other benefits, such as cash payments and use of the company's vehicles, materials, and supplies. Clearly, the employer had to make up the unpaid overtime payments; the question facing the Seventh Circuit was whether the employer also had to pay liquidated damages. The Seventh Circuit required liquidated damages, finding that the employer did not meet its burden of showing that it reasonably believed its actions were legal. Thus, it did not act in good faith, and liquidated damages were appropriate.

Many employees, especially those with family responsibilities, prefer comp time to overtime pay. However, the law requires comp time to be used in the same week as the overtime it compensates. If a nonexempt employee works more than 40 hours a week, overtime pay is required, even if the overtime was unauthorized. (The unauthorized work is a disciplinary, not a wage-and-hour, issue.) If supervisors are pressured to finish a certain amount of work in a certain amount of time, the company probably won't be able to claim that overtime was unauthorized. Raising output requirements or adding new projects may create an inference that overtime was required.

Wage-and-hour investigators look at real responsibilities and tasks and are not impressed by "title inflation," which makes a person sound like a manager when in fact he or she is really doing routine nonexempt tasks. A merger or acquisition could lead to reshuffling of titles and responsibilities and might result either in a promotion that makes a nonexempt person exempt or a demotion that has the contrary effect.

The following are some items that may require compensation or overtime:

- Rest breaks under 20 minutes
- Down time or on-call time that prevents the employee from pursuing personal business
- Preparation before shift; cleanup after shift
- Classes, meetings, and conventions that are mandatory rather than optional
- Unscheduled, or even unauthorized, work actually performed by the employee
- Travel time when the employee is away from home on business or moving between job sites (but not normal commuting)

If overtime is required, it must be paid at a rate of time-and-a-half, including shift differentials and call pay. If substantial bonuses are paid on a regular basis, they must be included in the hourly rate calculation.

As ¶23.8 shows, retaliation cases are a growing part of the employment discrimination caseload. In 1998, the Ninth Circuit tackled an FLSA retaliation case, in *Lambert v. Ackerly*, 156 F.3d 1018 (9th Cir. 1998). The plaintiffs used to work selling tickets for the Seattle SuperSonics. Initially, they were paid a $13,000 base salary plus commissions. The team made a $2000 allowance for overtime; after that, employees were told either to take comp time or stop working overtime. A productive sales rep could earn as much as $90,000 a year. The team changed the compensation system, telling the sales reps to work from 8:30 to 5:30 without overtime. The reps, not unnaturally, didn't like the new system and contacted the Department of Labor for information about overtime compensation. One of the plaintiffs claimed that the team's controller threatened her with firing if she kept up with the overtime issue. She, and five other people, were discharged. They sued under FLSA §215(a)(3)(the antiretaliation provision), which forbids discrimination against employees who file complaints or institute or testify at FLSA proceedings; they also claimed that their discharge violated the public policy of the state.

They did very well at the trial court level, getting not only compensatory damages but punitive damages and emotional distress damages. The Ninth Circuit dismissed the FLSA retaliation charges because the employees had not filed a complaint or testified at a hearing. Contacting the DOL doesn't reach the level of participating in formal legal proceedings.

Washington State law is more generous to employees: It bans retaliation against anyone who has complained to the employer or is "about to cause to be instituted" a wage and hour proceeding. Complaints by the plaintiff group therefore entitled them to protection against retaliation under state law, but not to punitive damages (because state law does not make this remedy available in wrongful termination cases).

The Fourth Circuit has ruled (*Ball v. Memphis Bar-B-Q Co.*, 228 F.3d 360 (4th Cir. 2000) that FLSA anti-retaliation protection is only triggered by the actual filing of a suit. Therefore, the anti-retaliation provision does not protect a person allegedly fired for saying that he would testify contrary to the company president's account of events that might be the subject of a future lawsuit. And, according to the Eleventh Circuit, punitive damages are not available for violation of the anti-retaliation provisions: *Snapp v. Unlimited Concepts, Inc.*, 208 F.3d 928 (11th Cir. 2000).

8.12 TRUST FUND TAX COMPLIANCE AND THE 100% PENALTY

The FUTA wage base remains at $7,000 for 2001. Employers in all states continue to pay a net FUTA rate of 0.8%. The state taxable wage bases for 2001 range widely, from $7,000 in several states (e.g., Florida; Nebraska) to $28,400 (Hawaii).

What is the status of nonqualified deferred compensation (e.g., "top hat" plans for executives) for Federal Insurance Contributions Act (FICA) and Federal Unemployment Tax Act (FUTA) purposes? IRS Final Regulations issued January 29, 1999, dealing with Code §3121, provide the answers. In general, wages are subject to FICA and FUTA when they are paid, or when they are considered "constructively" paid. Welfare plan benefits and severance pay are not considered deferred compensation. "Window benefits"—early retirement incentives that are available only for a limited time—are not considered deferred compensation if they are paid after January 1, 2000; before that, employers could elect to treat them as deferred compensation.

Nonqualified deferred compensation counts for FICA and FUTA either when the work giving rise to the compensation is done or when the right to collect the deferred amounts is no longer subject to a substantial risk of forfeiture—whichever comes later.

The Code includes "nonduplication" rules to make sure that the same amount is not subjected to FICA and FUTA both when the work is done and when the funds are actually paid out. Stock options are not considered deferred compensation as long as compensation is actually or constructively received in the year the option is exercised.

An IRS Field Service Memo from 1999, FSA 199948002, involves FICA treatment of bonuses to employees. The employer paid some bonuses in the year after the year to which they relate. Originally, the employer treated the bonuses as taxable income and FICA wages. Later, the employer took the position that the bonuses actually represented nonqualified deferred compensation to persons who had already paid the maximum FICA tax in the year to which the bonuses relate. But the IRS position is that the plan does not provide nonqualified deferred compensation, because employee participation can be terminated at any time at the employer's option, and employees could not enforce payment of the bonuses. Therefore, FICA tax was due in the year of actual payment.

A university offered early retirement incentives to both tenured professors and high-level administrators. According to the District of North Dakota, the payments to professors were made in exchange for surrender of contractual rights, and therefore were not FICA wages. But similar payments to administrators were subject to FICA. The court drew the distinction because administrators are at-will employees, but tenured professors cannot be dismissed except for grave cause: *North Dakota State U. v. U.S.*, 85 AFTR2d ¶2000-332 (D.N.D. 11/19/99).

Severance payments to retiring employees are subject to FICA under Code §3121(a). [*Abrahamsen*, CCH Unemployment Insurance Reporter (UIR) ¶16,429B (Fed.Cir. 2000).]

Larson v. U.S., 84 AFTR2d ¶99-5696 (D.Wa. 1999) upholds the imposition of the 100% penalty on an attorney who was the majority shareholder in a closely-held corporation, even though he was not an officer or director and was not involved in daily operations. Personal liability was deemed appropriate because he had the power to sign checks, control operations, and incur debt on behalf of the corporation; in fact, he took out a personal loan to pay taxes for the corporation.

Several cases from 2000 [E.g., *Karnofsky*, CCH UIR ¶16,473B (M.D. Fla.); *Battles*, CCH UIR ¶16,374B (D.Ala.); *Harris*, CCH UIR ¶16,353B (D.Fla); *Jepsen*, CCH UIR ¶16,354B (D.Ark).] reinforce the familiar theme that a business owner or top executive is a responsible person based on control of the business' finances—especially if other creditors were being paid at the time that trust fund taxes were **not** being paid.

8.13 TAX DEPOSITS: PAPER FORMS

The IRS is phasing out acceptance of paper forms from business filers with HR compliance obligations. Temporary and Proposed IRS Regulations provide that, for deposits after December 31, 2000, the Federal Reserve Bank of St. Louis—the sole Federal Reserve Bank still accepting paper coupons—would no longer do so. Because paper coupons are now down to 1/2 of 1% of all deposits, it is no longer cost-effective for the Federal Reserve system to handle them.

Businesses that are not eligible for, or are unable to use, the Electronic Federal Tax Payment System (EFTPS) can mail paper documents to Financial Agent, Federal Tax Deposit Processing, PO Box 970030, St. Louis, MO 63197.

8.14 PAYING TAXES ELECTRONICALLY

TD 8828, 1999-30 IRB 120, raises the threshold required for mandatory EFT payments from $50,000 to $200,000, for deposit return periods that begin after the year 1999. Taxpayers who first become subject to deposit in 1999 or later years get a one-year grace period to move from paper to electronic payment.

Since December, 2000, employers have been able to log on to http://www.ssa.gov to get a PIN number and password to be used in electronically transmitting W-2 and W-3 forms over the Internet. See Rev.Proc. 2001-9, 2001-3 IRB 328 for specifications for electronic and on-line filing of Form 940.

➠ TIP

940-EZ forms, and late or amended 940s, cannot be filed electronically. Information is available at http://www.irs.gov (or by calling the e-File Help line in Austin, Texas: (512) 460-8900) for online filing of Form 941.

Chapter 9

EMPLOYEE GROUP HEALTH PLANS (EGHPs)

9.2 CONTENT OF THE PLAN

On January 25, 2000, the Supreme Court affirmed (without opinion; #98-4112) the Seventh Circuit's decision in *Doe v. Mutual of Omaha.* The Seventh Circuit ruled that it is not a violation of ADA Title II (public accommodations) for either an insured or self-insured health plan to impose a lifetime cap on AIDS-related conditions that is much lower than the cap for other conditions (e.g., $25,000 versus $1 million). The court's rationale is that Mutual of Omaha didn't refuse to sell policies to people with AIDS, although admittedly the policy was worth a lot less to someone with AIDS or an AIDS-related condition than someone with other health problems.

A unionized company that wants its employees to pay 30% of the premium thereby has an obligation to release information to the union about the health care claims of nonunion employees and their dependents. Such information is not confidential, because the employer has opened up the issue of health care costs and cost containment [*U.S. Testing Co. v. NLRB,* 160 F.3d 14 (D.C. Cir. 1998)].

A self-insured health plan specifically excluded gastric stapling procedures used for weight loss. Therefore, the plan was correct to exclude coverage of complications of the stapling procedure, even life-threatening ones: *Carr v. Gates Health Care Plan,* 1999 WL 959648 (7th Cir. 1999).

International Brotherhood of Teamsters Health & Welfare Trust Fund v. Philip Morris, 68 LW 1311 (7th Cir. 11/15/99) holds that welfare benefit plans and health insurers can't bring antitrust or RICO suits against tobacco manufacturers, based on an allegation of harm in the form of benefits paid for tobacco-related illnesses. The so-called harm is too remote; a third-party payor can recover only based on contracts that provide for subrogation.

The Pension and Welfare Benefits Administration issued a major statement on the SPD requirements for health plans [62 FR 48376 (9/8/98)], dealing not only with the pension plan SPD (see Chapter 14) but with disclosures health plans must make with respect to Comprehensive Omnibus Budget Reconciliation Act (COBRA), Health Insurance Portability and Accountability Act (HIPAA) portability, and the Newborns' and Mothers' Health Protection Act.

Group health plan SPDs must include the following:

- Participants' cost-sharing obligations, such as premiums, deductibles, coinsurance, and copayments
- Caps (lifetime or annual) on plan benefits, or other benefit limits
- Coverage of preventive services
- Coverage (if any) of existing and new drugs
- Coverage of medical tests, devices, and procedures
- Which health care providers are inside the network
- Circumstances under which network providers must be used; coverage, if any, of out-of-network services
- How primary care and specialty providers must be selected
- Conditions for getting emergency care
- Requirements for preauthorization of treatment and utilization review

It's permissible for the SPD to include only a general description of the provider network, as long as the SPD discloses the availability of a separate document (furnished without charge) that lists all the network providers.

The Summary Plan Description for a health plan must describe the rights and responsibilities of employees and their families with respect to COBRA continuation coverage (see later)—(e.g., what constitutes a COBRA qualifying event; premiums ex-employees must pay for continuation coverage; notice procedures; how to make an election; and how long coverage will last). EGHP SPDs must either describe the plan's procedures with respect to qualified medical child support order (QMCSO) determination, or must inform participants and beneficiaries that, on request, they can get a free copy of the plan's QMCSO procedures. The description should be ample enough to assist potential alternate payees in enforcing their rights.

➠ TIP

A manual drafted for the administrative staff of a welfare benefit plan was not an SPD, even if the employee relied on it, because it was designed as an internal plan document, not a tool for employees to understand their benefits better [*Cooperative Benefit Plan Administrators Inc. v. Whittle*, 989 F.Supp. 1421 (M.D. Ala. 1997)].

9.2.1 Mental Health Parity

Extensive, significant interim regulations on implementation of the mental health parity rules were jointly published by the IRS, Department of Labor, and Department of Health and Human Services on December 22, 1997. The rules begin at page 66931 of Volume 62 of the *Federal Register*. The mental health parity requirement took effect for plan years beginning on or after January 1, 1998. It is scheduled to expire for services provided on or after September 30, 2001 (unless Congress chooses to extend it).

Under these rules, an EGHP that provides both medical and mental health benefits can satisfy the parity requirements in various ways:

- Not having any lifetime limit or annual dollar limitation on mental health benefits
- Using the same aggregate lifetime or annual dollar limits for physical and mental treatments
- Setting separate limits, as long as the mental health limit is not smaller than the limit for physical ailments
- Using a weighted limit for mental health benefits, to reflect the plan's differential treatment for different categories of physical illness

> **TIP**
>
> Note that if there is a separate limit for mental health benefits, benefits for treating substance abuse cannot be counted toward that limit.

The interim rule provides assistance in calculating the "increased cost" exception (parity is not required if it would increase the cost of the plan by 1% or more). It is estimated that 90% of plans will encounter cost increases of less than 1% and thus would not be entitled to exemption. Plans that claim this exemption must disclose to the Department of Treasury the notice that they give their plan participants and beneficiaries. (The interim rule provides model notices that can be used to comply with this requirement.)

In the same issue of the *Federal Register*, on page 66967, the IRS indicated that the text of those interim rules would also operate as IRS temporary regulations.

In mid-2000, the GAO published two reports about compliance with the Mental Health Parity Act of 1996. The GAO's conclusion was that as of December, 1999, 85% of employers who were surveyed responded that they were in compliance with the parity requirement of parity in annual and lifetime dollar limits in EGHPs (versus only 55% of employers who offered parity in 1996, before the statute took effect).

However, the GAO found that 87% of the plans that complied on this measure had at least one other design feature in the plan that is more restrictive for mental health than for other benefits. Only about 3% of the employers said that compliance increased their claims costs, and almost no employers dropped mental health coverage or other health benefits because they found the parity requirement so onerous. ["Mental Health Parity Act: Despite New Federal Standards, Mental Health Benefits Remain Limited," GAO/HEHS-00-95 (5/10/00); "Mental Health Parity Act: Employers' Mental Health Benefits Remain Limited Despite New Federal Standard," GAO/T-HEHS-00-113 (5/18/00).]

One of President Clinton's last acts before leaving office was an Executive Order requiring phasing in of mental health parity (including substance abuse treatment) in federal employment no later than January 1, 2001. This is a significant move because of the size of the federal workforce.

Most (32) of the states have some kind of mental health parity requirement of their own. Although originally fears were expressed that a mental health parity requirement would cause an explosion of employees seeking treatment for personal problems, the average cost increase due to health care parity is only 1.4%.

For one thing, a great deal of contemporary treatment for mental illness is short-term and biologically based, relying on antidepressants and other drugs rather than "talk therapy." The state laws are compatible with managed care, which also tends to limit lengthy hospitalizations and outpatient treatment.

In fact, enhanced treatment of mental illnesses can reduce other medical bills: employees who can cope with stress better are less likely to develop ulcers or have accidents, for instance.

Of the 32 states with parity requirements, 19 limit them to specific illnesses; typical choices are psychoses, major depressive disorders, obsessive-compulsive disorder, and/or serious biologically-based mental illness. One weakness of the state programs is that they often fail to cope with children's mental illness, because the biologically-based illnesses often do not manifest until adolescence. [See Erica Goode, "9 Million Gaining Upgraded Benefit for Mental Care," *New York Times* 1/1/01 p. A1.]

9.2.2 Maternity Stays

Interim and Proposed rules to implement the 1996 Newborns' and Mothers' Health Protection Act were issued jointly by the IRS, Pension and Welfare Benefit Administration, and Health Care Financing Administration. See 63 FR 57,545 for the interim rules and 57,565 for the proposed rules; both were published on October 27, 1998. The interim rules make it clear that, when a baby is delivered in the hospital, the stay begins at the time of delivery (or the last delivery, in a multiple birth). If the mother is admitted to the hospital after delivering elsewhere, the stay begins at the time of admission.

The 1998 rules forbid health plans to punish health care providers for complying with the Health Protection Act. It is improper to make payments or incentives to either a mother or a health care provider to induce an earlier check-out from the hospital. However, it is permissible to offer postdischarge follow-up after an early discharge, as long as the services obtained do not exceed those that would be provided during the 48- or 96-hour stay required by the Health Protection Act. Plans are not permitted to offer benefits that are less generous during an extended than during a normal maternity stay, and they may not increase the mother's co-payment obligations during the extended period.

9.2.3 Other Inclusion Issues

In 1999, more and more plans began to include at least some coverage of acupuncture, aromatherapy, homeopathy, reflexology, massage, and other alternatives to conventional Western medicine. Often, this was a win-win proposition for the plan: adding such coverage increased employee satisfaction, while also reducing plan costs.

Voucher plans—a new way to provide care, rather than a new type of care—also gained attention.

Alternative and Complementary Care

Alternative medicine is used instead of conventional Western care. Complementary medicine is used in conjunction with it. In 1997, according to the AMA, Americans actually made more visits to alternative practitioners than to family physicians, and out-of-pocket spending on alternative care was $27 billion—close to the $29 billion patients spent out-of-pocket on visits to traditional physicians. (Of course, employers spent heavily on conventional medical care.)

In 1998, more than 30 insurance companies included alternative care in their health plans. A November 1997 study by Landmark Health care shows that 62% of respondents think that access to alternative care is an important factor in choosing a health plan; 45% would be willing to pay extra for such access; and 42% used alternative care in 1996.

Employers considering adding alternative/complementary medical coverage to their plans are not just concerned about cost, but also the effectiveness of the treatments and the legitimacy of the providers. Most plans provide reimbursement only for treatment by licensed alternative practitioners who maintain appropriate liability insurance. [William Atkinson, "A New Twist on Health Care," *HR Magazine,* 6/99, p. 66.]

An April 1999 survey of members of the Society of Certified Employee Benefit Specialists yielded 534 questionnaires, 382 from corporate members. Close to half (45%) of the respondents had personally used at least one method of alternative care in the previous year, usually massage (54%) or herbal medicine (50%). About one-fifth of employers (19%) have yielded to employee demand, and provide at least one alternative-care benefit (usually acupuncture). Two-thirds of survey respondents expect alternative-care coverage to increase. See "Health Benefits for Alternative Medicine: Is There a Fit?" http://www.ifepb.org/recen99a.html.

Defined Contribution and Voucher Plans

Some employers are beginning to think that just about anything they do in the health benefits arena is bound to be controversial, so they're bowing out. There's an increasing trend toward offering employees health care vouchers and letting them make health care decisions—and, not incidentally, take the heat off the employers! This trend is explored by Ron Winslow and Carol Gentry, "Health-Benefits Trend: Give Workers Money, Let Them Buy a Plan," *Wall Street Journal,* 2/8/00, p. A1.

In effect, the voucher works like a defined-contribution or 401(k) plan, shifting control to the workers—but also putting them at risk if they make bad or simply unlucky choices.

In a voucher plan, the employer agrees to give employees a fixed amount that they can use to choose among a menu of health care choices. That way, the employer's exposure is limited, and is not subject to price increases by health care insurers and providers. If employees want a plan that is more expensive than the employer contribution, they have to make up the difference themselves.

Vouchers can save money for employers (unless, down the road, they get hit with major lawsuits!), but do not necessarily have the motivational effect that underlies the provision of benefits. Employers concerned with finding employees in a tight labor market may have to maintain their traditional benefit levels to attract workers.

EBRI's 1999 Health Insurance Preference Survey (discussed in the WestGroup Employment Alert issue of 6/10/99, p. 7) found that about two-thirds of respondents were satisfied with their current ratio of benefits to cash compensation, and would prefer not to get higher cash compensation if the result would be that they would have to shop for, purchase, and maintain their own health coverage. Another 20% would be willing to take a pay cut to get better health benefits; only 8% would rather have more cash and lower benefits. The older the worker, the more likely they were to prefer employer-based to individual health insurance.

When the Employee Benefits Research Institute (EBRI) held its Members' Conclave in December 2000, cost trends such as extremely high premium increases for managed care sparked interest in defined contribution health plans. [EBRI Members' Conclave 12/7/00 Fact Sheet, http://www.ebri.org/conclave/fact3.pdf.] In a fixed-dollar contribution plan, the employer offers a choice of health plans and gives each worker a certain amount of compensation to buy insurance. Employees who want a more expensive policy must use their own pre-tax dollars and pay the difference. In a fixed-percentage contribution plan, the employer contributes a percentage of the premium, and the employee pays the rest.

If the employer does not maintain a health plan, it could give the employees a one-time raise that they can use as they wish, including securing individual insurance coverage. But, according to a survey by the KPMG Peat Marwick and Kaiser Family Foundation Health Research and Educational Trust, at least 50% of employers say they are very unlikely to switch to a defined contribution health plan within the next five years. One major disincentive is that employees tend to see this as a cut in benefits, and therefore are less motivated.

Self-Insured Plans

As insurance premiums increase, employers give more serious consideration to self-funding employee health care. See http://benefitsboard.net/showthread/php?threadid-7530 (no www) for an interesting discussion on tactics for self-insuring health care, including the pitfalls of doing so. Vicki Lankarge's "How to Make Claims Under a Self-Insured Health Plan," http://www.insure.com/health/dol help.html provides useful information for employees working for self-insured employers.

Participants in the discussion cited reasons like avoiding the benefit mandates imposed on insured plans and ability to benefit from the investment return on funds escrowed for health claims.

However, a self-insured plan has a heavy administrative and disclosure burden (and the plan can no longer rely on getting its SPDs supplied by the insurer!). Reinsurance is vital, because even a young and healthy employee group can incur catastrophically high claims if, for example, an employee is in a serious accident or has a multi-handicapped child. Furthermore, health care providers tend to shift costs onto self-payors. One way to cope is to use a Blue Cross or other insurance entity as a Third-Party Administrator, because that may give your plan access to their discount structure. Discussants warned that, if a company has an unsuccessful experiment with self-insurance, it will have to maintain the self-insured plan for a while after returning to the insurance system, in order to handle claims already incurred during the self-insurance regime.

Michael A. McKuin's Web page, "The Stop-Loss Shuffle," [http://members.aol.com/mmckuin/stoploss-page1.html] gives some important insights into stop-loss coverage for self-insured plans. He warns that plans are at risk of conflict of interest if they get stop-loss coverage from the same company that provides TPA services, because the coverage is provided by a party in control of the plan and plan assets.

In a specific stop-loss plan, the insurer agrees to reimburse the employer or other plan sponsor for any claim that exceeds a specified amount (known as the retention). An aggregate stop-loss plan covers all claims above the retention in a particular year.

In effect, a stop-loss plan is really an insurance policy with a very high deductible. But from the insurer's viewpoint, a specified stop-loss plan is more favorable, because although the insurer collects premiums in either case, it has no direct liability to the employees covered by a stop-loss plan, and cannot be sued by them for allegedly improper denials of claims or refusals to pre-approve treatment. A stop-loss plan ends on a particular date, and the insurer is not responsible for claims that accrued by that date but have not yet been filed. In contrast, an insured plan is responsible for such "tail" or IBNR (Incurred But Not Reported) claims.

Contraception

A December 14, 2000 EEOC decision [Available at http://www.eeoc.gov/docs/decision-contraception.html] agrees with the charging parties, a group of female employees, that it violates Title VII for a plan to fail to cover prescription contraceptive drugs and devices when it covers other types of preventive medical care, and when it covers vasectomy and tubal ligation (permanent surgical methods of contraception). The agency says that this is discrimination on the basis of sex (in that only women use birth control pills, diaphragms, and IUDs) and pregnancy.

The EEOC's rationale is that the PDA forbids discrimination on the basis of potential as well as actual pregnancy. Employers can lawfully exclude coverage of abortion, but not of contraception. The employer said that contraception was not covered because the plan only covers abnormal health conditions, but the plan covers sterilization of healthy persons who wish not to procreate in the future.

Furthermore, the EEOC notes that health plans often cover vaccination and preventive examinations, which operate like contraception in that they prevent healthy employees from encountering unwanted health conditions. The EEOC required the plan to cover the full range of available prescription contraceptives, because a woman employee's needs might change in the course of employment.

9.2.4 Domestic Partner Benefits

EBRI notes that the most usual definition of domestic partner involves several elements:

- The partners are adults.
- They are not close blood relatives.
- They have a committed, exclusive personal relationship.
- They share their financial lives, e.g., by owning property together or having joint bank accounts.

Employees seeking coverage for domestic partners should be asked to prove the nature of the relationship, although care should be taken to avoid invasions of privacy.

Domestic partner benefits, so far, have not proved very expensive for employers. Only a small percentage of the workforce will be participating in domestic partnerships (the vast majority are either married or single), and many domestic partners already have employment-related coverage.

Although companies that cover same-sex couples do have some financial risk of encountering AIDS-related health costs, they have a lower financial risk of pregnancy, pregnancy complications, and costs for care of premature infants than EGHPs in general. Furthermore, many domestic partners are young and healthy, so they make few claims on the EGHP. ["Basic Facts About Domestic Partner Benefits," http://www.lambdalegal.org/cig-bin-pages/documents/record?record=17; "Facts from EBRI: Domestic Partner Benefits" (March 1999), http://www.ebri.org/facts/0399afact.htm.]

According to the Human Rights Campaign, as of August, 2000, there were 3,572 companies, institutions, and government units that already offered or were about to offer domestic partner benefits—this was 25% higher than the tally from a year earlier. Of the Fortune 500 companies, 70 offered domestic partner benefits in 1999 versus 102 in 2000. Furthermore, 2000 was the year in which the Big Three automakers (Ford, GM, and DaimlerChrysler, with an aggregate of 466,000 hourly and salaried workers) as well as Coca-Cola added domestic partner benefits.

About two-thirds of the companies that offer domestic partner benefits do so to both same-sex and heterosexual couples. The other third rely on the rationale that benefits should be limited to same-sex couples because male-female couples have the option of marrying and thereby qualifying for conventional family benefits.

Note that, under Reg. §1.106-1, employees are not taxed on coverage provided to their spouse or dependents—but there is no regulatory language about domestic partners. Therefore, unless the relationship is recognized by the state as spousal, or unless the domestic partner qualifies as a dependent under Code §152(a)(8) (i.e., the employee domestic partner provides at least half the support for a domestic partner who shares his or her household), the employee will have taxable income equal to the value of the dependent coverage. However, if local law makes it illegal to cohabit, or for persons of the same sex to cohabit, Code §152(b)(5) does not permit the domestic partner to be considered a dependent.

If the domestic partner is a dependent, then the cost of the domestic partner benefits is exempt from FICA and FUTA. If the cost is taxable to the employee, both FICA and FUTA will apply in addition to income tax. Under Reg. §1.61-21(b)(1), the gross income for the employee is the fair market value of the taxable fringe benefit minus any amount the employee paid for it. However, because the employee has already been taxed on this cost, neither the employee nor the domestic partner will be taxed on fringe benefits (e.g., health insurance reimbursement) actually provided under the plan. [Norihiko Shioruzu, "Gay Couples to Get Benefits at Auto Makers," *Wall Street Journal* 6/9/00 p. A3; No By-Line, "More Companies Offering Same-Sex Partner Benefits," *New York Times* 9/26/00 p. C2; No By-Line, "Health Benefits for Employees' Domestic Partners Become More Popular But Carry Tax Costs," *Benefits and Compliance Alert* 7/12/00 p. 6.]

A state university's denial of health insurance benefits to the same-sex domestic partners of family members has been held to violate the Oregon state Constitution. *Tanner v. Oregon Health Sciences University*, 971 P.2d 435 (Ore. App. 1998) holds that unmarried same-sex couples constitute a true class. They are not permitted to marry, and therefore discrimination against them represents unconstitutional discrimination on the basis of sexual orientation and not, as the university claimed, a distinction on the basis of marital status.

According to the Southern District of New York, neither Title VII nor the Equal Pay Act is violated when a company grants domestic partner benefits to same-sex couples but denies them to unmarried heterosexual couples: *Foray v. Bell Atlantic*, 67 LW 1774 (S.D.N.Y. 6/7/99). The court's rationale is that male–female couples who want access to family benefits have the option of getting married to secure them, whereas male–male or female–female couples do not have this choice.

According to *Irizarry v. Chicago Board of Education*, 69 LW 1128 (N.D. Ill. 7/26/00), the practice of limiting domestic partner benefits to same-sex couples furthers the legitimate government interest of recruiting and retaining qualified employees who have same-sex life partners.

9.2.5 Dental Plans

Dental coverage is extremely common: in 1997, 93% of companies in a William M. Mercer survey offered dental plans, although 37% made it an optional rather than a standard benefit. Nearly all (86%) provided dental coverage on a fee-for-service basis, but 29% had both managed care and fee-for-service components in the dental plan.

An emerging new form (which has picked up speed since the American Dental Association endorsed it in 1996) is the direct reimbursement plan, now offered by thousands of companies (although there is no authoritative survey of the total number of these plans). These are fee-for-service plans, where employees choose their own dentists, and most dental services and procedures are eligible for coverage.

The plans set a limit; up to the limit, the employee is entitled to payment of a percentage of dental expenses. The most common system is for the plan to pay the first $100 in expenses in full, then pay 50% of the next $1800 of expenses, phasing out at the plan limit of $1000. Companies like these plans because they are very easy and inexpensive to administer, either in-house or through a TPA. Originally, the plans were set up so that patients paid the dentist, then got reimbursed by the plan; many such plans today assign benefits (i.e., the plan pays the dentist, so the patient is not out-of-pocket). [Nancy Hatch Woodward, "Less Painful Dental Plans," *HR Magazine*, 9/99, p. 92. The American Dental Association, (800) 232-7698, can provide referrals for companies that want to create a plan.]

9.2.6 Prescription Drug Coverage

Prescription drug costs are among the fastest-growing components in the health care cost equation, and many managed care plans show prescription cost increases of 15–20% a year. One important factor in the cost explosion is the introduction of high-priced drugs for previously untreatable conditions.

The typical pharmacy plan requires beneficiaries to make a copayment (usually somewhere between $5 and $25 per prescription filled), with the result that the plan, and therefore the employer, bears the brunt of cost increases. That makes it important for employers to find cost-control strategies. (See Miles Z. Epstein & David G. Epstein, "Prescription for Success," *HR Magazine,* 6/99, p. 73.)

Some that have worked:

- Working with a PBM (pharmacy benefit management) company to take advantage of economies of scale in drug buying. PBMs have 115 million members, and handle about 60% of retail drug prescriptions. PBM can offer the average employer savings of 20–25%. Allan Zimmerman of the PBM National Prescription Administrators Inc. says, "If an employer is transitioning to a PBM from a fee-for-service plan, it can expect to save 10% to 15% on administrative costs, 5–10% on claims adjudication costs and 5–15% by limiting coverage for expensive or cosmetic drugs via formularies." Some PBMs share the risk of price increases by offering a guarantee, such as accepting half the risk if the plan's average price per prescription goes up by more than a specified percentage. But employers who get a deal of this kind have to realize that the PBM won't renew a contract that led to a major loss. From the employer's viewpoint, it's better if the PBM charges per claim processed, not per transaction, because only one-third of claims are actually processed, and many claims are rejected.
- "Therapeutic substitution" means the use of generics. Employees often respond to advertisements by asking for brand-name drugs, so giving them financial incentives to accept generic drugs can save money for the plan. One possibility is a three-tier copay system. For instance, employees might have to pay $5 for a generic prescription, $10 for a brand-name prescription that is in the plan's formulary, and $25–$30 for a brand-name drug outside the formulary.
- A formulary is a list of drugs classified on the basis of price and effectiveness. A positive formulary lists the accepted drugs; a negative formulary lists those that are considered inappropriate; many plans have both.
- Require prior authorization of prescriptions, so that doctors will at least try the least expensive drug before moving to something more expensive.
- Educate doctors and employees about the need for cost-effective prescribing. Sometimes doctors prescribe a more expensive drug because they have genuine evidence that it is more effective or has fewer side effects; but they may

also prescribe the drug that the drug company has spent the most to promote!

- Exclude coverage of lifestyle drugs such as Propecia or Viagra.
- Make high users (e.g., those filling over $500 in prescriptions per year) responsible for larger copayments.
- Place an annual limit (usually $300–$2000) on benefits; more predictable plans make budgeting easier for the employer.

9.2.7 Women's Health and Cancer Rights Act

The Women's Health and Cancer Rights Act of 1998, P.L. 105-277, became law on October 21, 1998. If an EGHP covers mastectomies, the Act requires it also to cover reconstructive breast surgery if the patient wants it and her attending physician prescribes it. This includes reconstruction of the mastectomized breast; surgery on the other breast to balance the patient's appearance; prostheses; and treatment of physical complications of mastectomy. The deductibles and coinsurance imposed on reconstructive surgery must be comparable to those imposed on other benefits under the plan. The Act is effective for plan years beginning on or after October 21, 1998.

EGHPs (and the insurers and HMOs that provide the medical and surgical benefits) are required to provide two forms of notice to plan participants. There was a one-time, "start-up" notice requirement that had to be satisfied by January 1, 1999. There is also an ongoing obligation to notify new plan participants of their rights under this Act, as soon as they become participants; notice must be renewed annually.

The notice must satisfy the Department of Labor requirements for Summary Plan Descriptions (see 29 CFR §2520.104b-1). The notice describes the types of reconstructive surgery covered, the applicable deductibles and coinsurance, and the fact that copayments for reconstructive surgery may not exceed those required for other types of care. It is not necessary for both the EGHP and the insurer or HMO to furnish the notice, as long as one of them does.

In May 1999, the Departments of Labor and Health and Human Services asked for public comments on the WHCRA coverage and notice requirements, receiving many responses that are summed up in an October 20, 1999 DOL notice.

According to the notice, health plans, unions, and insurers have a key role to play in informing women (employees and spouses of employees) of their rights as cancer patients, but they should be given some flexibility in how they carry out this role. The annual notice doesn't have to be given in the first year of enrollment (because it would only duplicate the initial enrollment notice). Annual notices must be delivered by a method that is reasonably likely to get the information to the plan participant, i.e., first-class mail or e-mail.

Furthermore, the notice doesn't have to be sent separately; it can be included with the SPD, Summary of Material Modifications, or Summary Annual Report; with a benefits newsletter or union newsletter; open enrollment information for the plan; or other written plan communications.

The DOL has furnished this model annual notice that will satisfy the compliance burden:

"Did you know that your plan, as required by the Women's Health and Cancer Rights Act of 1998, provides benefits for mastectomy-related services including reconstruction and surgery to achieve symmetry between the breasts, prostheses, and complications resulting from a mastectomy (including lymphedema)? Call your Plan Administrator [insert phone number] for more information." [The Women's Health and Cancer Rights Act of 1998: Questions and Answers Annual Notice Requirement Update, 10/20/99, http://www.dol.gov/dol/pwba/public/pubs/final1&a.htm.]

Health Promotion Measures

According to Hewitt Associates, 91% of U.S. companies undertake at least some health promotion efforts in the interest of keeping down health costs. Only 62% did so in 1992 and 89% did in 1996, so this is clearly a trend. The older and more stable an industry's workforce, the more likely it is to add health promotion to the plan. The two most popular health promotion measures are health screening (for blood pressure or cholesterol levels), offered at 78% of respondent companies, and education and training (offered by 76% of survey respondents)—(e.g., seminars and workshops; substance abuse counseling). Over one-third of respondents (39%) used financial incentives or disincentives (e.g., raising or lowering health premiums based on health or disease factors in the employee's lifestyle). About one-quarter (27%) gave employees questionnaires or risk appraisals.

This information comes from the Hewitt Newsstand online newsletter, http://www.hewitt.com/news/pressrel/1998/11-19-98.htm. The full study, "Health Promotion/Managed Health Provided by Major U.S. Employers in 1997," can be ordered for $50 a copy from Hewitt Associates Publications Desk, 100 Half Day Road, Lincolnshire, IL, 60069, (847) 295-5000.

See 66 FR 1420-1435 (1/8/01) for HCFA rules on bona fide wellness (health promotion) programs. To sum up, employers will not be penalized for discriminating against employees in poor health if they offer favorable treatment (such as premium discounts; rebates; reduced co-payment responsibilities) to employees who engage in health promotion practices such as quitting smoking and exercising.

The Pension and Welfare Benefits Administration (PWBA) published a Final Rule covering SPD requirements (for pension as well as welfare plans) at 65 FR 70226-70244 (11/21/00), discussed further at ¶14.2.

9.2.8 [NEW] Non-discrimination

On January 5, 2001, HHS, the PWBA, and the IRS jointly issued an interim final regulation on discrimination based on health factors. The stated effective date of the rule is the first day of the first plan year beginning on or after July 1, 2002. NOTE: This was one of the regulations whose effective date was delayed because of President Bush's Executive Order; see the Introduction for details.

This interim final rule implements IRC §9802/ERISA §702 (added by HIPAA), which prohibits discrimination in health coverage. Group health plans and insurers are forbidden to discriminate against individual participants or beneficiaries on the basis of any "health factor" of the individual employee. Nor can a higher premium be charged than that which would apply to a similarly situated individual without the health factor. A health factor is defined to mean:

- Health status
- Mental or physical condition
- Claims experience
- Past health care
- Medical history
- Genetic information
- Disability
- Insurability (including conditions caused by domestic violence and hazardous sports activities).

Group and self-insured plans must make coverage uniformly available to all similarly situated individuals. Benefit restrictions must also apply uniformly to all similarly situated individuals. Benefits can legitimately be limited or excluded in relation to a specific disease or condition, for certain types of drugs or treatments, or based on a determination that a procedure is experimental or not medically necessary—as long as all similarly situated individuals, not just those with health factors—are affected.

> **TIP**
>
> Whether a plan provision complies with HIPAA doesn't determine whether or not it violates the ADA.

According to the interim final rule, modifying a plan to restrict benefits for the treatment of a condition for which an individual has already filed a claim is considered to violate HIPAA if the plan amendment takes effect before the beginning of the next plan year—unless there are other facts on record to show that the plan was changed for reasons independent of the claim.

The interim final rule forbids "list billing" (using separate individual rates in connection with a group health plan, varying because of health factors)—even if the employer does not pass along the higher costs to employees who do have health factors. Underwriting can still be used to set group premiums, but the insurer has to use claims experience as part of rate-setting for the whole group.

Employees can be placed in valid employment-based classifications consistent with the employer's usual business practices: e.g., full-time vs. part-time employees, unionized vs. non-unionized employees, participants vs. beneficiaries, beneficiaries of full-time employees vs. beneficiaries of part-timers, employees in different occupational classes or work locations. In fact, health benefits can differ by occupation or geographic location even if this is based on health factors of the entire group. What is forbidden is taking individual health factors into account.

The general rule is that plans may not deny enrollment or increase premiums or co-payments because a person is unable to engage in normal life activities, although distinctions can be drawn between employees based on the services they render to the company.

➠ TIP

It would not violate the anti-discrimination rules to offer benefit packages to current employees that are not available to COBRA-qualified beneficiaries—but it WOULD violate COBRA. However, both COBRA and the anti-discrimination rules permit charging a higher premium for COBRA coverage during the disability extension than during other COBRA periods.

The interim final rule forbids "non-confinement clauses"—i.e., provisions that deny eligibility to a plan participant or beneficiary who is hospitalized on the date coverage would otherwise become effective. As a general rule "actively at work" clauses that deny coverage or raise co-payments for persons who are out sick on the day coverage would otherwise begin are not permitted. However, the plan or insurer can require that the individual begin work before coverage actually becomes effective.

However, employers are permitted to provide MORE favorable treatment for persons with above-average medical needs. For instance, it is acceptable to extend the period of coverage for disabled former employees, or to cover a disabled dependent child who has reached an age at which dependent coverage would ordinarily terminate. If the only way to provide coverage to a person with a health factor is to charge him or her more than a person without the factor, that is permissible.

Certain plans are exempt from the interim final rule, such as benefits that are exempted under HIPAA itself (e.g., long-term care insurance); single-participant plans (although states are allowed to regulate them); and self-funded plans that make an election under 45 CFR §146.180 to opt out of the non-discrimination requirements.

Recognizing that this lengthy, complex rule could be hard to understand or apply in practice, the Department of Labor published questions and answers about the rule at http://www.dol.gov/dol/pwba/public/pubs/faqs.htm. The DOL's interpretation is that EGHPs are not allowed to make passing a physical examination a condition of enrollment (even for late enrollees). Health status questionnaires can be used, but it is not allowed to condition eligibility on having a certain number of "health points."

Nor may a plan waive its pre-existing condition limitation after six months for individuals who did not make any claims since enrollment because all similarly situated individuals must be treated similarly.

The Q&A clarifies that it is permissible to distinguish between beneficiaries based on their relationship to the employee (spouse vs. dependent child, for instance) or on the basis of the age or student status of dependent children.

9.4 [NEW] LABOR LAW ISSUES IN THE EGHP

Unilaterally changing the health plan after a bargaining impasse, to require employees to pay much higher out-of-pocket costs, violates the Labor Management Relations Act: *Loral Defense Systems-Akron v. NLRB*, 68 LW 1400 (6th Cir. 12/8/99). The employer hadn't fully disclosed the proposal during the unsuccessful bargaining process. The employer had reserved the right to amend or modify the health plan, but the Sixth Circuit considered the changes tantamount to replacing the old plan, not amending it.

9.5 CLAIMS PROBLEMS

The Eastern District of Wisconsin found that it was arbitrary and capricious for a plan to deny coverage of a medically necessary feeding tube, for a patient who was unable to swallow, on the grounds that meals were available in the hospital: "An administrator is not free to give ordinary words bizarre or obscure interpretations." See *Schneider v. Wisconsin UFCW Unions*, 13 F.Supp. 2d 837 (E.D. Wis. 1997).

Even if symptoms begin earlier, a disease is not a "preexisting condition" if it was not diagnosed until the policy is in effect. A Wisconsin woman made two emergency room visits in May 1996 when she experienced stomach pains. On both occasions, she was told her condition was trivial and sent home. Her health insurance policy became effective on June 18, 1996. In late June, she was admitted to the hospital, where she was finally diagnosed with advanced cancer that killed her a few weeks later. The insurer in *Ermenc v. American Family Mutual Ins. Co.*, 1998 Westlaw 484640 (Wis. App. 1998), took the position that her cancer was a preexisting condition, so her hospital bills were not covered. The court was unimpressed—although she had some illness before the policy became effective, the actual cancer diagnosis occurred after the effective date.

In the view of the Tenth Circuit [*Healthcare America Plans Inc. v. Bossemeyer*, 166 F.3d 347 (10th Cir. 1998)], there is no ERISA violation when an EGHP administrator denies benefits for high-dose chemotherapy for breast cancer on the grounds that the treatment is experimental. The plan at issue defined experimental treatment as treatment not generally accepted by the medical community. Because that is a discretionary standard, the standard of review of plan decisions is whether or not they are arbitrary and capricious. To the Tenth Circuit, the exclusion for high-dose chemotherapy was reasoned and valid and therefore survived court review.

The Eleventh Circuit upheld a requirement in a self-insured health plan that all suits protesting internal appeals decisions be filed within 90 days. Although this is a short time frame, it was not inappropriate, in that the health plan had procedures for expediting decisions. (The court would not make a general ruling that a 90-day limitation would be permissible in all cases, only under the facts of this particular case.) See *Northlake Regional Medical Center v. Waffle House Sys. Employee Benefit Plan*, 160 F.3d 1301 (11th Cir. 1998).

9.5.1 [NEW] PWBA Final Rule On Claims Procedure

On November 21, 2000, the PWBA finalized the rule discussed in the previous Supplement. The Final Rule, affecting 29 CFR Part 2560, appears at 65 FR 70246-70271. [AON Consulting published a helpful chart of the new provisions, which can be found at http://www.fei.org/gr/download/DOL_Revises_Claims_Procedures.pdf] NOTE: This rule, although controversial, was NOT affected by the incoming Bush administration's moratorium on regulations that were not final as of the change of administration.

The Final Rule applies to ERISA health and disability plans(See ¶10.8 for more about disability plans), dental and vision plans, and health Flexible Spending Accounts—but not to plans offering long-term care benefits. DOL is using this process as a kind of test bed for broader procedural standards for reforming claims administration of pension plans, but the current rules apply only in the health arena. It preempts state laws that are contradictory, but not state laws that provide even more extensive protection to health plan beneficiaries.

The impact of the Final Rule is to make plans speed up their decision-making about health claims and appeals of denied claims, especially in situations where an employee files a claim for urgent care.

An important distinction is drawn between pre-service claims—advance approval of health care services that the employee wants—and post-service claims—medical care that has already been provided. The distinction is valid because in a post-service claim, there is far less urgency because the employee has already been treated, and the question is who will pay the bill, not whether care that might be necessary will be provided or not.

The Final Rule obligates plans to give a decision within 15 days on ordinary pre-service claims, and within 72 hours for urgent care claims, whereas decisions on post-service claims can wait for 30 days. The plan can get one extension of time of up to 15 days for adjudicating pre- or post-service claims, but not urgent claims. Furthermore, if the plan takes the position that a defective claim was filed (e.g., not all information fields are filled in), it must notify the claimant; it can't reject the claim on the basis of its procedural defects.

When a plan makes "concurrent care decisions" (such as utilization review decisions about whether to approve continuation of treatment that has already started), the employee must be given a right to request review before the plan terminates or even reduces his or her benefits. Employees must be given enough advance notice to use the appeal rights under the plan. If the request to extend benefits is deemed urgent by the treating physician, the plan must resolve the dispute within 24 hours.

Once the decision has been rendered, and is unfavorable to the claimant, the claimant must be given a chance to appeal. In the case of urgent care claims, the appeal decision must be rendered within 72 hours for urgent care claims (the plan is obligated to abide by a treating physician's characterization of a claim as urgent), 30 days for a pre-service claim, and 60 days for post-service claims. The rule expands the length of time employees have to appeal a denial. Under prior rules, they had 60 days to appeal; now it is 180 days, and their right to sue is expanded.

Under the new rule, employers must also give a greater degree of disclosure. Employees are now entitled to a detailed explanation of the plan's claims procedures and detailed reasons why claims have been denied, including copies of internal protocols used to make claims determinations. The rule imposes an additional obligation: health plans must have a mechanism for ensuring consistency of decision-making, so that, for instance, employees don't have to hope that they're lucky enough to have their claims reviewed by Larry Lenient instead of Martha Meanie.

Health plans may not impose any fees or costs on employees who appeal claims denials. The claims reviewer must not be the person who issued the initial denial, and must not be a subordinate of that person. Claims are reviewed on a de novo standard—that is, whether the reviewer made the right decision, not merely whether he or she abused his or her discretion. The plan has to consult appropriate health care professionals whenever there is an issue of medical judgment (e.g., whether treatment is or was necessary). When employees appeal a claims denial, they are allowed to introduce new facts that they did not raise earlier—even if those facts would not be admissible as evidence in a lawsuit.

The rule gives plans two options: they can have either a single level of review of claims denials, or two sequential levels of review (like a trial court and an appeals court). But if they impose a second level of review, they don't get any additional time to review the claim—both levels of review must be completed within the normal time frame.

Health plans are allowed to include an arbitration requirement in the claims procedure—but all employees are entitled to full disclosure of how arbitrators are chosen and how the procedure works. Furthermore, the claimant must agree to arbitration, and can't be compelled to arbitrate unwillingly. Arbitration can only be used as an intermediate step after the plan's own internal appeals procedure has been completed.

9.7 THE EMPLOYER'S RIGHT OF SUBROGATION

A health plan can recover the "reasonable" value of services provided to injured employees, defined as the fee-for-service fee schedule. Its right of subrogation is not limited to the actual amount paid to the health care providers because of the discounted rates paid by health plans: *Ince v. Aetna Health Management Inc.*, 1999 U.S. App. LEXIS 6352 (8th Cir. 4/9/99).

Several employees sued Aetna Health Management, which processed the claims, charging that Aetna (and the plan's HMO, MedCenters Health Care) violated their ERISA fiduciary duty by receiving subrogation in excess of the cost of the benefits. The Eighth Circuit didn't agree. Although it was possible that Aetna's control over plan administration made it a fiduciary, it was not a violation of duty to recover the "reasonable value" of the services. This case is discussed in Thompson's Coordination of Benefits Handbook: see http://ww.thompson.com/tpg/pen_ben/cobs/cobsjuly99.html.

In *John Deere Health Benefit Plan v. Chubb*, 45 F.Supp.2d 1131 (D.Kan. 1999), a participant in a self-insured health plan died. Her estate sued for medical malpractice, and won, and the plan asserted a subrogation claim against the estate for $266,000. The plan had promulgated two subrogation provisions: a detailed discussion in the plan document and a cursory statement in the SPD referring to the plan's right to seek recovery against a tortfeasor (but not mentioning the right to seek recovery against the plan participant or participant's survivors).

The SPD said that the plan document controlled in all situations where it conflicted with the SPD. Nevertheless, the District Court found that the SPD controlled, and because it was defective (failing to warn participants of their vulnerability to subrogation), the plan's subrogation claim should be denied.

There is a California state anti-subrogation statute. It says that a health insurer cannot be reimbursed out of a victim's medical malpractice recovery. The statute has been upheld as enforceable and not preempted by ERISA. The Sixth Circuit's rationale [*Medical Mutual of Ohio v. deSoto*, 69 LW 1345 (6th Cir. 11/30/00)] is that although the law is related to employee health benefits, it is not preempted by ERISA because ERISA has an exception for laws that represent state regulation of insurance.

In late 2000, it looked like the Supreme Court was going to tackle the issue of subrogation. It granted certiorari in the case of *Reynolds Metals Co. v. Ellis*, #99-1787, 202 F.3d 1246 (9th Cir. 2000). In this case, Mr. Ellis became a paraplegic as a result of a 1994 automobile accident. He received over $500,000 in health insurance payments. His settlement in the accident case was greater than the amount of health benefits. He refused to reimburse the health insurer, which sued him in federal court. The District Court and Ninth Circuit dismissed the case, finding that in such situations ERISA does not permit a suit against the injured employee—any remedies must be sought in state court.

The Ellis case did not become the vehicle for the Supreme Court to resolve the conflict between the Ninth Circuit and several other Circuits that do permit a federal suit in this situation, because both sides settled the case and withdrew their application for certiorari. On January 22, 2001, however, the Supreme Court granted certiorari in another Ninth Circuit case, *Great-West Life Insurance Co. v. Knudson*, #99-1786, so (unless this one washes out too!) the next supplement should explain the Supreme Court's resolution of this issue.

In a Sixth Circuit case from 2000, an employee received about $18,000 in medical expense reimbursement after a car accident. She got a tort judgment of $25,000 against the other driver; one-third of this amount went to the employee's lawyer as a contingent fee. The plan's subrogation clause allowed the plan to recover benefits already paid, to the extent of "any payment resulting from a judgment or settlement." The question in *Smith v. Wal-Mart Associates Group Health Plan*, 2000 U.S. App. LEXIS 33993 (6th Cir. 2000) was whether the attorney's one-third share of the judgment should have the effect of reducing the amount that the plan could receive. The Sixth Circuit said yes, because the employee herself received only two-thirds of the $25,000; the plan would have to sue the lawyer to recover the rest of the funds it advanced.

TIP

This problem can be avoided by drafting the plan's subrogation provision to make it clear that the plan is entitled to recover against the full, unreduced amount of a judgment or settlement.

9.8 HEALTH CARE COST TRENDS

A study by William M. Mercer Inc., published in January 1999, shows that 1998 was a year in which health care trends turned around. Between 1994 and 1997, health care costs remained more or less level (rising 2.5% in 1996, and only 0.2% in 1997); but in 1998, average health care costs went up a painful 6.1%.

For the first time, HMO membership declined: In 1998, 47% of employees got their coverage from HMOs or point-of-service (POS) plans, versus 50% in 1997. The 1998 HMO enrollment was 29% of the insured workforce; POS plans covered 18% of insured workers. However, enrollment in preferred provider organizations (PPOs) went up: 35% in 1997, 40% in 1998. (The percentages can exceed 100%, because employers can offer multiple plan options.)

In 1998, the average cost of health coverage (including both active and retired workers) was $4164 per person per year. Since the 1997 figure was $3924, the Mercer survey showed that health care costs were on the rise again. A key factor in the increase was a 13.8% jump in costs of covering prescription drugs; a trend predicted for 1999 was employer requirements of higher copayments for prescriptions. These figures come from Ron Winslow, "Measure of HMO Membership Falls for First Time," *Wall Street Journal*, 1/26/99, p.B7; "Growth in Health Plan Costs Held to 0.2 Percent in 1997," *Compensation and Benefits Update*, 3/11/98, p. 4. Also see Ron Winslow, "Health-Care Inflation Kept in Check Last Year," *Wall Street Journal*, 1/20/98, p. B1, and "Co-Payments Rise for Prescriptions," *Wall Street Journal*, 1/12/99, p. B1, tracing CIGNA Corp.'s experience with rising drug costs.

The low-hanging fruit has been harvested. One perspective is that employers, by switching from indemnity to managed care, have already taken the simplest step to reduce costs. Another perspective is that insurers that offer managed care plans have now more or less eliminated the competition and are in a position to raise premiums.

As predicted, small employers faced significant cost increases in 1999, described by the *New York Times* as "some of the steepest price increases for health insurance in almost 10 years" (see Jennifer Steinhauer, "Health Insurance Costs Rise, Hitting Small Business Hard," *NYT*, 1/19/99, p. A1). January 1999 increases for businesses with over 100 employees averaged 6% nationwide, but small businesses faced increases from 10 to 13%. Some small New York firms were told to pay 30% increases to maintain coverage—with the result that many of these businesses changed carrier, increased the employee share of the premium, or dropped coverage.

The Towers Perrin Health Care Cost Survey released on January 10, 2000 (see "Towers Perrin Survey Projects Double-Digit Growth in Health Care Costs in 2000," http://www.towers.com/towers/news/pr20000110.html) projects the first double-digit cost increase for almost a decade. The cost of large EGHPs was expected to go up an average of 12%, with double-digit increases forecast for several years after that. Data for this survey comes from 228 employers, most of them in the *Fortune* 1000.

Later that same year, the BLS Employment Cost Index showed that benefit costs for private employers went up 6% between September 1999 and September 2000. This was far higher than the average for the previous five years (2.26% a year). ["Benefit Costs for Private Employers Jump Six Percent in 2000," http://www.us.deloitte/com/pub/iq/vol10/iq10.htm].

According to the Center for Studying Health System Change, in 1999 health care costs went up 6.6%, again well over the recent average (annual increases averaging 2.4% for the period 1993-1997). Prescription drug cost increases accounted for 44% of the increase, versus 32% stemming from increases in physician fees, 21% from hospital outpatient treatment, and only 3% from inpatient hospitalization. In 1999, health insurance premiums went up 8.35% (versus only an average of 2% a year from 1994-1998). The cost of self-insured plans went up a comparatively modest 7.1%—with the result that the percentage of employees covered by self-insured plans increased from 48% to 51% from 1999 to 2000 alone. ["Study Finds Pharmaceuticals Cause Large Portion of Rising Health Care Costs," *WestGroup Employment Alert* 12/7/00 p. 9.]

Factors driving cost increases include more utilization of sophisticated (and expensive) prescription drugs as well as increasing health care utilization by an aging population. As the federal government cuts back on Medicare spending, health care providers often react by shifting costs to EGHPs.

Employees' average percentage contribution to the cost of care is still 21%—the same as in the 1999 survey; the average dollar contribution is $40/month out of a total cost of $195/month. For family coverage, employees contribute an average of $123/month, 23% of the $545/month cost of coverage (slightly lower than in 1999). Given the tight labor market, employers are reluctant to make employees pay a lot more for health coverage, for fear that that would be the last straw leading employees to job-hop. Covering an early retiree is usually more expensive than covering an active employee, whereas covering an over-65 retiree is less expensive because of the role of Medicare benefits.

The average cost of dental plans for 2000 is estimated at $24/month for employee-only coverage and $69/month for family coverage.

Managed care costs increased slightly—but only slightly—less than indemnity costs: 11% for indemnity, 10% for HMOs and PPOs, 8% for Point of Service (POS) plans. In other words, managed care is not holding the line on cost increases.

Hewitt Associates also predicted EGHP rate increases of 8–10%, and an average yearly cost per employee of $4853 in 2001. See http://www.hewitt.com/news/pressrel/1999/11-08-99.htm.

Looking at the problem from another angle, HCFA found that all private spending on health care increased 6.9% in 1998 (as compared with 4.8% in 1997). The total U.S. health care bill was $1.1 trillion (about $4,100 per person). Insurance premiums went up 8.2%—much, much more than the 1995 increase of 2.8% or the 3.3% and 3.5% rate of increase in 1996 and 1997, respectively. Spending on prescription drugs was the fastest-growing component in the health care cost equation: a total of $90.6 billion in 1998, or 15.4% above 1997 levels. [News item, "U.S. Health Care Costs Rose Faster in 1998," *N.Y.T.* 1/11/00, p. F14.

For more information, see the EBRI Health Benefits Databook (12/99), 200 pp.; devine@ebri.org.]

Not everyone who lacks health insurance is unemployed—or even employed by a company that does not have a health plan. Employers who offer health plans sometimes find that workers, especially lower-paid workers, are offered health coverage but decline to accept it. Employee Benefit Research Institute (EBRI) figures show that, in late 1997, the average worker would pay $396 for health insurance coverage for him- or herself under an employer plan—and would pay about $1600 for family coverage. A person earning $7 an hour (i.e., not a minimum-wage worker) would have to devote 11% of gross pay just to purchase family coverage.

Nor does mere enrollment in an EGHP always solve an employee's health-care-cost problems. A study by Consumers Union shows that in 1996, per capita health care costs for Americans were $3778. Families earning between $30,000 and $40,000 had average out-of-pocket health care costs of about $1500 (e.g., about 4.5% of earnings). But there were over two and a half million families that spent more than 30% of their earnings for out-of-pocket health care costs. More than 11 million families spent "only" 10% or more of their income on health costs—and 9 million of those families had insurance coverage for every member. (These figures come from a news item, "Health Policies Don't Cover Many Expenses," *WSJ*, 1/23/98, p. B7B.) The problem, then, is not just the large number of uninsured persons, but those who have nominal insurance coverage that imposes severe financial burdens both on them and on their employers.

9.10 MANAGED CARE

Legal issues about managed care come up in several forums. Federal litigation is still extensive. Many attempts are made to sue in state court (which often provides a quicker resolution, and access to more remedies, than the federal system). In addition to individual suits, sometimes attempts are made to litigate in class-action form. The two major issues are denial of care desired by patients and malpractice (i.e., the quality of care that is actually received).

A high volume of both federal and state legislation has been introduced, and some bills have even passed. However, vital issues remain to be resolved about the extent to which ERISA preempts the discussion of liability of managed care organizations.

See the Alliance for Health Reform's excellent, balanced discussion, "Resolving Health Plan Disputes," April 1999, which can be found at http://www.allhealth.org. The brief document covers topics such as internal and external review of MCO denials of claims, litigation issues, and a telephone list of experts.

William M. Mercer figures, quoted in Nancy Ann Jeffrey' s article "Test Over Time," *WSJ*, 10/23/97, p. R6, show that, although the market share of HMOs has remained fairly constant since 1994 (23% in 1994, 27% in 1995 and 26%), other forms of managed care have grown. In 1993, for instance, HMOs had a 19% market share; point-of-service (POS) plans were a minor player, at 7%; PPOs had a 27% share; and traditional indemnity plans captured almost half the market, at 48%.

The established principle under which employers escaped liability—because the HMO provided the actual treatment—and the HMO escaped liability—because ERISA preempts state law but says virtually nothing about the obligations of HMOs to employees who are denied care or who are injured by negligent care—is beginning to erode.

Early in 1999, the Supreme Court, in *Humana Inc. v. Forsyth*, #97-303, 525 U.S. 299 (Sup.Ct. 1999), permitted EGHP members who alleged that they were overbilled as part of a conspiracy to force them to make excessive copayments to sue for insurance fraud under RICO. (Therefore, treble damages became a possibility.) The defendant, naturally, claimed that the McCarran-Ferguson Act precluded the RICO suit, but the Supreme Court held that RICO does not invalidate or supersede state insurance laws, so the RICO suit is not barred by the McCarran-Ferguson Act.

But see *Maio v. Aetna Inc.*, 221 F.3d 472 (3rd Cir. 2000), holding that HMO subscribers cannot use the Racketeer Influenced and Corrupt Organizations Act (RICO) to charge an HMO with fraudulent failure to disclose its practices of restricting coverage to enhance profits, thus forcing subscribers to overpay for inadequate coverage. The Third Circuit said that a RICO suit requires actual, not hypothetical injury to the "business or property" of the plaintiffs, a burden that was not met in this case.

The Supreme Court returned to EGHP ERISA issues in April 1999. The decision in *UNUM Life Insurance Co. of America v. Ward*, #97-1867, 526 U.S. 328 (Sup.Ct. 1999), is that ERISA does not preempt state "notice-prejudice" laws. A notice-prejudice law prevents an insurer from denying a claim based on late filing, unless the delay was prejudicial to the insurer's interests. But this decision, although a setback for insurers, doesn't harm employers who administer EGHPs, because it says that although the employer is the insurer's "agent," the employer's role "relates to" an ERISA plan and therefore is preempted by ERISA.

In mid-2000, the Supreme Court decided, in *Pegram v. Herdrich*, #98-1949, 530 U.S. 211 (Sup.Ct. 2000) that when an HMO, acting through its doctors, makes a mixed decision about medical treatment and health plan eligibility, the HMO is NOT acting as a fiduciary. Therefore, even if patients' allegations that the plan denies them necessary treatment in order to enhance its profits are true, they do not state a cause of action for breach of fiduciary duty.

According to the Eastern District of Pennsylvania, four of the federal Circuit Courts say that there can be a fiduciary duty to disclose only if the plan participant asks specific questions, or if the fiduciary knows something about the individual circumstances of the plan participant indicating that non-disclosure will be harmful. In this analysis, a plan participant who does not allege denials of care, inadequate care, or rejected inquiries has no case (especially when a lot of the information in question was available on the insurer's Web site): *Peterson v. Connecticut General Life Ins. Co.*, 2000 U.S. Dist. LEXIS 16522 (E.D. Pa. 2000).

ERISA doesn't preempt an employee's state-law claims against an insurer who denied benefits under an individual disability policy that had been converted from a group policy. The employer was no longer involved, so ERISA was no longer the governing statute [*Demars v. CIGNA Corp.*, 173 F.3d 443 (1st Cir. 1999)].

ERISA does not preempt state medical malpractice suits against HMOs, based on vicarious liability theories, where the HMO arranged the health care provided to employees: *Hinterlong v. Baldwin*, 68 LW 1335 (Ill.App. 11/4/99). The Illinois Court of Appeals conceded that the HMO was a welfare benefit plan, but the medical malpractice action did not "relate" to the plan, because the malpractice claim could be decided without interpreting the plan documents with respect to plan administration or denial of plan benefits.

In mid-2000, the Fifth Circuit ruled that a Texas statute allowing health plans (including HMOs) to be sued for malpractice or negligent treatment decisions is not preempted by ERISA: *Corporate Health Insurance Inc. v. Texas Dep't of Insurance*, 215 F.3d 526 (5th Cir. 2000). The rationale is that the quality of medical care is a traditional and appropriate subject of state regulation. Furthermore, this Texas law specifically excludes state regulation of coverage decisions—which would be preempted by ERISA.

Hull v. Fallon, 1999 WL 637073 (8th Cir. 1999): ERISA preempts a medical malpractice claim against an MD-plan administrator who denied benefits for a particular test, in that he was acting as an administrator, not as a doctor, in making the decision.

One of the most contentious issues is the extent to which states can regulate HMO internal operations such as their review of claims denials (see ¶9.10.9, below), and whether litigation belongs in state or federal court.

In *Hill v. Blue Cross/Blue Shield of Alabama*, 2000 U.S. Dist. LEXIS 15132 (N.D. Ala. 2000), a plan participant brought a state-court suit against the insurer of his insured plan for fraud and for bad-faith denial of a benefits claim. The insurer removed the case to federal court. But, because of *UNUM v. Ward*, the Northern District determined that the claims related to insurance and therefore should be in state court. However, the Northern District of Alabama also said that self-insured plans cannot be sued in state court in this situation, because self-insured plans are not subject to state insurance regulation, and therefore the suit is preempted by ERISA. This conclusion was also reached in *Selby v. Principal Mutual Life Insurance*, 2000 U.S. Dist. LEXIS 1495 (S.D.N.Y. 2000) and *Lewis v. Aetna U.S. Healthcare, Inc.*, 78 F.Supp.2d 1202 (N.D. Okla. 1999).

Washington State's statute, requiring HMOs to provide acupuncture, massage, chiropractic, and other alternative medical treatments, is not preempted by ERISA [*Washington Physicians Service Association v. Gregoire*, 147 F.3d 1039 (9th Cir. 1998)].

ERISA does not preempt a surviving spouse's medical malpractice, breach of contract, and breach of fiduciary duty suit against an HMO primary care doctor who delayed referring the decedent to a medical specialist [*Nealy v. U.S. Healthcare*, 67 LW 1586 (N.Y. App. 3/25/99)].

A similar result was reached in *DeLucia v. St. Luke's Hospital*, discussed in Shannon P. Duffy's article, "When Quality, Not Quantity of Care Is at Issue, ERISA Doesn't Apply," http://www.lawnewsnet.com/stories/A1763-1999May25.html. In this case the parents of a deceased premature infant went to state court and sued the HMO that denied coverage of a breathing monitor. The HMO tried to remove the case from state to federal court, claiming ERISA preemption. The ERISA argument was unsuccessful, because the case involved a simple allegation of improper medical care—a classic state-law medical malpractice case. The employer plan had no meaningful involvement in the case.

A tragically similar case, *Bauman v. U.S. Healthcare Inc.*, 1 F.Supp.2d 420 (D.N.J. 1998), involves the death of another newborn. HMO policy called for discharge within 24 hours (but see ¶9.2.2 for current law about mandated coverage of longer maternity stays). The baby died of meningitis shortly after discharge. The parents sued the company that owned the HMO, the hospital, and the doctor who discharged the baby without detecting the soon-to-be-fatal infection. The claims against the HMO included negligently adopting a policy that encouraged or required premature discharge, with reckless indifference to the risks of the policy. According to the District Court for the District of New Jersey, these claims were not preempted by ERISA, because ERISA §502(a) (claims for benefits due under the plan) was not involved. The parents' claim was not for plan benefits, but was based on negligence in crafting the structure of the plan. However, the court did dismiss the parents' claim (on ERISA preemption grounds) that the plan promised them a home visit that was not delivered.

The Department of Labor has filed amicus curiae briefs in close to two dozen Court of Appeals cases dealing with the question of whether ERISA preempts state-law negligence claims against HMOs: see Barbara Yuill, "Official Lists Current Amicus Briefs of Labor Department on Medical Malpractice," 68 LW 2249 (11/2/99). DOL says that there are three separate issues to be considered, depending on the role that the HMO plays.

If the HMO actually provides or arranges the medical care by hiring doctors or entering into contracts with them, there is a potential for vicarious liability based on the quality of care provided by those doctors, or the HMO's negligent hiring and/or supervision of the individual doctors. The DOL's analysis is that ERISA preemption is not appropriate in such cases, because questions of plan interpretation and administration do not arise.

However, DOL does think that preemption is appropriate to the extent that the HMO acts as a plan administrator itself. To the extent that the HMO operates as an insurer (by taking a fixed fee from the employer plan in exchange for providing health care), the DOL view is that state regulation is possible. It's true that this HMO role relates to an employee benefit plan, but it escapes ERISA preemption because it falls under the insurance exception.

According to a news item appearing on page B6 of the January 5, 2000 issue of the *Wall Street Journal,* a jury in Florida state court awarded $29,000 for fraud and breach of contract, $1 million for intentional infliction of emotional distress, and $78.5 million in punitive damages against Humana Inc.

The plaintiff was notified in 1995 that therapy for his daughter, who has cerebral palsy, would be terminated because her condition was no longer "catastrophic." Eventually, some of the benefits were reinstated, but not to their original levels. Unsurprisingly enough, Humana is appealing the verdict, which it describes as "erroneous and excessive."

When a patient of a Medicare HMO dies, the Medicare Act does not preempt state-law claims of wrongful death or negligence or misconduct on the part of the HMO [*Wartenberg v. Aetna U.S. Healthcare Inc.*, 2 F.Supp. 2d 273 (E.D.N.Y. 1998)].

See Nancy Ann Jeffreys' article, "Test Over Time," *WSJ,* 10/23/97, p. R6, for criticism of HMO handling of the needs of chronically ill enrollees. People suffering from asthma, diabetes, kidney problems, or other chronic ailments may find that the plan offers inadequate coverage for medications and devices needed to control symptoms, as well as cuts back on physician visits needed to monitor their condition.

HMOs are facing another court challenge: from a former participating doctor who is suing under the ADA, charging that his HMO contract was terminated because he provided adequate (and therefore high-cost) care to disabled individuals, as well as from chronically ill persons charging that it violates the ADA to discriminate against them. This approach raises interesting legal issues because it moves the case from the ERISA to the civil rights arena. [Milo Geyelin, "A Disabled Attorney Puts Civil-Rights Spin on HMO Litigation," *Wall Street Journal,* 1/26/00, p. A1.]

The Center for Studying Health System Change, in collaboration with the Robert Wood Johnson Foundation, suggests that employers need to take the next step: not just having managed care plans, but a coordinated "managed competition" strategy that impels competition among insurers. (See "Study Suggests Few Employers Use Managed Competition Principles," *Compensation and Benefits Update,* 7/29/98, p. 5.)

Managed competition advocates suggest that employers adopt a policy of "equal dollar contribution" (i.e., to determine the amount they will contribute toward employees' insurance). Employees who want a more expensive plan have to pay the difference themselves.

For managed competition to be effective, employees must have detailed information about competing plans. The survey criticized employers' performance in this regard. Even among the large (over 500 employees) companies, the ones with the greatest HR resources, only 22% gave employees information beyond basic plan descriptions.

Quite apart from legal problems (although a wider range of liability, and larger verdicts, will place further strain on them), HMOs are facing financial problems. According to Martin D. Weiss, chairman of Weiss Ratings, most HMOs lose money on their operations. In 1998, nine HMOs failed financially, and in 1999, 16 HMOs did so (a 78% increase).

Plans that failed in 1999 include Harvard Pilgrim of New England, Sunstar Healthplan, Premier Health Care, and Xantus Healthplan of Tennessee. Harvard Pilgrim, with assets of $83 million, was by far the largest of the failed plans; the next-largest, Sunstar, had assets of only $20 million ["Financial Scorecard for 1999," http://news.excite.com/news/bw/000110/fl-weiss-ratings, 1/10/00; no www]. So, among the manifold other factors in choosing a Managed Care Organization (MCO) to contract with, employers must ponder the ongoing solvency of the MCO itself, and the potential impact of the organization's bankruptcy or financial problems on the sponsor company and its employees.

9.10.8 Employer Liability for HMO Actions

According to an Information Letter issued by the Department of Labor on February 19, 1998, it may be a breach of fiduciary duty for health plan trustees to choose health care providers merely based on cost considerations, without considering quality. In this context, quality involves issues such as the number and qualification of doctors in the health plan; employees' access to those doctors; the provider's past record; ratings and accreditation; and consumer satisfaction. Therefore, merely accepting the provider that posts the lowest bid is not necessarily appropriate fiduciary conduct, if the low-cost provider is not also a quality provider. This DOL letter is discussed in the RIA *Compensation and Benefits Update*, 3/25/98, p. 3.

9.10.9 State Regulation of Managed Care Plans

Families USA has published a useful summary of state laws involving managed care, with a chart indicating which states have which types of law: "State Managed Care Patient Protections," dated October 1999. It can be downloaded from http://www.familiesusa.org/hitmisup.htm. These state laws tackle the ERISA preemption problem by being limited to individuals who are not EGHP participants.

The types of legislation covered are:

- Emergency room: MCOs must cover emergency room care under any circumstance in which a prudent layperson would seek emergency treatment, even if the patient does not get prior authorization before getting emergency care.
- Access to providers: legislation dealing with access to specialists; ability of chronically ill individuals to see a specialist without a time-wasting prior visit to a generalist; access to gynecologists or obstetricians as primary care physicians.
- Continuity of care: continued reimbursement for treatment by one's physician, after that physician ceases to be part of the MCO network.

- Drugs: ability of patients to get coverage for prescription drugs they need, even if these drugs are not in the plan's official formulary.
- Ombudsman or consumer assistance program to help patients pursue complaints against MCOs.
- Gag rules: laws forbidding MCOs to limit the disclosure of treatment options to those covered by the plan.
- Physician incentives: bans on offering doctors financial incentives to refrain from providing needed care.
- Right to sue: ability to sue health plans for failure to exercise due care in issuing treatment decisions.
- Appeal or review procedures administered by someone outside the plan itself ("external appeals").

According to 68 LW 2174 (9/28/99), four-fifths of the U.S. population lives in states that require managed care organizations to have an external appeals process for claims denials (i.e., denied claims must be reviewed by someone outside the organization). Thirty-one states and the District of Columbia have such laws, 13 of them enacted or revised in 1999. However, few consumers actually use the appeals provisions, probably because procedures are new and not well-publicized. It's very possible that some, or all, of the state laws will be invalidated by courts on ERISA preemption grounds.

In early 2001, the Blue Cross Association's BCBS HealthIssues.com reported on state legislation about health care for 2000. [See http://bcbshealthissues.com/overview/vthl?PROACTIVE_ID=c5cecfcfcfc5cecfcbcbc7cdcfc6cacfc5c.] Blue Cross identifies managed care reform, including a requirement of a review authority external to the plan, as an important legislative theme for 2000.

Most state legislatures at least considered a bill expanding the right of HMO enrollees to sue their plans. However, although legislation of this type was introduced in 32 states, it passed in only four (Maine, Oklahoma, Washington, Arizona). In Maine and Oklahoma, plan enrollees can sue their plans for harm that results directly from health care treatment decisions rendered without ordinary care. In Arizona, suit can be brought to recover damages caused by rejection of claims, or delay in granting benefits, when the plan knew it did not have a reasonable basis for denial or delay. Washingtonians can sue when a plan fails to adhere to the accepted standard of care, with the result that an enrollee suffers substantial harm. The Maine and Oklahoma statutes impose damage caps; in the other states, any amount of damages can be sought and awarded.

However, because of 11 laws passed in 2000, the majority of the states now have "external review" statutes. That is, someone who does not work for the health plan is empowered to make decisions that bind the health plan. About half of external review decisions favor the enrollee, and about half uphold the plan.

Managed care reform was also a focus of proposed federal legislation, but at press time, no comprehensive federal law on this subject had been passed.

Two very similar cases, involving individuals who claim that they would not have suffered paralysis if their HMO had certified treatment more rapidly, reached different results. To the Eastern District of Louisiana, ERISA preempts the claim [*Benoit v. W.W. Grainger Inc.*, 67 LW 1271 (E.D. La. 10/21/98)]. But a Pennsylvania state court ruled a couple of months later that ERISA does not preempt the suit; HMOs should be prepared to suffer financially if they operate negligently [*Pappas v. Asbel*, 67 LW 1416 (Pa. 12/23/98)].

9.14 TAX IMPLICATIONS OF HEALTH PLANS

A partnership sought an IRS Private Letter Ruling as to the status of its plan for "medical consumer cards" issued by a managed care company to the partners and employees of the partnership. The consumer cards provided discounts on noncore items (e.g., dental and vision care) that were not part of the basic health plan. There would be a fee for the card, although it was not clear whether the partnership or the individual users would pay the fee. The company had no financial risk stemming from use of the cards.

In PLR 9814023, the IRS ruled that the partnership' s distribution of the cards constituted a fringe benefit. Employees would not have gross income because of the issuance of the card, because for them, the cards were part of an accident and health insurance plan excluded from gross income by Code §106(a). When the employees use the card to get a discount, they do not have compensation income. After all, the employer doesn't pay them; the participating health care providers extend them a discount.

At the partnership level, the cost of buying cards for partners was not deductible, because the plan did not conform to the definition of "insurance." The partnership didn' t ask the IRS about the tax status of cards provided to employees, but probably those costs would be deductible, because the plan had been ruled to fit the insurance definition for employees although not for partners. See "Mixed Tax Results for Employee Medical Discount Cards," *Compensation and Benefits Update*, 4/22/98, p. 4.

9.15 COBRA CONTINUATION COVERAGE

In 1998, the Supreme Court resolved an important COBRA question, in *Geissal v. Moore Medical Corp.*, #97-689, 524 U.S. 74 (Sup.Ct. 1998). Under *Geissal*, it is legitimate for an employer to terminate COBRA coverage if and when the employee gains access to other coverage subsequent to making a COBRA election. However, it is not permitted for the employer to terminate COBRA eligibility on the basis of coverage that the employee had access to prior to the election.

If an individual elects COBRA coverage and becomes disabled during the continuation period, the Fifth Circuit allows extension of coverage as long as the individual complies with the requirements set out in the health plan's SPD. Coverage cannot be denied based on limitations that appear in the formal text of the plan (or even in the COBRA statute or regulations) but are not included in the SPD.

According to the plan text (and COBRA), an additional 11 months of COBRA coverage would be provided based on notice that the Social Security Administration had ruled the applicant was disabled before the initial 18-month COBRA continuation period ended. But the SPD, the document available to the employee and his wife, said that the COBRA period could be extended based on notice to the employer within 60 days of the Social Security Administration determination of disability. The couple met this requirement, so the Fifth Circuit found them entitled to a COBRA extension even though the disability occurred after the employee terminated employment and initially became COBRA eligible. The case is *Fallo v. Piccadilly Cafeterias Inc.*, 141 F.3d 580 (5th Cir. 1998).

An Eighth Circuit case from 2000, *Marsh v. Omaha Printing Co.*, 2000 Westlaw 959609 (8th Cir. 2000) says that the 11-month extension requires having a Social Security Administration disability determination, so delays by the SSA can result in loss of the extension. The rationale is that, although the delay is not the disabled person's fault, it also prevents the disabled person from notifying the employer of his or her disability, making it unfair to impose an obligation on an employer who has not had notice.

The case of *Rittenhouse v. Professional Micro Systems, Inc.*, 1999 U.S. Dist. LEXIS 21695 (S.D. Ohio 1999) involves an employer whose group health policy allowed a disabled person to self-pay for six months, followed by 18 months of COBRA coverage. The plaintiff became disabled and could not return to work. The employer mistakenly informed him that he could continue the self-payments indefinitely. He did not receive a COBRA notice. The insurer terminated coverage when it learned that the ex-employee had been self-paying for 24 months. The plaintiff sued his ex-employer for $19,000 worth of unpaid medical expenses, plus additional coverage and the statutory penalties for failure to give COBRA notice.

In the Southern District's view, the plaintiff had already received more than the 18 months of COBRA coverage he was entitled to, so additional coverage was inappropriate. The plan documents clearly set a six-month limit. The breach of fiduciary duty claim was dismissed because the plaintiff asked for money damages instead of equitable relief. Claims against the insurer were dismissed, because under COBRA, the employer, as plan administrator, has sole responsibility for giving notice.

However, the court would not grant summary judgment for the employer on the issue of statutory penalties for failing to provide notice. The SPD did not provide adequate notice; COBRA requires that a notice be furnished after a qualifying event, even if the employer is acting in good faith.

A former employee and her husband, whose qualifying event was termination of her employment, brought suit to prevent the employer from changing their

COBRA coverage from a Preferred Provider Organization to a Point of Service plan. But the Tenth Circuit affirmed the District Court's dismissal of the case: under ERISA §601, it is legitimate to modify coverage for COBRA -qualified beneficiaries to reflect changes made in the coverage provided to active employees. [*Besting v. America West Holdings Corp. Inc.*, 2000 U.S. App. LEXIS 31222 (10th Cir. 2000).]

If a former employee needs only a certain amount of COBRA coverage (e.g., X months of coverage until he or she becomes eligible under a new plan), and asks for that amount of coverage, COBRA does not permit the plan to force the ex-employee to pay for a full 18 months of retroactive coverage: *Popovits v. Circuit City Stores Inc.*, 1999 WL 499487 (7th Cir. 1999).

In the case of *Lloynd v. Hanover Foods Corp.*, 1999 WL 1084262 (D.Del. 1999), a factory worker was fired for leaving a spice out of the ravioli she was assigned to prepare, and then failing to report the omission. The employer did not inform her about COBRA, treating the employee's conduct as sabotage and therefore as gross misconduct that would justify exclusion from COBRA.

But, to the District Court, the employee's mistake was merely ordinary negligence, so she was entitled to COBRA notice. The employer was ordered to pay $3,000 worth of medical expenses she had encountered, plus a civil money penalty of $25,250 ($50/day) for willful failure to give the COBRA notice, plus attorneys' fees and costs.

A terminated employee indicated an intention to elect COBRA coverage, but never paid the initial premium. She incurred medical expenses, and sought reimbursement from the plan, asking the plan to deduct the continuation coverage premium from the requested reimbursement. The plan refused to do this. The court agreed [*Goletto v. W.H. Braum Inc.*, 1999 WL 1096042 (D.Kan. 1999)]: ERISA §602(2)(C) allows a plan to terminate coverage retroactive to the date of the qualifying event. A contrary result would let employees gamble by applying for COBRA coverage, but withholding the premium until they encountered medical expenses that they wanted the plan to cover.

An employer that mistakenly extended continuation health benefits after the collectively bargained date was not estopped from terminating the coverage as soon as it discovered the mistake—even though the ex-employee's wife had racked up a $45,000 hospital bill in the meantime. The Seventh Circuit, in *Coker v. TWA*, 165 F.3d 579 (7th Cir. 1999), decided that it was not reasonable for the plaintiff to rely on the mistaken communications from the employer, given that the employee was given written materials at the time of the layoff, explaining the benefits.

Even a plan that allows retirees continued coverage at their own expense for an indefinite period of time (i.e., after the COBRA period expires) still has an independent obligation to issue COBRA notice at retirement, because retirement is a COBRA event [*Mansfield v. Chicago Park District Group Plan*, 997 F.Supp. 1053 (N.D. Ill. 1998)].

An invalid foreign divorce that was later nullified was not a COBRA-qualifying event—the event is finalization of the divorce, which cannot occur if the decree is invalidated: *Phillips v. Saratoga Harness Racing Inc.*, 103 F.Supp.2d 127 (N.D.N.Y. 2000).

The employer's business records, showing that COBRA notice was mailed, are adequate evidence to prove notice, even though the employer couldn't find a copy of the actual letter that was sent to employees. (The plaintiff didn't dispute receiving a standard notice form.) See *Roberts v. National Health Corp.*, 133 F.3d 916 (4th Cir. 1998).

DOL Advisory Opinion 99-14A is that it is sometimes permissible for a health plan to satisfy the COBRA notice requirement by mailing a single notice to multiple beneficiaries living at the same address, i.e., one first-class mailing covering employee, spouse, and dependent children. There must either be a separate election notice in the mailing for each person, or an explanation of the independent right each one has to elect coverage. [http://www.corbel.com/newssftu25.asp].

COBRA Regulations

On January 7, 1998, the IRS published a Notice of Proposed Rulemaking at 63 FR 708. The proposals conform COBRA to HIPAA, the Small Business Job Protection Act, and various other statutes. As a result of these changes, qualified beneficiaries can get 29 months (rather than the original 18) of COBRA coverage with respect to the same qualifying event if

- They are all qualified with respect to a termination of employment or a reduction in hours.
- They became disabled, within the Social Security Act definition, within the first 60 days of COBRA continuation coverage.
- They have given the plan administrator a copy of the determination of disability, within the initial 18-month COBRA period and also within 60 days of the date the determination was issued.

During the extended period (after 18 months, before the 29 months have expired), the employer can charge a premium of 150% of the applicable premium, rather than the normal 102% limit. Charging the 150% premium will not violate the IRC §9802(b) prohibition on premium discrimination on the basis of health status. If a second qualifying event occurs during a disability extension, then COBRA coverage can last for 36 months; the 150% premium can lawfully be charged until the 36-month period ends.

HIPAA creates entitlement to COBRA coverage for children born to or adopted by covered employees during a period of COBRA coverage. The maximum coverage period for the child runs from the date of the employee's qualifying event—not the child's birth or adoption. The effect is that the child's COBRA coverage ends at the same time as other family members' coverage.

The January 7, 1998 rule makes it clear that Medical Savings Accounts are not subject to the COBRA continuation coverage obligation. Neither are plans substantially all of whose coverage is for "qualified long-term care services," as defined by IRC §7702B; the plan can use any reasonable method of deciding whether it falls into this category.

In February 1999, the IRS went ahead and finalized COBRA regulations first proposed in 1987. The 1999 final rule, found at 64 FR 5160 (2/3/99), is fairly similar to the 1987 proposal. However, the final rule implements *Geissal.* It allows a measure of employer discretion in defining how many "plans" are maintained for COBRA purposes. It includes rules for coping with EGHPs in corporate transitions (see Chapter 31). It clarifies that COBRA does not apply to most medical flexible spending accounts. If the EGHP provides both core health coverage and noncore coverage (e.g., vision and dental), it is no longer necessary to allow qualified employees to elect only the core coverage.

Taking leave under the Family and Medical Leave Act (FMLA) is not in and of itself a COBRA qualifying event. But if an employee who was covered by the EGHP before or during the FMLA leave fails to return to work after the FMLA leave, there is a qualifying event for this person (and any dependent who is at risk of losing health coverage) as of the last day of the FMLA leave. The employer is not allowed to require the ex-employee to reimburse the employer for health premiums paid during the leave.

These regulations apply to qualifying events that occur in plan years beginning on or after January 1, 2000. In the interim, plans are required to comply in good faith with reasonable interpretations of Code §4980B (the statutory provision governing continuation coverage).

T.D. 8928, 66 FR 1843 (1/10/01) supplements the February, 1999 Regulations, and makes some of the 1999 proposals Final Regulations. Because the effective date of the Treasury Decision is January 10, 2001, it is not subject to the Bush Administration moratorium suspending effectiveness of the late-Clinton-era regulations. In general, T.D. 8928 applies to qualifying events that occur on or after January 1, 2002.

Under T.D. 8928, all benefits offered by a business are treated as a single plan—unless the governing instruments make it clear that the benefits come from separate plans.

For plans that claim COBRA exemption on the basis of having fewer than 20 employees, the calculation for part-time employees will be made on the basis of full-time equivalents (i.e., 80 persons working 10 hours a week = 20 FTEs), no matter how they are scheduled, so employers will have less incentive to manipulate scheduling.

With respect to business reorganizations, the 1999 Proposals have been finalized. The purchaser in an asset sale (i.e., a sale of a substantial asset such as a plant or a corporate division, or substantially all the assets of a trade or business) will be treated as a successor employer if the seller entirely ceases to provide group health plans, and the buyer continues business operations relating to the assets. Other kinds of transfers, including bankruptcy-related transactions, are considered asset "sales" if they have the same effect.

One way in which T.D. 8928 departs from the 1999 proposals is that the proposal said there was no COBRA event when the purchaser maintained the plan for the entire 18 months or other applicable COBRA coverage period. However in the Treasury Decision, in an asset sale, employees have a qualifying event if they terminate employment and do not receive continuation coverage from the successor, even if they are then re-hired in the same job.

9.16 HEALTH INSURANCE PORTABILITY

The mental health parity rules discussed previously also affect HIPAA. See 62 FR 66957-66961 (12/22/97) for the Pension and Welfare Benefit Administration's amendments to 29 CFR Part 2590 Subpart B, explaining the portability implications of mental health parity.

Also at the end of 1997, the IRS, the Department of Labor's Pension and Welfare Benefits Administration, and the Department of Health and Human Services jointly published a "clarification of regulations" that appears at 62 FR 67688 (12/29/97). This document makes it clear that health insurance portability is not required for certain health flexible spending arrangements (FSAs). In technical terms, such FSAs are "excepted benefits" under ERISA §§732 and 733(c) and IRC §§9831 and 9832(c). Another implication is that FSA coverage is not "creditable coverage" that triggers portability rights under HIPAA.

According to this document, a health FSA is a "benefit program that provides employees with coverage under which specified, incurred expenses may be reimbursed (subject to reimbursement maximums and any other reasonable conditions) and under which the maximum amount of reimbursement that is reasonably available to a participant for a period of coverage is not substantially in excess of the total premium (including both employee-paid and employer-paid portions of the premium) for the participant's coverage." As the document notes, FSAs usually cover medical expenses excluded by the primary EGHP.

The FSA is excepted from HIPAA if the employee's maximum FSA benefit for the year is not greater than twice the employee's salary reduction election under the FSA for the year, as long as the employee has other EGHP coverage and provides at least some benefits that are not excepted benefits.

What about employees or dependents of employees who, prior to HIPAA, were turned down for group health plan coverage because of health status? Another IRS/DOL/HCFA clarification, also published in the *Federal Register* on December 29, 1997 (62 FR 67689), forbids group health plans and group insurance coverage to continue excluding those people from plan enrollment or coverage.

Plans are not allowed to establish rules for initial or continued eligibility based on "health status-related" factors—(e.g., health status; medical condition; claims experience; receipt of health care; medical history; genetic testing; insurability; or disability). Employees and their dependents cannot be required to pass a physical examination in order to enroll in the health plan, even if they are late enrollees.

A person who enrolls post-HIPAA cannot be treated as a late enrollee if he or she was previously denied enrollment for health status-related reasons, or if he or she thought it was futile even to apply.

Slightly earlier, Proposed and Temporary Regulations were issued: 62 FR 60165 and 60196 (11/7/97), dealing with changes in cafeteria plan elections, as well as HIPAA conformity for plans dealing with COBRA, medical child support orders, and Medicare/Medicaid eligibility. The effective date of this rule was delayed until 12/31/98.

On December 15, 1999, the IRS, Department of Labor Pension and Welfare Benefits Administration, and the Department of Health and Human Services signed a Memorandum of Understanding, effective retroactive to April 21, 1999. The MOU requires the various agencies to coordinate their HIPAA regulations, so that agencies that have joint enforcement responsibility will be carrying out consistent rules. The agencies also agree to coordinate their enforcement efforts to avoid duplication. The MOU appears at 64 FR 70164 (12/15/99).

HCFA's Program Memorandum 00-04 says that HIPAA forbids the use of "actively at work" provisions (i.e., only people who are working on the day on which a plan changes its carrier will be entitled to coverage under the new plan) to discriminate on the basis of disability and other health factors.

9.17 MEDICAL SAVINGS ACCOUNTS

MSA implementation is discussed in "How the MSA Works and Why You Should Reconsider It," http://solution.westgroup.com/employeebenefits/Nolink/hc_dec.htm (12/99).

Although the MSA pilot project was initially scheduled to expire on October 1, 1999, it was extended by IRS Announcement 99-95, 1999-42 IRB 520. The Community Renewal Tax Relief Bill of 2000 (H.R. 5652), passed on December 15, 2000, renames the account the Archer MSA (after Representative Bill Archer, a Texas Republican) and extends their life for another two years. The existing limitations on the program remain, including the cap on the number of participants. For 2001, the deductible on an MSA covering only one participant is $1,600 ($50 above the previous limit). The family coverage limit is also increased $50, to $2,400, and the limit on out-of-pocket expenses goes up $100, to $3,200.

The unpopularity of MSAs continues; as of September, 2000, only about 100,000 accounts had been set up. Many insurers dropped the accounts for lack of interest. There are many factors in the lack of success. Small employers are not usually innovators; some state laws prevent small employers from offering the accounts at all; and the rules are so rigid that it is unattractive to drop existing coverage to adopt an MSA. Furthermore, even if the accounts operate as planned, they would not necessarily be adequate to pay high medical bills. [Jennifer Steinhauer, "A Spending Account in Need of a Cure," *New York Times* 9/3/00 Bus. 11.]

9.18 QMCSOs

A 1998 law, the Child Support Performance and Incentives Act, P.L. 105-200, imposes the obligation on state child-support enforcement agencies to protect the rights children have to medical coverage under their parents' separation and divorce documents.

The Department of Labor and HHS joined forces to publish a Final Rule setting the text for the National Medical Child Support Notice: see 65 FR 82128 and 82154 (12/27/00). State agencies are required to use the form no later than October 1, 2001 to enforce child support orders, but they have the discretion to start using it earlier.

Originally, the Final Rule was supposed to take effect January 26, 2001, for notices received after that date. However, the PWBA published a notice in the January 26, 2001 *Federal Register* delaying the effective date of the regulations to March 27, 2001 (as a result of the Bush administration moratorium on the regulations published at the end of the Clinton administration). The Notice includes Parts A and B. Part A, the Employer Withholding Notice, informs the employer of the facts of the medical support order. The employer has an obligation either to:

- Inform the child-support enforcement agency that forwarded the order that the employer doesn't provide health care coverage to the employee who is the subject of the order,
- Inform the agency that the person named in the order is no longer an employee (the agency must also be notified if the employee is later terminated), OR
- Forward Part B of the form to the plan administrator within 20 business days, if health care coverage for a child is applicable.

Then the plan administrator determines whether the child or children covered by the order are enrolled in the health plan; if so, any appropriate withholding is taken from the employee's wages to provide medical coverage for the children. These deductions cannot exceed the amount of medical support specified by the order, and are also subject to federal and state limitations on wage assignments. Employers are subject to ERISA and state-law sanctions if they fail to carry out the wage deductions or, on the other hand, if they fire or discipline employees because they have medical child-support obligations.

Part B, the plan administrator's responsibility, is sent to the child-support enforcement agency. The form indicates whether the administrator deems the notice to be a valid QMCSO and, if so, what coverage options are available and which option the child(ren) has(have) been enrolled in. The administrator has 40 business days to determine the validity of the alleged QMCSO.

9.19 MEDICARE AS SECONDARY PAYOR (MSP)

Hewitt Survey: Employers React to Medicare Managed Care Changes

Before 1999, the Medicare system made provision for managed care, but generally in the form of HMOs (already familiar to benefit professionals because of their role in the EGHP). As of January 1999, the federal government planned to phase out Medicare HMOs in favor of an assortment of Medicare+Choice (M+C) managed care plans. Senior citizens would have a choice between getting their care through the conventional Medicare program or from an M+C plan.

In August 1998, Hewitt Associates received survey responses from 350 employers dealing with their reactions to the new program. Most of the employers said that they were aware of the transition to Medicare's new managed care format, but only 17% had even a tentative policy for communicating with employees and retirees about the new program or changing their retiree health plans. About a third of them plan to give their employees written information about Medicare+Choice; about 10% planned to outsource employees' and retirees' questions about M+C to an outside contractor.

About a third of the survey respondents had experience in sponsoring a Medicare risk HMO for older employees and retirees. Two-thirds of survey respondents planned to sponsor at least some medical coverage for individuals who retired at or after 65. Three-quarters of respondents considered offering M+C HMO coverage for this purpose in the future; 60% considered offering a POS HMO. PPOs were under consideration by 55% of respondents, but very few were interested in offering the other M+C alternatives (private fee-for-service plans; provider-sponsored organizations [PSOs]; or medical savings accounts [MSAs]).

9.20 CONSUMER PROTECTION FOR PATIENTS

HIPAA §264 set up two alternatives: either for Congress to enact standards to protect the privacy of individual health information by August 21, 1999, or for HHS to promulgate final regulations if Congress fails to act. In fact, Congress did not pass legislation. HCFA finalized privacy regulations in the December 28, 2000

Federal Register, starting at page 82511. The proposals discussed in the previous supplement covered only information transmitted electronically; the final rule is much broader, because it covers traditional paper-based documents as well as their electronic counterparts.

As initially published, the rules were supposed to take effect as of February 26, 2003, with small health plans with annual receipts below $5 million getting an extra year to get into compliance. However, a notice published in the Federal Register on February 26, 2001 (page 12433) defers the effective date of the regulations to April 14, 2001 and therefore also defers the compliance date.

Although the privacy rules are lengthy, detailed, and very sweeping, many employers will not be directly affected, because the obligation to protect privacy falls on the health insurer, not the employer. There is one important exception: self-insured plans are subject to HIPAA's mandate of protecting the privacy of individually identifiable health information (i.e., information about a particular person, not about the employee group in general—and not information from which identifying factors have been removed), and not giving out such information without consent of the patient.

Sponsors of self-insured plans will therefore have to create privacy policies, appoint someone ("privacy official") to implement these policies, make sure that health records cannot be accessed by unauthorized persons, and set up procedures for getting authorization from employees for use of their confidential health information and handling complaints of alleged improper disclosure or misuse of information. These internal operational changes will have to be mirrored in amendments to the SPD and other plan documents.

Even if information is used properly (e.g., sent to claims processing firms or HMOs, or used for utilization review), the self-insured plan will be responsible for making sure that such "business associates" maintain the confidentiality of the data.

Violation of the privacy rules can be penalized by up to $100 per violation per person, with a maximum of $25,000 a year. Knowing misuse of health information is also subject to criminal penalties.

HCFA released interim final regulations (if that isn't a contradiction in terms) on August 20, 1999, affecting 45 CFR Part 150. See 64 FR 45786. The regulations spell out HCFA's enforcement powers in situations in which states fail to enact necessary legislation, or enact but fail to enforce, consumer health statutes (HIPAA, Mental Health Parity, Women's Health and Cancer Rights Act, Newborns' and Mothers' Health Protection Act). When state enforcement fails, HCFA can impose penalties on health insurers or plan sponsors that violate the statutes. Penalties can be as high as $100 per day per person affected by noncompliance with the protective statutes: 42 USC §300gg-2(b)(2)(C); 45 CFR §150.301.

The Healthcare Research and Quality Act of 1999, signed by President Clinton on December 6, 1999, reauthorizes the operations of the Agency for Health Care Policy and Research, but gives it a new name, the Agency for Healthcare Research and Quality (AHRQ). The agency's mission is to undertake and publicize research about medical health care quality, including prevention of errors. AHRQ's Public Affairs Office telephone number is (301) 594-1364; its web address is http://www.ahrq.gov. See http://www.ahrq.gov/news/ahrqfact.htm for background on the agency.

Chapter 10

FRINGE BENEFITS

10.1 [NEW] INTRODUCTION

In November, 2000, the IRS issued Publication 15-B, Employer's Tax Guide to Fringe Benefits. (It can be accessed at http://www.fedworld.gov/pub/irb-pdf/p15b.pdf.) This document does not make any really major changes, but it does reflect the increase in the value of the transportation benefit for qualified parking from $175 to $180 (for 2001). The combined limit for transit passes and van pools is still $65, but an automatic increase to $100 is scheduled for years after 2001.

EEOC directives do not have the force of law, and even Regulations promulgated by this agency have frequently been declared invalid. Nevertheless, you should consult Section 3 of the EEOC's Compliance Manual, issued October 3, 2000, and available at http://www.eeoc.gov/docs/benefits.html for information about EEOC policy on how employers can avoid discrimination on the basis of age or handicap, and what is necessary to furnish "equal" benefits when it comes to disability benefits, life and health insurance, pensions, early retirement, and severance.

The revised Compliance Manual permits employers to reduce long-term disability benefits to account for Social Security Disability Income, Worker's Compensation, and other non-age-based government benefits. Long-term disability benefits to older workers can also be reduced by pension benefits that derive from employer contributions, if: the worker voluntarily opts to receive the pension (at any age), or the worker has reached the later of 62 or the plan's Normal Retirement Age (NRA) and is eligible for an unreduced pension. In plans partially funded by employee contributions, the employer is only permitted to reduce benefits traceable to its own contributions.

The EEOC position is that disability retirement benefits are not equal if they are calculated based on the number of years the employee would have worked until NRA, because that favors younger employees. But disability benefits under government programs can legitimately be used to reduce disability retirement benefits paid by the employer.

10.3 STOCK OPTIONS

In Announcement 2000-97, 2000-48 IRB 557 (11/27/00), the IRS published new codes that were supposed to be used on 2001 W-2 forms to identify reportable income from exercise of non-statutory stock options. Code V on Box 12 of the W-2 identifies Income from Exercise of Non-statutory Stock Options, and is also reflected in Boxes 1, 3, and 5 (but only up to the Social Security wage base for Box 5).

However, on January 18, 2001, the IRS reversed itself and placed a two-year moratorium on the collection of payroll and withholding taxes on Incentive Stock Options and employee stock purchase plans. The moratorium's purpose was to give the IRS time to figure out how to regulate the tax consequences of options without discouraging companies from offering them and thereby enhancing productivity.

In the late 1990s, as tech stocks boomed, award of stock options became much more common, especially as a way for start-up companies to attract top talent. A Watson Wyatt survey of 1352 companies, released in early 2000, showed that in 1999, nearly 19% of all workers in surveyed companies were eligible for stock options.

A Towers Perrin report released on October 16, 2000 showed that more than 11 million U.S. employees were covered by long-term incentive plans, the most common of which were stock option plans. But many employees were not knowledgeable about stock options—and, in the current stock market climate, where many options are "under water" (i.e., the option exercise price is actually higher than the actual price at which the stock trades), stock options do not create much of an incentive. [See http://www.ebri.org/conclave/fact11.pdf, EBRI Members' Conclave fact sheet on stock options, dated 12/7/00.]

The grant and exercise of stock options creates significant accounting problems. The basic accounting document is the 1972 APB Opinion No. 25, "Accounting for Stock Issued to Employees," supplemented by FASB Statement No. 123, "Accounting for Stock-Based Compensation." However, the financial and accounting landscape has changed significantly in the intervening decades, and FASB issued an Exposure Draft on 3/31/99: "Accounting for Certain Transactions Involving Stock Compensation." FASB received many comments on this contentious issue. They are summed up in FASB's "Stock Compensation: Interpretation of Opinion 25," http://www.rutgers.edu/Accounting/raw/fasb/project/stockcom.html. The comments should be influential in shaping the final interpretation that FASB announced would be issued early in 2000.

The rules of Opinion 25 are limited to common-law employees subject to payroll tax. FASB says that Opinion 25 does not apply to grant of options to independent contractors and service providers (e.g., an Internet start-up's law firm). If the option grantee is a leased employee, options granted by the lessee come under Opinion 25 in the lessee's financial statements only if the employees are common-law employees of the lessee, with payroll taxes being remitted by the lessor. The lessee must set the employee's compensation level, including the number and value of options in the grant, and the employee must be allowed to participate in the lessee's employee benefit plans. Similarly, Opinion 25 does not apply to stock options or awards to outside directors.

If the grantee of a nonvested option continues to provide services to the grantor, but either becomes or ceases to be a common-law employee, and if the change in status does not change the terms of the option significantly, then the compensation cost of the grant is accounted for under Opinion 25, or the Statement 123 fair value method, as if the option was granted as of the date the worker's status changed. But if there is a significant change in terms, the modified option must be treated as a new grant subject to the accounting rules that apply to the grantee's changed status, and compensation cost is fully recognized over the balance of the vesting period.

A discount of up to 15% is permissible in an ESOP, which can then be treated as a noncompensatory plan, because such a discount "is no greater than would be reasonable in an offer of stock to stockholders or others."

A phantom stock plan (which provides cash rewards based on changes in the price of the company's stock, although participants in the plan are not granted actual shares of stock) is not a pension plan for ERISA purposes, and therefore the federal courts have no jurisdiction over claims brought the employees asserting that they were entitled to receive phantom stock awards that were not provided to them: *Emmenegger v. Bull Moose Tube Co.*, 68 LW 1368 (8th Cir. 11/24/99). (You might call it the case of the phantom phantom stock.)

10.4 INSURANCE FRINGE BENEFITS

On January 13, 1999, the IRS issued a proposed revision for the "Table I" rates used under Code §79 to determine if employees have taxable income due to the employer's payment of insurance premiums over and above the pure cost of insurance. For most employees, the new rates are significantly lower—the older the employee, the more marked the effect. The IRS decided to lower the insurance costs to reflect increases in life expectancy. The new rates became effective on July 1, 1999; see 64 FR 29788 (6/3/99).

Employee's Age	Prior Law	Revised Rates
≯25	.08	.05
25–29	.08	.06
30–34	.09	.08
35–39	.11	.09
40–44	.17	.10
45–49	.29	.15
50–54	.48	.23
55–59	.75	.43
60–64	1.17	.66
65–70	2.10	1.27
>70	3.76	2.06

IRS Notice 2001-10, 2001-5 IRB 1 clarifies the IRS' earlier rulings on split-dollar insurance in the employment context (but doesn't deal with the use of split-dollar as a way to make charitable gifts). [Aon Consulting has an excellent online explanatory paper, "Split Dollar Tax Treatment Could be Changed Significantly," http://www.aon.com/intelligence/pdf/alert/AL010206.pdf (2/6/01).] The IRS' definition of split-dollar is the joint purchase of insurance on the life of an employee, by the employer and employee, subject to a contract that allocates the policy benefits between the employer and employee.

Split-dollar arrangements rely on the increase in cash value in a whole life policy. In the conventional arrangement, the employer pays the premiums, and the death benefit minus the cash value goes to the beneficiary designated by the employee, but the cash value goes to the employer at the employee's death or when the arrangement ends. An "equity" split-dollar arrangement entitles the employer to repayment of the premiums it paid, and nothing more. A "reverse" split-dollar plan gives the cash value to the employee and the death benefit net of cash value to the employer.

The IRS' previous split-dollar rulings (Rev.Rul. 64-328; Rev.Rul. 66-110), which date all the way back to the 1960s, refer to two forms of contract. Under the first type of arrangement, the endorsement method, the employer owns the insurance policy and endorses the contract to specify what can be paid to the employee's beneficiary. The employee owns the policy under the collateral assignment method. The employer makes loans to the employee to pay the premiums, and the employer's interest in the policy proceeds serves as collateral for the loans.

According to Notice 2001-10, there are no published rulings covering the equity split-dollar arrangements that have become popular recently. In such arrangements, part of the cash surrender value of the policy belongs to the employee. Usually, the employer's interest in the cash surrender value is limited to the sum of the premium payments it has made. Therefore, all the economic benefit from the return on the employer's investment goes to the employee.

Code §83 provides that a life insurance contract is property to the extent of its cash surrender value. Therefore, the IRS position is that an employee's beneficial interest in cash surrender value is includible in gross income, because it is property transferred in connection with provision of services. If the employee is the beneficial owner from the inception of the arrangement, there has been no transfer and therefore no income under §83 is involved.

If there is a reasonable and bona fide expectation that the employer will be repaid for its share of the premiums at a date in the future that is either fixed or determinable, then the arrangement can be treated as the employee's use of loans from the employer to acquire life insurance—not an arrangement under which the employer acquires the life insurance contract and provides potentially taxable benefits to the employee under the contract. Code §7872 deals with below-market loans; interest that is not charged to a borrower might constitute compensation income.

As the IRS admits, in the past it has not been common to apply §7872 to impute compensation income from the deemed loans. The IRS says that it will use the following guidelines until it develops final rules based on public comments:

- The parties' characterization of the employer's payments will be accepted by the IRS as long as the characterization does not contradict the clear substance of the transaction; all parties treat the transaction consistently; and the parties adopt accounting conventions that are consistent with the characterization.
- The employer's payments can be treated as loans. The employee will **not** have compensation income equivalent to the value of insurance protection, and the cash surrender value will **not** be considered a §83 transfer. But the employee will have gross income if the loan is not repaid in accordance with its terms. Furthermore, §72 makes actual distributions under the life insurance contract includible in gross income.
- Failure to consistently treat the employer payments as a loan will be deemed characterization of the transaction as a non-loan. Economic benefits must be accounted for accordingly. Therefore, the employer will be treated as having beneficial ownership of the policy through its share of premium payments. The employee has compensation income, under §61, equal to the value of each year's life insurance protection, minus any amount paid by the employee. Dividends and similar distributions under the insurance contract are also income for the employee under §61. Any substantially vested interest in the policy's cash surrender value (minus any amount paid by the employee to acquire the interest) will be treated as §83(a) compensation income.
- If the employer pays the premiums but doesn't acquire a beneficial interest in the policy, and has no reasonable expectation of repayment, then the employer's payments under the split-dollar plan are included in the employee's gross income under §61.

Earlier rulings allowed either P.S. 58 rates (based on 1946 mortality tables; originally published in Rev. Rul. 55-747) or lower one-year term rates published by employers to be used to value split-dollar arrangements. However, the IRS' current position is that the P.S. 58 rates no longer represent the market value of insurance protection.

For tax years ending on or after January 1, 2002, the IRS will **not** accept the P.S. 58 rates as proper valuation for life insurance protection, because the IRS believes that the P.S. 58 rates significantly overstate the value of the policy benefits allocated to the employer, with the result that the employee's share of the premium is much less than the employee's actual share of the benefits under the policy.

The Notice includes a premium rate table (Table 2001) for valuing current life insurance protection on a single life for either a split-dollar or a qualified retirement plan. Table 2001 reflects the actuarial assumptions used in Table I currently used to value group-term life insurance. However, Table I uses five-year age brackets; Table 2001 has a separate rate for each age. Taxpayers can also use lower premium rates published by an insurer that are available to all standard risks for initial issue one-year term. For periods after 12/31/03, the IRS will insist on verification of the actual availability of the rates.

Table 2001 provides that, for $1000 worth of life insurance, the §79 extended and interpolated annual rate for a person aged 30 is $0.87, versus $0.99 at age 35, $1.10 at age 40, $1.53 at 45, $2.30 at 50, $4.15 at 55, $6.51 at 60, and $11.90 at 65.

The result of implementation of Notice 2001-10 is that, after 2003, employers will have to use Table 2001 or one-year term rates to value traditional split-dollar plans. Employees participating in reverse split-dollar plans will probably have to report much more income, because the Table 2001 rates are a lot lower than the P.S. 58 rates. The IRS has not yet set its final policy for treatment of equity split-dollar.

A September 1998 case, *Cehrs v. Northeast Ohio Alzheimer's Research Center*, 155 F.3d 755 (6th Cir. 1998), involves an employer that had a life insurance plan. A disabled employee was told that he did not fit the plan's definition of disability, so the employer would not maintain his life insurance coverage. However, the employer did not give any reason for the determination or how to appeal it. After the ex-employee's death, his family sued under ERISA §503. The employer's litigating position was that the employee failed to mitigate (reduce) his damages by investigating and discovering that the employer's position was incorrect. The Sixth Circuit rejected this argument, taking the position that when a plan fails to provide statutorily mandated notices, employees essentially can't mitigate their damages; and requiring them to do so would reward plans for failure to provide the required notices.

The estate of a wrongfully terminated employee was entitled to recover the face value of the employer-provided life insurance forfeited by the discharge, minus the proceeds of the insurance policy the deceased ex-employee purchased as a replacement: *Sposato v. Electronic Data Systems Corp.*, 188 F.3d 1146 (9th Cir. 1999).

The Ninth Circuit held that the proper measure of damages was the amount of insurance, not just the premiums that the employer would have paid.

A plan participant who had an employer-sponsored life insurance policy died during medical leave. The insurer said she was not an "active employee" at the time of her death, and therefore refused to pay under the policy. The employee's widower sued the insurer for wrongful denial of benefits and breach of fiduciary duty. The Fourth Circuit [*Tester v. Reliance Ins. Co.*, No. 97-1589, 2000 U.S. App. LEXIS 23724 (4th Cir. 2000).] did not reach the fiduciary claim because it found that benefits were wrongfully denied. In the court's analysis, the term "active" was ambiguous, and if applied with undue strictness would terminate coverage for any employee who ever missed work because of illness. Furthermore, the insurer continued to accept premiums on behalf of the employee, who was treated by the employer as being on an approved leave of absence.

When Kenneth Howell died in 1996, he had a life insurance policy under a welfare benefit plan. In 1994, his second wife (he already had three children from a prior marriage) sued for divorce. In 1995, a family court ordered both spouses to refrain from transferring or otherwise disposing of marital assets during the divorce proceedings; proceedings were still pending when he died. However, contrary to the court order, he changed the beneficiary designation from his second wife to his children.

His pension fund brought an interpleader action under ERISA [*Central States, Southeast & Southwest Areas Pension Fund v. Howell*, 227 F.3d 672 (6th Cir. 2000).] The court order didn't qualify as a QDRO, because it omitted mandatory information such as the number of payments and how the participant's benefits were to be allocated. Because there was no QDRO, ERISA preempted state-law allocation principles, and the beneficiary card filed with the plan (directing payment to the children) governed. However, the case was remanded to the District Court to see if a constructive trust should be imposed (i.e., whether the benefits should be treated as if a trust had been established with provisions reflecting equity and justice).

Preemption was also asserted in *Armstrong v. Columbia/HCA Healthcare Corp.*, 2000 U.S. Dist. LEXIS 17640 (S.D. Tex. 2000). In many cases, employees sue employers in state courts over plan disputes. The employer then tries to get the case removed to federal court on the grounds that ERISA preempts the employee's claim. In this case, the employee paid for life insurance covering his spouse, supplementing the coverage paid for by the employer. The employee said that his payments should be treated as a separate plan with no employer contributions. But the court said that the supplemental coverage was part of a larger plan that was preempted by ERISA.

A group of retirees from a Blue Cross plan tried to enforce the pre-1998 terms of the plan, before life insurance coverage was significantly reduced. They say that they were protected by an implied contract, because the employer promised them benefits for life, and that therefore they were vested in the benefits although in general ERISA does not provide for vesting of welfare benefits. In late 2000, the Southern District of New York ruled [*Byrnes v. Empire Blue Cross/Blue Shield, N.Y.L.J.* 10/26/00 p. 34 col. 2 (S.D.N.Y.)] that the most relevant document is the SPD as of the time of retirement—which provided that benefits did not vest until retirement, and reserved the employer's right to change the plan. Therefore, the employees could not get the court to enforce the pre-1998 plan terms, and the employer won on the ERISA §502(a) claims of wrongful reduction of benefits and the fiduciary breach claim.

10.5 CAFETERIA PLANS

Proposed and Temporary Regulations for bringing cafeteria plans into conformity with HIPAA were published at 62 FR 60165 and 60196 (11/7/97). In March, 2000, IRS replaced the 1997 Temporary Regulations with final regulations in T.D. 8878, 65 *Federal Register* 15548, 2000-15 IRB 857 (3/23/00). The new regulations sought to clarify the circumstances under which employees participating in cafeteria plans can change their elections with respect to accident, health, or group-term life insurance coverage (e.g., when a Qualified Medical Child Support Order is granted; when eligibility for Medicare or Medicaid is gained or lost). T.D. 8878 was supposed to be effective for plan years beginning one or after January 1, 2001.

At the beginning of 2001, however, the IRS issued a revision, T.D. 8921, 66 *Federal Register* 1837 (1/10/01). T.D. 8921 modifies the T.D. 8878 final Regs. by allowing cafeteria plan participants to increase or decrease their coverage whenever they have a change of status event.

They were always allowed to do so based on marriage or divorce; thanks to T.D. 8921 they can also do so when a dependent is born or adopted. An employee who decreases or cancels coverage because of coverage under a spouse's or dependent's plan has to certify that he or she is obtaining other coverage. The election can be changed to conform to a domestic relations order—but only if the spouse or former spouse actually provides coverage for the child. T.D. 8921 also allows elections to be changed when the employee's responsibility for payments under the plan increases or decreases significantly.

NOTE: T.D. 8921 was not affected by the moratorium imposed by President Bush on late Clinton-era regulations.

10.6 FLEXIBLE SPENDING ACCOUNTS (FSAs)

At the end of 1997, the IRS, the Department of Labor's Pension and Welfare Benefits Administration, and the Department of Health and Human Services jointly published a "clarification of regulations" that appears at 62 FR 67688 (12/29/97). The document makes it clear that health insurance portability is not required for certain health flexible spending arrangements (FSAs). In technical terms, such FSAs are "excepted benefits" under ERISA §§732 and 733(c) and IRC §§9831 and 9832(c). Another implication is that FSA coverage is not "creditable coverage" that triggers portability rights under HIPAA.

According to this document, a health FSA is a "benefit program that provides employees with coverage under which specified, incurred expenses may be reimbursed (subject to reimbursement maximums and any other reasonable conditions) and under which the maximum amount of reimbursement that is reasonably available to a participant for a period of coverage is not substantially in excess of the total premium (including both employee-paid and employer-paid portions of the premium) for the participant's coverage." As the document notes, FSAs usually cover medical expenses excluded by the primary EGHP.

The FSA is excepted from HIPAA if the employee's maximum FSA benefit for the year is not greater than twice the employee's salary reduction election under the FSA for the year, as long as the employee has other EGHP coverage and provides at least some benefits that are not excepted benefits.

A 1999 IRS Technical Advice Memorandum, TAM 199936046 says that it's permissible for a cafeteria plan to offer supplemental cancer and hospital coverage (over and above the normal health plan). Such coverage is treated as an IRC §106 accident and health plan notwithstanding the fact that premium is waived after hospitalization or cancer diagnosis, and even though cash benefits are paid to cancer patients. See "Supplemental Insurance Policies May be Offered Under a Flex Plan, IRS Says," http://www.thompson.com/tpg/pem_ben/flex/flexnov99.html.

In late 2000, IRS officials informally confirmed that employer funds in an FSA remaining unspent at the end of a year could be carried over to the following year, as long as the money is used only for medical reimbursement—but would be forfeited when the employee retires or otherwise terminates employment. It was less clear whether unspent funds could be used to pay COBRA or retiree health premiums, but the IRS position is that cashout is inappropriate, because a plan that distributes cash is not an insured arrangement. [The Segal Company Capital Checkup, "IRS Confirms Rollover Option Available for Employer Funds in FSA," http://www.segalco.comcapchkp111700.html, 11/7/00.]

In 1999, a Freedom of Information Act (FOIA) request resulted in the release of an IRS General Information Letter issued in 1997. General Information Letters are not binding on the IRS, but do indicate trends and areas in which official guidance may later appear. This letter indicates that FSAs may be able to reimburse orthodontia costs "up front," rather than making individual reimbursements keyed to individual treatments. Usually, orthodontists get a large downpayment, then bill for additional services. The Letter says that employers can either reimburse employees for amounts they have paid, when the employee submits a dentist's bill, or can require a schedule of treatments and reimburse employees as the treatments are actually given. See "IRS Gives Employers Something to Smile About," http://www.watsonwyatt.com/homepage/us/new/Insider/new/2000/2000/2000_01_04.asp.

According to Hewitt Associates (call 847-295-5000 for more information), about 17.5% of the workforce participates in health care FSAs. Ninety-one percent of the employers who implement FSAs have forfeitures in the plan, averaging $136 per employee per year. The survey of about 500 employers showed an average 1997 FSA contribution of $744 per employee for health care accounts, $2848 for dependent care accounts.

10.8 DISABILITY PLANS

The Seventh Circuit's decision in *Doe v. Mutual of Omaha* has been affirmed, without opinion, by the Supreme Court (#98-4112, 1/25/00). Title II (the public accommodations title) of the Americans with Disabilities Act is not violated when an insured or self-insured health plan imposes a lower cap on benefits for AIDS-related than for other illnesses and conditions. The Supreme Court refused to grant privileged status to diseases that do cause ADA disability over other diseases that do not.

Corley v. Kimberly-Clark Tissue Co. Pension Plan, 1998 U.S. Dist. LEXIS 9381 (S.D. Ala. 1998), involves a pension plan that limited disability retirement benefit eligibility to persons unable to hold any paying job, with medical certification that the inability is expected to be lifelong. The plaintiff's own doctor said that the plaintiff could not do heavy manual labor but could do light to medium work. In light of this, his application for disability retirement was rejected. The doctor revised his opinion but never indicated that the plaintiff was completely unable to work. The pension plan's physician opined that the plaintiff was unable to perform any job currently available with the employer—which is not the same thing as complete inability to undertake paid work. The District Court upheld the denial of benefits. The plan did not act arbitrarily or capriciously, and there was no abuse of discretion. The evidence did not show eligibility for the benefit—only inability to retain the preinjury job.

An attorney had heart surgery and was unable to return to work. Although six doctors said that he couldn't work, one doctor said that his inability to work was motivational in nature. The employer cut off his disability benefits based on that one opinion, and the insurer affirmed the denial, describing litigation as a "sedentary" occupation. The attorney sued under ERISA §502(a)(1)(B), the cause of action for recovery of benefits due under a plan.

In *Kearny v. Standard Insurance Co.*, 175 F.3d 1084 (9th Cir. 1998), the Ninth Circuit ruled that the plan, which required "satisfactory written proof of disability" as a prerequisite to paying benefits, did not explicitly give discretionary authority to the plan administrator. Therefore, the administrator's decisions should be reviewed on a de novo basis, subject to objective standards. Since there were certainly material issues of fact as to what a litigator's job entails and the plaintiff's ability to perform the job, the lawyer's claim should have proceeded to trial.

Disability benefits that are reduced on the twenty-fifth anniversary of the former employee's hiring, to the level of the pension he or she would have received after retiring with 25 years of service, remain disability benefits and do not become pension benefits as a result of the reduction. Therefore, under *Picard v. Comm'r*, 165 F.3d 744 (9th Cir. 1/26/99), benefits received under the plan remain tax-free under IRC §104(a)(1).

On February, 17, 1998, the Israel Discount Bank filed a settlement with the EEOC, under which the bank agreed to parity between mental and physical disabilities in its long-term disability plan: See 66 LW 2519. The case's docket number is 95-CV-6964 (S.D.N.Y.).

If the employee pays all the premiums for long-term disability insurance, and the employer's only role is to administer the payments (without endorsing the policy), then ERISA does not preempt a suit by the employee against the insurer, claiming that benefits were cut off in bad faith after the employee refused to take an independent medical examination. There are three tests for deciding whether ERISA preempts litigation about a disability policy:

- Was there a "plan, fund or program"? In this case, a plan was clearly present—but it was not an ERISA plan.
- Does the arrangement qualify for the ERISA safe harbor? It does if the employer does not make any contributions to the plan; the plan is completely voluntary; the employer does not profit from the plan (other than receiving a reasonable administrative fee); and the employer allows one or more insurers to publicize the availability of the program, but does not endorse or recommend it.
- Is the employer's sole function under the plan collection of premiums, or is there deeper employer involvement?

In the judge's view, in the case of *Bagden v. Equitable Life Assurance Society of the United States*, an employer can be neutral even if it is involved in program administration. The most important criterion is whether a reasonable employee would believe that the program was part of the employer's own benefit package, or that the employer controlled the program. But in this case, the employer properly gave information about the program but did not endorse it. Since ERISA preemption was not triggered, the employee is at liberty to sue the insurer for terminating her disability benefits.

Bagden is discussed in Shannon P. Duffy's article, "Employee-Paid Disability Policy Falls Under ERISA Safe Harbor," from *The Legal Intelligencer.* The article is available at http://www.lawnewsnetwork.com/practice/employmentlaw/news/A1399-1999May12.html.

Nor does ERISA preempt an employee's state-law claims about an insurer's denial of benefits under an individual disability policy converted from a group policy [*Demars v. CIGNA Corp.*, 173 F.3d 443 (1st Cir. 1999)]. The employer is no longer involved, so neither is ERISA.

A plan participant who was denied benefits under a long-term disability plan brought suit under ERISA §502(a)(3) and got a default judgment covering disability expenses, medical benefits, prejudgment interest, and attorneys' fees [*Rogers v. Hartford Life & Accident Insurance Co.*, 167 F.3d 933 (5th Cir. 1999)]. When the plan got the court to reopen the case, the Fifth Circuit reduced the damages, on the grounds that the cost of medical treatment lay outside the disability plan's contract. The *Mertens* case [508 U.S. 248 (Sup. Ct. 1993)] says that §502(a)(3) remedies are purely equitable; compensatory damages are unavailable.

The Department of Labor's final rule on claims procedures, published at 65 *Federal Register* 70246 (11/21/00), discussed in greater detail in ¶9.5.1, sets the time frame for resolving disability claims. At the initial level, claims must be resolved within 45 days of the time the plan receives the claim. But, as long as the claimant receives a notice explaining the reason for the delay, resolution can be deferred for 30 days for factors beyond the control of the plan, with a second 30-day extension possible. If the decision is adverse to the claimant, the appeal usually has to be decided within 45 days, with a possible extension of 45 days if the plan is unable to complete review within the original time period.

Although the general rule is that the Mental Health Parity Act, 42 USC 300gg (see ¶9.2.1), does not cover disability plans, employers must beware of the argument that distinguishing between physical and mental disabilities violates the Americans With Disabilities Act. The argument pro and con can be found in "Post-Employment Fringe Benefits and the ADA: Suing for Differential Disability Coverage," *WestGroup Employment Alert*, 7/9/98, p. 1.

There's an outside chance that the distinction will be penalized under Title III of the ADA (the ban on discrimination in public accommodations). However, cases such as *Ford v. Schering-Plough Corp.*, 145 F.3d 601 (3rd Cir. 1998) *cert. denied* 119 S.Ct. 850, *EEOC v. C.N.A. Insurance Co.*, 96 F.3d 1039 (7th Cir. 1996), and *Parker v. Metropolitan Life Ins. Co.*, 121 F.3d 1006 (6th Cir. 1996) either find that there was no discrimination or find that the discrimination, if any, is between different classes of disabled individuals, whereas the ADA only bans discriminating between disabled and nondisabled persons.

ADA Title IV immunizes insurer and benefit plan decisions based on underwriting, classifying, or administering risks, as long as the decisions are not a subterfuge to escape ADA compliance. Therefore, decisions that have actuarial support are likely to qualify for this safe harbor. However, *Lewis v. Aetna Life Ins. Co.*, 7 F.Supp.2d 743 (E.D. Va. 1998), does not allow safe harbor characterization for a distinction between physical and mental disabilities for which actuarial support was not proven.

At least according to the First Circuit, a Social Security Disability Insurance (SSDI) determination is relevant to the question of whether a person receiving LTD benefits continues to be disabled—but it is not controlling, because ERISA-regulated disability plans and SSDI have different standards. [*Pari-Fasano v. ITT Hartford Life and Accident Ins. Co.*, 2000 U.S. App. LEXIS 26656 (1st Cir. 2000).]

The question of when a person is totally disabled has occupied several courts.

Friedrich v. Intel Corp., 181 F.3d 1105 (9th Cir. 6/29/99) involves a self-funded long-term disability plan that excluded "mental, emotional or psychiatric illness or disorder of any type," but covered disability confirmed by "objective medical findings" such as lab tests and diagnostic scans. The plaintiff was terminated in October 1993, suffering from symptoms that were diagnosed both as major depression and as Chronic Fatigue Syndrome (CFS). Eventually, he qualified for Social Security disability benefits.

Five doctors retained by Intel issued reports that the plaintiff was suffering from a noncovered psychiatric illness, and there was no objective evidence of organic illness. However, the District Court granted LTD benefits to the plaintiff, and the Ninth Circuit affirmed. To the Ninth Circuit, Intel had failed to provide an adequate appeals procedure. It was proper for the courts to use a de novo standard (receiving new evidence), and it was held that the plaintiff presented appropriate evidence that CFS is a coverable organic illness; that there was objective proof of his health status; and that any psychiatric problems were secondary to physical illness.

In *Perlman v. Swiss Bank Corp. Comprehensive Disability Protection Plan*, 68 LW 1282 (7th Cir. 11/2/99), the plaintiff employee was seriously hurt in an automobile accident, and collected disability benefits for a year and subsequently for two shorter periods. However, she returned to work and worked successfully for two years, at which point she quit and applied for disability benefits, which were denied. The Seventh Circuit upheld the denial, finding that it was not arbitrary or capricious, because the plaintiff had not submitted evidence of any change in condition that would make it impossible to work after two years of acceptable performance.

According to *Kimber v. Thiokol Corp.*, 68 LW 1335 (10th Cir. 11/10/99), it was not arbitrary or capricious for a plan administrator to abide by the plan's two-year cap on benefits for mental disabilities. Nor was it an ADA violation to have separate caps for physical and mental ailments. ADA Title II doesn't require a long-term disability plan for state employees to have the same level of benefits for mental and physical ailments: *Rogers v. Dep't of Health & Environmental Control*, 67 LW 1671 (4th Cir. 4/8/99).

Weyer v. Twentieth Century Fox Film Corp., 68 LW 1432 (9th Cir. 1/3/00) holds that ADA Title I was not violated by different caps for mental and physical ailments. In this case, the plaintiff was totally disabled and couldn't perform essential functions even with accommodation; Title III was not violated because there was no public accommodation involved, and insurance underwriting decisions are entitled to safe-harbor protection.

According to the Seventh Circuit, the plaintiff in *Feldman v. American Memorial Life Insurance Co.*, 1999 U.S. App. LEXIS 29360 (7th Cir. 11/9/99) was not "totally disabled" throughout the 90-day elimination period in her disability insurance policy. Therefore, her ERISA §510 claim, that the employer fired her to prevent her from collecting benefits, had to fail, because she never became eligible for the benefits and therefore the employer's motivation in terminating her could not have been to keep her from receiving benefits she had earned.

The Northern District of Georgia did not allow a Long Term Disability insurer to recover three years of overpayments made to a partially disabled person who gave the insurer proper notice that he was working part-time (which would have entitled the insurer to terminate payments). However, ERISA does allow the insurer to terminate the payments on a prospective basis. [*Burger v. Life Ins. Co. of North America*, 103 F.Supp.2d 1344 (N.D. Ga. 2000).]

ERISA doesn't preempt a state (in this case, Oklahoma) "notice-prejudice" law. A notice-prejudice law prevents an insurer from denying a claim based on untimely notice of the covered event, unless the insurer actually suffers a disadvantage because of the delay. *Daug v. UNUM Life Insurance Co.*, 1999 WL 238236 (10th Cir. 1999) involves a long-term disability policy. *Cisneros v. UNUM*, 134 F.3d 939 (9th Cir. 1999), *cert.denied* 119 S.Ct. 1495, reaches a similar conclusion about the California notice-prejudice law.

The employee in *Whatley v. C.N.A. Insurance*, 1999 U.S. App. LEXIS 22504 (11th Cir. 9/20/99) lost his job on September 29. He claimed that he became totally disabled on October 3, and applied for disability benefits. The benefits were denied, on the basis that he must not have been disabled on September 29, because he was working on that day, so any disability would not be covered by the employer's long-term disability plan because it arose after employment was terminated. The District Court granted summary judgment for the employer. The evidence showed that the plaintiff's work performance was poor, and he needed frequent rests, but the District Court's view was that work performance, even poor performance, ruled out a contention of total disability before his termination.

The Eleventh Circuit reversed, finding that even though the employee went to work, he might have been totally disabled at the end of September. Summary judgment was inappropriate because fact questions remained to be settled; for instance, medical evidence about the actual onset of total disability.

The District Court, as affirmed by the Ninth Circuit, found that the plaintiff was not "totally disabled," as defined by the plan, because the plan's standard was inability to engage in any occupation or employment, and several doctors testified that the plaintiff was capable of performing most sedentary or light-duty jobs: *Goodberry v. Northrop Grumman Long Term Disability Income Plan*, 1999 U.S. App. LEXIS 29507 (9th Cir. 11/4/99). The plan did not provide for discretionary authority for the plan administrator or its fiduciaries, so the standard of review for the courts was de novo. The plaintiff asserted that the District Court should have required the plan to consult a vocational expert, but the courts did not view this as necessary for a plan that sets the standard of disability as inability to engage in any occupation, because a vocational expert would have nothing to contribute to such a determination.

An employee with a herniated disk received benefits under an employer-sponsored LTD plan that was both insured and administered by Hartford Life. At first, he submitted a doctor's statement that he was totally unable to work for an indefinite period. After neck surgery, his condition improved and he was able to return to part-time work. Surveillance videos showed him driving a truck and carrying heavy objects. Hartford notified him that benefits would be terminated because he was no longer totally disabled. He appealed within the 60-day time limit, providing additional information. The insurer did not respond. The employee sued to continue the benefits. The trial court granted summary judgment for the insurer, on the grounds that there had been no abuse of discretion.

On appeal [*McGarrah v. Hartford Life Ins. Co.*, 2000 U.S. App. LEXIS 31388 (8th Cir. 2000).] the employee said that, by ignoring his appeal, the insurer lost the right to have its decisions reviewed deferentially by the court. But, according to the Eighth Circuit, even though this was a serious irregularity in procedure that violated the LTD policy's own claims procedure as well as Department of Labor regulations, deferential review was still appropriate because the employee had no real evidence that the insurer acted arbitrarily, and there was a great deal of evidence that he was no longer totally disabled and therefore that benefits were properly terminated.

In the view of the Ninth Circuit, the ADEA may be violated by calculating disability retirement benefits using the age at the time of hiring. The plan calculated the benefit on the basis of years of service lost due to disability, based on the length of service between age 55 (presumed retirement date) and the age at which the disabled individual became a public employee. Under *Hazen*, calculations based on actual years of service are acceptable, because a younger person might have more years of service, and vice versa.

However, this is a slightly different question because the age at hire had a strong effect on the potential disability benefit. The Ninth Circuit remanded the case to the District Court for disposition: *Arnett v. California Public Employees Retirement System*, 67 LW 1742 (9th Cir. 6/2/99).

In late 1999, the Eighth Circuit offered yet another lesson in the importance of careful drafting of plan documents. Ceridian Corporation used to pay insurance premiums for disabled individuals as part of its long-term disability plan. When it discontinued this practice, a group of disabled ex-employees sued. The SPD reserved the right to amend the plan, but didn't specify whether the plan could be amended with respect to people who were already disabled at the time of the change. [*Barker v. Ceridian Corp.*, 1999 U.S. App. LEXIS 26470 (8th Cir. 10/21/99) *cert. denied* 99-1506 (5/30/00)].

The Eighth Circuit found that the SPD provision was ambiguous, so testimony about the company's intentions should be admissible. The Eighth Circuit found that the District Court's pro-employer verdict was clearly erroneous, and therefore ordered Ceridian to continue paying for insurance for the group of ex-employees already disabled at the time of the change in the plan.

Another employer fared better in amending its disability plan: see *Anderson v. Intermountain Power Service Corp.*, 1999 U.S. App. LEXIS 25629 (10th Cir. 10/14/99). After the plaintiff became disabled and began to collect long-term disability benefits, the plan informed him that he would have to pay health insurance premiums to maintain his health coverage. He made partial but not full payments, and his health insurance was cancelled.

He sued the former employer on ERISA and disability discrimination claims, but lost at both the District Court and Court of Appeals levels on all the claims. The plan had validly reserved the right to amend its terms. Canceling coverage for late payment was not a breach of fiduciary duty. The plan had no legal obligation to accept partial payments; accepting some partial payments as an accommodation to the ex-employee did not waive the right to enforce the payment provisions at a later time.

The Standard Insurance Company introduced an innovation that can be used for policies purchased on or after January 1, 2001: instead of making disability payments by check or electronic transfer, the insurer issues a debit card (carrying the VISA logo) that can be used in stores and ATMs. Disability payments are deposited into the card account; balances can also be transferred to the disabled person's bank account. Automatic electronic crediting of the amounts not only saves paperwork for the insurer, it reassures disabled people because they don't have to worry about checks that are delayed or lost. [Vicki Lankarge, "The Standard Introduces a Debit Card for Disability Payments," http://www.insure.com/health/securecard101.html.]

Nancy Hatch Woodward's article, "Supplemental LTD Plans Can Reduce Executive Discrimination," *HR Magazine* ,12/98, p. 68, points out that most long-term disability (LTD) plans have maximum benefits of $5000 a month. Even though their maximum replacement level is 60% of prior income, this amount is still uncomfortably small for highly compensated employees—especially since an LTD plan replaces only salary income, not bonuses or stock options.

An employer that has only minimal LTD protection may be at a disadvantage when trying to recruit employees in a market that offers much higher benefits. It's true that executives tend to work in "safe" jobs where there are few industrial accidents, but 90% of disability stems from illness rather than accident, so this argument is not very compelling.

TIP

No doubt your workforce would prefer you to respond by increasing the limits on the disability plan for everyone—but that's expensive. A good compromise is to offer individual supplemental disability policies over and above the group plan. A supplemental plan can have higher limits and replace all compensation, not just salary.

Usually, employers pay for the base plan (generating taxable income for the employee), but employees pay for the supplements; group premiums are 5 to 20% lower than individual premiums, so employees still benefit. If the employee pays all, the employer can open up the plan to everyone, not just executives, although executives tend to have more disposable income and therefore find such plans more appealing than rank-and-file workers do.

How can disability costs be brought under control? Successive surveys by Watson Wyatt Worldwide, in conjunction with the Washington Business Group on Health, suggest that integrated disability management (for both occupationally- and nonoccupationally-caused disabilities) can save money. Using a single source to manage rehabilitation of injured workers and administer disability and Worker's Compensation benefits is an effective tactic. The report, published in the fall of 1999, is "Staying@Work: Focusing on What Works." Call (800) 388-9868 or go to http://www.stayingatwork.com for purchase information. Also see "Survey Finds that a Coordinated Disability Management Strategy Reduces Worker Absences," http://www.spencernet.com/Archive/News111400.html; Dianne Dyck, "Disability Management Best Practices," http://www.benefitscanada.com/Content/2000/11-00/disability.html, showing significant reductions in absence and major cost savings deriving from commitment to coordinated disability management.

See §10.14, later in this chapter, for the *Parker-Hannifin* case.

Although it involves an individual policy, a 1999 case from the Eastern District of New York may provide some guidance. The issue in *Mossa v. Provident Life & Casualty Insurance Co.*, 36 F.Supp. 2d 524 (E.D. N.Y. 1999) (see Bill Alden, "Disability Policy Clause Interpreted by Federal Judge," *New York Law Journal*, 2/17/99, p. 1), was when benefits can be terminated on the grounds that the person can engage in "any gainful occupation." The opinion requires consideration of the individual's earnings history and availability of jobs in the relevant geographic area—a position shared by most of the courts that have had to interpret such clauses.

10.9 EDUCATION ASSISTANCE

The Ticket to Work Act, P.L. 106-170, also includes some miscellaneous tax provisions, such as an extension of the tax deduction for employer-provided, undergraduate-level education assistance until 12/31/01. The education provision is §506 of the Act.

The IRS revised Publication 508, "Tax Benefits for Work-Related Education," in November, 1999. It can be ordered from (800) 829-3676 or downloaded from http://ftp.fedworld.gov/pub/irs-pdf/p508.pdf.

A Hewitt Associates survey of 460 companies revealed that about half (46%) imposed a maximum on the educational assistance they would provide an individual in any year; the median figure was $3000, but some paid quite a bit more, in line with the rising cost of tuition. A number of companies raised their reimbursement levels to encourage employees to take two courses a semester rather than one (so they could complete their coursework faster). On the other hand, few companies reimburse for more than two classes a semester—a heavy course load is likely to cut into workplace productivity.

Many companies offer higher reimbursement for graduate than for undergraduate courses. Reimbursement is the key word: Only 5% pay in advance, and 76% wait for the employee to finish the course (and almost two-thirds reimburse only if the grade is C or better; some offer a base level of reimbursement, and enhance it if the employee gets an A or a B). Most companies reimburse the related cost of books and school fees, but 23% limit reimbursement to the actual cost of tuition. There is an increasing trend for employers to require that the courses be work related.

Traditional on-campus university courses are not the only option. Many employers see the benefit of using television, video, or the Internet for distance learning, which is much more adaptable to employees' work and family schedules. See Dale K. DuPont, "Tuition Aid That Makes the Grade," *HR Magazine*, 4/99, p. 75.

10.13 MISCELLANEOUS FRINGES

During 1999 and 2000, when talk of a New Economy was at its peak, many established "bricks and mortar" businesses feared that Internet "dot-com" companies would raid their best talent. Therefore, a spiral developed to add more benefits and more valuable and innovative benefits, everything from providing Internet-based portals to allow employees working long hours to do errands at work, to allowing employees to bring pets to work.

With the collapse of the dot-com boom, it is less likely that employers will suffer the same pressure, but certain trends may remain: allowing employees more discretion to customize benefit packages; allowing them to sell or exchange vacation and personal days; providing "health lifestyle credits" for healthful and safety-promoting behavior; or even backing away from formal benefits programs and simply increasing cash compensation somewhat so employees can use the money as they see fit. [Karen Lee, "Full Plate," *Employee Benefit News* 10/1/00, http://www.benefitnews.com/subscriber/00_10/feature1.html]

10.14 VOLUNTARY EMPLOYEE BENEFITS ASSOCIATIONS (VEBAs)

An employer could deduct only the part of the VEBA contribution that was used to fund long-term disability benefits. The portions that funded postretirement benefits and medical benefits for union members were not deductible, because the employer failed to satisfy the IRC §419A(c)(2) requirements for accumulating assets to prefund the benefits [*Parker-Hannifin Corp. v. Comm'r*, 139 F.3d 1090 (6th Cir. 3/23/98)].

10.15 VACATIONS AND VACATION BANKING

The "group emergency pool" technique can be used to maintain the paycheck of sick employees who would not otherwise be entitled to pay. It works especially well in smaller companies that can't afford a short-term disability plan. Employees donate unused vacation days, and the donor's salary is contributed to the sick employee. Theoretically, at least, employees who benefit from the pooling system will donate some of their own time when they get better.

Many variations and administrative structures are possible. There can be an anonymous pool, or the donors can be identified so the recipients can thank them. The company can allow pooling of vacation time only, sick leave only, or both. Usually, the maximum donation is 80 hours, because there are sound reasons for requiring employees to take at least some vacation time. A person who never takes vacations could be a workaholic who needs to slow down before he or she burns out—or an embezzler who has to keep watch over a dishonest scheme.

A donation plan can be calculated on an hour-for-hour basis; or, if employees with widely disparate wage scales are involved, on a dollar-for-dollar basis. Employers who want to implement a plan of this type should be sure to communicate it to employees and maintain written policy guidelines. Employees should not be put under pressure to donate; it should be a voluntary program. To avoid potential liability, make sure that pregnancy-related and HIV/AIDS-related requests are handled on a par with other sick day requests. For information, see Carla Joinson, "Time Share," *HR Magazine*, 12/98, p. 104.

Not only can vacation days be donated; they can also be purchased and sold. In 1994, Hewitt Associates surveyed about 500 companies and found that 15% allowed buying and selling of vacation days; 24% allowed this in 1997. After all, from the corporate viewpoint, the same number of work days are put in; all that changes is the identity of the people doing the work. Eighteen percent of the survey respondents allowed selling of vacation days, and 12% allowed buying. Where both are permitted, there are more would-be buyers than sellers: 25% of employees want to buy more vacation days, and only 10% want to sell. Even if the program has no net cash effect on payroll, it can be effective, because it's an incentive for employees to feel more in control of their schedules. (These figures come from Kate Walter's "Time For Sale" on p. 131 of the October 1998 issue of *HR Magazine.*)

Typically, vacation-sale plans allow the purchase or sale of up to five days. Employees get a monthly or quarterly statement of their vacation "balances." IRS regulations call for the purchase/sale decision to be made at benefit enrollment time. They also require employees to use up their regular days off before their purchased days.

If regular vacation days are on a "use it or lose it" basis, the same can be true for purchased days; or unused days can be banked toward a sabbatical or cashed out. (Year-end extra cash is especially welcome for holiday purchases.) The employer can deduct the cost of purchased days from the purchaser's paycheck, and the cost can be spread out over the entire year. Vacation day sales can be added to a flexible benefit program that includes flex credits and cash.

In the 1998 Eighth Circuit case of *Mange v. Petrolite Corp.*, 135 F.3d 570 (8th Cir. 1998), the plaintiff employees took voluntary retirement or voluntary separation as part of a reduction in force. The company's vacation policy treated vacation benefits as vesting at the end of the fiscal year. The plaintiffs claimed that their vacation vested on the last day of employment, and therefore they're entitled to be paid for unused vacation days. Their claim did not succeed in court, because the RIF programs didn't cover pay for unused vacation days, and the employees waived their claims under the regular plan by accepting the RIF incentives.

10.18 ERISA REGULATION OF WELFARE BENEFIT PLANS

A brokerage firm created an association of small firms (those with under 225 employees) so the members could maintain a self-funded health benefit plan. The Third Circuit ruled that the members lacked the requisite commonality of interest, and therefore the plan was not an "employee welfare benefit plan" as defined by ERISA [*Gruber v. Hubbard Bert Karle Weber Inc.*, 159 F.3d 780 (3rd Cir. 1998)].

Where failure to make complete disclosure could be harmful to benefit participants, a benefit plan administrator has a fiduciary duty to give complete and accurate information about the plan; it's not enough simply to answer participants' questions, if it's clear that the participant is unaware of important features of the plan [*Krohn v. Huron Memorial Hospital*, 173 F.3d 542 (6th Cir. 1999)].

Vega v. National Life Insurance Services Inc., 68 LW 1154 (9/21/99) involves a plan sponsored by a married couple who owned a business. The plan administrator (which, as it happened, was a subsidiary of the insurer who wrote the plan's policies) denied a health claim for the wife, based on information from her doctor that the claim was for surgery contemplated before the policy was obtained.

The Fifth Circuit heard the case twice (first by a panel including some of the judges, then the entire court). The second time, the Fifth Circuit decided that even if a plan administrator experiences a conflict of interest when denying a claim (which, in this case, would have been paid by the administrator's parent company), ERISA does not impose an additional duty of reasonable investigation before denying the claim. However, when a court reviews the transaction to see if there was an abuse of discretion by the administrator, the conflict of interest is relevant evidence. But even an administrator who has a conflict of interest can reach a valid decision.

This case is also interesting because it takes the position that a business owner can be treated as an employee, and therefore as a plan participant for ERISA purposes, as long as there is at least one participant in the plan besides the owner and his or her spouse.

Chapter 11

EARLY RETIREMENT AND RETIREE HEALTH BENEFITS

11.1 INTRODUCTION

P.L. 106-170, the Ticket to Work Act, makes it easier for disabled people to return to the workforce without sacrificing public-sector health benefits. It also contains various other provisions, including reauthorization of IRC §420, which was scheduled to expire 12/31/00. Section 420 authorizes "401(h) plans": i.e., use of a pension plan's surplus assets to provide retiree health benefits. Under P.L. 106-170 §535, 401(h) plans are authorized until 12/31/05.

See IRS Proposed Regs, REG-116468-00, RIN 1545-AY43 [Discussed at http://www.benefitslink.com/taxregs/1.420-1-prop.shtml.] for an explanation of how to apply the minimum cost requirements in 401(h) plans. If the employer fails the minimum cost requirement test, the transfer of plan assets to the 401(h) plan will not be valid for tax purposes. The employer is at risk of losing qualification if the employer's action reduces the number of persons receiving health benefits under the plan by 10% or more in any year. It is assumed that the buyer of a business will not cover retirees from the seller company, so such corporate transitions are always treated as employer action to see how many individuals have lost health benefits.

One alternative that is gaining attention is "phased retirement," a means of keeping older employees on the payroll on a reduced basis. That way, employees can keep working in a less pressured environment and the employer can defer having to replace experienced workers. Furthermore, as Ellen E. Schultz points out [" 'Phased Retirement' Option for Workers in Mainly a Boon for Their Employers," *WSJ* 7/27/00 p. A6.] this can be a potent money-saving device—especially if it enables the employer to eliminate early-retirement subsidies on a prospective basis.

Assume, for instance, that the phased retiree takes a lump sum pension payout but continues to work part-time. That one-time payment will probably be less than what the company would have to pay if the employee continued to work full-time for longer, because pensions are typically based on compensation in the last years of the career. The example Schultz gives is a person who would have an annual pension of $36,286 if he or she retired at 65 after working for the same company for 40 years, earning $50,000 a year. If he or she takes out a $263,250 lump sum at age 55 and works for 10 more years, the pension will be based on only 10 years' service, not 40, so the pension will be only $9,071 a year.

Under current law, employees are not allowed to take pension payouts until they have reached normal retirement age or are disabled, so federal legislation has been introduced to create incentives for phased retirement by allowing pension payments to begin before the NRA.

In early 1999, the Sixth Circuit adopted the Third Circuit rule, previously expressed in *Fischer v. Philadelphia Electric Co.*, 96 F.3d 1533 (3rd Cir. 1996): A revised early retirement incentive has received "serious consideration," and therefore must be disclosed to potential early retirees, once senior managers discuss the proposal for purposes of implementation. Thus, *McAuley v. IBM Corp.*, 165 F.3d 1038 (6th Cir. 1999) permits retirees to sue for breach of fiduciary duty when their ex-employer adopts an early retirement plan more favorable than the plan they accepted.

EEOC Manual

The update to Section 3 of the Compliance Manual issued by the EEOC in late 2000 [Number 915.003 (10/3/00) benefits rule, http://www.eeoc.gov/docs/benefits.html] has a good deal to say about early retirement incentives. An early retirement incentive (ERI) program is lawful as long as it's voluntary. The EEOC will not get involved if the employer chooses to:

- Set a minimum age or minimum number of years of service for employees who participate
- Have a window (i.e., make the incentive available only for retirement between January 1 and April)
- Limit the ERI to a manager, a department, a particular facility, etc.

However, ERI benefits can't be reduced or denied for older employees versus similarly situated younger employees unless the employer qualifies for one of five defenses: equal cost; subsidizing a portion of the early retirement benefit; integrating the incentives with Social Security; the incentives go to a tenured faculty member; or the plan is consistent with the objectives of the ADEA.

An ERI is not voluntary if a reasonable person informed of its terms would conclude that there was no choice but to accept, Relevant factors in the analysis include, e.g., adequate time to decide; absence of coercion; lack of negative consequences for older employees who turn down the offer; and whether a particular employee had legal advice when deciding.

The revisions to the Manual say (at page 36): "On the other hand it is not coercion for an employer to notify its workforce that layoffs will be necessary if insufficient numbers of employees retire voluntarily, unless older workers are the only ones threatened. It is also not coercion that an employer's offer was "too good to refuse."

The equal cost defense is seldom available in connection with ERIs, because the cost of early retirement benefits generally does not increase with the employee's age.

The EEOC allows the employer to limit the ERI or pay higher ERI benefits to younger employees where the benefits are used to bring early retirees up to the level of the unreduced pension that they would receive under a defined benefit plan at Normal Retirement Age (NRA). But the subsidized pension can't be greater than the pension of a similarly situated older employee who has reached NRA.

It is also permissible to offer an ERI to bridge the gap to Social Security eligibility, for a person who has not yet reached Social Security early retirement age. The employer also has the option of bridging the gap until the normal Social Security retirement age. However, the supplement can't get greater than the Social Security benefit that the employee will eventually receive as an early or normal-age retiree.

The EEOC says that equal severance benefits are required for all similarly situated employees irrespective of their age. Employers may not deny severance because the employee is eligible for a pension, although sometimes pension benefits can be offset against the severance pay. Denying recall rights to older workers operates as involuntary retirement. The cost of providing severance does not rise with the employees' age, so employers are not allowed to assert an equal cost defense.

However, retiree health benefits can legitimately be offset against severance if the retiree is eligible for an immediate pension; the retiree actually receives health benefit coverage; and retiree benefits are at least comparable to Medicare in type and value. If the retiree is over 65, benefits must be at least comparable to one-fourth of the value of Medicare benefits. The offset itself must be reduced by any percentage by which the pension is reduced for retirement before Normal Retirement Age (NRA), and any percentage of the premium that the retiree has to pay for retiree health coverage.

The EEOC considers an ERI to ignore age as a criterion for treating employees—and therefore consistent with the purpose of the ADEA—as long as it gives all employees above a certain age:

- A flat dollar amount (e.g. $20,000)
- Additional service-based benefits (for instance, $1,000 for each year of service)
- A percentage of salary

- A flat dollar increase in pension benefits, such as an extra $200 a month
- A percentage increase (e.g., 10%) in pension benefits
- Extra years of service and/or age used in pension computations.

Case Law

In *Bins v. Exxon Co.*, 189 F.3d 929 (9th Cir. 8/30/99): the Ninth Circuit also adopts the *Fischer* "serious consideration" test, so in this Circuit, disclosure of proposals that are material to the retirement decision is required even if the employee doesn't ask.

On rehearing (220 F.3d 1042, 9th Cir. 2000), the Ninth Circuit mandate to the fiduciary to give complete and accurate information about plan changes under "serious consideration", in response to employee queries, was affirmed. But the Ninth Circuit did not impose a duty to volunteer information absent an inquiry, and did not require the employer to report changes to an employee who inquired in the past, unless the employer volunteered to supply updated information.

Another Ninth Circuit case from 1999, *Wayne v. Pacific Bell* (189 F.3d 982), rules that discussion of a particular early retirement proposal during collective bargaining is tantamount to serious consideration of the proposal, even if that particular proposal is never adopted.

Hudson v. General Dynamics Corp., 69 LW 1304 (D.Conn. 9/28/00) finds a breach of fiduciary duty with respect to two employees who inquired, but were not told that an early retirement program was under serious consideration—but dismisses the claims of 87 other employees who either failed to ask, or whose inquiries preceded the company's serious consideration of the superior program.

In the view of the Seventh Circuit, it does not violate ERISA to deny early retirement to employees who are deemed especially valuable, if the plan gives management discretion as to whether early retirement is in the company's best interests. A company's standards (as opposed to rules) are supposed to be applied flexibly and with discretion, and implementation of this standard was not so arbitrary or capricious as to violate ERISA [*McNab v. General Motors*, 162 F.3d 959 (7th Cir. 1998)].

Another General Motors case, this time in the Third Circuit, says that the LMRA and NLRA do not preempt early retiree's claims under state law that the employer fraudulently induced them to accept early retirement. [*Voilas v. General Motors*, 170 F.3d 367 (3rd Cir. 1999)].

An early 1998 case arose because a plant closed, then was re-opened by a new owner who required the former employees to re-apply for their old jobs, cut wages, reduced benefits, and changed the seniority schedule. According to the Tenth Circuit, there was no "permanent shutdown" of the plant, and therefore the original employer's "forced termination" provision did not come into play, and the plaintiffs were not entitled to early retirement benefits [*Dycus v. PBGC*, 133 F.3d 1367 (10th Cir. 1998)].

A "suspension" of benefits (for exceeding the plan's limitation on postretirement employment) is not considered a "reduction" in benefits subject to the ERISA anti-cutback rule. Therefore, tougher limitations on post-retirement employment, adopted six years after the plaintiff retired, permitted the employer to suspend retirement benefits without violating ERISA [*Spacek v. Maritime Association,* 134 F.3d 283 (5th Cir. 1998)].

It is a breach of fiduciary duty to inform potential early retirees that lump-sum payouts are available, without also disclosing the IRC §415 limitations on rollovers and pointing out that failure to make a rollover will result in immediate taxation. See *Farr v. U.S. West Communications, Inc.,* 58 F.3d 1361 (9th Cir. 1998). The fiduciaries' common-law duty of loyalty requires them to deal fairly and honestly with plan participants, so it is a violation to give them incomplete information.

Five years after her early retirement, a US West retiree found out that her lump-sum check was much smaller than it should have been because the plan calculated the death benefit incorrectly. She pursued the plan's administrative remedies to get the amount she (and other early retirees in similar situations) should have received. The claim was denied; she appealed it to the former employer's Employee Benefits Committee, which agreed that she was right and said that the company was applying to the IRS to fix the problem.

The retiree, S.A. McElwaine, kept trying to find out what was happening, but couldn't get any helpful information. She knew that the statute of limitations would expire, and her claim would become time-barred, in May of 1996. In March 1996, she sued US West in federal court. In the same month, US West proposed to the IRS that it would pay $20 million to about 3,000 early retirees whose lump sum benefits were incorrectly calculated.

In August 1996, the IRS approved the proposal, ordering payments to begin within 90 days. In November 1996, Ms. McElwaine received about $10,000. Her suit was dismissed because of the payment. In June 1997, Ms. McElwaine sued to recover attorneys' fees and costs under 29 USC §1132(g)(1), which allows courts to award attorneys' fees to plan beneficiaries who win ERISA suits. The District Court rejected this claim, saying that US West had already promised to pay additional benefits when the suit was filed. But the Ninth Circuit disagreed (*McElwaine v. US West,* 9th Cir. 5/10/99; see http://www.thompson.com/tpg/pen_ben/mend/mendsept1.html). The federal claim was filed before US West made an enforceable promise to make payments to the group of early retirees. The statute of limitations was close to expiration, so it made sense for Ms. McElwaine to preserve her claim by filing suit. Therefore, she was awarded attorneys' fees and costs for the period between March 1996 (when her suit was filed) and September 1996 (when US West disclosed its agreement with the IRS), plus fees and costs for appealing the District Court's denial of her fee claim.

A university offered early retirement incentives to both tenured professors and high-level administrators. According to the District of North Dakota, the payments to professors were made in exchange for surrender of contractual rights, and therefore were not FICA wages.

In contrast, similar payments to administrators were subject to FICA. The court drew the distinction because administrators are at-will employees, but tenured professors cannot be dismissed except for grave cause: *North Dakota State U. v. U.S.*, 85 AFTR2d ¶2000-332 (D.N.D. 11/19/99).

A downsizing employer discovered that it couldn't provide early retirement incentives to all the upper-management employees it wanted to target without making the pension plan discriminatory. So the employer set up a separate system of enhanced lump-sum separation benefits that were not part of the qualified pension plan.

The plaintiffs in *Piner v. DuPont*, 2000 U.S. App. LEXIS 29016 (4th Cir. 2000) weren't unhappy participants in the plan—they were ineligible employees who sued for fiduciary breach and statutory penalties for failure to provide disclosure documents, on the grounds that all employees should have been eligible for the program. But the District Court, affirmed by the Fourth Circuit, granted summary judgment for the employer on the ERISA claims: "ERISA simply does not prohibit an employer from offering some employees and not others access to separate, additional plans with enhanced benefits," and there is no obligation to provide documents to employees who are not eligible for the plans covered by such documents.

ERISA §204(g) was at issue in *Bellas v. CBS*, 221 F.3d 517 (3rd Cir. 2000) (the Supreme Court denied certiorari in January 2001).The plaintiff worked for CBS between 1964 and 1997, when he was terminated for lack of work. Prior to 1994, the predecessor employer's pension plan offered permanent job separation benefits to employees terminated for lack of work. A 1994 amendment narrowed the definition of "permanent job separation," and the benefit was eliminated entirely for terminations occurring after September 1, 1998. The plaintiff would have qualified for benefits under the pre-1994 rule. He sued the employer, charging that the change in benefit definition and eventual elimination of the benefit violated ERISA §204(g) (the "anti-cutback" rule).

The Third Circuit agreed with him, reading the legislative history of the Retirement Equity Act to mean that benefits greater than the actuarially reduced normal retirement benefit, triggered by an unpredictable contingent event (e.g., being laid off) is a retirement-type subsidy which accrues when the benefit program is created. The Fifth and Ninth Circuits also take this position, but the Sixth and Eleventh Circuits accept the employer's argument that job separation benefits do not accrue until the layoff actually occurs.

The practical significance of the *Bellas* decision [As explained by Joseph S. Adams, "Court Rules Supplemental Benefits Must Stay in Plan," http://www.benefitslink.com/articles/mend001012.shtml.] is that, in Circuits that follow this theory, employers can only decrease early retirement benefits and subsidies prospectively. That is, once a person satisfies plan requirements, the plan cannot be amended to reduce or eliminate the early retirement benefit that has already accrued.

Therefore, employers may have to budget a much larger amount than they anticipated when they amended the plan.

11.2 EARLY RETIREMENT INCENTIVES: ADEA ISSUES

The Urban Institute, a nonpartisan research facility, has published three papers in its "Retirement Project" series. Number 3, "Incentives for Early Retirement in Private and Health Insurance Plans," by Daniel Dulitzky, can be downloaded from http://www.urban.org/retirement/briefs/3/brief_3.html.

Dr. Dulitzky notes that growth of the U.S. population is slowing down as lifespans increase. Therefore, in the future, the ratio between senior citizens and people of conventional working age will be much higher. In 1950, there were about seven times as many people aged 20-64 as over 65; by 2030, there will only be about three times as many people in the younger than in the senior-citizen age group. Therefore, it will be hard for employers to recruit the new workers they need, and to earn enough to support large pension commitments. It will be necessary to keep older workers in the workforce for longer, or to get them to reverse retirement decisions.

The Social Security retirement age (the age at which an unreduced benefit is payable) is gradually being increased from 65 to 67, and the Social Security system includes incentives for workers to delay their retirement (because they will get a larger Social Security benefit if they do). However, many private pension plans do the opposite: they provide incentives for early retirement, because the employer wants to cut its workforce or because the employer fears the high cost of providing EGHP coverage for older employees.

A 1996 study cited by Dulitzky shows that employee health care coverage costs twice as much for a male worker aged 45-54 as for his 25- to 34-year-old counterpart. For the 25-34 age group, health care costs represent 6% of average earnings, and 8.4% of average earnings for the 45-64 group.

NOTE: One of the typical features of a conversion from a conventional defined-benefit plan to a hybrid cash-balance plan (¶12.4.6) is the elimination of subsidies for early retirement.

See ¶26.3 for the EEOC's Final Regulation on how to draft a waiver that is valid under the Older Workers Benefit Protection Act.

Although the Older Workers Benefit Protection Act mandates a 21-day period during which employees can consider whether or not to accept an early retirement offer, the offer need not remain irrevocable during that period. The employer retains the option of canceling the offer [*Ellison v. Premier Salons Int'l Inc.*, 164 F.3d 1111 (8th Cir. 1999)].

The key question is OWBPA compliance, which in turn depends on the way the waiver is drafted and the circumstances surrounding its signing. The Seventh Circuit gave effect to a clear, unambiguous waiver signed by a lawyer (!) employed by a corporation. Presumably, he was able to understand the document. Even though he believed he was given the choice of resigning and being terminated because of his age, he was still bound by the waiver he signed: *Lloyd v. Brunswick Corp.*, 180 F.3d 893 (7th Cir. 1999).

However, given the possibility of fraud that the company used to induce employees to sign waivers, the Tenth Circuit refused to give effect to those waivers: *Bennett v. Coors Brewing Co.*, 189 F.3d 1221 (10th Cir. 1999).

Also see Simon J. Nadel, "Exchanging Enhanced Severance Packages for Waiver of Legal Rights Raises Questions," 68 LW 2243 (11/2/99).

11.3 RETIREE HEALTH BENEFITS

A William M. Mercer survey of companies with 500 or more employees reveals that in 1994, 40% provided retiree health coverage, a percentage that had declined to under 25% by 2000. [Milt Freudenheim, "Cuts in Health Benefits Squeeze Retirees' Nest Eggs," *NYT* 12/31/00 p.Bus8. Also see Ellen E. Schultz and Robert McGough, "Health Advisory: Investors Should Do a Checkup on Firms that Use Medical Plans to Lift Profits," *WSJ* 10/25/00 p. C1, reporting on a practice of using investment profits from retiree health benefit trusts and reductions in health care cost inflation to improve stockholder opinions of the companies' overall financial prospects—an especially timely warning now that health care cost inflation is heating up and stock market returns are down.]

In 1994, 43% of respondents provided health coverage for retirees who were too young to qualify for Medicare, a percentage dropping to 31% in 2000. For very large companies (5000 or more employees), it was more likely that retiree health coverage would be offered, but even there, the trend was to cut costs by raising deductibles, eliminating prescription drug coverage, capping benefits, or maintaining the plan for current retirees but excluding new hires from retiree health plan participation.

See GAO/HEHS-98-133, "Private Health Insurance: Declining Employer Coverage May Affect Access for 55- to 64-Year Olds," (6/1/98), describing the effect of declining employer participation in retiree health coverage on the access of the "near elderly" to health insurance.

This report notes that, according to the consulting firm Foster Higgins, the average cost to the corporation of providing retiree health coverage was $5210 for 1996 (a figure that hadn't changed much since 1993). Peat Marwick figures show a fall in the cost of early retirement coverage, from $5748 in 1993 to $5460 in 1995. Other Foster Higgins data shows that, in 1997, 12% of survey respondents said that, during the two years prior to the study, they had raised the plan contribution required of retirees; 6% had increased retirees' deductibles and copayments; 4% restricted eligibility; and 8% moved retirees from an indemnity to a managed care plan.

Peat Marwick looked at the amount that retirees had to pay toward the cost of their own family benefits. In 1995, the percentage contributed by retirees ranged from 41 to 53% (analyzed by size of firm—200 workers or over 5000 workers; the smaller the firm, the larger the retirees' responsibility), an average of $2040 to $3048 a year. The overall nationwide average was 45%, or $2340 a year. The number of retirees who declined to enroll in COBRA plans went up between 1994 and 1997, often because of the expense.

To the extent that employers provided retiree benefits at all, they were likely to subject the obligation to some sort of "cap" (i.e., a yearly or lifetime maximum); they also tended to make eligibility requirements stricter. The decline in employment-related retiree health coverage opens up some opportunities for sale of acute health insurance to the near elderly. Such clients then become a good market for Medigap insurance once they reach the age of Medicare eligibility.

According to the Third Circuit, it is a violation of the ADEA for the employer to provide health benefits to its Medicare-eligible employees via an HMO, while providing greater benefits through a separate POS plan for employees who are not eligible for Medicare (because they are under 65). The HMO plan cost less than the POS plan, so the Third Circuit did not accept the equal-cost defense asserted by the employer, although it did remand the case back to the District Court to allow the employer to introduce evidence on the cost issue. [*Erie County Retirees Ass'n v. Erie County, Pa.*, 200 F.3d 193 (3rd Cir. 2000).] The District Court had ruled for the employer, saying that the ADEA does not apply to benefits for retirees. The Third Circuit found the legislative history ambiguous on this point, but said that it was age discrimination to impose HMO participation only on over-65 retirees.

According to the Northern District of Illinois, given that retirement is a COBRA event, a plan has an independent duty to issue a COBRA notice at retirement, even if retirees are given access under the plan to health coverage for an indefinite period of time, not limited by the COBRA period: *Mansfield v. Chicago Park District Group Plan,* 997 F.Supp. 1053 (N.D. Ill. 1998).

In a unionized environment, when the Collective Bargaining Agreement determines retiree benefit rights "for the term of the agreement," it is not an ERISA violation to terminate retiree health and life insurance benefits after a contract ends. In other words, it's a new ball game each time the CBA is re-negotiated. See *Pabst Brewing Co. v. Corrao,* 161 F.3d 434 (7th Cir. 1998).

ERISA fiduciary duty was not breached by transferring the obligation to provide some retiree health benefits to a new company formed when a corporate division was spun off: *Sengpiel v. B.F. Goodrich Co.,* 156 F.3d 660 (6th Cir. 1998). To the Sixth Circuit, the new entity's reduction of retiree health and life insurance benefits was lawful, because the power to alter benefits was retained in the plan documents. The reduction should be analyzed as a plan amendment, modification, or termination—that is, a business decision—rather than a fiduciary decision involving discretionary issues in plan administration.

Chapter 12

SUBSTANTIVE LAW OF PENSIONS

12.1 INTRODUCTION

The plan limits for the 2001 tax year (published in IR-2000-82, Notice 2000-66, 2000-52 IRB 600) are:

- §415(b)(1)(A) defined benefit plan annual benefit: $140,000 (formerly $135,000)
- §415(c)(1)(A) maximum contribution to a defined contribution plan: $35,000, after several years at $30,000
- §414(q)(1)(B) definition of a highly compensated employee (HCE): $85,000 a year
- §401(a)(17), 404(l) limit on annual compensation used in calculations: $170,000
- For 2001, the Social Security wage base (the amount that is subject to FICA tax) is $80,400
- Maximum 401(k) deferral remains $10,500

For a look at the fixed annuity, a major funding mechanism for pensions, see Jeremy Alexander's "Fixed Annuities Play Major Role in Pensions," *National Underwriter*, 9/28/98, p. 21. A fixed annuity is an investment contract that guarantees a particular rate of return. Alexander reports that, of 295 fixed annuities studied by Beacon Research, about half could be used to invest corporate pension contributions, and nearly all (94.1%) accepted IRA rollovers.

Plan sponsors favor fixed-annuity investments because they are safe and predictable. Furthermore, defined benefit plans take the risk that they will have to contribute more to satisfy the funding obligation as interest rates rise; fixed annuities eliminate this risk. It should also be noted that, if a defined benefit plan is fully invested in guaranteed-rate contracts, Pension Benefit Guaranty Corporation (PBGC) insurance will not be required because of the shift of risk to the insurance company.

The insurance companies that sell fixed annuities can perform many administrative chores, and they make it easy to annuitize the pension obligation when the employee retires. (The insurer may even perform the annuitization at no charge to the plan.) To the extent that the plan still wishes to make minimum distributions to participants who have reached 70 1/2 (or is obligated to do so, in the case of employee-stockholders), "withdrawal without liquidation" (permitted by about one-third of the fixed annuities studied) can meet this need by receiving set payments under the fixed annuity, usually deriving from interest, at stated periods.

The Beacon Research study also shows that 60.5% of fixed annuity plans require funding with a single premium, 33.1% set the premium flexibly, and 6.4% use a basis of a single premium but allow enhancements.

EBRI's ninth annual Retirement Confidence Survey, released in December 1999, concludes that the great majority of Americans (70%) have retirement savings—even more than the 1998 figure of 68%. About half (46%) of workers expect that their own contributions to the employer plan will be a major source of retirement security; 40% predict that employer contributions will yield a major retirement income stream. [SOURCE: "EBRI Retirement Survey: More Americans Are Saving and Planning for Retirement But Gaps Remain," http://news.excite.com/news/pr/991210/dc-ebri-retirement.]

The Pension Research Council of the Wharton School has released a detailed report, "New Trends in Pension Benefit and Retirement Provisions," PRC WP 2000-1 (January 2000), covering trends since 1980. Free downloads are available from http://prc.wharton.upenn.edu/prc/prc.html. (There's no www in this URL.) The report, prepared by Olivia S. Mitchell and Erica L. Dykes, concludes that:

- Benefit and vesting formulas can influence workers' decisions to retain their jobs or leave.
- Investment decisions by employees (e.g., in defined contribution plans) are strongly influenced by employer communications.
- In 1985, 89% of employees in medium-sized or large firms were covered by defined benefit plans; but in 1997, only half of such workers were covered by a defined benefit plan.
- Between 1980 and 1997, defined benefit plans became much more likely to impose minimum age and/or service requirements for participation (68% vs. 59%).
- Nearly all defined benefit plans use cliff vesting (96% in 1997, 89% in 1980), usually at five years. The percentage of plans offering early retirement has remained constant at about 95% since 1980.
- Flat-dollar benefits (often associated with collective bargaining agreements) are less important than ever before: 30% of participants in 1980, 23% in 1997,

were entitled to defined benefits of this type. Throughout this period, about two-thirds of benefits were calculated based on employee earnings, usually earnings at the end of the career, and usually involving only base pay, not bonuses, commissions, or shift differentials. The fraction of earnings included in the calculation usually varied by year of service, rather than remaining constant for all calculation years.

- About three-quarters of defined benefit plan participants had disability coverage in 1997; coverage peaked at 90% in 1989, then dropped.
- In 1991, only 14% of defined-benefit plan participants had a lump-sum option, but by 1997, 23% of participants had this choice.
- Defined contribution plans gained significantly in popularity during the 1980–1997 time frame; many companies have both defined benefit and defined contribution plans.
- Profit-sharing plans have become less popular, and stock and stock bonus plans are not commonly offered, but 401(k) plans have gained in popularity: 45% of employees had CODAs in 1995 versus only 26% in 1985.
- Employees typically are given more investment discretion over their own plan contributions than over employer contributions to defined contribution plans.

To be able to retire in comfort, a person covered by a 401(k) plan (but no other plan) will have to deposit the equivalent of about seven years' pay into the account; at least four years' pay in the account will be required if it supplements other employer plans. That's the conclusion of "Benefit Adequacy in the Age of 401(k)," http://www.watsonwyatt.com/homepage/us/new/Insider/april99/4_99.htm. This article contains an "adequacy matrix," comparing the required savings level for employees based on age and years of service.

The Urban Institute (Washington, D.C.) has published a Final Report, #06750-003, "What Happens When You Show Them the Money? Lump-Sum Distributions, Retirement Income Security, and Public Policy," (November 1999). It was compiled by Leonard E. Burman and Norma B. Coe of the Department of the Treasury and William G. Gale of the Brookings Institution.

The report concludes that employees who receive lump sum distributions from their pension plans usually don't take advantage of the option to roll over the lump sum to an IRA or another qualified plan. Instead, they tend to spend the money (although large sums are more likely to be rolled over than small ones), which can have policy implications if the workers sacrifice their long-term financial stability for short-term advantage.

Hewitt Associates found similar results in its September 1999 survey. Hewitt found that 57% of job-switchers opt to take their 401(k) balances in cash; 37% rolled over the funds to an IRA, and only 6% rolled over the balance to the new employer's qualified plan. Small balances were much more likely to be taken in cash than large ones. More than three-quarters of balances under $5,000 were taken in cash; so were about a third of balances between $25,000 and $50,000, and even 17% of balances between $50,000 and $100,000. ["Hewitt Study Shows More than Half of 401(k) Plan Participants Opt for Cash When Changing Jobs," http://www.businesswire.com/webbox/bw.091399/192561563.htm.]

In the view of the Third Circuit, it is not a breach of fiduciary duty for an employer to buy GICs for individual accounts from a company that later was seized by regulators. *In re Unisys Savings Plan Litigation*, 74 F.3d 420 (3rd Cir. 1999), *cert. denied* 519 U.S. 810 holds that the employer did not fail in its duty of prudence. Investment responsibility was delegated to appropriate parties, who made an adequate investigation prior to purchase. The bad result was unfortunate, but not a fiduciary breach.

12.3 FACTORS IN QUALIFICATION

IRS Notice 99-44, 1999-35 IRB 326, explains the implications of the repeal of the §415(e) combined limit for limitation years beginning on or after 1/1/00. Under prior law, there was a ceiling on total contributions made on behalf of a person covered by both a defined benefit and a defined contribution plan. There are some fairly complex rules for the consequences of various types of plan amendments, effect of the repeal on the plan's nondiscrimination testing, and for increasing benefits of persons who were already retired when the combined limit was eliminated, so this is an important area to discuss with your counsel.

For Final and Temporary IRS Regulations, allowing the Commissioner to grant relief for a plan that would otherwise be disqualified, if it adopts retroactive remedial amendments to eliminate the invalid provision, see 65 FR 5432 (2/4/00).

12.4 PENSION PLAN STRUCTURES

A state cannot use its Disposition of Unclaimed Property Act to seize unclaimed benefits from a defined benefit plan. *Commonwealth Edison v. Vega*, 174 F.3d 870 (7th Cir. 1999) says that ERISA preempts the state law, because states do not have the power to take over pension plan operations by recouping unclaimed benefits.

A "floor-offset" plan is a hybrid plan, where the defined benefit portion of the plan guarantees a floor level of benefits, offset by the annuity the retiree could purchase at retirement with the balance in the defined contribution portion of the plan. *Lunn v. Montgomery Ward & Co. Retirement Security Plan*, 166 F.3d 880 (7th Cir. 1999), holds that an employee who retired four years after normal retirement age was not entitled to additional retirement benefits to make up for the reduced duration of benefits. The court upheld the general floor-offset structure, finding that it does not violate ERISA's antiforfeiture provisions or benefit accrual requirements.

Rev.Rul. 2000-8, 2000-7 IRB 617 and IRS Announcement 2000-60, 2000-31 IRB 149 reflect the IRS' desire to increase the number of plans that include automatic enrollment features, because such features tend to increase plan participation.

Rev.Procs. 2000-40 and -41, 2000-42 IRB 357 and 371, provide the procedure under which the sponsor or administrator of any defined benefit plan subject to Code §412 or ERISA §302 can get the Secretary of the Treasury to approve a change in the plan's funding method under Code §412(c)(5)(A):

- Shift from the entry age normal method to the unit credit method of complying with the minimum funding method
- Using the aggregate method, but with the normal cost level as a dollar amount instead of a level percentage of compensation
- Changing the method of valuing assets
- Changing the valuation date from the plan year's first day to its last day
- Changing the plan year (which of course also changes the valuation date)
- Changing the software used to carry out the valuation, if this has the result of changing the specific computations
- Changing the method of determining the cost of ancillary benefits.

The IRS will approve a change in funding method only if both the proposed new method and the form of transition are acceptable. The IRS has jurisdiction to review the appropriateness of a change that has a significant effect on the plan's minimum funding requirement or full funding limitation.

The request, which should be directed to the IRS Commissioner. TE/GE Attention: T:EP:RA PO Box 27063 McPherson Station Washington, DC 20038, is due at the close of the plan year in which the change will be effective. The IRS can extend the due date by up to 2 1/2 months, on a discretionary basis, if the plan submits a statement giving adequate reason for the delay.

In 2000, the *Wall Street Journal* reported on strategies used by large companies (e.g., IBM, KMart, Dow Chemical) to reduce their pension obligations, reducing future benefit accruals without unlawfully reducing benefits already accrued. For instance, if a plan is frozen, additional service does not increase the benefit, and can have the effect of making an underfunded plan compliant or even overfunded.

Companies interested in reducing pension costs can cap the years of service that will be counted toward a pension, and can base the benefit on high-five, last-five, last-10, or career-average compensation instead of high-three, which tends to result in a larger pension obligation. In essence, a cash balance plan has the same effect as a career average computation in reducing the employer's obligation. They can reduce the "multiplier," i.e., define the pension as 1% rather than 1.5% of the chosen compensation figure per year of service. [Ellen E. Schultz, "Pension Cuts 101: Companies Find Host of Subtle Ways to Pare Retirement Payouts," *WSJ* 7/27/00 p. A1.]

Defined Contribution Plans

Between 1980 and 1996, the number of participants in defined contribution plans went up 155%, rising from 20 million to 51 million, whereas the number of participants in defined benefit plans (once considered the conventional choice for retirement planning) was nearly unchanged, going up only 8% (38 million to 41 million). A study by the Investment Company Research Institute ["Defined Contribution Plan Distribution Choices at Retirement," http://www.ici.org/pdf/rpt_annuitization.pdf] shows that employees who were richer at the time of retirement usually deferred receiving their distributions or rolled them over to an IRA, whereas those with lower current income tended to annuitize or take installment payments.

Seventy percent of defined contribution plan participants had access to multiple distribution alternatives—of that group, 90% could take a lump sum, 72% could take an annuity, 70% could take installment payments, and 68% had the option of delaying distributions until the required beginning date even if they retired earlier. Of those who had choices, 47% took the lump sum, 26% deferred the first payment, 23% took an annuity, and only 10% opted for installment payments.

Most participants who took a lump sum had professional advice, and acted prudently by re-investing in a diversified IRA portfolio. The larger the lump sum, the more likely it was to be invested; only 8% spent the entire lump sum, and 26% spent some of it (an average of 25% of the total account balance). Those who spent the entire defined contribution lump sum payout tended to have small distributions from that plan, ongoing income from Social Security and other plans, and also frequently used the sums sensibly, e.g., for health care and reducing their debts.

On October 6, 2000, Proposed Regulations were published at 65 FR 59774-59780 covering the non-discrimination requirements for "new comparability plans." These are defined contribution plans that are allowed to perform cross-testing and demonstrate non-discrimination under Reg. §1.401(a)(4)-(8) by reference to their benefits rather than the employer's contributions. Employers adopt new comparability plans because they permit a much higher allocation rate for highly compensated employees than for other employees. Also see Notice 2000-14, 2000-10 IRB 737 (2/24/00) for the IRS' opinions on issues raised by such plans.

12.4.3 401(k) Plans

The 401(k) plan, also known as a CODA (for "Cash or Deferred Arrangement"), is a form of deferred compensation under which employees are given the choice either to receive up to $10,500 (for 2001) of their compensation in cash immediately or have the compensation placed into an account where it will accumulate until retirement. The incentives for employees to do this are freedom from taxation on the appreciation in the value of the account until retirement, and the practice of many employers to match part of the employee contribution (although tax law does not require employers to do this). Typically, the plan will place the responsibility for allocating the employee contribution portion of the fund on the employee, who is given a choice of several investment alternatives, such as stock and bond funds. The employer will determine the investment of its own matching contribution.

Under Revenue Procedure 2000-27, 2000-21 IRB 1016, it is permissible to distribute a person's 401(k) asset balance on the basis of separation from service whenever substantially all the assets of a trade or business are sold to an unrelated employer—even if most of the employees continue to work for the successor orporation.

An IRS Private Letter Ruling from 2000 allows the employer to offer a disability income feature inside a 401(k) plan, in that buying a long-term disability policy doesn't violate the Internal Revenue Code or destroy the qualification of the plan. Under this PLR, the employee who elects to have part of his or her salary deferrals used to buy LTD insurance is not taxed currently, and amounts paid under the policy are not taxed to the employee if they are paid to the plan—only if they go directly to the employee. This extends the existing possibility of buying life insurance in a 401(k) plan. [April K. Caudill, "IRS Private Ruling Allows DI Policy in 401(k) Plan," *National Underwriter* 10/16/00 p. 33.]

401(k) Utilization

Since its origin in a minor section of the Tax Reform Act of 1978, the 401(k) plan has grown from about 7 million participants in 1985 to about 34 million participants in 340,000 plans (the estimated figure for 1999).

Whether or not employees will accept 401(k) participation has a lot to do with their planning horizons: those who think only two years ahead are much less likely to join the plan. As a recruitment and retention incentive, more and more companies are speeding up the time at which employees will be eligible—52% of surveyed plans now allow eligibility within three months of hiring (up from 32% in 1998), and 37% (was 24%) allow deferral from the paycheck even in the first month of employment.

For the 1999 plan year, the Profit Sharing/401(k) Council of America (PSCA) surveyed about 800 plans—423 of them 401(k) plans, 89 profit-sharing only, the other 294 hybrids. The survey [For ordering information, see http://www.psca.org/43rd.html; the survey is $75 for PSCA members, $195 for non-members.] showed 82.5% of employees in the companies surveyed had 401(k) balances, averaging deferrals of 5.4% of pay for lower-paid and 6.4% for higher-paid employees. The average employer contribution to 401(k)s was 4.7%.

Over half (51.2%) of survey respondents offered 10 or more fund options for investing the deferred amounts, with an average of 12. Close to half (46.8%) of the surveyed plans were self-trusteed, versus 28.1% with bank trustees. About a third of plan assets were invested in mutual funds (36.7%), 18.3% of assets managed by banks, 16.8% by insurance companies, 11.0% by investment advisors, and 9.7% by brokerage firms.

According to a study performed by EBRI and the Investment Company Institute, in 1999, the average account balance for all 401(k) active participants grew by 18% (remember, this was at the height of the bull market). The average balance was $55,502 but that masks very wide variations based on factors such as length of plan participation, compensation and deferral levels, and investment performance. So 42% of participants had small balances—up to $10,000—whereas only 15% had balances over $100,000. [Danny Hakim, "Controlling 401(k) Assets," *NYT* 11/17/00 p. C1; Alicia H. Munnell, Annika Sunden and Catherine Taylor, "What Determines 401(k) Participation and Contributions?" WP #2000-12 from The Center for Retirement Research, http://www.bc.edu/bc_org/avp/csom/executive/crr/wp_2000-12.shtml; "Workers Have Less of a Wait to Save for Retirement," http://www.psca.org/pr40.html (12/6/00); "Latest EBRI/ICI Analysis: Average 401(K) Balance Grew 18% in 1999," (PR Newswire) http://www.benefitslink.com/articles/feeds/982183337.shtml.]

However, other research indicates that in many large companies, 401(k) participation is low—and vesting is very low. Ironically, the IRS antidiscrimination rules give employers an incentive to exclude younger, low-paid workers from plan participation, because if they were allowed to participate but didn't do so, the plan might flunk the antidiscrimination tests. In companies that have a mobile workforce, forfeitures are common, i.e., employees leave before vesting. If the company then reallocates the forfeited amounts among the remaining employees, it's likely that the best-paid employees, who are also the most likely to stay, will get the benefit. See Ellen E. Schultz, "Many Workers are Missing Out on 401(k) Plans," *Wall Street Journal,* 12/16/99, p. C1.

Trends and Predictions

In March 1998, David L. Wray of the Profit Sharing 401(k) Council of America and securities analyst Kathleen Hartman identified more than a dozen directions that they predict the 401(k) market will take,[3] such as

- Continuing increase in 401(k) participation rates
- Higher percentages of salary being saved
- Even greater investment of 401(k) balances in equities
- Higher balances for participants
- Near-universal permission for employees to direct the investment of their own contributions; majority permission of employees to allocate employer matches
- More use of Internet/intranet in 401(k) management and communications
- Lower fees thanks to market pressures
- Legislative changes (such as increasing the percentage that can be contributed to a defined-contribution plan) that will benefit lower-income employees

Nondiscrimination Tests

401(k) plans must not discriminate in favor of highly compensated employees. There are various technical requirements for satisfying the nondiscrimination test, but safe harbors are also permitted to simplify plan administration. If safe harbor matching or nonelective contributions are made on behalf of all eligible rank-and-file employees, and if employees are given adequate notice of their rights, then the plan will probably be held to satisfy the Actual Deferral Percentage (ADP) test and Actual Contribution Percentage (ACP) test and thus to be nondiscriminatory.

See IRS Notice 98-52, 1998-46 IRB 16, for safe harbor rules for plan years beginning after 12/31/98 (including companies that offer more than one 401(k) plan). Notices to employees do not have to be issued before 3/1/99. If the employer just makes the basic, safe harbor matching contributions, the plan will automatically qualify as nondiscriminatory. If it makes additional matching contributions, however, the contributions must be limited as described in the Notice to prevent discrimination in favor of highly compensated employees.

Under the safe harbor, the employer has to match $1 for every $1 deferred by the employee, up to 3% of the employee's compensation. If the employee chooses to defer 4 or 5% of compensation, the employer can match 50 cents for each $1 deferred at this level but cannot offer any further match after matching $3 for the first 3% and $1 for 4 to 5%—the maximum employer match is thus 4% of compensation. Nonelective nonmatching contributions by the employer must contribute 3% for all participants, whether or not the participants are highly compensated.[4]

Notice 98-52 permits the company to defer amending the plan to comply with the safe harbor requirement until it makes other plan amendments to phase in changes based on the Small Business Job Protection Act of 1996.

IRS Notice 2000-3,2000-4 IRB 413, gives guidance on the safe harbor nondiscrimination rules for 401(k) plans enacted by the Small Business Job Protection Act of 1996, covering plan years beginning after 12/31/98. Earlier IRS guidance, Notice 98-52, 1998-46 IRB 16, establishes a safe harbor for plans that achieve the required level of matching or nonelective contributions for all rank-and-file employees who are eligible for the plan, and that give employees a timely explanation of their 401(k) rights.

Notice 2000-3 builds on this by giving employers until 5/1/00 to furnish the notice, if they qualify for the safe harbor for the first time in the year 2000. Notice can be sent electronically. Employers get until December 1 of each plan year to decide whether to contribute 3% to the 401(k) plan. Employer matches can be calculated based on compensation for a payroll period, month, or quarter, not just a whole year. If the plan qualifies for the safe harbor for the first time in 2000, it is permissible to defer giving the safe harbor notice to employees until May 1, 2000. In the Notice, the IRS also asked for comments about keeping plans nondiscriminatory in the wake of a merger or acquisition; the IRS plans to publish guidance on this issue later in 2000.

Rev.Rul. 2000-8, 2000-7 IRB 617, settles the "opt in" vs. "opt out" question. That is, a 401(k) plan can permissibly be drafted to take an automatic, fixed percentage from the employee's compensation, and put it into the 401(k) plan, if the employee has **not** opted out of the plan.

Also note that, because of IRS Notice 99-5, 1999-3 IRB 10, hardship withdrawals from 401(k) plans cannot be rolled over unless the employee is at least $59^1/_2$ or has separated from service. Therefore, an in-service hardship distribution is not subject to 20% withholding like other one-time distributions from qualified plans. The employee has the right to waive withholding; if he or she does not, withholding should be done at a 10% rate. This rule took effect 1/1/00, no matter what the plan year is.

401(k) Plan Fees and Management

The Department of Labor's Pension and Welfare Benefit Administration (PWBA) has released guidance about 401(k) plan fee structures, which can be found at http://www.dol.gov/dol/pwba/public/pubs/401kfe~1.htm. The purpose of this document is to improve investment decision making by 401(k) plan participants, so you may wish to print it out and distribute it to employees (or make it available on your HR Internet or intranet site). The checklist for 401(k) fees on page 5 of this six-page document is especially handy.

The PWBA report groups fees into three categories: plan administration fees; investment fees (the major component); and individual service fees for optional features, such as plan loans or investment advice. The fees may be payable to the employer, if it furnishes services directly, or to outside service providers. In a bundled arrangement, all fees are funneled through one provider that coordinates the services. In an unbundled arrangement, the fees of the trustee, communications firm, investment manager, or other provider will be charged separately.

12.4.6 Cash Balance Plans

A cash balance plan is a hybrid plan that has many features like a conventional defined benefit plan, but also some features more like a profit sharing or 401(k) plan. For legal purposes, a cash balance plan is obligated to follow the requirements for defined benefit plans.

The plan is set up so that the corporation's books reflect an individual account for each participant. The employer funds the plan each year, based on a percentage of pay. (The §415 limit applies.) The final pension that the employee receives reflects two elements: an annual benefit credit (a stipulated percentage of pay), plus annual interest credited at the rate specified by the plan. The individual-account feature makes the cash balance plan more portable than the conventional defined benefit plan.

When the employee retires, the retirement annuity is based on the vested account balance. The practical effect is that, although accrual increases in the later years of employment in most defined benefit plans, accrual is greater in the early years of a cash balance plan. Defined benefit plans often subsidize early retirement, but cash balance plans seldom do.

The IRS' definition of a cash balance plan (see 64 FR 56579): "A cash balance plan is a defined benefit pension plan that typically defines an employee's retirement benefit by reference to the amount of a hypothetical account balance. In a typical cash balance plan, this account is credited with hypothetical allocations and interest that are determined under a formula set forth in the plan. The crediting of hypothetical allocations and hypothetical interest has been described as resembling the allocation of actual contributions and actual earnings to an employee's account under a defined contribution plan, such as a profit-sharing plan.

In recent years, existing defined benefit plans covering a significant number of employees have been changed into cash balance plans. This change, made by amending the existing plan, is commonly referred to as a conversion. In a conversion, the new cash balance benefit formula generally applies to new employees and may also apply to employees who had already earned benefits under the plan before the conversion. The law protects benefits earned before the conversion by prohibiting a plan amendment that reduces those benefits. See Kenneth R. Elliott and James H. Moore, Jr., "Cash Balance Pension Plans: The New Wave," BLS Compensation and Working Conditions Online (Summer 2000), http://www.bls.gov/opub/cwc/2000/Summer/art1abs.htm.

In some conversions, however, employees who already earned benefits may not earn additional retirement benefits for varying periods of time after the conversion. This effect, often referred to as a 'wearaway' or 'benefit plateau,' continues until an employee's benefit under the ongoing cash balance formula 'catches up' with the employee's protected benefit."

What is wearaway? A report from the ERISA Advisory Council report defines it this way: "As a transition device—called 'wearaway'—plans often promise employees they will receive the greater of their frozen benefit under the previous formula or their total benefit under the cash balance formula. (1) For employees at or near early retirement age, the value of the 'old-plan' benefit may be so much larger than the accruals under the cash balance formula that they effectively accrue little or nothing for a prolonged period, until the old-plan benefit is worn away."

A History of Controversy

From the historical viewpoint, cash balance plans trace their authorization to a sentence in the preamble of IRS Proposed Regulations published on September 11, 1991, creating a safe harbor. The Prop. Regs. say that changing a defined benefit plan's accrual pattern "will not cause a cash balance plan to fail to satisfy the requirement of section 411(b)(1)(H)." [Ellen E. Schultz, "Inquiry Sought Into History of Pension Rule," *WSJ*, 1/14/00, p. A4, and "How a Single Sentence from IRS Paved Way to Cash Balance Plans," *WSJ*, 12/28/99, p. A1, also available at http://public.wsj.com/careers/resources/documents/20000114-schultz.htm (no www).]

This portion of the Reg. has never been finalized, but the IRS has permitted numerous conversions, including some involving major corporations such as IBM, CitiGroup Inc., AT&T, Bell Atlantic, CIGNA Corp., Aetna, Eastman Kodak, and CBS. These plans might have operated in obscurity, if it were not for Ellen E. Schultz of the *Wall Street Journal*, whose coverage of cash balance plan conversions has brought this issue to public attention.

It should be noted that in September 1999, in response to bad publicity, IBM backpedaled and doubled the number of employees allowed to remain in the old plan and thus not subject to conversion. See Ellen E. Schultz, Jon G. Auerbach, and Glenn Burkins, "Boomer Backlash," *Wall Street Journal*, 9/20/99, p. A1; Richard J. Oppell Jr., "I.B.M. Does An About-Face on Pensions," *N.Y.T.*, 9/20/99, p. B1.]

Although it usually permits conversions, the IRS has agreed that Onan Corporation's cash balance plan, whose tax-exempt status is under challenge in the Tax Court, and which is being sued for age discrimination in the District of Indiana, should be disqualified.

Cash Balance Plans: Pros and Cons

The employer's motivation for adopting its first plan in cash balance form, or for converting a defined benefit to a cash balance plan, is the ability to retain the difference between the plan's actual investment return and the rate of return promised to employees. The plan can become self-funded if the gap is wide enough to relieve the employer of the need to make further contributions. See Graham A. Mitenko, Michael J. O'Hara, and Gerald V. Boyles, "Cash Balance Pension Plans" (presented to American Academy of Financial and Economic Experts, March 1999, and available at http://cba.unomaha.edu/faculty/mohara/web/CPBB-INET.html; no www).

In testimony before the Senate Committee on Health, Education, Labor & Pensions, IRS Chief Counsel Stuart Brown said that the IRS is reviewing cash balance plans with regard to rates of accrual; protection of benefits accrued before conversion to cash balance; and whether benefit accruals are illegally reduced "because" of age. However, he stated that mere correlation between age and benefit reductions is not necessarily unlawful discrimination, because a plan is not discriminatory for tax purposes unless the accrual rate is reduced **because** of the attainment of a particular age. Mr. Brown testified that there is no legal protection of the employee's expectation that the plan's formulas will not change. [Glenn Burkins, "IRS Says Cash Balance Plans Don't Discriminate," *Wall Street Journal*, 9/22/99, p. A2. The hearing is summarized in Colleen T. Congel, "Treasury Official Tells Senate Labor Panel Resources Exist to Study Cash Balance Plans," 68 LW 2171 (9/28/99), and a transcript of the hearing is available at http://www.senate.gov/~labor/hearings/septhear/092199wt/body_092199wt.htm.]

According to *Eaton v. Onan Corp.*, 117 F.Supp.2d 812 (S.D. Ind. 2000), converting a defined benefit plan to a cash balance plan does not violate the ADEA or ERISA's ban on age discrimination in benefit accruals. The court said that the

ERISA provisions do not apply to employees younger than the plan's Normal Retirement Age.

In September 1999, the IRS issued a memo from Employee Plans Division Director Carol Gold to division chiefs, stating that the decision to approve or deny an application for cash balance conversion will be made by the national office, not the local field offices. In other words, technical advice is required. The memo was interpreted to impose a freeze on approvals: Richard A. Oppel Jr., "Cash-Balance Pension Plans Under Scrutiny by Tax Agency," *N.Y.T.*, 9/17/99, p. C1.

In October 1999, the IRS sought public comments (64 FR 56578,10/20/99) on cash balance plans, especially conversions. Possible tax issues: rate of accruals vis-a-vis §411(b); whether accrued benefits are protected as required by §411(d)(6); and whether benefit accruals are reduced on account of age, which is prohibited by §411(b)(1)(H).

The Department of Labor's PWBA weighed in to the debate on November 30, 1999, via a document intended to inform plan participants: "Cash Balance Plans Questions & Answers," http://www.dol.gov/dol/pwba/public/pubs/cashbq&a.htm. It distinguishes not only between cash balance plans and conventional defined benefit and defined contribution plans, but also between cash balance plans and 401(k)s.

The PWBA lists four main differences (besides the fact that legally speaking, a 401(k) is a defined contribution plan):

- 401(k) plan participation is elective; participation in a cash balance plan isn't.
- The employer bears investment risk in a cash balance plan, but the employee does in a 401(k).
- Cash balance plans have to offer Qualified Joint and Survivor Annuities (QJSAs); 401(k)s don't.
- Cash balance plans, but not 401(k) plans, are PBGC-guaranteed.

The PWBA report says that the legality of "wear-away" is being "closely studied" by the EEOC, IRS, and DOL, but doesn't indicate what the conclusion will be. Question 11 says that neither ERISA nor the Tax Code obligates employers who convert to a cash balance plan to give employees the option of remaining in the old plan. The employer can simply replace the old formula with the new formula for all participants, as long as benefits already accrued as of the date of the conversion are not reduced. Or, the employer can keep current employees under the old plan formula, applying the new formula only to those hired after the change; or, some employees can be "grandfathered in" and given an option to receive their pension under the old formula.

At least 15 days' notice must be given in advance of adoption of a plan amendment that significantly reduces the rate of benefit accrual in the future. It may also be necessary to issue a revised SPD and/or Summary of Material Modification.

If the converted plan does offer choices to participants, and if they have to sign a waiver as part of the option process, make sure that the waiver conforms to OWBPA standards.

Employee benefits attorney Hugh Forcier, in "Understanding the Assault on Cash Balance Plans," http://www.faegre.com/article_print.asp?id=349, rebuts three arguments against cash balance plans.

- It has been asserted that the rate of accrual decreases with age in a front-loaded cash balance plan with a level pay credit, but Forcier says this is not a correct analysis. The true rate of benefit accrual is the pay credit (e.g., 4%) which stays level and does not decline with age. Forcier points out that, in cases involving Georgia Pacific and First National Bank of Boston, the courts rejected the argument because allowing it would give participants more than they actually expected from the plan.
- Another contention is that cash balance plans discriminate against older workers, who get a lower benefit at age 65 than they would have received if the plan had never converted, and may receive less than some younger workers. Forcier's reply is that some employers continue the old plan for some participants and most provide "considerable transition relief." Anyway, courts will look at the percentage of pay dedicated to the pension in each year, and older workers get the same percentage as younger ones. In effect, the old pension formula favored older workers; but that doesn't mean the employer has to maintain the old formula forever. Switching to an age-neutral formula is permissible.
- Forcier's contention is that wear-away is not inherently related to age. For instance, it does not affect older employees hired after a cash balance plan is already in place, only those who were pension plan participants at the time of the conversion. Therefore, any ADEA challenges would have to be phrased as disparate impact claims, and it's far from clear that ADEA disparate impact claims are even permitted at all.

What are the arguments against cash balance conversions? It has been asserted that the traditional defined benefit plan doesn't respond to current workforce needs. By encouraging early retirement, it makes it hard for employers to hang on to mature workers whose skills are needed. Some employers also say that they need cash balance plans as incentives for a younger, more mobile workforce, who would be attracted by the ability to roll over a lump sum from the cash balance plan to an IRA or another qualified plan.

However, because cash balance plans can still impose participation and vesting requirements, the end result is that workers who leave before vesting, or when only a small part of the account is vested, don't benefit from cash balance plans. [See Ellen E. Schultz, "Young and Vestless," *Wall Street Journal,* 12/16/99, p. A1.]

See http://www.cashpensions.com for a site marshalling the arguments against cash balance plans, and tracking efforts by employees to fight against these plans and to get court and legislative support for their position.

"Whipsaw" and Financial Factors

The "whipsaw" issue arises because Code §417 specifies the interest and mortality assumptions that are mandatory for use in conversion from annuity to lump-sum payment. When a worker covered by a defined benefit plan terminates employment, the sponsor must calculate the present value of any lump-sum distribution.

This is done by projecting the account balance that would be available at normal retirement age (using PBGC-authorized interest rate assumptions), finding the value of the annuity that could be purchased with that sum, and using the PBGC interest rate assumptions again to reconvert the annuity to a lump sum that represents the present value of the participant's account.

Under the fact circumstances of some cash balance plans, applying the whipsaw calculation increases the lump sum available to certain plan participants. Naturally, then, the plan sponsors want to argue that they can bypass the whipsaw calculation; advantaged participants want to argue that it must be applied.

IRS Notice 96-8 creates a safe harbor for some cash balance plans that use acceptable interest rates. However, at least two cash balance plan sponsors have defeated challenges by plan participants, even though they did not satisfy the safe harbor criteria.

In 2000, the Court of Appeals reversed the District Court in two important cases about cash balance plans.

Esden v. Bank of Boston, 229 F.3d 154 (2nd Cir. 2000) is a class action alleging that the plan's calculation of lump-sum distributions violated the ERISA anti-forfeiture rule.

The plan projected cash account balances that would be taken as lump sums using an interest rate lower than the minimum interest rate guaranteed by the plan. (The interest rate used for the lump-sum calculation was 4%, well below the 5.5% rate used to accrue interest credits). When the projection was discounted back to present value, participants received less than the actuarial equivalent of the normal balance. Part of the benefit was also contingent on the distribution option chosen, which was alleged to violate ERISA §203(a) and Code §411(a)(2).

The Second Circuit adopted the IRS view (expressed in Notice 96-8), that "whipsaw," the result of projecting the account value with a rate below the guaranteed rate, violates ERISA because the participant is entitled to the present value of the accrued benefit. According to the Second Circuit, a variable interest rate is permissible as long as it is definitely determinable and does not grant discretion to the employer to set the amount after establishing the plan.

Lyons v. Georgia-Pacific Corp., 2000 Westlaw 1140673 (11th Cir. 8/11/00) holds that the lump sum benefit under a defined benefit plan must be calculated by using the PBGC discount rate to discount the normal retirement benefit to present value. The District Court treated the IRS Regulations about the discount rate (Reg. §1.411(a)-11) as "unreasonable," (66 F.Supp.2d 1328 (N.D. Ga. 1999)), but the Eleventh Circuit upheld their validity. [These cases are discussed in "Whipsawed," http://www.plansponsor.com/content/magazine/Whipsawd.]

The whipsaw problem is most acute for disputes about cash balance plan administration before 1995, because in 1994, PBGC interest rates were significantly raised to match the interest rate on 30-year Treasury bonds. The higher the interest rates used, the less likely participants are to protest. ["Cash Balance 'Whipsaw,'" http://www.assetpub.com/psmay99/may99PS074_right.html.]

Watson Wyatt Worldwide has calculated the impact of cash balance conversion, based on a 30-year career for a person hired at a starting salary of $45,000, who receives a 3% raise each year, ending up with a final salary of $106,000. Watson Wyatt's calculations involve four permutations: a traditional versus a cash balance plan, and a 30-year career at one company versus three 10-year stints at different companies.

Assuming that the conventional defined benefit pension for the hypothetical workers equals 1.25% of final pay times years of service, the final value of the defined benefit pension after a 30-year career is $377,600, as compared with only $248,700 in the cash balance plan, calculated at 5% of salary subject to a 6% interest rate assumption.

For the person who held three jobs over the 30-year period, the conventional defined benefit pension's final value was $289,200 (lower because the final pay for the first two jobs was lower, depressing the total) and $295,800 for the cash balance plan (assuming that the balance from the first two jobs was rolled over to an IRA earning 7.5% a year). In other words, participating in a cash balance versus a defined benefit plan doesn't make much difference for a job-hopper, but is very significant for employees who spend their entire career with a single company. [Richard A. Oppel Jr., "No Small Change as Pension Plans are Converted," *N.Y.T.*, 10/24/99, Business p.12. "Meeting the Challenge of Cash Balance Transitions," an article in Watson Wyatt's online newsletter, contains some interesting information and metrics about design and implementation of cash balance formulas: http://www.watsonwyatt.com/homepage/us/new/Insider/October99/10_99.htm. Also see R. Evan Inglis and Richard R. Joss, "Smoothing the Way for Cash Balance Plans," *HR Magazine,* 12/99, p. 77.]

Accounting issues are tackled by Alex T. Arcady and Francine Mellors, "Cash Balance Conversions: Assessing the Accounting and Business Implications," http://www.aicpa.org/pubs/jofa/feb2000/arcady.htm. For accounting purposes, despite its hybrid features, a cash balance plan is a defined benefit plan. Therefore, its accounting treatment is controlled by FASB Statement No. 87 (Employers' Accounting for Pensions), No. 88 (Employers' Accounting for Settlements), and No. 132 (Employers' Disclosures About Pensions and Other Postretirement Benefits.) An actuary will be required to calculate the new assumptions and the effect of the changed assumptions on plan balances. It may be necessary to footnote the company's financial statements to reflect the conversion.

The conversion is a negative plan amendment. The financial benefits to the company must be recognized prospectively on financial statements, in that the prior service cost of the pension plan is reduced.

12.5 NONQUALIFIED PLANS

For more information about funding methods for nonqualified plans, see Jinny St. Goar, "Nonqualified Successes," *CFO Magazine,* 10/99, also published as http://www.cfonet.com/html/Articles/CFO/1999/99OCnonq.html. More and more corporations seek certainty by funding their nonqualified benefits instead of keeping them on a pay-as-you-go basis, but about half of nonqualified plans remain unfunded.

Because they are not fettered by the maximum limitations placed on qualified plans, St. Goar notes that nonqualified plans can provide much larger benefits; as much as 90% of a top executive's luxurious retirement package can derive from nonqualified plans.

QSERPs

Qualified Supplemental Executive Retirement Plans (QSERPs) are another means of enhancing retirement benefits for executives. In some ways, QSERPs are similar to top hats or excess benefit plans, but they are qualified plans. Therefore, the employer gets a current tax deduction; employees get more certainty that benefits will eventually be paid; and the employee is not taxed on the benefits until they are actually paid out. To have a QSERP plan, the employer must satisfy the nondiscrimination requirements for qualified plans, and must keep the benefits within the IRC §415 limits.

However, the nondiscrimination requirements don't always impair QSERP funding, because tax law allows integration of the employer's contributions to Social Security, which represent a significant portion of lower-paid employee's compensation.

Adopting a QSERP can be simple: The corporation can simply amend the plan documents to include an annual list of people or job titles that get additional benefits of $X/year. QSERP amounts are usually subtracted from amounts that would otherwise be payable under nonqualified plans. However, if the QSERP is a defined contribution plan, the IRC limit on contributions to ALL defined contribution plans is still only $30,000 per person. If the employer is already making contributions for the executive at or close to the maximum, there may be little or no leeway for the QSERP. [Information about QSERPs: Watson Wyatt Insider electronic newsletter, Vol. 9 Issue 10 (10/99); http://www.watsonwyatt.com/homepage/us/new/Insider/October99/10_99.htm.]

TIP

The interaction of income and estate tax rules can subject nonqualified benefits that are inherited by the executive's heirs to cripplingly heavy taxation. See David Baum, "Benefit Conversion Option: Planning for Succeeding Generations," at http://www.benefitslink.com/articles/benconversion.shtml for some estate planning insights.

12.5.1 Taxation of Participants of Nonqualified Plans

In 1996, the Tax Court decided that §83(a) requires inclusion in income as soon as vacation and severance pay benefits are secured with a letter of credit, because the employee is deemed to have received those amounts [*Schmidt Baking Co. v. Comm'r,* 107 TC 271 (1996)]. Congress overturned that result by legislation, passing §7001 of the Internal Revenue Service Restructuring and Reform Act of 1998 (IRSRRA), P.L. 105-206, adding a new IRC §404(a)(11). The new section makes it clear that deeming is not proper—amounts are not included in taxable income until they are actually received. See IRS Notice 99-16, 1999-13 IRB 10, for information about how to make accounting changes to conform to the IRSRRA requirements.

12.6 FACTORS IN CHOOSING A PLAN FORM

IRS Announcement 99-2, 1999-2 IRB 44 (12/29/98), encourages employers that do not have plans to permit employees to invest, via payroll deductions, in either regular or Roth IRAs. The Announcement explains how to adjust withholding taxes to compensate for deductible IRA contributions.

DOL's Interpretive Bulletin 99-1, "Payroll Deduction Programs for Individual Retirement Accounts," was published in the Federal Register on June 18, 1999, at 64 FR 32999-33003, explaining a 1975 DOL regulation that allows employers to use payroll deductions to send money to employees' IRAs, without the arrangement constituting a "plan" subject to ERISA. This regulation helps employees by making it easier for them to save for retirement, so DOL gives employers safe harbor relief. In fact, when it enacted the Taxpayer Relief Act of 1997, Congress went on record (H.R. Rep. No. 220, 105th Congress) that employers that do not have retirement plans should be encouraged to set up payroll deduction systems so their employees can use IRAs to save for retirement.

29 CFR §2510.3-2(d) says that an IRA payroll deduction plan is not a "plan" subject to ERISA if:

- The employer doesn't make any contributions.
- Employee participation in the arrangement is completely voluntary.
- The employer's only involvement is letting employees participate (but not endorsing participation), making payroll deductions, and sending the deducted amounts to the IRA sponsor.
- The employer can collect reasonable reimbursement for its services, but no other compensation.

Although employers must remain neutral, it's all right for them to provide educational materials about IRAs and the value of saving for retirement, but they must make it clear that the employer only administers the payroll deductions and doesn't contribute to the plan. The employer can also distribute literature prepared by the IRA sponsor, and even display its own logo on the materials.

The employer can either select a single IRA sponsor, or have criteria for selecting high-quality sponsors; but it's not permissible for the employer to negotiate special terms with the sponsor for its own employees that are not available to everyone else who buys IRAs through that sponsor. It's permissible for the employer to absorb the sponsor's fee for administering the program, and to assume the in-house costs of running the payroll deduction plan, but not to pay administrative, investment management, or other fees that the sponsor would otherwise charge employees. On the other hand, it is also permissible for the employer to charge the sponsor reasonable compensation for the administrative services the employer performs, but not to make this a profit center.

Appropriate disclosures to employees include:

- There are other ways for employees to fund IRAs.
- IRAs are not suitable for everyone.
- IRAs work the same way whether or not payroll deductions are involved.

12.7 BASIC REQUIREMENTS

Effective in 2000, combined limitation (§415(e)) on allocations to defined contribution plus accrued benefits from defined benefit plans no longer applies for individuals who participate in both types of plans. However, it is permissible for plans to continue to include language imposing a combined limitation. Defined benefit plans are allowed to increase benefits beginning in 2000 to reflect repeal of the combined limitation—for retirees as well as active employees.

For the year 2001, the defined benefit limit is $140,000, rather than the earlier figure of $135,000.

Rev.Rul. 99-51, 1999-50 IRB 652 involves a company that divided its defined benefit plan into two plans: one for HCEs, the other for rank-and-file employees. The IRS concedes that assets and liabilities were properly allocated between the two plans.

At first, the sponsor company froze benefit accruals to the plan for HCEs, as of the date of the spin-off of the new plans. Next, the company amended the plan for rank-and-file employees to include HCEs, providing for benefit accruals for the entire period of service by the HCEs. In effect, they were covered by both the operating and the frozen plan for their pre–spin-off service. The Revenue Ruling holds that the spin-off tactic violates §401(a)(4) by discriminating in favor of the HCEs by providing them with duplicative coverage. The sponsor could have achieved the desired results without violating §401(a)(4) either by instituting a nonqualified plan for the HCEs, or by integrating the rank-and-file plan with Social Security.

The IRS allowed defined contribution plans to have broader discretion in eliminating unpopular benefit forms (e.g., annuities, in-kind distributions) from defined contribution plans. ["IRS Relaxes Protected Benefit Rules," CIGNA'S Pension Analyst October 2000, http://www.cigna.com/professional.] The sponsor of a defined contribution plan can eliminate the installment and annuity periodic payment options, but money-purchase plans must always offer payment in the form of Qualified Joint and Survivor Annuity (QJSA).

There are four permissible ways to move account balances from one plan to another: a direct rollover; an elective transfer of a 100% vested benefit; a "transaction transfer" available only in between defined contribution plans of the same type (i.e., money purchase to money purchase, 401(k) to 401(k), etc.) and only in part of a merger or acquisition; and an "employment change transfer" (for instance, going to work for a different division of the same employer, but where a different pension plan is involved).

12.10 EMPLOYEE CONTRIBUTIONS

On January 25, 1999, the Supreme Court decided the extremely significant case of *Hughes Aircraft Co. v. Jacobson*, #97-1287, 525 U.S. 432. The case involved Hughes Aircraft Company's defined benefit retirement plan. Unlike most defined benefit plans, this one mandated employee contributions, and a large part of the plan was attributable to employee contributions.

The Hughes plan operated at a surplus, and the employer suspended its contributions in light of the surplus. It also amended the plan to provide for early retirement benefits and to add a new benefit structure for new participants. Under the new structure, employee contributions were not required; the plan was funded with the surplus from the older plan.

The plaintiff employees contended—unsuccessfully—that the employer had an obligation to share the plan surplus with the employees who contributed to it, rather than using the surplus to reduce the employer's future obligations. In the view of the Supreme Court, the very nature of a defined benefit plan is that the employer assumes and controls the risk. If the plan operates at a surplus, it is not improper for the employer to apply that surplus toward other obligations—because the employer is always obligated to provide the vested benefits specified in the plan. In this analysis, Hughes did not violate ERISA, because it did not cease to furnish vested benefits as defined by the plan.

Nor did the Supreme Court accept the employees' argument that Hughes improperly terminated the old plan. Instead, the court held that an amendment creating a new benefit structure is permissible—and should not be treated as the creation of a second plan—if there is only one pool of assets used to fund both obligations. The old plan was not terminated merely because an additional benefit structure was added, because payments would continue to be made to longer-serving employees on the basis of the original plan.

For a later case dealing with pension surplus, see the Second Circuit's April 1999 ruling that New Coleman Holdings Inc., a unit of Sunbeam Corp., was entitled to the surplus (approximately $14 million) in the pension plan of one of its controlled companies. The surplus derived from investment gains. The investment was intended to fund future benefits, and the District Court held that plan participants were entitled to the money. The Second Circuit reversed, on the grounds that participants in the defined benefit plan would get their promised benefits, and so were not harmed; the corporation was entitled to reap the benefit of the investment success.

12.11 LEASED EMPLOYEES

According to *Bronk v. Mountain States Telephone & Telegraph Inc.*, 98-1 USTC ¶50,316 (10th Cir. 1998), ERISA does require that employees be permitted to participate in the plan once they have satisfied the plan's age and service requirements. However, it does not violate ERISA to draft the plan in such a way that leased employees—even leased employees who are common-law employees—are excluded from all participation. See IRS Notice 84-11, Q&A 14: "[IRC]§414(n)(1)(A) requires only that a leased employee be treated as an employee; it does not require that a leased employee be a participant in the recipient's qualified plan."

Similarly, in the view of the Eleventh Circuit (*Wolf v. Coca-Cola Co.*), it is legitimate to draft a plan to exclude certain categories of employees, including leased employees, even if the leased employees fit the definition of common-law employees. The Eleventh Circuit didn't find it necessary to follow *Vizcaino*, because Microsoft's plan purported to cover all common-law employees. As the *Wolf* court reads it, standing to sue under ERISA requires not only common-law employee status, but also eligibility under the plan.

In April, 2000, the IRS released a TAM (informational memorandum that does not have the full force of a formal regulation) about workers who claim that they were inappropriately treated as independent contractors or as employees of a leasing company or professional employer organization.

As long as plan participation is limited to employees on the payroll record, coming under specified job codes or work status codes, and as long as contingent workers are fully informed that they are not entitled to plan participation, the IRS did not see any violation of §410 or Reg. §1.401(a)-3(d), even though certain workers were excluded. The plan was not ambiguous and did not give the employer inappropriate discretion to exclude workers. The IRS inquired as to whether the job categories served an independent business purpose, and found them valid. The IRS also approved a plan provision that said that workers would not be retroactively admitted to plan participation even if an administrative agency or court treated them as employees rather than contractors—the IRS treated this provision as improving the stability and predictability of the plan. [Mary B. Hevener, "IRS Sides With Employers That Excluded Contract Workers From Its Qualified Retirement Plans," FindLaw Library (Summer 2000).]

Attorney Sheldon M. Geller provides some guidelines in "Employee Staffing and Plan Design," *The CPA Journal* (November 2000), http://www.cpa.journal.clm /1100dept/d116700a.htm. He suggests that employers who use temporary services to get workers might wish to:

- Amend their plans to exclude the employees of staffing companies, even if they are re-classified as common-law employees
- Review welfare plans to exclude re-classified employees
- Give the plan administrator full discretionary authority, especially with respect to eligibility for participation
- Ask temporary or leased employees to waive participation, even if re-classified
- Examine the tasks assigned to independent contractors to make sure they are not performing as employees.

He also suggests that Third Party Administrators check with plan sponsors to make sure that they have provided a complete census of workers, and do not mistakenly exclude persons who should be covered and/or counted in performing non-discrimination testing.

12.13 WHICH PLANS ARE MOST POPULAR?

In 1998, the total assets in all defined contribution plans maintained by large employers grew by 19%. However, in that year, defined benefit plans covered almost twice as many workers as defined contribution plans, had about 55% more overall assets, and paid approximately 30% more benefits than their defined contribution counterparts. Those findings come from the Committee on the Investment of Employee Benefit Assets, covering more than 150 of the largest corporate pension funds in the U.S.

Among large companies, it was just about universal (99%) to maintain both types of plan. Only 16% sponsored cash balance plans (see §12.4.6). Overall, defined benefit plans were invested 62% in equity, 28% in bonds and other fixed-income vehicles, and 10% otherwise. Defined contribution plans were 31% invested in equity, 38% in employer stock, 22% in fixed-income vehicles, 7% in balanced fund, and 2% other. [Summary of findings: http://news.excite.com/news/pr/991110/dc-cieba-401k-survey; no www. CIEBA's site is http://www.plansponsorexchange.com.]

See EBRI Issue Brief No. 229, "Retirement and Health Data" at http://www.ebri.org/ibex/ib229.htm (1/01) for general background information on employment-based retirement systems, such as the aggregate financial assets and holdings of pension plans; general trends in the 401(k) market; account balances and asset allocations for 401(k)s; IRA assets; and the rate at which retirement assets are rolled over.

In 1999, fueled by a long-running bull market, the trend was for companies to experience very low pension costs. (It would not be surprising to find that this trend reversed in 2000 and 2001!) In 1995, for instance, the corporate pension cost for the S&P 100 was close to $5 billion, which declined to about $2 billion in 1998—and only $155 million in 1999! In fact, some plans earned enough in the stock market to actually contribute to corporate earnings instead of being an expense. Pension costs were also lowered by factors such as downsizing and shift to cash balance plans. [Ellen E. Schultz, "Companies' Pension Costs Plunged in '99," *WSJ* 6/6/00 p. A2.]

EBRI has traced pension access trends for men and women of working age (18-62) between 1989 and 1998. Both men and women have tended to increase pension wealth over this time period, although men did better because of their generally more risk-tolerant investment strategy. In 1989, for example, 43% of women and 53% of men were pension participants. The percentage of participant women increased slightly, to 45%, and men's participation rate declined to 52%, in 1998. In both years, women earned about 57% as much as men.

In constant 1998 dollars, the average balance in women's defined contribution plans went from $15,372 in 1992 to $25,020 in 1998 (an increase of 53%). In comparison, the average balance for men went from $41,149 to $57,230 (a smaller increase, of 39%). So women benefited more, in part because they became less conservative in their investing strategy. However, the average male participant had a larger defined contribution plan balance than the average female participant, because of men's typically greater earnings and more consistent workforce participation. [EBRI Issue Brief No. 227, http://www.ebri.org/ibex/ib227.htm (11/00).]

12.14 PBGC PREMIUMS

A PBGC news release of 11/23/99 (see http://www.pbgc.gov/pr0008.htm) announces that safe harbor relief will be more freely available for plans that would otherwise encounter late payment penalties on their estimated payments of PBGC premiums. (The PBGC doesn't have authority to waive interest on underpayments, so interest payments will still be due.) Plan administrators will not face late payment penalties based on undercounting the number of plan participants, if they rely on the participant count for the previous year's premium payment.

Furthermore, if a plan corrects its underpayment before receiving a PBGC notice about it, the penalty is only 1% a month, rather than the 5% a month imposed on companies that do not self-correct.

The full text of the announcement can be found in the 11/26/99 issue of the *Federal Register.*

Although concerns have been voiced about the long-term viability of the PBGC, it achieved its third straight surplus year in 1998 (following 20 deficit years). For the year ending 9/30/98, the PBGC single-employer program had assets of

$17.6 billion versus $12.6 billion in liabilities. The agency covered about 42 million employees; 209,300 of them received $848 million in insurance payments in FY 1998. 1998 was a year in which comparatively few plans terminated, so the PBGC was not stressed by major new obligations.

In October of 1998, the GAO studied the long-term prospects of the agency in a Letter Report, "Pension Benefit Guaranty Corporation: Financial Condition Improving, But Long-Term Risks Remain," GAO/HEHS-99-5, dated 10/16/98. The GAO's conclusion was that most insured, underfunded plans have strengthened their financial status, which is hopeful for the PBGC's long-run stability. The PBGC's forecasting methodology has become more sophisticated, so there will be fewer surprises. However, there are still some large underfunded plans that might make large calls on the PBGC in the future.

Over time, many small plans have terminated, so that although the number of participants has increased since the 1980s, the number of PBGC-insured plans has been cut in half.

REFERENCES

[1]"401(k) Plan Sponsorship Growth 1994–1998," performed with Booz-Allen & Hamilton Inc.; see http://www.psca.org/grow401k.html.

[2]"Trends in the 401(k) Market," *West Employment Alert*, 4/16/98, p. 4.

[3]For safe harbor modifications of Notice 98-52, see "Recent IRC Changes Make 401(k) Plans, SIMPLEs More Attractive," *Compensation and Benefits Update*, 12/30/98, p. 1.

[4]Ellen E. Schultz and Kyle Pope, "CBS Is Replacing Its Pension Program With Cash-Balance Plan, Stock Options," *WSJ*, 3/24/99, p. B10.

[5]The main guidance comes from Notice 96-8, IRB 1996-6 (2/5/96). It requires that the lump sum distribution from a cash-balance plan must be computed by determining the hypothetical balance in the plan projected out to normal retirement age, then making sure the employee receives at least the present value of that sum. There were earlier regulations in 1991, amended in 1993. See Colleen T. Congel, "Cash Balance Pension Plan Growth Fuels Congressional, Regulatory Action," 67 LW 2531 (3/16/99).

[6]Frances A. McMorris, "Sunbeam Unit Is Entitled to Surplus in Pension," *WSJ*, 4/5/99, p. B2.

[7]"Pension Benefit Posts a Surplus of $5 Billion," *WSJ*, 3/30/99, p. A17.

Chapter 13

PLAN ADMINISTRATION

13.2 CREATING A PLAN

The IRS has engaged in ongoing efforts to allow plans to correct failures without becoming disqualified. The efforts began with Rev.Proc. 98-22, 1998-12 IRB 12, and have continued with Rev.Proc. 99-31, 1999-34 IRB 280, culminating in Adv.Rev.Proc. 2000-16, 2000-6 IRB 518, which consolidates several earlier programs for voluntary return to compliance.

The latest entry is Rev.Proc. 2000-17, 2000-589 IRB 7. A single voluntary correction program, VCP, now combines the former VCR, Walk-in Cap, and TVC programs. Plan sponsors can submit anonymous requests for information. When plan assets are transferred, or plans are merged in connection with mergers and other corporate transactions, the surviving entity is entitled to an extended self-correction period to repair plan problems.

For information about the PBGC's insurance program for 1999 (the last year for which data analysis is complete), see The PBGC Pension Insurance Data Book 1999, http://www.pbgc.gov/publications/databooks/databook.htm.

13.3 CLAIMS PROCEDURE

NOTE: See ¶9.5.1 for the Department of Labor's November 21, 2000 Final Rule on claims procedures for health and disability plans.

A self-insured health plan imposed a 90-day time limit for filing suits based on internal appeals of claims denials. The Eleventh Circuit found this requirement to be valid [*Northlake Regional Medical Center v. Waffle House Sys. Employee Benefit Plan*, 160 F.3d 1301 (11th Cir. 1998)]. The court declined to impose a general rule that a 90-day limitation is always permissible, but under the facts of the case, and given that the plan had procedures for expediting decision making, the limitation was appropriate and not overreaching.

A Ninth Circuit case from 2000, *Chappel v. Laboratory Corp. of America*, 2000 U.S. App. LEXIS 28645 (9th Cir. 2000) involves a plan that required a claimant who challenged a claims denial to request arbitration within 60 days. The arbitrator's decision would be final and binding, and would completely preclude an ERISA suit. Claimants had to pay part of the cost of arbitration, and they were not entitled to recover attorneys' fees even if they prevailed against the employer.

The Ninth Circuit ruled that the arbitration clause (which was reflected in the plan's SPD) was valid. But it reversed the District Court's dismissal of the plaintiff's claim for breach of fiduciary duty. The plan administrator should not have relied completely on the SPD to inform plan participants of their obligation to arbitrate their claims instead of litigating them. Therefore, if the claimant can show that he did not get timely and effective notice of the duty to arbitrate, he can get another chance to go to arbitration. Once arbitration has been completed, he has exhausted his administrative remedies under the plan and will be permitted to use the court system.

ERISA's required claims procedure means that claimants must be able to appeal benefit denials—which includes the right to review pertinent documents. The plan participant who sued in *Simpson v. Ameritech Corp., Inc.*, 2000 U.S. Dist. LEXIS 14607 (E.D. Mich. 2000) said she was denied access to documents relevant to denial of her claims for long-term disability benefits. The Eastern District of Michigan said that she didn't even ask for the documents until the appeals process was complete, so she was not entitled to relief. The document disclosure requirement is intended to make appeals more efficient, a purpose that cannot be served by requesting documents after completion of the appeal!

However, an earlier case, *Ellis v. Metropolitan Life Ins. Co.*, 126 F.3d 228 (4th Cir. 1997) says that the DOL regulations imply a requirement that the plan administrator or fiduciary inform participants of their right to review documents.

Third Party Administrators (TPAs)

The plans that provide pension and health benefits to about two-thirds of covered workers in the United States use some degree of third party administration. A TPA can be any kind of outsourcing firm that handles administrative tasks, from a consulting firm to a company that handles all kinds of benefits administration tasks. There are no federal licensing rules for TPAs, although many states do impose their own licensing laws, which can be quite restrictive.

TPAs usually arrange stop-loss protection for the plan in the form of back-up insurance benefiting the plan (not the employee) in case of unexpectedly high claims. Having a stop-loss plan does not convert a self-insured plan into an insured plan for ERISA purposes. [See Frederick D. Hunt, "Everything You Wanted to Know About TPAs But Were Afraid to Ask," http://users.erols.com/spba/p0000010.html; no www.]

13.4 STANDARD OF REVIEW

The main question is whether decisions are reviewed de novo, based on objective standards, or whether deference is granted and the inquiry is merely whether the administrators acted in an arbitrary and capricious fashion.

According to the Ninth Circuit, a disability plan that requires "satisfactory written proof" of disability, but does not say in so many words that the plan administrator has discretionary authority, is subject to de novo review of the objective correctness of the administrator's decisions [*Kearney v. Standard Insurance Co.*, 175 F.3d 1084 (9th Cir. 1998)].

In contrast, the Seventh Circuit case of *McNab v. GM*, 162 F.3d 959 (7th Cir. 1998), involved an early retirement plan that gave management discretion to reject early retirement applications from employees who were deemed especially valuable and therefore whose early retirement was contrary to the company's best interests. The court interpreted this as a standard rather than a rule (i.e., something that can be applied flexibly and with discretion). Denial of early retirement to the plaintiffs was not sufficiently arbitrary or capricious to constitute an ERISA violation.

Unless the plan specifically gives the administrator discretionary authority, courts reviewing claims disputes should use a de novo standard not only to see if the administrator interpreted the plan's language correctly, but with respect to the administrator's determinations of fact issues.

In this case, the question was whether the job of Director of Nursing was sedentary or not, in order to determine whether an employee was "totally disabled" in terms of performing that job. [*Kinstler v. First Reliance Standard life Ins. Co.*, 1999 WL 388022 (2nd Cir. 1999).]

The definition of disability was also at issue in a later case, *Harte v. Bethlehem Steel Corp.*, 214 F.3d 446 (3rd Cir. 2000). The plan administrator interpreted "compensable disability incurred during the course of employment" strictly, limiting it to work-related disabilities eligible for Worker's Compensation. Under this interpretation, the employee had a break in service and therefore a much lower pension.

The Third Circuit said that the administrator's decision, reviewed under the abuse of discretion standard, was reasonable. However, there was also a fiduciary duty to inform, which may have been breached because the participant was not informed in time to take action. A prudent fiduciary should have known that the worker would not think he had experienced a break in service, because he received plan benefits and had not been informed of the limitation to work-related disabilities.

To the Fourth Circuit, the arbitrary and capricious standard of review applies only if the plan gives the administrator discretion; de novo review is required for all other plans. The long-term disability plan construed in *Feder v. Paul Revere Life Insurance Co.*, No. 97-2346 (4th Cir. 2000) said that a physician was eligible if he or she was totally disabled and unable to perform professional duties. Total disability meant injury or sickness that completely precluded work and made the doctor unable to perform the central duties of the medical specialty.

The plaintiff, a surgeon, was terminated in 1993, and submitted a LTD claim for disabling mental illness. Benefits were paid as of February 1994; in June 1996, the insurer gave notice that benefits were being terminated because the doctor no longer qualified. The District Court granted summary judgment for the plan, because its decision was not arbitrary or capricious, but the Fourth Circuit reversed because the insurer did not reserve discretion. It merely required submission of written claims, which is an inevitable part of all insurance claims processes.

According to the Seventh Circuit, for a sponsor to reserve discretion, the plan documents must say more than that claimants must prove or give satisfactory proof of entitlement to benefits. The rationale of *Herzberger v. Standard Insurance Co.*, No. 99-1944 (7th Cir. 2000) is that an ERISA plan is a contract, which is interpreted by courts and not the party who drafted the language. However, the court approved this language as adequate to secure deferential review: "Benefits under this plan will be paid only if the plan administrator decides in his discretion that the applicant is entitled to them."

Yochum v. Barnett Bank, 2000 U.S. App. LEXIS 30207 (11th Cir. 2000) involves an employee who worked for a bank that was sold to NationsBank. The first employer's severance plan denied severance benefits to anyone who rejected a written offer of comparable employment. The plaintiff was offered a job that would result in forfeiture of his stock options and would reduce the duration of his salary guarantee from two years to one year. He did not accept the job, and went to work for a competitor.

Based on his rejection of a "comparable" job, the plan's administrative committee refused to pay severance benefits to him. The District Court reviewed this decision under the arbitrary and capricious standard, and affirmed it.

However, on appeal, the Eleventh Circuit reversed the District Court. It did not require de novo review (because discretion had been reserved), but imposed a heightened arbitrary and capricious standard because the committee had a conflict of interest and made its decision based on "false and incomplete" information. The committee did not examine the employment contract, and did not realize that the salary guarantee was cut down to only one year. This case highlights the importance of drafting the plan to cope with potential corporate transitions, and of preventing conflicts of interest. [See "Denial of Severance Benefits Was Reversed Where Committee's Decision Was Based on 'False and Incomplete' Information," http://www.ebia.com/weekly/articles/ERISA001207Yochum.html.]

13.5 ADMINISTERING THE CLAIM

A 1998 case from the Northern District of California [*Bankamerica Pension Plan v. McMath*, 1998 Westlaw 422323 (N.D. Cal. 1998)] finds that it was proper for a plan to give effect to an unsigned form that changed a beneficiary designation. The employee didn't know that the form was not signed, and otherwise complied with the plan's requirements, so it was not arbitrary or capricious to carry out his wishes even though the technical requirements of the plan were not satisfied.

Vega v. National Life Insurance Services Inc., 68 LW 1154 (9/21/99) involves a plan sponsored by a married couple who owned a business. The plan administrator (which, as it happened, was a subsidiary of the insurer who wrote the plan's policies) denied a health claim for the wife, based on information from her doctor that the claim was for surgery contemplated before the policy was obtained.

The Fifth Circuit heard the case twice (first by a panel including some of the judges, then the entire court). The second time, the Fifth Circuit decided that even if a plan administrator experiences a conflict of interest when denying a claim (which, in this case, would have been paid by the administrator's parent company), ERISA does not impose an additional duty of reasonable investigation before denying the claim. However, when a court reviews the transaction to see if there was an abuse of discretion by the administrator, the conflict of interest is relevant evidence. But even an administrator who has a conflict of interest can reach a valid decision.

This case is also interesting because it takes the position that a business owner can be treated as an employee, and therefore as a plan participant for ERISA purposes, as long as there is at least one participant in the plan besides the owner and his or her spouse.

A fiduciary, including a life insurance company, has a right under ERISA §502(a) to seek appropriate equitable relief from the courts in order to enforce plan provisions. Therefore, the fiduciary can bring an interpleader action (a suit asking for court guidance on how to dispose of funds whose ownership is disputed) if there are conflicting claims (based on the beneficiary designation and community property laws) to insurance proceeds. [*Aetna Life Ins. Co. v. Bayona,* 2000 U.S. App. LEXIS 22625 (9th Cir. 2000).]

13.6 PLAN AMENDMENTS

As a general rule, Code §411(d)(6) prevents plans from adopting amendments that eliminate optional forms of benefits, but the Secretary of the Treasury has the power to permit exceptions to this rule. A recent example is found in IRS Notice 98-29, 1998-22 IRB 8. In mergers, for instance, the surviving plan may find itself saddled with a confusing variety of optional plans, which can be time-consuming and expensive to administer. The IRS is considering a relief provision, under which a defined contribution plan could be amended to pare down the number of payment options, as long as participants would have a choice of at least one lump sum and one multipayment form of distribution. Another possibility is to allow cancellation of payment options that are extremely unpopular with participants, or those that affect only a very small portion of the benefit.

13.7 [NEW] INVESTMENT-RELATED COSTS

The Department of Labor's Letter 2001-01A (1/18/01) includes an advisory opinion and six hypotheticals to clarify the types of expenses that can properly be charged to a plan. [See "DOL Provides New Guidance on Payment of Expenses from Plan Assets," http://www.benefitslink.com/print.php.] Some DOL regional offices distinguish between "settlor" and "administrative" functions when they audit a plan. In this reading, settlor expenses such as designing and establishing a plan are normal business expenses for the plan sponsor, and can't be charged to the plan, whereas ongoing administrative expenses are chargeable.

To clear up the disparities among the offices, the DOL advisory opinion letter says that plan expenses to maintain tax qualification, perform non-discrimination testing, and obtain an IRS determination letter are properly chargeable to the plan, even though the employer does derive financial advantage from the plan getting and maintaining tax qualification.

If plan fiduciaries determine that taking the charge is prudent, and costs are reasonable, the plan can legitimately be charged the communication costs; costs of computing the implications of a plan-to-plan transfer of assets; non-discrimination testing; plan amendments to comply with tax changes; and costs of outsourcing administrative tasks (e.g., to a TPA).

However, design studies, amendments required by corporate transitions, union negotiating costs, cost studies for new benefits designs, and FASB 88 statement costs are not chargeable to the plan.

Although defined contribution plans often consider the investment-selection process to be completed once they select a vendor, the fiduciaries still have a duty to monitor the vendors and the investments they recommend. The typical range of compensation for vendors is 20-50 basis points (i.e., one-fifth to one-half of one percent), from the plan or as revenue sharing from products. Plan vendors are offering both more and more flexible investment options. However, vendors are biased toward their own products, or those that generate the highest fees—not necessarily the best products for the plan and its participants. [Richard M. Todd, "Keys to Prudent Plan Investment Selection," RIA *Pension & Benefits Tax*, http://www.riatax.com/weekly/pension.shtml.]

13.8 MINIMUM FUNDING

Defined benefit plans seeking to change their asset valuation technique or funding methods are given additional flexibility by Rev.Proc. 99-45, 1999-49 IRB 603 (12/6/99). For instance, in some cases it is merely necessary to make the plan administrator aware of a changed funding method before the plan's Form 5500 is filed; he or she does not have to give affirmative consent to the change. However, some plans with negative unfunded liability are not allowed to change funding methods. Rev.Proc. 99-45 is effective for plan years beginning on or after 1/1/99.

13.9 ACCOUNTING ISSUES FOR PENSION PLANS

➠ **TIP**

Check the PBGC's Website each month, at http://www.pbgc.gov/interest.htp, for updated interest rates used each month for

- valuation of lump-sum payments from the plan
- variable-rate premiums
- valuation of annuity benefits
- PBGC charges on employer liability, unpaid contributions, and unpaid premiums

Rates are updated on the fifteenth of every month.

The site includes FAQs about premiums, standard terminations, and plan coverage, as well as the text of regulations, technical updates, and opinion letters.

You can e-mail PBGC staffers for assistance with problems of various kinds:

- Premium calculation and payment: premiums@pbgc.gov
- Coverage and standard terminations: standard@pbgc.gov
- Distress terminations: distress.term@pbgc.gov
- Early warning program: advance.report@pbgc.gov
- ERISA §4010 reporting: ERISA.4010@pbgc.gov
- Reportable events: post-event.report@pbgc.gov
- General legal questions: AskOGC@pbgc.gov
- Problem resolution officer for practitioners: practitioner.pro@pbgc.gov
- Other: Ask.PBGC@pbgc.gov

For more information about the expanding role of PBGC's online presence, see PBGC Technical Update 01-1 (1/19/01), http://www.pbgc.gov/legal_info/tech_updates/tech01-1.htm.

13.10 ROUTINE TAX COMPLIANCE

Rev.Rul. 86-142 states IRS' position that employers are entitled to deduct (as Code §162 ordinary and necessary business expenses) the **recurring** expenses of plan operation and administration that the employer pays directly. However, an August

1999 Tax Court case, *Sklar, Greenstein & Scheer, PC v. Comm'r*, 113 T.C. No. 9, allows an employer maintaining a money purchase plan to deduct the expenses of suing the plan's investment manager. The Tax Court agreed with the company that the expenses were ordinary and necessary, and rejected the IRS requirement that the expenses "recur"; after all, the text of §162 doesn't require that.

See IR-2000-83, published in the *Federal Register* issue of December 6, 2000, for temporary and proposed regulations on deposit of federal employment taxes. Starting January 1, 2001, approximately one million small businesses have been permitted to make quarterly rather than monthly payments of employment taxes. The rule applies to cumulative taxes of up to $2,500 for the quarterly or annual period (increased from $1,000 under prior law). Furthermore, instead of making a deposit, the employer can remit the full liability with a timely return.

The IRS' Website includes "Q and A for Businesses Filing Taxes Electronically," http://www.irs.gov/elec_svs/qa-bus.html, which includes links to topics such as filing Form 941 with a personal computer or touch-tone telephone, filing Form 940 electronically under the e-file and On-Line Filing programs, using magnetic tape to file Forms 940 and 941, and the FIRE system, which covers filing of 1042-S, 1098, 1099, 5498, 8027, and W-2G. This group of information returns can be filed electronically, with a modem or on magnetic tape (including floppy disks).

13.11 ROUTINE PBGC COMPLIANCE

The current basic flat-rate premium for single-employer pension plans remains at $19 a year for each participant. Underfunded plans are subject to an additional variable-rate charge of $9 for every $1000 of unfunded vested benefits. For premium payment years beginning on or after January 1999, the required interest rate under 29 CFR §2006 is 4.30%. See http://www.pbgc.gov/premiums.htp.

On January 14, 1999, the PBGC established a toll-free telephone hot line (800-736-2444) for the assistance of plan administrators who have questions about plan coverage, premiums, or plan terminations. See the PBGC's press release, http://www.pbgc.gov/1999form.htm.

At the end of 2000, the PBGC issued Technical Update 00-6 (12/20/00), http://www.pbgc.gov/legal_info.tech_updates/tech00_6.htm, explaining the simplified premium form, 1-EZ, which is included in the 2001 premium payment package. Starting with the 2001 plan year, single-employer plans can use the 1-EZ form instead of Form 1 and Schedule A, as long as they are exempt from the variable rate premium. Exemption is available if the plan has no vested participants on the premium snapshot date; if it is funded exclusively by individual insurance contracts; if it has fewer than 500 participants and has no unfunded vested benefits; if the sponsor's contributions for the prior plan year were at least as great as the full funding limitation; or if the plan is terminating via a standard termination on or before the snapshot date.

A PBGC Final Rule appearing in the *Federal Register* on December 14, 1998 (63 FR 68684) amends 29 CFR Part 4007 to provide that the final filing due date for a calendar-year plan's premium declaration will be October 15. In other words, the date is the same for the declaration as for the extended due date for Form 5500. The Final Rule makes corresponding changes in the treatment of the declaration for fiscal-year plans, which are now due on the fifteenth day of the tenth full calendar month of the premium payment year. (Adjustments are made if the plan changes its plan year, or if it is a new or newly covered plan.)

Plans will not face late-payment penalties if they base their PBGC premium payments on the previous year's participant count, and it later turns out that the plan had more participants than expected. However, interest will still be due on the underpayment, because the PBGC has discretion to waive penalties but not interest. Companies that correct their underpayments before being notified by the PBGC will have to pay a penalty of only 1% per month, not the normal 5%. The notice was published in the November 26, 1999 issue of the *Federal Register*, see the PBGC News Release of 11/23/99, http://www.pbgc.gov/pr0008.htm.

A Final Rule published in December, 2000, effective January 1, 2001, simplifies the administration of premium payments: 65 *Federal Register* 75160-75164 (12/1/00). The administrator can pay a prorated premium for a short plan year, instead of paying the full premium and getting a refund or claiming a credit against a future premium payment. A short plan year might occur during a plan's first, partial year; in the year of termination; or when a trustee is appointed under ERISA §4042.

The Final Rule also changes the definition of "participant," so that the plan can exclude from the count (and not pay premiums for) a person who has no accrued benefits and to whom the plan has no other benefit liabilities. The upshot is that a new plan doesn't have to pay premiums for its first year unless it credits service before the beginning of the plan.

In October, 2000, the PWBA, IRS, and PBGC, acknowledging the numerous and sweeping changes in the rules, announced relief for plans unable to file timely Form 5500s. PWBA's Leslie B. Kramerich announced that filers unable to meet a deadline should attach a statement to the form when it is finally filed, explaining the reasons for delay. Late filers will not be penalized solely on the basis of late filing, if they provide a reasonable rationale for failing to meet the deadline. [PWBA Press Release USDL:01-1 (10/6/00), http://www.dol.gov/dol/pwba/public/media/press/pr100600.htm]

13.11.1 CHANGES IN FORM 5500 COMPLIANCE

In February 2000, the DOL, IRS, and PBGC announced significant changes in the structure and filing methods for Form 5500, the Annual Return/Report for Employee Benefit Plans. Instead of having a long form and two abbreviated forms, the agencies have drafted a single three-page Form 5500 that will be used by all filers. (The new Form 5500 is reproduced in the Forms section of this book.) The new Form 5500 goes to the Pension and Welfare Benefits Administration (PWBA), part of the DOL, and not to the IRS, where the earlier 5500 series-forms were filed.

In addition to the basic Form 5500, up to 13 schedules may be required. Some of them are new additions; others are revised from previously required schedules:

- Schedule A: information on contracts with insurance companies
- Schedule B: actuarial information about defined benefit plans
- Schedule C: information on service providers
- Schedule D: information about certain funding mechanisms
- Schedule E: ESOP data
- Schedule F: information about fringe benefit plans
- Schedule G: disclosure of transactions such as loans and leases that are not exempt
- Schedule H: large-plan financial statements
- Schedule I: the small-plan equivalent
- Schedule P: files about tax-exempt pension trusts
- Schedule R: information (e.g., funding requirements; distributions) about pension plans
- Schedule T: support for tax qualification of pension plans
- Schedule SSA: information submitted to the Social Security Administration about ex-employees who have rights to receive future benefits under the plan

The schedules to be submitted depend on the type of plan and its characteristics. Fringe benefit plans need only file Schedule F, whereas large pension plans will probably have to complete all the schedules except Schedules F and I. Unfunded excess benefit plans, unfunded top hat plans, unfunded or insured discriminatory welfare benefit plans, and welfare plans with fewer than 100 participants that are unfunded or fully insured, are all exempt from filing the new Form 5500.

Starting in July 2000, when forms are due for 1999 plan years, the EFAST computerized system goes into effect. Plan years beginning in January, 2001 or later can take advantage of the expansion of the EFAST electronic filing system (http://www.efast.dol.gov).

For all prior years, plans had to obtain paper forms and file hard copies. Because of a Final Rule published in 65 *Federal Register* 75160-75164 (12/1/00), effective January 1, 2001, forms and instructions can be downloaded as PDF files for Windows, Mac, or Unix. EFAST filers can use either a machine print or hand print version, both of which are computer-scannable.

PWBA Press Release USDL: 01-13 (12/29/00) includes tips for preparing the forms:

- For forms filed on paper, send the originals—photocopies might be rejected
- Do not use felt tip pens, because they bleed through
- Do not make manual entries on machine-print forms
- Do not staple paper forms—use binder clips or other removable fasteners.

Publication EFAST A is the user's guide to electronic filing of 5500 and 5500-EZ forms: see http://www.efast.dol.gov. A list of approved software vendors and developers can be found at http://www.efast.dol/gov/softcos.htm.

Chapter 14

PLAN DISCLOSURE

14.1 INTRODUCTION

The Taxpayer Relief Act of 1997 freed plan administrators of the requirement of filing SPD and SMM copies with the Department of Labor routinely, although the documents still must be furnished if the DOL requests them. However, in August 1999, the DOL proposed a Rule (see 64 FR 42797) making plan administrators personally liable for civil penalties if they fail to honor a DOL request. The request is proper only if it is made on behalf of plan participants, beneficiaries, prospective beneficiaries (including those covered by a QDRO or QMCSO), and their representatives, who ask the DOL for help.

The administrator must pay any penalty personally, not using plan assets for this purpose. DOL can make multiple requests for the same SPD or other document, if several individuals ask the DOL for help with that document. The civil penalty for failing to comply with each request can be up to $100/request/day, but subject to a limit of $1000 per violation. If there is more than one administrator, each is jointly and severally liable for the penalties.

Administrators can apply for relief by explaining, not more than 30 days after a DOL request, that matters beyond the administrator's control prevented compliance.

> **TIP**
>
> See ¶ 12.4.6 for the disclosure requirements when a defined benefit plan is converted to a cash balance plan.

14.2 SPD

The PWBA published a Final Rule governing SPDs for pension, health, and welfare benefit plans on November 21, 2000, at 65 FR 70226-70244. (See ¶9.5.1 for discussion of the Final Rule on claims procedures for health plans, also published on November 21.) The effective date for the SPD Final Rule is the first day of the plan's second plan year that begins on or after January 22, 2001. The PWBA's estimate is that 50% of health plans and 30% of pension plans will have to revise their SPDs, SMMs, or both and distribute complying disclosure materials by the end of 2002. That adds up to 1.2 million plans and 36 million participants who are affected.

Under the Final Rule, all health plans SPDs (even those for HMOs that qualified for an exemption under the earlier rules) must disclose:

- The participants' cost-sharing obligations (such as deductibles and coinsurance)
- The annual and lifetime caps placed on benefits
- The extent (if any) to which preventive services are covered
- The extent to which accepted and new drugs are covered
- Extent of coverage of medical tests (although really detailed explanations can be saved for the SMM, as long as the SPD contains basic information)
- How the plan creates its network of providers
- The extent to which participants are required to get their care within the network, and when out-of-network care will be covered (e.g., in emergencies). The plan can simply inform participants of their right to request a detailed schedule of covered drugs and procedures, but they must be furnished automatically with a list of the health care providers within the network, because choice of a provider is such a significant decision. Another permissible option is for the SPD to give a general description of the provider network and give all participants a separate provider list, free of charge to them.
- Rules for coverage of emergency care
- Requirements for pre-authorization of treatment, and utilization review of ongoing treatment
- Information about the required length of hospital stays for childbirth, including descriptions of the federal law and any additional protection furnished by state law
- Either a description of claims procedures, or a statement that a free copy of the claims procedure is available on request
- Disclosure of COBRA rights.

According to the PWBA, the SPD must explain the role (if any) of health insurance in the plan, "particularly in those cases where the plan is self-funded and an insurer is serving as a contract administrator or claims payor, rather than as an insurer."

Under the PWBA Final Rule, the SPDs for pension and welfare benefit plans must disclose:

- Procedures for QDROs and QMCSOs, either through a description in the SPD itself or disclosure that the administrator will provide a free copy of a separate document on request
- The extent of the sponsor's reserved rights to terminate the plan or eliminate benefits
- Current information on PBGC coverage and ERISA rights

After reviewing comments, the PWBA concluded that the current disclosure requirements give adequate information about cash balance plan conversions and operations, so the agency declined to impose any special requirements. It continues to seek comments about possible changes in the SPD requirements and standardized language for cash balance plan disclosures.

With respect to plan terminations, SPDs must include:

- A summary of the plan's provisions authorizing the sponsor (or anyone else) to terminate the plan or eliminate benefits in whole or in part
- The circumstances under which termination of a whole plan or benefit elimination might occur
- Summary of plan provisions about the benefits, rights and obligations of participants and beneficiaries when the plan is terminated. Pension plan SPDs must summarize the accrual and vesting consequences of termination.
- How the plan's assets will be allocated and disposed of at termination.

According to the Middle District of Alabama, a manual for a welfare plan's administrative staff was not an SPD because it did not contain enough comprehensive information, even if the plaintiff relied on its provisions, because it was designed as an internal plan document rather than guidance for employees. Therefore, the plan was able to enforce the terms of the manual even though it was not published as an SPD [*Cooperative Benefit Administrators Inc. v Whittle*, 989 F.Supp. 1421 (M.D. Ala. 1997)].

Also note that, in *Fallo v. Piccadilly Cafeterias Inc.*, 141 F.3d 580 (5th Cir. 1998), an employee was entitled to an 11-month COBRA extension (after the normal 18-month period) because his wife became disabled during the 18-month period. The terms of the plan itself echoed the COBRA statute, requiring that notice of the Social Security Administration's determination of disability be given before the initial 18-month period expired. But the SPD merely required that notice be given to the plan within 60 days of the SSA disability determination and did not rule out extensions for disabilities beginning late in the initial 18-month period. The SPD was the document given to the employee, and therefore it was the document that was given effect by the Fifth Circuit. The moral? Make sure that the SPD is an accurate reflection of all facets of the plan, including its limitations.

In *John Deere Health Benefit Plan v. Chubb*, 45 F.Supp.2d 1131 (D.Kan. 1999), a participant in a self-insured health plan died. Her estate sued for medical malpractice, and won, and the plan asserted a subrogation claim against the estate for $266,000. The plan had promulgated two subrogation provisions: a detailed discussion in the plan document, and a cursory statement in the SPD referring to the plan's right to seek recovery against a tortfeasor (but not mentioning the right to seek recovery against the plan participant or participant's survivors).

The SPD said that the plan document controlled in all situations where it conflicted with the SPD. Nevertheless, the District Court found that the SPD controlled, and because it was defective (failing to warn participants of their vulnerability to subrogation), the plan's subrogation claim should be denied.

According to the prominent accounting and consulting firm Deloitte, employees usually win cases involving SPDs, because the language is construed against the employer. A continued high volume of litigation can be predicted (especially in connection with 401(k) plans)—particularly as employees look for someone to blame for poor investment returns during a stock market downturn!

Deloitte advises against "stonewalling" on disclosure; it's hard to imagine any benefits gained by "playing it close to the chest" that won't be outweighed by the difficulty and expense of litigation. Furthermore, if there is a lawsuit, a great deal of information will be made available (and often publicized) because of the discovery process. ["Employee Plan Disclosures: It's Cheaper to Communicate Than to Litigate," (no by-line), http://www.us.deloitte.com/pub/iq/vol18/iq07.htm.]

14.4 OTHER NOTICES

FASB Changes

In 1998, the Financial Accounting Standards Board (FASB) revised three of its existing statements (No. 87, "Employers' Accounting for Pensions," No. 88, "Employers' Accounting for Settlements and Curtailments of Defined Benefit Pension Plans and for Termination Benefits," and No. 106, "Employers' Accounting for Postretirement Benefits Other Than Pensions"). The new statement, No. 132, "Employers' Disclosures About Pension and Other Postretirement Benefits," streamlines the reporting process by eliminating some noncritical disclosures but increases the amount of information that must be disclosed about changes in the employers' benefit obligations and the fair values of plan assets. Another objective is to increase the standardization of retiree benefit disclosures.

The statement is effective for fiscal years beginning after December 15, 1997. If a company includes comparative information about pre-1998 years, it must restate the disclosures for earlier periods as long as the information is readily available.

Notice of Amendments Reducing Benefits

The IRS issued Final Regulations on December 14, 1998 (T.D. 8795; see 63 FR 68678) explaining the requirements of ERISA §204(h) (for defined benefit plans) and ERISA §302 (for certain individual account plans), with respect to the plan administrator's obligation to give notice of plan amendments that significantly reduce the rate of future benefit accruals. (The Final Regulations replace the Temporary Regulations of T.D. 8631, which appeared at 60 FR 64320 on 12/12/95.) The Final Rule is effective for amendments adopted on or after December 12, 1998.

Under ERISA §204(h), the administrator is obligated to give written notice to participants, alternate payees, and unions (in a unionized workplace) of plan amendments that significantly reduce the rate of future benefit accruals (i.e., that have the effect of changing the annual benefit that will eventually be paid when the employee reaches normal retirement age; for an individual account plan, that have the effect of changing the amounts allocated to participants' accounts in the future). Notice, disclosing the text of the plan amendment and its effective date, is due after the amendment is adopted and at least 15 days before its effective date. The notice requirement applies even if the amendment also triggers the need for a summary of material modifications (SMM), which is in fact provided to the employees.

The plan administrator can use any method reasonably calculated to get the notice to employees: hand delivery; first class mail to the employee's last known address; or delivery in combination with any other required notice.

The plan amendment will not become effective as to *any* plan participant if the administrator intentionally omits to provide the necessary notice. If some but not all persons who were supposed to get the notice were notified, the amendment does not become effective as to those who were not notified.

Example 2, Question 5 of the Final Rule says that, if a plan is amended to modify the actuarial factors used to convert an annuity to a lump sum distribution, the amendment does *not* affect the annual benefit commencing at normal retirement age. Therefore, notice is not required.

Question 6 defines the plan provisions that must be taken into account in determining whether the rate of future accruals has been reduced:

- Dollar amount or percentage of compensation on which benefit accruals are based
- Amount of disparity in a plan using permitted disparity
- Definition of service or compensation taken into account in accruing benefits
- Method of calculating average compensation
- Defined benefit plan's definition of normal retirement age
- Denying future participation to current participants
- Benefits offsets
- Minimum benefit provisions

- Individual account plan formulas for contributions and forfeitures
- Target benefit plan actuarial assumptions

Donald P. Carleen's "IRS Guidance on Amendments Reducing Plan Benefit Accruals," *N.Y.L.J.*, 10/29/99, p.3, is a helpful discussion of these issues.

QJSA Notices

An IRS Notice of Proposed Rulemaking (REG-109481-99, RIN 1545-AX34, 66 FR 3916-39020 (1/17/01), discussed in http://www.benefitslink.com/taxregs/annstart-proposed-2001.shtml] involves Code §417, which allows a married plan participant whose spouse consents to choose a different distribution method for pension benefits instead of the conventional Qualified Joint and Survivor Annuity. The original rule was that, within a reasonable time before the annuity starting date, the plan must provide the participant with a written description of the QJSA, the right to waive it and elect a different form of benefit payment, and the rights of the spouse.

The Small Business Jobs Protection Act (SBJPA) enacted Code §417(a)(7), allowing the QJSA disclosure statement to be provided after the annuity starting date, as long as the period for making the election to waive the QJSA is at least 30 days after the notice is rendered. The IRS proposal (effective for plan years beginning on or after January 1, 2002) permits the explanation to be furnished either on or after the annuity starting date and permits a retroactive starting date if the plan makes provisions for it and the participant so elects.

Proper Use of Electronic Media

As Chapter 5 shows, corporations are turning more and more to computers, the Internet, and their own intranets as effective, cost-efficient distributions mechanisms for communicating with employees. Some employer-employee communications are simply an internal policy matter, so the corporation can adopt any communications medium that it chooses. However, others are government mandated, such as required communications about tax and employee benefit matters.

In late 1998, the IRS proposed rules for transmitting information about plan distributions and securing employee consent to elections via electronic media. See 63 FR 70071 (12/18/98).

Code §411(a)(11) does not allow involuntary cash-outs of plan balances over $5000. However, employees can consent to a lump sum distribution. Regulation §1.411(a)-11(c)(2) imposes a prior-notice requirement (i.e., for the employee's consent to be valid, he or she must have received an explanation of the distribution options under the plan and have been notified of the right to defer the distribution and also defer taxation). Code §402(f) mandates notice of the income tax withholding requirements that apply to eligible rollover distributions, and §3405(e)(10)(b) requires notice to recipients of distributions that are *not* eligible rollover distributions of their ability to direct that income tax not be withheld from the distribution.

The Taxpayer Relief Act of 1997 (TRA '97) directed the IRS to start coming up with rules for integrating computer technology into plan administration and the disclosure process. The December 1998 proposals make it clear that a plan [or a 401(k) plan] will not lose its qualified status merely because it uses paperless electronic methods to give notice and secure consents—provided, of course, that proper standards are satisfied.

A satisfactory electronic notice

- Is at least as comprehensible to the average participant as the written notice it replaces
- Contains as much information as the paper version
- Is written (e.g., e-mail or Website) rather than oral (e.g., automated telephone system) if it is complex enough to require writing; the §3405(e)(10)(B) notice is simple enough to be given via telephone, whereas the others require writing
- Advises its recipient that, if he or she wishes, a paper version of the notice will be furnished at no charge; the paper version must be the employee's own copy, which can be saved for reference; posting to a corkboard will not suffice
- Uses any currently available technology, or technology that will be developed in the future, that satisfies the standards

A consent form under §411(a)(11) can be either a written paper document or "an electronic medium reasonably accessible to the participant" (although the latter opens up questions of signature and authentication). The proposal suggests that passwords and/or PINs can be used to make sure that only the participant, and not an unauthorized person, renders the consent.

The IRS declined to use the 12/18/98 proposal as a means of responding to suggestions about electronic media for waivers of the QJSA and QPSA, or for notices rendering a 401(k) plan nondiscriminatory under the safe harbor provision, but noted that guidance will be provided in the future.

T.D. 8873 contains Final Regulations, effective for plan years beginning on or after January 1, 2001, for using electronic media to notify plan participants, and gain their consent, with respect to distributions from the plan. It was published at 65 FR 6001 (2/8/00). Specifically, all of these can legitimately be transmitted electronically to participants, rather than being distributed in print form:

- §411(a)(11) notice of distribution options; right to defer distribution; participant's consent to a distribution
- §402(f) rollover notice
- §3405(e)(10)(B) withholding notice

Furthermore, the plan is allowed to give the §411(a)(11) and 402(f) notices more than 90 days before a distribution, as long as they offer a summary of the requisite notices within the 90-day period before the distribution. Participants must always be given the option of receiving a printed-out version of the electronic notice, and the plan is not allowed to charge them for exercising this option.

Also see IRS Notice 99-1, 1999-2 IRB 8, and Announcement 99-6, 1999-4 IRB 24. The former explains how pension and benefit plans can perform "paperless" administration of tasks such as enrolling participants and designating beneficiaries; the latter allows W-4P forms to be transmitted electronically. Note that these are strictly tax rules; they do not address ERISA issues that arise out of use of electronic communications.

Chapter 15

DISTRIBUTIONS FROM THE PLAN

15.1 INTRODUCTION

T.D. 8794, published at 63 FR 70335 (12/21/98), contains IRS Final and Temporary Regulations for implementing the TRA '97 increase in the possible "cash-out" from $3500 to $5000. That is, although a plan can permit retirees to take their entire interest in the plan in a lump sum, a plan cannot "cash out" (force acceptance of a lump sum) except for very small amounts: IRC §411(a)(11).

> **TIP**
>
> T.D. 8794 generally applies to distributions made on or after 3/22/99, but most of the requirements can be applied retroactively to plan years beginning on or after 8/6/97.

The "look-back" rule is eliminated for most distributions. The look-back rule allowed cash-out of a present value that does not exceed the cash-out limit at the time of the current distribution, without regard to the value of the benefit at an early distribution. But the T.D. 8794 temporary regulations provide that a participant who has commenced distributions of an optional form of benefit is entitled to at least one more payment; and if the present value was greater than $5000 at the beginning of the distribution of the optional form of benefit, then cash-out of the remaining nonforfeitable accrued benefit is not required. The present value is calculated with the interest rate and mortality tables that the plan uses on the annuity starting date.

The calculation of the accrued benefit under §411(a)(7)(B)(i) does not have to include any service with respect to which the employee has already been cashed out at a level below $3500, and that cash-out occurred in connection with the termination of the employee's plan participation. T.D. 8794 temporary regulations provide that a cash-out of up to $5000 can be treated as part of termination of participation, if it could have been made due to termination of participation at a time when the present value was between $3500 and $5000.

It's permissible for a plan to be amended for plan years beginning on or after 8/6/97 to permit cash-out of up to $5000 with respect to benefits accrued before the amendment—even if the plan did not permit cash-outs before the amendment.

Rev.Rul. 2000-36, 2000-31 IRB 140, permits a plan to make the default method of handling involuntary cash-outs a direct rollover as prescribed by §401(a)(31), as long as the plan participants get adequate notice that they can forestall the rollover and get the cash instead.

On July 22, 1999, the PBGC announced a wider use of the Internet to find some 10,000 people entitled to more than $19 million in pension benefits, and issued an online guide, "Finding a Lost Pension." The PBGC has a Pension Search database, including last-known addresses of lost payees; see http://search.pbgc.gov (no www). The agency's intention is for members of the public to be able to go to the database; if they are listed there, they can notify the PBGC, verify their identity, and access the pension benefits (either immediately or at retirement age). A press release about the program is available at http://www.pbgc.gov/pnsrc99.htm.

T.D. 8873 contains Final Regulations, effective for plan years beginning on or after January 1, 2001, for using electronic media to notify plan participants, and gain their consent, with respect to distributions from the plan. It was published at 65 FR 6001 (2/8/00) and in 2000-9 IRB 713. Specifically, the following can legitimately be transmitted electronically to participants, rather than being distributed in print form:

- §411(a)(11) notice of distribution options; right to defer distribution; participant's consent to a distribution
- §402(f) rollover notice
- §3405(e)(10)(B) withholding notice

Furthermore, the plan is allowed to give the §411(a)(11) and 402(f) notices more than 90 days before a distribution, as long as they offer a summary of the requisite notices within the 90-day period before the distribution. Participants must always be given the option of receiving a printed-out version of the electronic notice, and the plan is not allowed to charge them for exercising this option.

Also see IRS Notice 99-1, 1999-2 IRB 8, and Announcement 99-6, 1999-4 IRB 24; the former explains how pension and benefit plans can perform "paperless" administration of tasks such as enrolling participants and designating beneficiaries; the latter allows W-4P forms to be transmitted electronically. Note that these are strictly tax rules; they do not address ERISA issues that arise out of use of electronic communications.

Beneficiary designation is a very important aspect of plan administration, and the plan's administrators need to know the appropriate party to receive distributions.

According to the Northern District of California, it is permissible, and not arbitrary and capricious, to give effect to an unsigned form for changing the beneficiary. In *Bankamerica Pension Plan v. McMath*, 1998 WL 922323 (N.D. Cal. 1998), the lack of signature was clearly an oversight; the participant didn't know that the form wasn't signed, and otherwise followed the requirements for changing the beneficiary.

In March, 2001, the Supreme Court (reversing the state trial court) held that ERISA preempts a Washington State statute calling for automatic revocation of beneficiary designations (for life insurance as well as employee benefits) when the employee spouse and the named beneficiary divorce. The Supreme Court's rationale is that beneficiary designation is a core ERISA area, so state law regulation is preempted. [*Egelhoff v. Egelhoff*, #99-1529, 69 LW 4206 (Sup.Ct. 3/21/01)]

Esden v. Bank of Boston, 229 F.3d 154 (2nd Cir. 2000), a class action against a pension plan, tackles some important issues affecting cash-balance pension plans. (These plans are discussed in more detail at ¶12.4.6.) The plaintiffs alleged that the plan's calculation of lump-sum distributions violated the ERISA anti-forfeiture rule.

The plan projected cash account balances that would be taken as lump sums using an interest rate lower than the minimum interest rate guaranteed by the plan. (The interest rate used for the lump-sum calculation was 4%, well below the 5.5% rate used to accrue interest credits). When the projection was discounted back to present value, participants received less than the actuarial equivalent of the normal balance. Part of the benefit was also contingent on the distribution option chosen, which was alleged to violate ERISA §203(a) and Code §411(a)(2).

The Second Circuit adopted the IRS view (expressed in Notice 96-8, 1996-1 C.B. 359) that "whipsaw," the result of projecting the account value with a rate below the guaranteed rate, violates ERISA because the participant is entitled to the present value of the accrued benefit. According to the Second Circuit, a variable interest rate is permissible as long as it is definitely determinable and does not grant discretion to the employer to set the amount after establishing the plan.

Lyons v. Georgia-Pacific Corp., 2000 Westlaw 1140673 (11th Cir. 8/11/00) holds that the lump sum benefit under a defined benefit plan must be calculated by using the PBGC discount rate to discount the normal retirement benefit to present value. The District Court treated the IRS Regulations about the discount rate (Reg. §1.411(a)-11) as "unreasonable," (66 F.Supp.2d 1328 (N.D. Ga. 1999)), but the Eleventh Circuit upheld their validity. [These cases are discussed in "Whipsawed," http://www.plansponsor.com/content/magazine/Whipsawd.]

15.1.1 [NEW] January 2001 Proposals

On January 17, 2001, the IRS published a Proposed Regulation at 66 FR 3928-3954, relating to the required minimum distributions from qualified plans, IRAs, and 403(b) and 457 (governmental) plans. The Proposal is a substantial simplification of the §401(a)(9) Proposed Regulations issued in 1987.

Under the 1987 schema, if the employee designated a beneficiary before the required beginning date (RBD), that designation could not be changed subsequent to the RBD, even if there were significant planning reasons for the change. Under most circumstances, unless the designated beneficiary was the employee's spouse, distributions of the balance remaining as of the employee's death would have to be completed relatively quickly.

Yet, for many people, it is preferable to "stretch out" the distribution as much as possible, not only to provide an income stream for a longer time, but to reduce the amount of taxable income each year. The Code provides excise tax penalties for failure to take the required minimum distribution (RMD)—there is no penalty for speeding up withdrawals if greater cash flow is desired under the employee's financial plan.

As a tax relief measure, then, the 2001 proposal permits the RMD to be calculated with a single Minimum Distribution Incidental Benefit (MDIB) table, found in Reg. §1.401(a)(9)-(2). It provides for required minimum distributions during the employee's life, ranging from 25.2 years (at age 70) to 1.8 years (at ages 115 and older!).

The same table can be used whether the beneficiary is the spouse, a natural person other than the spouse, or an entity such as a trust or a charity. (Under prior law, choosing a non-natural-person as a beneficiary would require a faster post-death distribution of the balance, because the entity does not have a life expectancy over which the balance could be distributed.)

The table uses a uniform assumption that the beneficiary is 10 years younger than the employee, and calls for distributions over the unisex life expectancy of a person 10 years younger than the employee. However, if the beneficiary is in fact the spouse, and he or she actually is more than 10 years than the employee, MRD calculations can be made based on the actual life expectancy, thus allowing even greater "stretch-out." If the employee does not designate a beneficiary, the RMD is calculated based on the employee's own life expectancy, reduced every year by one year.

As for post-death distributions, the 2001 proposal allows designation of a beneficiary up to the end of the year following the year of the employee's death. The beneficiary can be changed after the RBD. Where it is financially advisable, beneficiaries can cash out small account balances, or disclaim beneficiary status.

In general, distribution is required over the life expectancy of the designated beneficiary, based on the beneficiary's age as of the year of the beneficiary's death. If more than one beneficiary is designated (e.g., "My daughters Ernestine and Clara") then the beneficiary with the shortest life expectancy is treated as the designated beneficiary (whether the employee's death occurs before or after the RBD). Where no beneficiary has been designated as of the end of the year after the employee's death, then the balance must be distributed over five years.

If the employee is also a stockholder who owns 5% or more of the employer corporation's stock, he or she will have an excise tax penalty unless he or she starts receiving RMDs within the calendar year in which he or she reaches age 70 1/2. But employees who are not stockholders, or who own less than 5%, are not required to take RMDs until their actual year of retirement, even if they retire in their mid- to late seventies, or even their eighties.

If a QDRO (Qualified Domestic Relations Order) is in the picture (see below), then the ex-spouse who is entitled to some or all of the benefits will be considered a "spouse," even if the QDRO does not make explicit reference to §§401(a)(11) and 417. This is true even if the employee has more than one ex-spouse. Distributions to the alternate payee named by the QDRO must start by the employee's RBD. However, the calculation will be based on the employee's life expectancy, or on the actual joint life expectancies of the employee and ex-spouse, if the ex-spouse is more than 10 years younger than the employee.

The 2001 proposal is effective for distributions for 2002 and subsequent calendar years. For 2001 and other years before these Proposed Regulations are finalized, the plan sponsors are permitted, but not required, to follow the proposal and adopt the model plan amendment given in the Federal Register. Additional timing issues are addressed in Announcement 2001-18, 2001-10 IRB 791.

15.2 QJSA/QPSA PAYMENTS

Regulations

T.D. 8794, 63 FR 70335 (12/21/98), discussed previously, also affects QJSA/QPSA payments. Consent is required for distribution of any accrued benefit (including QJSA/QPSA); the look-back rule (discussed previously) is repealed.

T.D. 8796 promulgates Final Regulations, effective 12/18/98, for giving notice and receiving consent and elections under Code §§411(a)(11) and 417. It appears at 63 FR 70009 (12/18/98). T.D. 8796 finalizes (at long last!) regulations proposed in 1995.

Before the proposal, Regulation §1.411(a)-11(c) required the participant to be notified of rights at least 30, but not more than 90, days before the annuity starting date. Absent such notice, the participant's consent to a §411(a)(11) distribution would not be valid. The same timing requirement was imposed on waivers of the QJSA.

The Proposed Regulations allowed participants to elect distributions after receiving late notice; the plan would not fail in compliance just because a distribution is made less than 30 days after provision of the notice. In 1996, the Small Business Job Protection Act (P.L. 104-188) amended the Code to permit QJSA explanations to be given *after* the annuity starting date.

The Final Regulations unite the two approaches: It is permissible to start distributions less than 30 days after notice (but more than seven days after the notice). QJSA disclosure can be deferred until after the annuity starting date. However, a participant's election of form of distribution remains revocable until the annuity starting date or seven days postnotice—whichever comes later.

The Department of the Treasury issued REG-109481-99, RIN 1545-AX34, a Notice of Proposed Rulemaking (see http://www.benefitslink.com/taxregs/annstart-proposed-2000.shtml). The Small Business Jobs Protection Act enacted Code §417(a)(7), under which a plan can furnish the explanation of the QJSA and how to waive it after the annuity starting date, as long as the election period extends at least 30 days after the date the explanation is furnished. Effective for plan years beginning on or after January 1, 2002, the QJSA explanation can be furnished on or after the annuity starting date, and the notice how to handle a retroactive annuity starting date (which, however, is available only if the plan provides for it and the participant elects it).

The IRS allowed defined contribution plans to have broader discretion in eliminating unpopular benefit forms (e.g., annuities, in-kind distributions) from defined contribution plans. ["IRS Relaxes Protected Benefit Rules," CIGNA'S Pension Analyst October 2000, http://www.cigna.com/professional.] The sponsor of a defined contribution plan can eliminate the installment and annuity periodic payment options, but money-purchase plans must always offer payment in the form of Qualified Joint and Survivor Annuity (QJSA). 401(k) plans and profit-sharing plans (other than those that hold assets transferred from a pension plan) have leeway to eliminate all of their annuity and installment payouts, and require all balances to be taken in lump-sum form. However, the forms of payment that are eliminated must be "grandfathered"—persons retiring at about the time of the change must be granted access to the payment forms they expected during their careers.

It is permissible to amend the plan to require plan distributions in cash instead of marketable securities other than the employer's own securities—but if the employer adopted the practice of distributing its own securities, it must continue to do so.

There are four permissible ways to move account balances from one plan to another: a direct rollover; an elective transfer of a 100% vested benefit; a "transaction transfer" available only in between defined contribution plans of the same type (i.e., money purchase to money purchase, 401(k) to 401(k), etc.) and only in part of a merger or acquisition; and an "employment change transfer" (for instance, going to work for a different division of the same employer, but where a different pension plan is involved). The first two are traditional, the second newly adopted by the IRS.

Case Law

In a Washington State case [*Gardner v. Gardner*, 2000 Wash.App. LEXIS 2410 (Wash.App. 2000), it was conceded that the employee's surviving spouse, his second wife, was entitled to 50% of his pension, because she did not grant consent under the REA to naming a different beneficiary. The case controlled the disposition of the other 50% of the pension as between the children of his first marriage and the surviving second spouse. He failed to change the beneficiary designation after his divorce; in the divorce decree, the first wife waived her interest in the participant's property. At the time of his death, the first wife was named as primary beneficiary and the children of the first marriage as residual beneficiaries. The surviving spouse produced a subsequent designation form, signed by the decedent but not filed by the plan, naming her as the sole beneficiary.

Washington law revokes beneficiary designations to the ex-spouse when a divorce occurs, as if the non-employee spouse had predeceased the employee spouse, and therefore the surviving spouse was granted 100%, not just 50%, of the pension. But see ¶15.1 for the *Egelhoff* case.

Kopec v. Kopec, 68 LW 1253 (E.D.N.Y. 10/18/99) allows the IRS to levy against the entire balance of an IRA account that an employee-spouse funded with rollovers from a qualified plan. The Eastern District did not accept the employee's wife's argument that she never waived her survivorship interest, and therefore she had a 50% interest in the IRA account. Although her suit was brought under ERISA, the court treated the case as a tax-enforcement case under 26 USC §7426(a)(1), a claim of wrongful levy, which requires proof of title or ownership in the levied property. According to the Eastern District, the wife is still entitled to collect a survivorship annuity from the plan, and therefore she had no ownership interest in the IRA account, and therefore could not object to the IRS levy.

CIGNA Retirement & Investment Services has posted a helpful document, dated August 1999, explaining how to administer survivor benefits in a defined contribution plan. "Survivor Benefit Rules for Defined Contribution Plans" appears at http://www.cigna.com/retirement/sponsor/cpa9908.html.

15.5 ROLLOVERS

IRS Notice 2000-11, 2000-6 IRB 572 (1/21/00) explains how to notify employees when they receive a plan distribution that is eligible to be rolled over. The Notice includes a standard form that can be used by the plan; using the form provides a safe harbor if it is claimed that notice was inadequate.

Also note that, because of IRS Notice 99-5, 1999-3 IRB 10, hardship withdrawals from 401(k) plans cannot be rolled over unless the employee is at least 59½ or has separated from service. Therefore, an in-service hardship distribution is not subject to 20% withholding like other one-time distributions from qualified plans. The employee has the right to waive withholding; if he or she does not, withholding should be done at a 10% rate. This rule took effect 1/1/00, no matter what the plan year is.

15.7 QDROs

If a qualified domestic relations order (QDRO) satisfies ERISA, the plan administrator is required to abide by it, without inquiring as to its acceptability under state law. If the employee is opposed to the terms of the QDRO, he or she must litigate with the ex-spouse in state court, but the plan administrator is not liable for complying with the QDRO [*Blue v. UAL Corp.*, 160 F.3d 383 (7th Cir. 1998)].

Regulatory Guidance

The PWBA's Office of Regulations and Interpretations issued Advisory Opinion 2000-09A on July 12, 2000, providing guidance on ERISA §206(d)(3) issues. Its text can be found at http://www.dol.gov/dol/pwba/public/programs/ori/advisory2000/2000-09a.htm. The opinion explains the proper treatment of an order that names an alternate payee for a survivor benefit under a plan that limits beneficiary designation to a class consisting of the employee's spouse, minor children, and parents—but not including a former spouse.

The benefit is provided in addition to, not instead of, the QJSA. In the situation for which guidance was requested, the participant was married when he retired. He named his spouse as beneficiary of his defined benefit pension plan. He elected, and his wife consented, to take a single life annuity instead of the QJSA. At that time, the participant was also vested in the additional death benefit; he named his then-wife and children as beneficiaries and did not change the designation.

When he divorced, the divorce court assigned part of the retirement benefit to the ex-spouse, and provided that the additional death benefit would go to her. The plan administrator rejected the court order as a non-QDRO, saying that it attempts to require the plan to provide a form of payment (death benefit to ex-spouse) that is not offered by the plan.

However, the PWBA disagreed, stating that under ERISA §206(d)(3)(F), an ex-spouse must be treated as a surviving spouse to the extent provided by a QDRO. Furthermore, §206(d)(3)(B) provides for assignment of all or part of benefits payable with respect to a participant, not just those payable directly to the participant, because Congress' legislative intent was to let state courts and agencies be able to provide for transfer of all employment-related benefits earned by a person getting a divorce.

Under this analysis, the court order was a valid QDRO because the alternate payee had already been named to receive the death benefit, and at the time of the employee's retirement, she was still his spouse and therefore the normal recipient of the benefit.

A PWBA Advisory Opinion dated 9/29/99 (#99-13A, interpreting ERISA §206(d)(3)), gives advice to a plan administrator who wanted to know how to deal with a document that purports to be a QDRO, but which the administrator believes is a sham or at least questionable. In this particular case, the plan was an Employee Stock Option Plan (ESOP) that allows the alternate payee to get an immediate lump sum distribution of whatever plan benefits are assigned under a QDRO. Otherwise, lump sums are distributed only when a participant dies or terminates employment.

The administrator received a series of 16 alleged QDROs (many of them coming from the same lawyer) calling for lump sum distributions from the ESOP, but not referring to the employer's pension plan. The alleged QDROs reported the same address for the alternate payee and the plan participant (i.e., the spouses alleged to be separated or divorced). The administrator also became aware of a publication suggesting sham divorces (or sham marriages followed by sham divorces) as a way to gain access to ESOP balances during continued employment.

The advisory opinion (which can be accessed at http://www.dol.gov/dol/pwba/public/programs/ori/advisory99/99-13a.htm) says that plan administrators have a duty to determine that alleged QDROs really are qualified. "For example, if the plan administrator has received evidence calling into question the validity of an order relating to marital property rights under state domestic relations law, the plan administrator is not free to ignore that information."

If the administrator determines that this evidence is credible, the administrator must make a case-by-case determination of the validity of the order "without inappropriately spending plan assets or inappropriately involving the plan in the state domestic relations proceeding." The opinion suggests that appropriate action could include informing the court that issued the order of its possible invalidity; intervening in a domestic relations proceeding; or even bringing suit. However, an administrator who can't get a response from the court or other agency issuing the order within a reasonable time "may not independently determine that the order is not valid under state law."

At the American Society of Pension Actuaries' 1999 Annual Conference (held October 24-27), representatives of the Department of Labor answered questions posed by conference attendees. A transcript of the session is posted at http://www.aspa.org/govpages/99dolq&a.htm. Several of the questions involved QDROs. According to the DOL representative, the plan may neither impose a direct charge nor debit the plan account for determining whether an order is a valid QDRO, or for administering a QDRO.

Case Law

Where a QDRO transferred a portion of the lifetime annuity but did not specify that the ex-spouse was to be treated as a surviving spouse for the survivor annuity, it was proper for payments to stop after the participant's death: *Dorn v. IBEW*, 2000 Westlaw 530332 (5th Cir. 2000).

A plan participant had two children in a non-marital relationship. In 1981, the children's mother got a paternity and child support judgment with which the father did not comply. In 1991, a court order was issued requiring all pension plans to notify the mother before distributing any funds to the father of the children. In 1994, the IRS served a tax levy of more than $450,000 against the father. The pension plan informed the mother that the father's plan account would soon become payable, and that the IRS had asserted claims.

Before the mother could get a QDRO, the father died, having named someone else as his sole beneficiary. The plan filed an interpleader action to determine how survivor benefits should be distributed. The court gave the mother permission to suspend the interpleader proceedings to finalize the QDRO, under which she was entitled to about $325,000 in child support arrears and attorneys' fees.

The IRS (for reasons not described in the opinion) dropped its claim. The trial court, upheld by the Ninth Circuit, awarded $325,000 to the mother and the $40,000 balance in the plan to the designated beneficiary. According to *Trustees of the Directors Guild of America-Producer Pension Benefit Plans v. Tise,* 2000 U.S. App. LEXIS 31161 (9th Cir. 2000), ERISA does not require a QDRO to be approved before the participant's death, because Congress' intent was to protect ex-spouses and children, even if sometimes the effect is to frustrate the plan participant's own estate plan.

Participants in domestic relations proceedings should be given access to enough information to prepare a valid QDRO, so they should be allowed access to the SPD, other plan documents, and a statement of the participant's benefit entitlements. That way, it is less likely that an obviously invalid order, such as one calling for a form of benefit that the plan does not provide, will be submitted. The plan's determination process, including its schedule for making determinations and its review process, should also be disclosed.

The case of *Emard v. Hughes Aircraft Co.,* 153 F.3d 949 (9th Cir. 1998), involves the common situation in which a divorced employee failed to change the beneficiary designation to reflect remarriage. When the employee died, her surviving husband sued in state court on constructive trust and community property theories. According to the Ninth Circuit, ERISA did not preempt the state-law claims alleging that the failure to change the beneficiary was a mistake. Nor, in this analysis, does California community property law conflict with ERISA, so the widower's claims were allowed to proceed.

The Sixth Circuit took a somewhat different view of a similar case in *Hendon v. DuPont,* 1998 U.S. App. LEXIS 7573 (6th Cir. 1998). The separation agreement required the employee spouse to change the beneficiary designation, but this was not done. The Sixth Circuit said that breach of contract claim involving waiver of plan benefits was preempted by ERISA. Therefore, the plan was justified in distributing the benefits to the ex-spouse.

The Fourth Circuit, in *Metropolitan Life Insurance v. Pettit,* 164 F.3d 857 (4th Cir. 1998), also deemed ERISA to preempt suits to enforce agreements that are not QDROs but that purport to affect life insurance benefits under qualified plans. The Fourth Circuit specifically rejected the constructive trust theory that succeeded in *Emard.*

Who should get the benefits under an ERISA welfare benefits plan is a federal-law question, and therefore, in the Sixth Circuit view, ERISA preempts state-law claims that undue influence was exerted to get an employee to change his designation of beneficiary: *Tinsley v. General Motors,* 227 F.3d 700 (6th Cir. 2000).

Courts have identified at least two strands of analysis in dividing retirement benefits with a QDRO: the "separate interest" and "shared payment" method. The "separate interest" method is typefied by *In re Marriage of Shelstead,* 66 Cal.App.4th 893 (1998).

In this case, when the Shelsteads divorced, the court awarded the non-employee wife a 50% community-property interest in the employee husband's pension plan. The order said that, if the wife died before the husband, she would be able to designate a successor in interest to receive her community-property share. However, the California Court of Appeals determined that this divorce-related order was not a QDRO, because QDROs settle the rights of an alternate payee (i.e., a spouse, ex-spouse, or dependent of the employee spouse). The Shelsteads' order allowed the ex-wife to designate anyone she wanted, not just another alternate payee, so the order could be a valid QDRO.

➠ TIP

It's sensible to cope with the possibility that the non-employee spouse will die first; but to preserve QDRO status, make sure that only other alternate payees can be designated as contingent alternate payees.

If there's a valid QDRO, the alternate payee has to be afforded the status of an ERISA "beneficiary." However, sometimes the alternate payee is entitled to even more protection, as a "participant." If the QDRO is issued when the employee spouse's pension is already in pay status, the "shared payment" method is obligatory, and if the non-employee spouse dies first, his or her share of the QJSA reverts to the surviving employee spouse. The alternate payee is merely a beneficiary, and can only dispose of his or her interest in the plan by naming another alternate beneficiary as contingent alternate beneficiary in the QDRO.

However, if the "separate interest" method is available (typically, if the divorce occurs before the benefits are in pay status), the alternate payee's status is closer to that of a plan participant because the alternate payee can choose the form of pension payment. Some forms of payment (for instance, a term-certain annuity) give the payee the right to designate someone else to receive unpaid benefits at the payee's death. In this instance, the recipient is not named in the QDRO, which merely gives the non-employee spouse access to a separate interest in the plan.

In a defined contribution plan (including a 401(k) plan), the alternate payee always gets a separate interest. If the alternate payee receives a lump sum, he or she can dispose of it however he or she wishes. It's probably permissible for the QDRO to be drafted to allow the alternate payee to designate someone to receive the lump sum if he or she dies between the time that the QDRO is entered and the time the plan actually disburses the lump sum. [Resource: Darren J. Goodman, "Transferring the Alternate Payee's Retirement Benefits at Death: A Look at *Shelstead*," http://www.qdroprep.com/benefit.htm.]

These concepts came into play in the case of *Rich v. Southern California IBEW-NECA Pension Plan*, 1999 Daily Journal D.A.R. 6965 (Cal.App. 1999). [Darren J.

Goodman discusses this case in "Pension Plan Ordered to Restore Full Benefits to Participant at Alternate Payee's Death," http://www.qdroprep.com/pension.htm.] The QDRO directed that the community property portion of the employee spouse's $962/month pension be equally divided between employee and non-employee spouses, with payments continuing until the death of one of them. The non-employee spouse died in 1997, and the employee spouse applied to the plan to receive the entire benefit.

At trial, the employee spouse lost, based on the court's holding that the non-employee spouse had received a separate interest in the plan. But the appellate court disagreed, treating the QDRO as an order to pay the entire amount to the employee spouse for his life, then divide the benefit in half and pay half to the alternate payee. In other words, it was a shared payment, not a separate interest, division.

For the related concept of QMCSOs (Qualified Medical Child Support Orders), see HHS/DOL Final Rule on National Medical Child Support Notice, 65 FR 82128 (DOL) and 65 FR 72154 (HHS), both published on December 27, 2000. The Final Rule was supposed to be effective January 26, 2001 for notices received after that date, but because of the Bush Administration suspension of effectiveness of late-Clinton-era regulations, the PWBA published a notice in the January 26, 2001 Federal Register delaying the effective date until March 27, 2001. (State agencies have an obligation to start using the revised notice as of October 1, 2001 to enforce medical child support orders, but can use it earlier if they prefer.) See ¶9.18 for more on QMCSOs.

15.9 ANTI-ALIENATION RULES

ERISA preempts Illinois' Uniform Disposition of Unclaimed Property Act with respect to $125,000 in unclaimed pension benefits that Illinois said reverted to the state treasury. In the view of the Seventh Circuit, as expressed in *Commonwealth Edison Co. v. Vega*, 1999 WL 212210 (7th Cir. 1999), unclaimed benefits remain plan assets until they are accessed by a participant or beneficiary. If the state did have the right to appropriate unclaimed benefits, it would be violating ERISA by assuming a plan management role, in its own interests and contrary to the interests of plan participants and beneficiaries.

Although ERISA does include anti-alienation provisions, once benefits have been distributed in accordance with the plan, ERISA does not prevent the imposition of a constructive trust, for instance, when a family court order has been violated: *Central States Southeast & Southwest Areas Pension Fund v. Howell*, 227 F.3d 672 (6th Cir. 2000), also discussed at ¶10.4.

Chapter 16

PLAN TERMINATION

16.2 THE PBGC'S ROLE

For plans terminating in 2001, the PBGC has amended the Table of Maximum Guaranteed Benefits. The PBGC's monthly maximum guarantee for terminations in that year is $3,392.05 (i.e., $40,704.60/year), up from $3221.59 and $38,659.08, respectively, for terminations in 2000. See http://www.pbgc.gov/newsroom/press_releases/2000/pr01_05.htm. Another set of annually-updated PBGC figures, appearing at 65 FR 75165 (12/11/00), should be used in the year 2001 to evaluate the benefits of plans going through an involuntary or distress termination. The calculation required by 29 CFR Part 4044, Appendix D, determines the likelihood (low/medium/high) that a participant will retire early in various years. The calculation involves the Unreduced Retirement Age (URA): either normal retirement age (NRA) or the earliest age at which pension benefits are payable without actuarial reduction, whichever is earlier.

Year of Retirement	Low	Medium	High
2002	<442	442-1867	>1867
2003	<454	454-1915	>1915
2004	<466	466-1965	>1965
2005	<478	478-2016	>2016
2006	<516	516-2177	>2177
2007	<503	503-2122	>2122
2008	<516	516-2177	>2177
2009	<530	530-2234	>2234
2010	<543	543-2292	>2292
2011, later	<557	557-2352	>2352

For information about PBGC operations and the availability of benefits after a plan termination, see the *Pension Insurance Data Book 1999*, which can be accessed at http://www.pbgc.gov/publications/databooks/databook99.pdf.

When a single-employer plan terminates and its assets are insufficient to pay all the benefits, the PBGC intervenes. The PBGC has the power to assess penalties if the employer was late in premium payments or omitted to provide proper notices to employees.

A PBGC Proposed Rule, RIN 1212-AA95 (66 FR 2857; see http://www.benefitslink.com/pbgcregs/4071-proposed-2001.shtml) centralizes all the PBGC rules about penalties, putting them into 29 CFR Parts 4003, 4007, and 4071.

Under the proposal, the PBGC will waive all or part of a late payment penalty if the employer has reasonable cause for lateness (e.g., some kind of emergency). The penalty can be waived on a discretionary basis even if reasonable cause for the delay is not shown.

The PBGC's debt collection rules (29 CFR Part 4903) allow the agency to collect penalties from amounts (e.g., tax refunds) that the federal government owes the employer. But under the proposal, this collection technique can be waived if there is a safe harbor or other law or regulation calling for waiver; if the employer had reasonable cause not to pay, or to make only a partial payment; if the employer failed to pay because it interpreted the law inaccurately; or if collection would violate the purposes of ERISA (for instance, if the law changed just before a payment was made).

Section 32 of the proposal describes reasonable cause as circumstances beyond the employer's control, that could not have been avoided by exercising ordinary care and prudence. The larger the organization and the more staff it has, the higher the standard of care it will be held to. The larger the premium owed to the government, the more effort the employer will be expected to make to see that it is submitted on time!

Section 34 gives the definition of "reasonable cause" for this purpose; it includes the absence of the person who was supposed to make the payment; fire or other casualty; and reasonable reliance on incorrect advice given by the PBGC, either orally or in writing.

16.3 TERMINATION TYPES

The case of *Hughes Aircraft Co. v. Jacobson*, #97-1287, 525 U.S. 432 (Sup.Ct. 1999), discussed in connection with several other pension issues, also affects plan termination. *Hughes* involves a plan partially funded by mandatory employee contributions. At a time when the plan had a surplus, the employer suspended its own contributions and created a new, noncontributory plan for new plan participants. Participants in the existing plan charged the employer with ERISA violations in amending the plan. However, the alteration in plan structure did not constitute a voluntary termination under ERISA §4041(a)(1), and employees were not entitled to an order terminating the plan involuntarily.

The employees tried—but failed—to use a "wasting trust" theory: that the original plan was, in effect, wound up because it satisfied all of its objectives. The Supreme Court pointed out that this theory is inconsistent with ERISA's elaborate termination provisions.

Neither a standard nor a distress termination is appropriate as long as a plan continues to provide benefits to participants and accumulate funds for future benefit payments. The Hughes plan could not be characterized as "an enfeebled plan whose membership has dwindled to a mere remnant that would no longer benefit from the Plan's administration." Even though management exercised permissible discretion to change the plan terms, a viable plan remained.

A Final Rule, applicable to amendments adopted on or after 12/12/98, is published at 63 FR 68676 (12/14/98). It contains an example showing the application of ERISA §204(h) to some situations of defined benefit plans that cannot be terminated on the proposed termination date because of failure to satisfy all ERISA Title IV requirements.

If all of the requirements of Title IV are not satisfied, accruals will still cease if an amendment has been adopted that ceases accruals as of a specified date and §204(h) notice of that amendment, including a statement of its effective date, is given.

Question 16 in the Final Rule's Q&A explains that an amendment providing for the cessation of benefit accruals on a specified future date and for the termination of a plan is subject to §204(h). If the plan is terminated in accordance with ERISA Title IV, it is deemed to have satisfied §204(h) no later than its termination date, so no additional benefits have to accrue after the date of the termination. But if the amendment reducing future accruals is effective earlier than the termination date, then §204(h) does apply.

Also see 63 FR 38305 (7/16/98), explaining how to implement the increased "cash-out" that is now permitted when a plan terminates. That is, very small balances under $5000 (not just the earlier limit of $3500) can be distributed in lump sum form even if a lump sum is not requested by the participant.

PBGC No. 01-14 [12/22/00, reprinted at 65 FR 81456 (12/26/00)] is the PBGC's announcement of regulatory changes it proposes for payments to participants of terminated defined benefit plans taken over the PBGC. Under the proposal, plan participants would be allowed to select alternative annuity benefit forms (with the consent of the spouses of married participants). Furthermore, non-spouses could be designated as beneficiaries. The proposal distinguishes between separation from service and retirement, and determines who will inherit benefits due to a deceased participant. The proposal also simplifies the application of the maximum guaranteed benefit rules if the same individual is a plan participant but is also entitled to plan benefits as a survivor of another participant (i.e., married co-workers).

The PBGC proposes to make benefits available as straight life annuities and annuities for five, ten, or fifteen years certain and continuous. The proposal also refers to joint and 50, 75, or 100% survivor annuities and joint and 50% survivor "pop-up" annuities (the participant's benefit pops up to the unreduced level if the beneficiary dies before the participant). For joint life annuities, both parties would have to be natural persons, not, e.g., trusts or charities.

The PBGC's intention is to make all these forms available when the plan terminates, even if some of these options were not available when the plan was operating. The PBGC would have the power to add additional benefit payment forms by promulgating further regulations—although it does not anticipate doing so for particular plans, only overall.

The proposal defines the Earliest PBGC Retirement Date (EPRD), a concept that is needed because some plans allow the receipt of a lump sum significantly before normal retirement age. The EPRD is the earliest retirement date under ERISA Title IV—i.e., the earliest date to receive an immediate annuity (or lump sum, if the plan permits this). The EPRD is either the earliest annuity date or, for dates before age 55, either 55 or the time when the participant could retire, given consideration of all facts and circumstances.

The proposal calls for the PBGC to adjust the survivor's benefit under a joint and survivor annuity if the agency determines that there was an underpayment or overpayment as of the time of the first spouse's death.

Under current law, the PBGC imposes an aggregate limit on guaranteed benefits in three situations: the same person's benefits payable under multiple plans; the same person's benefits with respect to two or more participants; and benefits with respect to a participant who has more than one beneficiary. Under the proposal, the PBGC will waive the limit with respect to a person who is dually entitled to benefits as both worker and survivor, but aggregation will continue for multiple beneficiaries, who will have to divide the benefit.

Revenue Procedure 2000-17, 2000-11 IRB 766 explains how a plan can get a waiver of the 100% tax imposed by Code §4971(b) when accumulated funding deficiencies under §412 remain even after the 10% tax has been imposed. The Secretary of the Treasury can waive the 100% tax for certain terminated single-employer plans (even if the accumulated funding deficiency has not been reduced to zero). To qualify for the waiver, the plan must be terminated in a standard termination. All the Series 5500 forms must have been filed for all years, and any §4971(a) excise taxes must be paid up. Furthermore, the plan participants must not be entitled to any portion of whatever residual assets remain after the plan has satisfied its liability to participants and beneficiaries.

According to the Seventh Circuit, a plaintiff who alleges that he was entitled to full vesting of his account balances because the plan underwent a partial termination is entitled to use events from more than one plan year to establish that termination occurred. [*Matz v. Household International Tax Reduction Investment Plan*, 2000 U.S. App. LEXIS 23601 (7th Cir. 2000), discussed in "Partial Termination May

Occur Over Multiple Plan Years, Court Affirms," BenefitsLink 11/17/00; see *Sea Ray v. Robinson*, 164 F.3d 981 (6th Cir. 1999).]

The Sixth Circuit's rationale is that, if review was limited to a single year, employers would be able to escape liability by terminating some participants in late December, others in early January. The Seventh Circuit also required counting of both vested and nonvested participants to determine whether a partial termination occurred.

16.5 PLAN REVERSIONS

In *Shepley v. New Coleman Holdings Inc.*, 1999 WL 186182 (2nd Cir. 1999), a defined benefit plan was 100% employer-funded (i.e., no employee contributions were accepted). The employer terminated the plan and satisfied all of its liabilities; $14 million remained. Participants brought suit under ERISA §1344(d)(1)(C) to prevent the money from reverting to the employer. They were successful at the District Court level, but the Second Circuit ruled in favor of the employer, given that the plan documents authorized reversion of funds remaining after termination.

16.9 DISCLOSURE TO PARTICIPANTS

The PWBA Final Rule governing the content of Summary Plan Descriptions (SPDs) furnished to plan participants (65 FR 70226-70244 (11/21/00) requires that the document include, along with a great deal of other information:

- A summary of the plan's provisions authorizing the sponsor, or other party, to terminate the plan or eliminate some or all benefits
- Circumstances that might trigger termination or benefit elimination
- The benefits, rights and obligations of plan participants and beneficiaries if and when the plan is terminated. For pension plan SPDs only, an explanation of the accrual and vesting consequences of termination must be given—vesting is not an issue in welfare plan SPDs because such benefits do not vest.
- Disposition of plan assets upon termination.

Chapter 17

ERISA ENFORCEMENT

17.2 WHO IS A FIDUCIARY?

The scope of potential liability was expanded by a Supreme Court case, *Harris Trust v. Salomon Brothers,* #99-579, 530 U.S. 238 (Sup.Ct. 2000). The question, answered in the affirmative, is whether a party that is an ERISA party in interest, but not a fiduciary (e.g., a plan's employees and service providers) can be enjoined by a court or required to make restitution if the plan loses because the party in interest engaged in a prohibited transaction.

ERISA does not permit a fiduciary's investment client to sue the fiduciary for drafting a contract containing a noncompete clause that keeps an ex-employee of the fiduciary from providing independent services for the plaintiff [*Frank Russell Co. v. Wellington Management Co.,* 154 F.3d 97 (3rd Cir. 1998)].

The case arose when an investment capital manager quit his job to open up his own, competing firm. His employment agreement with the former employer barred him from doing business with the ex-employer's clients for five years. The plaintiff was a company that canceled its contract with the former employer in order to have the capital manager take care of its account. The plaintiff sought an injunction against enforcement of the noncompete clause.

Although the District Court granted a preliminary injunction, the Third Circuit reversed, finding that the plaintiff was unable to prove it was at risk of irreparable harm. The plaintiff charged the ex-employer with a violation of its ERISA fiduciary duty in accepting the plaintiff as a client without informing it of the noncompete clause. The Third Circuit was not persuaded by this argument and refused to impose additional fiduciary duties in situations not involving employees.

An investment broker and investment partnerships are not fiduciaries of a profit-sharing plan, and therefore are not liable for unanticipated taxes on the plan investments in a suit brought by the plan trustee. *Pedre Co. v. Robins,* 984 F.Supp. 235

(S.D.N.Y. 1997), reaches this result because the broker's role was purely administrative, with no fiduciary duties. In any event, there could have been no breach of fiduciary duty, because the broker made legal investments and the taxes were not attributable to fraud.

Harold Ives Trucking Co. v. Spradley & Coker Inc., 178 F.3d 523 (8th Cir. 1999) holds that, even though the service contract had language to the contrary, a Third Party Administrator (TPA) became a fiduciary by making an independent determination that a rehab facility was covered under the EGHP.

The stop-loss insurance carrier informed the TPA that excess coverage was not available for that facility. The TPA did not consult the plan administrator. The plan sued the TPA for fiduciary breach and breach of contract (the service agreement). The Eighth Circuit ruled that the TPA became a fiduciary by assuming the discretion to overrule the stop-loss carrier's coverage decision, and by failing to inform the plan administrator. Keeping the plan administrator out of the loop prevented the plan from appealing to the stop-loss carrier, and saddled it with $70,000 in rehab bills. The employer had a legal right to sue the TPA to recover this loss.

A consulting firm retained to prepare financial reports did not have, and did not assume, discretionary authority over the plan, and thus did not have fiduciary liability for not disclosing that the plan trustee had embezzled from the plan: *CSA 401(k) Plan v. Pension Professionals, Inc.*, 68 LW 1327 (9th Cir. 11/13/99). (DOL regulations state clearly that mere performance of consulting services does not make a firm a fiduciary.) The facts of the case are that when the firm discovered the wrongdoing, it conditioned its future services on the trustee repaying the money and disclosing to plan participants how and why underfunding had occurred. The trustee failed to do this, and the firm resigned as the plan's TPA.

A plan participant who claims that his or her lump sum benefits were miscalculated can only sue the employer for ERISA equitable relief if the employer was a fiduciary vis-à-vis the plan (e.g., performed administrative functions, not just sponsoring the plan). And if the plan, not the employer, has the primary responsibility for making the payments, it's inappropriate to sue the employer to collect additional benefits. See *Esden v. Bank of Boston*, 5 F.Supp.2d 214 (D. Vt. 1998). That is, equitable relief can only be ordered against a fiduciary.

The holder of a self-directed IRA was in complete control of the account, and therefore the brokerage firm that oversaw the account was not a fiduciary, and not liable for the holder's failure to designate his sister as beneficiary of the account: *Holtz v. JJB Hilliard W.L. Lyons Inc.*, 185 F.3d 732 (7th Cir. 7/15/99).

According to the plaintiff in *Group Dekko Services LLC v. Miller*, 717 N.E.2d 967 (Ind.App. 1999), she was fired because she protested the mishandling of an employee's benefit claim. (The plaintiff was a benefits administrator, afraid that she would be considered an ERISA fiduciary and held liable for the claim handling.) The court held that state wrongful discharge claims were preempted by ERISA, because determining her status as a fiduciary requires interpretation of the plan.

The Pension and Welfare Benefits Administration published a Final Rule on January 5, 2000 (65 FR 614) creating a safe harbor for insurance companies that manage pension funds as part of their general accounts. Insurance policies do become plan assets, but for policies issued on or before 12/31/98, the insurance company will not be an ERISA fiduciary as to the plan, if the insurer provides adequate annual disclosure to plan participants. Furthermore, if the insurer unilaterally modifies the policy in a way that has a material adverse effect on the policyholder, 60 days' advance notice is required.

17.3 FIDUCIARY DUTY

In mid-2000, the Supreme Court decided, in *Pegram v. Herdrich*, #98-1949, 530 U.S. 211 (Sup.Ct. 2000) that an HMO is not acting as a fiduciary when, acting through its doctors, it makes a "mixed" decision about medical treatment and health plan eligibility. Therefore, even if the patients are accurate in their contention that the plan denied necessary treatments in order to enhance its profitability, they have not stated a cause of action for breach of fiduciary duty.

A health plan can recover the "reasonable" value of services provided to injured employees, defined as the fee-for-service fee schedule. Its right of subrogation is not limited to the actual amount paid to the health care providers because of the discounted rates paid by health plans: *Ince v. Aetna Health Management Inc.*, 1999 U.S. App. LEXIS 6352 (8th Cir. 4/9/99).

Several employees sued Aetna Health Management, which processed the claims, charging that Aetna (and the plan's HMO, MedCenters Health Care) violated their ERISA fiduciary duty by receiving subrogation in excess of the cost of the benefits. The Eighth Circuit didn't agree. Although it was possible that Aetna's control over plan administration made it a fiduciary, it was not a violation of duty to recover the "reasonable value" of the services. This case is discussed in Thompson's *Coordination of Benefits Handbook*: see http://ww.thompson.com/tpg/pen_ben/cobs/cobsjuly99.html.

According to a letter issued by the Department of Labor on February 19, 1998, it may constitute a breach of fiduciary duty for health plan trustees to select health providers purely because they place the lowest bid, without consideration of quality. In this context, quality refers to issues such as the scope of the provider; the qualifications of its doctors; how easy it will be for plan beneficiaries to get access to the doctors; ratings and accreditation; appeals of coverage denials; and consumer satisfaction scores the provider has achieved elsewhere. (See RIA *Compensation and Benefits Update*, 3/25/98, p. 3.)

A Ninth Circuit case from late 2000 arose when a participant's claim for health benefits was denied as relating to a pre-existing condition. He lost his internal appeal of the denial. The participant was not informed that his sole further redress was to file for arbitration within 60 days—although he would have known this if he had consulted the SPD.

According to the court [*Chappel v. Laboratory Corp. of America*, 69 LW 1312 (9th Cir. 11/14/00)] failure to disclose the arbitration requirement violated ERISA

§404(a), which obligates fiduciaries to act solely in the interests of plan participants and beneficiaries. The fiduciary must provide written notice of the steps that must be taken to invoke arbitration. The arbitration clause was held to be enforceable, but the case was sent back to the District Court to handle the fiduciary breach claim against the plan administrator.

Employees sued for breach of fiduciary duty when their employer decided to terminate a retirement plan. According to the Eastern District of Louisiana, amendment or termination of a plan is not a fiduciary action (and therefore there can be no breach) if the plan has no accrued or vested benefits. However, the employer could not get summary judgment—the case had to be tried to find out if the employees were correct in their claim to have vested benefit rights. [*Musmeci v. Schwegmann Giant Super Markets*, 2000 Westlaw 798437 (E.D. La. 2000).]

"Serious consideration" of a new early retirement plan, requiring disclosure to potential early retirees (who need this information to decide whether to accept retirement incentives under existing plans or to hold out for a superior new package), occurs when senior managers discuss the proposal for purposes of implementation.

Using this test, which derives from *Fischer v. Philadelphia Electric Co.*, 96 F.3d 1533 (3rd Cir. 1996), the Sixth Circuit permitted a lawsuit for breach of fiduciary duty by a group of retirees who alleged that they were deprived of information about a later, superior retirement plan [*McAuley v. IBM Corp.*, 165 F.3d 1038 (6th Cir. 1/22/99)].

TIP

If silence could be harmful, a benefit plan administrator has a fiduciary duty to give complete and accurate information about the plan, even if the beneficiary hasn't asked for the information [*Krohn v. Huron Memorial Hospital*, 173 F.3d 542 (6th Cir. 4/1/99)]. Similarly, it is a fiduciary breach for a plan to inform potential early retirees that lump sum distributions are available, without also giving them information about the Code §415 limitations on rollovers and disclosing that amounts not rolled over are subject to immediate income taxation [*Farr v. U.S. West Communications Inc.*, 58 F.3d 1361 (9th Cir. 1998)]. The fiduciaries' common-law duty of loyalty requires honest, fair dealing with plan participants, so complete rather than partial information must be given.

Bins v. Exxon Co., 189 F.3d 929 (9th Cir. 8/30/99): also adopts the *Fischer* "serious consideration" test, i.e., disclosure of proposals that are material to the retirement decision is required even if the employee doesn't ask. On rehearing (220 F.3d 1042, 9th Cir. 2000), the Ninth Circuit requirement that the fiduciary must give complete and accurate information about plan changes under "serious consideration," in response to employee queries, was affirmed. But the Ninth Circuit did not impose a duty to volunteer information absent an inquiry, and did not require the employer to report changes to an employee who inquired in the past, unless the employer volunteered to supply updated information.

Similarly, *Hudson v. General Dynamics Corp.*, 69 LW 1304 (D.Conn. 9/28/00) finds a breach of fiduciary duty with respect to two employees who inquired, but were not told that an early retirement program was under serious consideration—but dismisses the claims of 87 other employees who either failed to ask, or whose inquiries preceded the company's serious consideration of the superior program.

Wayne v. Pacific Bell, 189 F.3d 982 (9th Cir. 1999) holds that discussion of a particular early retirement proposal during collective bargaining is tantamount to serious consideration, even if it isn't adopted, therefore the company has an affirmative duty to inform employees accurately about the proposal accepted by the union because of its materiality to the timing of retirement.

In 1991, Burlington Northern decided to use a voluntary severance plan to reduce its workforce. It was hard to get volunteers for past programs, because workers assumed that waiting would give them access to a better deal. The SPD for this program said that management had not decided whether additional offers would be made, "but if there are any additional plans, the benefits would not be as good as those contained in this plan." However, the SPD did reserve the sponsor's right to amend and/or terminate the plan at any time.

In 1995, the company did adopt a more generous plan. The Fifth Circuit suit [*McCall v. Burlington Northern*, #99-11147 (5th Cir. 12/26/00)] was brought by employees suing the employer, the plan, and the fiduciaries of the plan. Their contention was that they were entitled to the more generous benefits provided by the 1995 plan. They also added an ERISA §510 claim, alleging that the SPD was designed to mislead them in order to induce their resignation and surrender of better future benefits.

The District Court, affirmed by the Fifth Circuit, granted summary judgment for the defendants. There was no fiduciary breach, because the 1991 statement was truthful when it was made. The plan administrator did not abuse discretion by refusing to grant pre-1995 retirees the superior benefits under the 1995 plan. Although the 1991 SPD did say that benefits would not be enhanced, it did not specify remedies for breach of this pledge, and the employer showed its intent to retain flexibility by including the reservation of the right to change the plan. The §510 claim had to fail because of the determination that there had been no misrepresentation as of the time the original statement was made.

A beneficiary sued the plan fiduciary based on its allegedly inaccurate advice about the tax consequences of a benefit distribution. But this claim was unsuccessful, because the Southern District of West Virginia ruled that it is not a fiduciary breach to distribute benefits in accordance with the participant's own instructions; money already distributed to the participant cannot be paid to her again even if the advice was bad; and she sought compensatory damages that are not available under ERISA: *Glencoe v. TIAA*, 69 F.Supp.2d 849 (S.D.W.V. 1999).

The Ninth Circuit not only found a fiduciary breach, but held a plan manager personally liable for the plan's losses because he used plan assets to buy "inverse floaters," which are complicated derivative securities. In three separate transactions, he bought these extremely illiquid and risky securities, relying on the broker's representations about risk and resale opportunities. The purchases, motivated by trust in the broker, did not satisfy the standard of prudence. Fiduciaries must investigate their purchases in advance; relying on a trusted broker isn't good enough: *Gilbert v. EMG Advisors Inc.*, 1999 US App. LEXIS 4719 (3/8/99).

Gilbert follows the expected course of accusing a fiduciary of being too reckless, and lacking the necessary prudence. *Brown v. American Life Holdings*, 1999 US App LEXIS 21047 (8th Cir. 9/3/99) takes the opposite tack.

The plaintiff accused the administrative committee of an ESOP, the plan sponsor, and the trustees holding plan assets of committing a breach of fiduciary duty by investing too **conservatively**. The statute of limitations for a breach of fiduciary duty claim is either six years from the date of the breach, or three years from plaintiff's acquiring actual knowledge of the breach. The plaintiff in *Brown*'s position was that he knew about the transactions long before he knew that they breached the fiduciary duty.

However, the Eighth Circuit did not find this argument compelling, holding that he was aware of the breach more than three years before filing suit. Nor did the court believe that the fiduciaries had breached their duty. ESOPs are supposed to have significant investment flexibility, and are not required to diversify their portfolios. They are also exempt from normal ERISA bans on self-dealing and conflict of interest.

However, fiduciaries are not liable merely because an adverse consequence ensued under their stewardship. An employer's purchase of Guaranteed Investment Certificates (GICs) for individual pension accounts, from a company that was eventually seized by regulators, was not a breach of the employer's fiduciary duty. *In re Unisys Savings Plan Litigation*, 173 F.3d 145 (3rd Cir. 3/22/99) holds that the employer acted with adequate prudence in that it delegated investment responsibility to appropriate parties, who made an adequate investigation before recommending the ill-starred purchase. *Bussian v. RJR Nabisco Inc.*, 21 F.Supp. 2d 680 (S.D. Tex. 1998), reaches a similar conclusion for annuities purchased from an insurer that later became bankrupt.

Well, that's why they put erasers on pencils. If the sponsor is unaware of the error, it is not a breach of fiduciary duty for the sponsor to cite incorrect benefit figures from an actuary's report in a letter to a participant. If the participant knew the figure was inaccurate, but the sponsor didn't, it's permissible for the sponsor to make payments based on the actuary s figure rather than the (higher) true figure. See *Easa v. FTD Ass'n*, 5 F.Supp. 2d 522 (E.D. Mich. 1998). As the proverb says, "Love thy neighbor—but cut the cards." Double-check all figures and assumptions, even if a mistake won't land you in court.

An employee got a statement of benefits from her employer, showing a projected retirement benefit of $1672.86 a month. She decided to keep working rather than accept an enhanced early retirement benefit of $2139.40 a month. Three years later, the HR department told her that her actual retirement benefit would be about $200 a month lower than projected. The Eastern District of Pennsylvania dismissed all her claims (of breach of contract, estoppel, and breach of fiduciary duty): *Hofsas v. Montgomery Hospital Medical Center*, 2000 U.S. Dist. LEXIS 14602 (E.D. Pa. 2000).

The breach of contract claim failed because an ERISA plan participant's rights depend on the terms of the plan, which only entitled her to the lower benefit figure. There were no extraordinary circumstances that would estop the employer from following the terms of the plan, and a good-faith mistake in computation does not constitute a breach of fiduciary duty.

In that retiree health benefits do not vest at retirement, it is not a breach of fiduciary duty to transfer the benefit obligation to a new company formed in the spin-off of a corporate division [*Sengpiel v. B.F. Goodrich Co.*, 156 F.3d 660 (6th Cir. 1998), *cert. denied* 119 S.Ct. 1249].

17.6 PENALTIES FOR FIDUCIARY BREACH

In mid-2000, the Supreme Court ruled that a party in interest to a prohibited transaction with a plan can be liable under ERISA §502(a)(3) (civil action for relief, brought by a participant, beneficiary, or fiduciary)—even if the defendant is not a fiduciary: *Harris Trust v. Salomon Brothers*, #99-579, 530 U.S. 238 (Sup.Ct. 2000).

Unless the crime involved an ERISA pension plan, and restitution to the plan is ordered, a federal court sentencing a person convicted of a crime does not have the power to order that undistributed funds from the defendant's pension plan be used to pay restitution: *U.S. v. Jackson*, No. 99-50302 (9th Cir. 10/12/00); see http://laws.findlaw.com/9th/9950302.html.

A late 1997 case, *Schmidt v. Sheet Metal Workers' National Pension Fund*, 128 F.3d 541(7th Cir. 1997), arose when a plan employee mailed the wrong form to a participant. Without the correct form, the participant was unable to designate the desired beneficiary. The Seventh Circuit ruled that the plan's trustees were not guilty of fiduciary breach. They weren't responsible for the mistake, and the plan documents and SPD were correct.

17.14 ENFORCEMENT UNDER ERISA SECTION 502

A lawyer employed as a litigator underwent heart surgery and was unable to return to work. His disability benefits were terminated when one doctor said that his inability to work was motivational in nature, not physical. Several other doctors certified his disability. The insurer affirmed the benefits cut-off, on the grounds that litigation is sedentary work suitable for a recuperating heart patient. The Ninth Circuit, in *Kearney v. Standard Insurance Co.*, 175 F.3d 1084 (9th Cir. 1998), treated the plan, which required "satisfactory proof" of disability but did not explicitly give discretionary authority to the plan administrator, as one subject to objective standards and de novo review. Because there were material issues of fact as to the nature of a litigator's job, and the plaintiff's ability to perform it, the case had to proceed to trial; it could not be resolved by summary judgment.

According to the Third Circuit, a grant of interest on benefits wrongfully withheld for a while, but eventually paid, constitutes "other appropriate equitable relief," which can properly be the subject of an ERISA §502(a)(3)(B) suit [*Fotta v. Trustees of UMW Health Retirement Fund*, 165 F.3d 209 (3rd Cir. 1998)].

When benefits are denied under a long-term disability plan, and the participant sues under §502(a)(3), the participant cannot recover the expenses of medical treatment, because these are extracontractual, compensatory damages of the type ruled out by *Mertens* [*Rogers v. Hartford Life & Accident Ins. Co.*, 167 F.3d 933 (5th Cir. 1999)].

But note that, in the view of the Eighth Circuit, ERISA doesn't provide any additional relief for a plan participant who had to bring suit, and wait three and a half years, to collect payment under his 401(k) plan. Because he got the money eventually, and ERISA §502(a)(3) provides only equitable relief, and not compensatory damages, for breach of fiduciary duty, the court had no relief to grant: *Kerr v. Charles V. Vatterott & Co.*, 184 F.3d 939 (8th Cir. 7/12/99).

The DOL can bring suit under §502(a)(5) for equitable relief for employees misclassified as project, supplementary, or temporary rather than permanent, notwithstanding the employees' own rights to use ERISA administrative proceedings to obtain benefits: *Herman v. Time Warner*, 1999 WL 691904 (S.D.N.Y. 1999).

A benefit plan tried (but failed) with a creative theory in *Cement Masons Health & Welfare Trust Fund v. Stone*, 68 LW 1357 (9th Cir. 12/9/99). The plan tried to use ERISA's enforcement provisions to recover the amount it had paid for the medical care of a deceased worker. The plan sought recovery from the decedent's wife, who settled cases related to his death. It's true that 29 USC §1132(a)(3) allows a participant, beneficiary, or fiduciary to get an injunction or other equitable relief, but not to be reimbursed under a contract theory. This case also holds that, in an ERISA case where the plaintiff is not entitled to any equitable remedy, the case is dismissed on its merits, not for lack of subject matter jurisdiction.

ERISA does not allow extracontractual damages (such as paying medical bills to put an employee in the position he or she would have been in if the employer had lived up to its obligations) when benefits are wrongfully denied under an ERISA plan: *Rogers v. Hartford Life & Accident Insurance Co.*, 167 F.3d 933 (5th Cir. 1999). (In this case, it was a long-term disability plan.) After all, *Mertens* rules out compensatory damages, whether or not they are contractual.

17.15 [NEW] SECTION 510

ERISA §510 makes it unlawful to interfere with ERISA rights, or to discharge or discriminate against a plan participant for exercising ERISA rights. The defendant corporation in *Williams v. Mack Trucks, Inc.*, 2000 U.S. Dist. LEXIS 18758 (E.D.Pa.

2000) closed a plant, then later rehired some of the displaced employees. The corporation adopted a "pension liability avoidance policy" that denied rehiring to former employees who had credited service under the pension plan.

A group of ex-employees brought suit under §510, but lost. According to the Eastern District of Pennsylvania, the employer was not liable under §510, because that section requires an ongoing employment relationship, and thus does not apply to initial hires or re-hires.

17.16 OTHER ENFORCEMENT ISSUES

ERISA gives the federal courts subject-matter jurisdiction to hear interpleader actions (a case in which the holder of disputed property asks the court for guidance about what to do with the property) where an insurance company can't determine who is the proper beneficiary under a benefit plan. The insurance company is serving as a fiduciary, and interpleader is one of the types of equitable relief that can be granted to a fiduciary in order to enforce the terms of the plan: *Aetna Life Ins. v. Bayona*, 227 F.3d 1070 (9th Cir. 2000).

Schleibaum v. Kmart Corp., 153 F.3d 496 (7th Cir. 1998), involves a claim that the employer breached ERISA by failing to give adequate notice of benefit denial when it ceased payment of life insurance on behalf of an ex-employee whom the employer claimed was not permanently and totally disabled. After the ex-employee's death, his family sued under ERISA §503 (failure to provide mandated appeal information).

The defendant prevailed at the District Court level; the court took the position that the plaintiff should simply have bought his own insurance after the denial. The Seventh Circuit, however, found for the plaintiffs. The Seventh Circuit's position was that the employee should not have been forced to purchase the coverage.

Furthermore, the Seventh Circuit held that a plaintiff in such a situation is not required to mitigate (reduce) damages by investigating his or her rights, given that the employer controls information about the benefit plan. The case was remanded for determination as to whether the decedent was, indeed, disabled when the life insurance benefits were cut off. If so, the Seventh Circuit held the damages to be the face value of the insurance policy that should have been provided, not just the premiums the ex-employee would have paid under an individual conversion policy.

In general, standing to sue under ERISA (e.g., as a participant or beneficiary) is measured as of the time the suit is filed. However, in *McBride v. PLM Int'l Inc.*, 1999 WL 355936 (9th Cir. 1999), a whistleblower employee objected to the termination of an ESOP plan and to using the value of common rather than preferred stock to make termination distributions from the ESOP.

According to the Ninth Circuit, this employee was a plan participant, despite being fired and despite the termination of the plan. Therefore, he was a whistleblower, as defined by ERISA §1140, with standing to sue. As the Ninth Circuit pointed out, a contrary result would actually encourage employers to fire dissident employees and terminate plans—not exactly the results ERISA was supposed to achieve!

When does an ERISA cause of action accrue, in order to apply statutes of limitations and determine if a claim is time-barred (brought too late)? *Wetzel v. Lou Ehlers Cadillac Group Long Term Disability Insurance Program*, 1999 U.S. App. LEXIS 21327 (9/7/99) involves a claim for long-term disability benefits.

ERISA has an explicit statute of limitations for claims of breach of fiduciary duty, but not for participants' claims for plan benefits. By applying earlier cases, the Ninth Circuit decided that the crucial issue is whether the plaintiff provided proof of loss (i.e., proof of continuing disability) for each month. The general federal rule, which is that the claim accrues as soon as the claimant knew or had reason to know that his claim had been denied, would apply in any month in which adequate proof of loss was provided. But a separate three-year statute of limitations would be applied to determine whether claims were timely for each month in which adequate proof of loss was not submitted.

According to the Seventh Circuit, the plaintiff in *Feldman v. American Memorial Life Insurance Co.*, 1999 U.S. App. LEXIS 29360 (7th Cir. 11/9/99) was not "totally disabled" throughout the 90-day elimination period in her disability insurance policy. Therefore, her ERISA §510 claim, that the employer fired her to prevent her from collecting benefits, had to fail, because she never became eligible for the benefits and therefore the employer's motivation in terminating her could not have been to keep her from receiving benefits she had earned.

The trustees of a union pension and welfare benefit plan sued an employer for failure to make the required plan contributions. [*Brown v. C. Volante Corp.*, 1999 U.S. App. LEXIS 25350 (2nd Cir. 10/8/99).] The employer's argument was that the court didn't have jurisdiction over claims involving a time period when there was no signed collective bargaining agreement in place.

The court did not find this argument persuasive, because ERISA §515 (and 29 USC §1132(g)(2)) give the federal courts jurisdiction over claims for "promised contributions." Anyway, the Second Circuit found that the employer had, in effect, adopted the provisions of two collective bargaining agreements, including obligations to fund the plan, even though the agreements were never formally signed.

Chapter 18

LABOR LAW

18.1 INTRODUCTION

Although LMRA §301 says that labor unions can "sue and be sued" in federal court, that provision does not provide automatic federal jurisdiction when a union wants to sue in federal court. The union must abide by the normal rules of civil procedure, bringing suit in the federal courts only if a federal question is involved or only if the parties are citizens of different states and substantial amounts of money are involved [*K.V. Mart Co. v. United Food & Commercial Workers*, 173 F.3d 1221 (9th Cir. 1999)].

What is a federal question, anyway? The Supreme Court decided, in mid-1998 [*Textron v. UAAAIW*, #97-463, 523 U.S. 653 (Sup. Ct. 5/18/98)], that an allegation that an employer violated a collective bargaining agreement presents a federal question. But an allegation that the employer fraudulently induced the union into entering into a contract, and getting a no-strike pledge, by promising not to subcontract out work did not come under LMRA §301 and did not present a federal question.

It has long been accepted that unionized employees are entitled to have a union representative or other co-worker present at any investigatory interview that the employee reasonably believes could result in discharge, suspension, or other disciplinary action. In 2000, the NLRB extended the right to have a co-worker present to the non-union context: *Epilepsy Foundation of Northeastern Ohio*, 331 NLRB No. 92.

18.2 SOURCES OF LABOR LAW

Although the Norris-LaGuardia Act severely limits the availability of injunctions against unions, there are situations in which an injunction is appropriate. In

Burlington Northern Railway v. IBT Local 174, 170 F.3d 897 (9th Cir. 1999), for instance, an injunction was upheld to prevent a union from picketing a site where nonunionized contractors loaded goods onto trains. Because no collective bargaining agreement or organizing effort was at stake, there was no "labor dispute" as defined by the Norris-LaGuardia Act.

Richard R. Nelson sums up state labor laws passed in 2000 dealing with minimum wages, child labor, and anti-discrimination in an article in the January 2001 issue of the Bureau of Labor Statistics' Monthly Labor Review. The article "State Labor Legislation Enacted in 2000" can be read online or downloaded from http://www.bls.gov/opub/mlr/2001/01/art2exc.htm.

18.3 EMPLOYEE STATUS

In August, 2000, the NLRB issued a decision that is of explosive interest in an economy that features many non-traditional jobs (see §8.4). According to the NLRB, temporary workers can be included in the same collective bargaining unit as permanent employees, as long as the characteristics of the jobs are similar: *M.B. Sturgis Inc.*, 331 NLRB No. 173, http://www.nlrb.gov/slip331.html (8/25/00).

This is a reversal of earlier NLRB decisions saying that temporary workers could be organized in a permanent employees' bargaining unit only if neither the "supplier employer" (the company, e.g., a temp agency, that supplied the workers) nor the company where the services actually occurred (the "user employer") objected. As you can imagine, one or both usually did object! [This case is discussed in Nixon Peabody LLPs' Employment Law Alert Issue 71, January 2001, and Nicholas Kulish and Carlos Tejada, "Labor Board Allows Organizing of Temps," *WSJ* 8/31/00 p. A2.]

The NLRB ruled that the union has the right to show that the two companies are really joint employers of the workers, because they both determine the terms and conditions of employment. However, the user employer gets a chance to rebut the union's contention, by showing that the supplier employer has the real control over the workers.

Therefore, the law firm Nixon Peabody LLP suggests that user employers avoid giving referred employees the same uniforms, badges, or ID cards as their permanent work force. They should not be given copies of the policy manual or handbook, and the supplier employer rather than the user employer should be responsible for disciplining the referred employees.

Because "supervisors" are not allowed to organize, it often becomes important to determine if a particular person is a supervisor or a rank-and-file employee. Two cases involving employees of the nursing home chain Beverly Enterprises reached different conclusions. To the Fourth Circuit, licensed practical nurses (LPNs) are supervisors because they supervise nursing assistants; must use independent judgment at work; and, for two of the three shifts, are the most senior personnel available [*Beverly Enterprises v. NLRB*, 165 F.3d 307 (4th Cir. 1999)].

But the D.C. Circuit says that LPNs are not supervisors. They have mere paper authority and are not really able to exercise authority over the nursing assistants. Therefore, they are not supervisors and are entitled to unionize if they want [see also *Beverly Enterprises v. NLRB*, this time 67 LW 1460 (D.C. Cir. 2/2/99)]. The Seventh Circuit reached a similar conclusion in a non-Beverly case [*NLRB v. Gran Care Inc.*, 170 F.3d 662 (7th Cir. 1999)].

Integrated Health Services of Michigan v. NLRB, 68 LW 1207 (6th Cir. 9/17/99) says that nursing home staff nurses have authority to direct and discipline nursing assistants, and therefore are supervisors as defined by the NLRA and are not appropriate members of a bargaining unit with their subordinates. The Sixth Circuit also ruled that the NLRB has the burden of proving that a contested group of individuals are not supervisors; the employer is not required to prove that they are.

Two pro-union workers in *Dreyer's Grand Ice Cream, Inc. v. NLRB*, 140 F.3d 684 (7th Cir. 1998), held the job of "super-coordinator," in charge of several work teams (including interviewing job applicants, recommending hiring and pay raises, and disciplining team members). The super-coordinator job was eliminated after a year, and the two kept their increased salaries but were not promoted to the newly created position of "facilitator."

The former super-coordinators were fired after an attempt to unionize Dreyer's failed. The NLRB ordered reinstatement, and Dreyer's sought review on the grounds that even after the super-coordinator positions were eliminated, the two workers were supervisors who didn't belong in a bargaining unit. The employer lost: The Seventh Circuit upheld the NLRB, because the two did not continue to exercise authority after their demotion.

On another status issue, the NLRB ruled in January 2000 that a full-time paid union organizer who was denied employment as an electrician because of his admitted intention to organize the workplace was entitled to back pay for the period of time he was unable to work at that job. Furthermore, his union salary should not serve to reduce the back-pay award, because the NLRB treated it as "secondary employment," not interim earnings that would offset the award: *Ferguson Electric Co.*, 330 NLRB No. 75 (1/19/00).

18.4 ELECTIONS, CERTIFICATION, AND RECOGNITION

In September 1999, the NLRB revised the administrative manual it uses to process cases involving representation elections. The manual can be searched or downloaded from http://www.nlrb.gov. Printed copies, which cost $29, can be ordered from the Superintendent of Documents, U.S. Government Printing Office, Washington, DC 20402. The stock number is 631-000-00002-9.

In some recent cases, employer behavior was deemed to taint an election:

- Delivering paychecks at the voting site for a decertification election, rather than at the employees' workplaces [*United Cerebral Palsy Ass'n of Niagara County*, 327 NLRB No. 14 (1998)]. The NLRB requires a legitimate business reason for changing paycheck delivery within 24 hours of an election. Usually, increasing voter turnout is good—but in a decertification election, increased turnout favors the employer rather than the union.
- Telling workers that their yearly merit raises would end if the company unionized [*LaSalle Ambulance, Inc.*, 327 NLRB No. 18 (1998)]. The correct statement would have been that the yearly raises were a term or condition of employment, that could not be altered without bargaining, not a new issue which could not be implemented without bargaining.
- Telling employees that unless they returned to work the next day without a union contract, the business would be closed down, and its equipment sold or leased, was a threat—an unfair labor practice—rather than a permissible prediction of future events. It was a threat because it referred to events wholly within the employer's control [*NLRB v. Gerig's Dump Trucking Inc.*, 137 F.3d 936 (7th Cir. 1998)].

Contracting out in-house security functions (and, therefore, firing all the newly unionized employees) was held by the D.C. Circuit to violate the NLRA: *Reno Hilton Resorts v. NLRB*, 68 LW 1384 (D.C. Cir. 12/3/99). In this reading, although the hotel claimed that it outsourced as a response to declining revenues, it did not provide enough evidence of the connection between the two. The fact that outsourcing was a possibility before unionization also worked against the hotel's case.

The NLRB did not abuse its discretion in extending the certification year by six months, and by ordering the employer to reinstate its bargaining proposals, in a case where the employer withdrew all its proposals just before the certification year ended: *NLRB v. Beverly Health & Rehab Services*, 68 LW 1144 (8th Cir. 8/3/99).

It's true that announcing benefits right before an election can invalidate the election, but only if circumstances are right, as two contrasting NLRB decisions from 1999 show. In *Network Ambulance Services Inc.*, 329 NLRB No. 13, two new floating holidays were announced the day before the election. The NLRB found that the election was still valid because the holidays affected thousands of employees throughout the employer's parent company, and the announcement came at a logical point in the parent company's fiscal year. The fact that it was right before the election was purely coincidental.

However, the NLRB did consider the election in *Waste Management of Palm Beach*, 329 NLRB No. 20, to be tainted. A company-wide increase in employer contributions to the 401(k) plan was announced to employees in the unit facing an election three days before the election. Employees in the rest of the company didn't get the good news until later.

The Second Circuit ruled that it is permissible speech, and therefore not an unfair labor practice, for an employer to increase the amount of information available about existing benefits (information that the employer previously refused to disclose, on the grounds of "saving labor costs") just before the election. *Beverly Enterprises Inc. v. NLRB*, 66 LW 1569 (2nd Cir. 3/9/98), distinguishes improved access to information from actually increasing benefits just prior to the election.

It violates the NLRA to fail to give employees their regular annual across-the-board raise if the omission occurs during a union organizing campaign: *NLRB v. Aluminum Casting & Engraving Co.*, 69 LW 1272 (7th Cir. 10/13/00).

On October 27, 2000, the NLRB reversed its earlier decision against the General Electric Company. In July 1996, at 321 NLRB 662, the agency said that it was an unfair labor practice for GE to distribute anti-union handbills during an organizing drive. The handbills said, for instance, that union organization would lead to long, bitter negotiations and possibly an ugly strike. The D.C. Circuit enforced part of the NLRB decision (see 117 F.3d 627, D.C. Cir. 1997), but the Court of Appeals asked the NLRB to reconsider its decision about the handbills. The 2000 NLRB decision, 332 NLRB No. 91, finds that GE did not commit an unfair labor practice, because the handbills were fact-based, not coercive or threatening.

Using a supervisor (even a low-level one) as an election observer for the union invalidates a representation election, so the election results must be set aside: *Family Service Agency, San Francisco*, 331 NLRB No. 103 (7/24/00).

The D.C. Circuit refused to invalidate an election on the basis of unlawful surveillance even though pro-union employees photographed and videotaped other employees. The court did not find that they were acting as union agents who had a probable effect on the election outcome. Nor did the court find that the employees created an atmosphere of fear and reprisal such that a fair election would be impossible [*Overnite Transportation Co. v. NLRB*, 140 F.3d 259 (D.C. Cir. 1998)].

Also on the subject of surveillance, *National Steel & Shipbuilding Co. v. NLRB*, 156 F.3d 1268 (D.C. Cir. 1998), holds that the employer's videotaping of employees at union rallies outside the plant constituted interference with protected activities, because the employer failed to provide reasonable objective justification for the surveillance. Is this a double standard? The employer is in a more powerful position than a union seeking to organize, which probably explains the differing results.

In 1998, the NLRB eased up the rule in its case handling manual. The manual allows balloting by mail only if it is "infeasible" to hold the election via normal in-person balloting. The holding of *San Diego Gas & Electric*, 325 NLRB No. 218 (1998), is that voting by mail should be allowed not only in the fraught situation of an election during a strike or picketing, but when the potential voters would have to travel a significant distance to the polls and are so scattered that simply relocating the polling place wouldn't be effective. Another signal for mail balloting is a workforce with varying schedules that rule out assembling workers in one place at any particular time.

➡ TIP

Undocumented aliens are employees entitled to vote in representation elections—even if their status has been challenged under the IRCA [*NLRB v. Kolkka*, 170 F.3d 937 (9th Cir. 1999)]. The NLRB's position is that undocumented workers can also be awarded back pay when they fall victim to an unlawful layoff, up to the date the employer discovered the undocumented status (and, at least theoretically, would have dismissed the worker) [*Hoffman Plastics Compounds, Inc.*, 327 NLRB No. 86 (1998)].

When several unions engage in joint picketing as part of an organization drive, one union will not be vicariously liable for unfair labor practices of another union merely because they share the common goal of organizing the workplace [*Washington v. HCA Health Services of Texas Inc.*, 152 F.3d 464 (5th Cir. 1998)].

Where the NLRB is called in to resolve a challenge to a representation election, and the membership of the stipulated bargaining unit is ambiguous, the NLRB only has the power to ignore the stipulation and analyze the bargaining unit under the "community of interest" standard if the NLRB is able to discern the parties' intent from the stipulation: *Associated Milk Producers Inc. v. NLRB*, 68 LW 1248 (D.C. Cir. 10/22/99).

An employer can permissibly forbid employees to display any decals not issued by the employer (including, of course, pro-union decals) on their hard hats. According to the Fourth Circuit (*Eastern Omni Constructors Inc. v. NLRB*, 170 F.3d 418 (4th Cir. 3/9/99), the ban served a legitimate function because the employer-issued decals promoted workplace safety by identifying workers certified to use particular pieces of equipment. The employees' free expression was not stifled because they could display union insignia on their other clothing.

January 1999 marked the first time that the NLRB made petition forms for representation cases available online (on its Web site, http:www.nlrb.gov). A June 1998 pilot project for online access to charge forms for unfair labor practices was considered a success, leading to expansion of the program. The usefulness of making the representation petition available from the site will also be assessed after a six-month trial.

18.4.1 Access by Nonemployees

The NLRB found that a grocery chain can permissibly bar nonemployee labor organizers from a public snack bar and could have them leave front sidewalks that the grocery chain was responsible for maintaining. Federal labor was not violated, because the company maintained a consistent ban on solicitation (union solicitation was not singled out). Furthermore, a nearby parking lot was available for solicitation, so the grocery chain's actions did not completely preclude the union from getting its message across. See *Farm Fresh Inc.*, 326 NLRB No. 81 (8/27/98).

The Ninth Circuit held that it was an unfair labor practice for a store to have union representatives arrested for picketing and handbilling in the store's private parking lot: *NLRB v. Calkins*, 187 F.3d 1080 (9th Cir. 8/11/99). The court refused to apply *Lechmere* on the grounds that that case was decided under Connecticut law, which permits union organizers to be excluded from private property as trespassers. Under California law, protection of free speech rights is broader, and entitles union representatives to picket and distribute literature on private property.

The Tenth Circuit ruled that the City of Denver could legitimately bar musicians' union picketing and leafleting at the pedestrian walkway of the city-owned arts center: *Hawkins v. Denver*, 170 F.3d 1281 (10th Cir. 3/10/99). The walkway was not a public forum, and had no history of being used for public expressive activities.

18.5 PREVENTIVE LABOR RELATIONS

J. Derek Braziel's white paper, "Avoid the Union Label: How to Fight Organizers Without Violating the Law," http://www.lawnewsnetwork.com/practice/employmentlaw/papers/lawfirm/A1667-1999May21.html, provides some insights about labor's sometimes successful new push to organize. According to Braziel, in 1998 unions won more representation elections than they lost (whereas in other years in the 1990s, the majority of organization drives failed). Unions are targeting new workplaces and new employee groups and are also using new media tactics to make their message seem more appealing (and to publicize alleged employer improprieties).

The practice of salting, mentioned at ¶1.7, involves job applications by confessed union organizers, who then claim to be the victims of antiunion animus if their applications are not accepted. If the application is accepted, of course, the activist will try to convert other employees to the pro-union cause.

> **➠ TIP**
>
> If you're asked to "review" a petition signed by employees, or union authorization cards—don't do it! The result could be authorization of the union without an election.

Although it is an unfair labor practice to threaten employees or punish them for pro-union sentiments, it is perfectly permissible and fair to communicate to employees your honest opinion about why continued nonunion operation serves everyone's best interest, and to publicize facts about the union that could serve as dinsincentives to joining up.

18.6 THE COLLECTIVE BARGAINING PROCESS

"Regressive bargaining"—withdrawing an offer if the union is unable to meet the employer's time frame—has been upheld by the NLRB in *White Cap, Inc.*, 325 NLRB No. 220 (1998), unless it is done specifically for the purpose of avoiding a contract. Where the employer has a legitimate business reason for wanting to resolve the issue quickly, regressive bargaining is permissible.

During the course of unproductive negotiations, a union adopted a "work to rule" slow-down strategy. The employer's response was a lock-out. The NLRB, in the matter of *Central Illinois Public Service Co.*, 326 NLRB No. 80 (1998), agreed with both sides. The slow-down was deemed to be protected activity, but the employer was not out of line either. The lock-out was not inherently destructive of union rights and was motivated by a desire to get the negotiations back on track, rather than by antiunion animus.

The Third Circuit found it to be an unfair labor practice for an employer to refuse to complete a questionnaire about its utilization of nonunion personnel (during scheduled plant shutdowns for maintenance purposes) to perform work otherwise covered by the collective bargaining agreement. Under *NLRB v. PSE&G*, 157 F.3d 222 (3rd Cir. 1998), the union needs this information to represent its members.

In the course of negotiations for a plant-closing agreement, the employer said that it was considering moving the operation, including moving to distant states. What the employer **didn't** mention was that it had already bought a new plant seven miles away from the location to be closed. The union was fooled, and concentrated on negotiating for better severance pay rather than transfer benefits. Once the union found out, it complained to the NLRB. The NLRB demanded, and the Eighth Circuit upheld, renegotiation because employers can't take advantage of deception about their intentions. [*NLRB v. Waymouth Farms, Inc.*, 1999 WL 181974 (8th Cir. 1999).]

Unilaterally changing the health plan after a bargaining impasse, to require employees to pay much higher out-of-pocket costs, violates the Labor Management Relations Act: *Loral Defense Systems-Akron v. NLRB*, 68 LW 1400 (6th Cir. 12/8/99). The employer hadn't fully disclosed the proposal during the unsuccessful bargaining process. The employer had reserved the right to amend or modify the health plan, but the Sixth Circuit considered the changes tantamount to replacing the old plan, not amending it.

18.7 UNION SECURITY

Under a late-1998 Supreme Court decision, *Marquez v. Screen Actors Guild*, #97-1056, 525 U.S. 33 (11/3/98), a union does not breach its duty of fair representation if it enters into a collective bargaining agreement that contains a union-security clause that reproduces the wording of NLRA §8(a)(3).

The plaintiff, an actress, claimed that she should have been notified of her right not to join the union and to pay the union only for its representational activities. The plaintiff also challenged the 30-day grace period in the collective bargaining agreement (CBA), but the Supreme Court upheld the Ninth Circuit: Claims of this type fall within the NLRB's primary jurisdiction and cannot be originated within the federal court system.

A union can include organizing expenses as an element in the agency fees that it charges to nonmembers. According to the NLRB [*United Food & Commercial Workers,* 329 NLRB No. 69 (9/30/99)], this is permissible because of the positive effects that unionization has on wage scales, thus benefiting even workers who prefer not to join.

Where the collective bargaining agreement contained a provision permitting the employer to contract out preventive maintenance work, the employer was justified in contracting out some routine preventive maintenance work after a piece of equipment had been shut down. [*International Paper Co. v. United Paperworkers Int'l Union,* 215 F.3d 815 (8th Cir. 2000).]

The Fourth Circuit reversed the NLRB, [*Dorsey Trailers Inc. v. NLRB,* 69 LW 1348 (4th Cir. 12/1/00)] holding that a company did not violate the NLRA by closing its Pennsylvania plant and opening a plant in Georgia during a strike. The move was economically motivated and would have occurred even without anti-union animus. Furthermore, relocation is a core entrepreneurial decision (under *First National Maintenance v. NLRB,* 452 U.S. 666 (Sup.Ct. 1981)), and the Fourth Circuit does not consider relocation to be a term or condition of employment.

18.9 LABOR ARBITRATION

The Supreme Court decided in March, 2001 that the Federal Arbitration Act is generally applicable to employment contracts. Although the language of the FAA exempts "contracts of employment of seamen, railroad employees, or any other class of workers engaged in foreign or interstate commerce," the exemption is limited to transportation workers, and does not extend to all workers involved in interstate commerce. Therefore, pre-dispute arbitration clauses are not necessarily unenforceable merely on the grounds that they involve workers in interstate commerce. [*Circuit City Stores, Inc. v. Adams,* #99-1379, 69 LW 4195 (Sup.Ct. 3/21/01)]

An employer demonstrated improper antiunion animus by firing an employee who disobeyed an order that forbade him to change his lunch hour to attend a co-worker's arbitration hearing. The discharged employee helped his co-worker prepare for the arbitration hearing, and therefore had a legitimate interest in attending even though the case did not fall under *Ohmite. Ohmite Manufacturing Co.,* 290 NLRB 1036 (1988), says that refusal to allow an employee to attend an NLRB hearing is unlawful only if the employee has a real need to attend the hearing, or if the employer acts out of an improper motive. The D.C. Circuit did find an improper motive in the case of *Cadbury Beverages Inc. v. NLRB,* 160 F.3d 24 (D.C. Cir. 1998): animus against the union.

LMRA §301 permits a federal District Court to enforce a subpoena duces tecum (for production of documents) issued by a labor arbitrator to a person or entity that is not a party to the collective bargaining agreement [*AFTRA v. WJBK-TV*, 164 F.3d 1004 (6th Cir. 1999)]. However, the labor arbitrator cannot order non-parties to appear and testify, only to produce documents.

18.10 STRIKES

A restaurant supervisor who was friendly with, and liked by, employees was fired. The Seventh Circuit held [in *Bob Evans Farms Inc. v. NLRB*, 163 F.3d 1012 (7th Cir. 1998)] that employees who went out on strike in sympathy were overreacting to management's action. Therefore, the strike did not constitute protected concerted activity.

It's hard to accumulate evidence that dozens or hundreds of employees weren't really sick when they claimed to be, but if you have the evidence, it's proper to impose discipline on employees who falsely claim illness. Be sure, however, that discipline is applied fairly and uniformly. Don't target members of a particular ethnic group or union activists while allowing sick-out violations by others.

If you have already experienced a sick-out, a sensible response is to add a uniformly enforced policy that employees who take sick days will be charged with a personal day unless they have a doctor's note diagnosing an actual illness.

TIP

Strikes are not the only hostile labor activity you may encounter. An article by Emily Nelson and J. C. Conklin, "Leery of Strikes, More Workers Stage Sickouts," *WSJ*, 1/12/99, p. B1, deals with job actions in which workers (especially public employees and others who are not supposed to strike because their jobs affect the public interest) agree to call in sick on particular days in lieu of a strike. The article quotes labor law professor Marina Angel, who says that a sick-out is really an unlawful partial strike. It can be especially damaging to employers, who could simply bite the bullet and hire permanent replacements in the wake of a lengthy strike but can't replace employees when a day off is taken here and there.

The LMRA preempts state-law claims for fraud and breach of contract brought by striker replacements who were laid off six months after the strike was settled. They alleged that they were promised they would not be laid off, but their lack of seniority meant that they were in fact laid off when business failed to pick up once the strike ended. The Ninth Circuit held that the state claims were preempted by federal law because it was necessary to interpret the CBA to determine the rights of the replacements. [*Aguilera v. Pirelli Armstrong Tire Co.*, 223 F.3d 1010 (9th Cir. 2000).]

A union was guilty of unfair labor practices by distributing handbills at a construction site that resulted in a secondary boycott when neutral employees walked off the job. Although the handbill directed employees not to walk out, there was substantial evidence that the union sought to promote an unlawful secondary boycott. [*Warshawsky & Co. v. NLRB*, 68 LW 1058 (D.C. Cir. 7/9/99).]

18.11 THE WARN ACT

WARN Act notice must be given to laid-off employees who have a legitimate expectation of recall. *Kildea v. Electro-Wire Products Inc.*, 144 F.3d 400 (6th Cir. 1998), says that such employees fall under the definition of affected employees because of the likelihood that plant closing will lead to job loss.

A company's entire sales force was brought to several centralized locations cross-country and fired. Before their discharge, the salespersons worked all over the United States, with an administrative center in Virginia. The District Court treated the Virginia center as a "single site of employment" from which there could have been a WARN Act mass layoff.

However, on appeal, the Third Circuit found that there were real issues of fact as to whether all sales staffers took orders from, and reported to, the Virginia location. The relevant regulation, 20 CFR §639.3(I)(6), defines three categories of employment sites: home bases; places from which work is assigned; and places where reports are received. So the appeals court in *Ciarlante v. Brown & Williamson Tobacco Corp.*, 143 F.3d 139 (3rd Cir. 1998), sent the case back to the District Court for a factual determination.

Although the WARN Act refers to a "group" of laid-off employees, employers cannot avoid the application of the act by performing layoffs one at a time. Instead, all economically motivated layoffs during the 90-day period must be aggregated to see if the limit of 50 has been reached: *Hallowell v. Orleans Regional Hospital*, 69 LW 1096 (5th Cir. 7/18/00).

A company can't avoid its WARN Act responsibilities merely by filing a bankruptcy petition. However, once things have gone further than that, and the company is no longer operating as a going concern, but is simply winding up its affairs in preparation for liquidation, it is no longer an "employer" for WARN Act purposes. Therefore, the company is not liable for back pay if it does not give the WARN Act notice: *Official Committee of Unsecured Creditors v. United Healthcare System Inc.*, 68 LW 1393 (3rd Cir. 12/29/99).

Back pay and damages that are awarded under the WARN Act are not "wages" that are subject to a West Virginia statute mandating timely wage payments [*Conrad v. Charles Town Races Inc.*, 67 LW 1220 (W. Va. 7/15/98)]. The state court took this position even though WARN Act damages are described in the WARN Act itself as back pay.

18.13 SHARED LIABILITY

In the view of the Sixth Circuit, vested benefits under a collective bargaining agreement are transferable when the employer transfers employees to another one of its locations, which is covered by another collective bargaining agreement with another union. [In this case, *Anderson v. AT&T Corp.*, 147 F.3d 467 (6th Cir. 1998, *cert. denied* 119 S.Ct. 851), the benefit was a special wage-incentive payment that was due as long as the employee continued to be employed.]

18.14 EMPLOYER DOMINATION

Once again, the NLRB found employee participation companies formed by the employer to be "labor organizations" improperly dominated by the employer [*EFCO Corp.*, 327 NLRB No. 71 (12/31/98)]. Committees dealing with employee benefits, employee policies, and safety issues were forbidden, but the employee suggestions committee was permitted to stand, because it did not deal with management on subjects that fall under the ambit of collective bargaining. The text of the decision can be found at http://www.nlrb.gov/slip327.html.

In the fall of 1999, the NLRB ruled that Polaroid's employee participation committee—which discussed issues such as family leave, termination policy, and ESOPs—was an impermissibly employer-dominated labor organization, in violation of NLRA §8(a)(2). See *Polaroid Corp. & Scivally*, 329 NLRB No. 47 (9/30/99). The NLRB naturally can't come out against workers conveying their opinions to management, but in the NLRB's view, appropriate ways for a company to get employee input include suggestion boxes and employee surveys, but not "sweetheart" organizations.

18.15 NLRB JURISDICTION

The Seventh Circuit upheld the NLRB's imposition of a corporate-wide remedial order against a corporation that operates about 900 separate nursing homes. Remedies at the corporate level were proper because violations were detected in a number of facilities, not just one, and the company is centrally administered. [*Beverly California Corp. v. NLRB*, 227 F.3d 817 (7th Cir. 2000).]

Fines imposed by the NLRB on a union that violated a consent decree are not punitive in nature. Therefore, the NLRB is not required to provide all the safeguards of criminal law before imposing the fine: *NLRB v. Ironworkers Local 433*, 169 F.3d 1217 (9th Cir. 3/12/99).

Chapter 19

Unemployment Insurance

19.1 INTRODUCTION

HR consulting firm Laurdan Associates Inc. reports that the amount per employee paid by employers for federal and state unemployment taxes decreased slightly between 1997 and 1998. In 1997, the figure was $210, versus $207 per employee in 1998. In 1996, the average duration of unemployment benefit payments was 14.9 weeks, and this too dropped slightly, falling to 14.6 weeks in 1997. In 1996, 33.4% of claimants exhausted their benefit eligibility, versus 33.1% in 1997. See Robert W. Thompson, "Unemployment Insurance Costs Dropped From 1997 to 1998," *HR Magazine*, 12/98, p. 12.

For unadjusted and seasonally adjusted data on the number of unemployment insurance claims, with an analysis of trends in high-unemployment states, you can check out the Department of Labor's Web site, http://www.dol.gov/dol/opa/public/media/press/eta/ui, or http://doleta.wsdc.org/newsroom/press/2000, or call (202) 219-6871 for the Unemployment Insurance Weekly Claims Reports.

Robert Kenyon Jr. and Loryn Lancaster summarize the federal and state legislation introduced and passed in 2000 in laws affecting unemployment insurance in "Changes in Unemployment Insurance Legislation in 2000," published in the January 2001 issue of the *Monthly Labor Review*. You can download the article from http://www.bls.gov/opub/mlr/2001/01/art4full.pdf.

19.2 ELIGIBILITY FOR BENEFITS

A claimant for unemployment benefits was the treasurer of the corporation of which he was also a 25% shareholder. According to the New Jersey Superior Court, he was not "unemployed" when the corporation stopped operating but had not yet dissolved or applied for bankruptcy protection. In this reading, as long as a 5% or greater stockholder holds corporate ownership or continues to own stock, unemployment benefits are not available. [*Fernicola,*, CCH Unemployment Insurance (UI) Reporter ¶8637 (N.J. Super. 2000).]

In the view of the Arkansas Court of Appeals, benefits should have been granted to a person discharged for pleading "no contest" to a domestic violence felony; the charges were not work-related, and did not harm the employer's interests: *Baldor Electric Co.*, CCH UI ¶8501 (Ark.App. 2000).

The Wisconsin Circuit Court said that an individual can apply for benefits and bypass the search for work if he or she has a reasonable expectation of reemployment; absolute certainty is not required: *Thomas,* CCH UI ¶9510 (Wis.Cir. 2000). So the claimant, who was #2 on the seniority list for a brewery whose purchaser signed a Collective Bargaining Agreement calling for recall on the basis of seniority, could reasonably expect to be called back to work when the brewery re-opened, and could collect unemployment benefits in the interim even though he had not looked for another job.

Benefits were denied to a person who quit to get a higher-paid job, and then was laid off from that job through no fault of his own. In this reading, the offer of higher pay somewhere else is not good cause for leaving a job, because the first employer was not at fault. [*Total Audio-Visual Systems, Inc.*, CCH UI ¶8484 (Md.App. 2000).]

However, severing a relationship with a temporary placement agency in order to take a full-time, permanent job constitutes good cause for quitting temporary work: *Duby,* CCH UI ¶8896 (Fla.App. 2000), so benefits could be granted after the loss of the permanent job.

Ability to work is another important criterion. In *Daniels,* CCH UI ¶9022 (Ia.Dist.Ct. 2000), the claimant was told by her doctor to find a job she could do sitting down when she was seven months pregnant. Her job as blackjack dealer required standing for the entire shift. The employer put her on medical leave, and she was denied unemployment benefits because the medical restriction made her unable to work.

In contrast, in another contemporary Iowa case, *Priority Express Inc.*, CCH UI ¶9026 (Ia.Dist.Ct. 2000), benefits were granted to a truck driver whose work-related back injury required her to drive a vehicle with an automatic transmission. The employer transferred her away from the only route that had a truck she could drive. The District Court treated her leaving the job as justified by the employer's refusal to accommodate her disability-related needs. (Perhaps the two cases were decided differently because only the second medical condition was work-related).

However, the employee still has to participate in the process. The Washington Court of Appeals denied benefits to a claimant who developed sensitivity to the chemicals used in his job (washing trucks). The employer moved him to working in an outside tunnel; he still had problems. The company's HR director suggested that he seek accommodation under the ADA, but he chose to quit instead. Benefits were denied because he failed to exhaust all the reasonable alternatives before leaving the job. [*Woods*, CCH UI ¶9022 (Wash.App. 2000).] And unemployment benefits can't be paid at the same time as Worker's Compensation benefits, even if there is no statutory bar to duplicate benefits, because one benefit is premised on ability to work—the other on inability to work: *Ballard*, CCH UI ¶8594 (Ind.App. 2000).

In a 1998 Missouri appellate case, a truck driver was fired after failing a drug test. When he applied for unemployment benefits, his employer said that benefits should be denied because he was fired for good cause. The ex-employee's argument was that the drug test lab report was just hearsay and not admissible. The employer's rebuttal was that evidence law makes documents kept in the course of business admissible under the "business records" exception.

The trial court agreed with the fired employee, because the report was prepared in the course of the lab's business, not the trucking company's business. But the appellate court said the trial court misread the business records hearsay exception. According to the appellate court [*Associated Wholesale Grocers v. Moncrief*, 970 S.W.2d 425 (Mo. App. 1998)], *anybody's* business records can be introduced, as long as they were kept in the normal course of business, were made close enough after the event to be reliable, and there are other reasons for considering the records to be reliable.

In another case involving drugs, the employer's policy called for termination of any employee found with a detectable level of alcohol or illegal drugs. The plaintiff of *Smith v. Zero Defects Inc.*, 1999 WL 330163 (Ida. 1999) tested positive for amphetamines in a random test; he was not impaired at that particular time. However, Idaho, like Nebraska, Nevada, Oklahoma, and Utah, but unlike Arizona, Kansas, Oregon, and Washington, considers violation of an employer's zero-tolerance policy to constitute misconduct serious enough to prevent receipt of unemployment insurance benefits, even if the employee was not currently impaired at the time of the test. In other words, off-duty drug use can be serious enough to prevent the user from receiving unemployment benefits.

It did not constitute disqualifying misconduct for an employee to refuse to take a drug test ordered by the employer (on his own time, without compensation) after the employee had been written up for insubordination. [*Andrews*, CCH UI ¶8878 (Ore.App. 2000).] The company policy of requiring a drug test after all reprimands was not reasonable, in cases (like this one) where there was no evidence of drug use.

19.7 DOL PROPOSAL FOR EXPANDED ELIGIBILITY

A Notice of Proposed Rulemaking, issued by DOL on December 3, 1999 (64 FR 67972), asks for comments on the agency's proposal that state unemployment agencies make voluntary payments to parents who need time off from work to care for a newly born or adopted child. The program is known as BAA[Birth and Adoption]-UC. (The proposals affect 20 CFR Part 604.) The DOL acted in response to a 5/24/99 President's Executive Memorandum that tells the Secretary of Labor to participate in the evolution of mechanisms for providing unemployment benefits as partial wage replacement for new parents.

The legal issue is whether new parents are "able and available" for work. The proposal's position is that families, and the economy as a whole, will be best served by a period of time when parents stay at home with newborns and new adoptees before returning to the workforce. Eligibility is limited to a one-year period beginning with the week of birth or placement for adoption. The proposal allows states to limit compensation to "approved leave" negotiated between parents and employers, with a specified date for return to work.

The Federal Register notice says that states can pass laws and start an unemployment program for new parents at any time after a Final Rule is enacted; if they want to pass laws based on the proposed rule, the laws should have a proposal for amendments to comply with the final federal rule. DOL will take three years to evaluate data from at least four state programs.

DOL finalized the rule, with no significant changes, as the Birth and Adoption-Unemployment Compensation (BAA-UC) program, 65 FR 37209 (6/13/00).

Also see *Wilson*, CCH UI ¶8227 (Del.Super. 2000), holding that an employee who quits because a shift change conflicted with parental obligations is entitled to benefits because there was a good cause to quit.

Chapter 20

Worker's Compensation

20.1 INTRODUCTION

In the year 2000, several states raised the maximum WC benefit that can be paid for disability or death. In Georgia, for instance, the weekly maximum benefit for temporary partial disability went up to $250 (from $233.33); the maximum death benefit went from $100,000 to $125,000. In Minnesota, the maximum weekly compensation benefit is now $750 rather than $615. Nebraska renamed its Second Injury Fund the Workers' Compensation Trust Fund. You can see Glenn Whittington's summary of 2000 legislative changes in Worker's Compensation in the January, 2001 issue of the *Monthly Labor Review*, published by the Bureau of Labor Statistics, at http://www.bls.gov/opub/mlr/2001/01/art3exc.htm.

On March 3, 1999, the Supreme Court decided a Worker's Compensation (WC) case, *American Manufacturers Mutual Insurance Co. v. Sullivan*, #97-2000, 526 U. S. 46 (Sup.Ct. 1999). Under Pennsylvania's WC Act, once liability is no longer contested, the employer or its insurer has an obligation to pay for all reasonable or necessary treatment. However, an insurer, or a self-insured employer, is permitted to withhold payment for disputed treatment pending utilization review by an independent third party.

The *Sullivan* plaintiffs brought a civil rights suit claiming violation of the Due Process clause of the Constitution. They sued state officials, WC insurers, and a self-insured school district, charging that benefits had been withheld without notice, thus depriving the employees of a property right.

Their claims did not succeed. In the Supreme Court's analysis, private insurers are not "state actors" subject to the Due Process clause when they use the utilization review process. The employees do not gain a property right until the treatment has been found reasonable and necessary. Therefore, there was no requirement of giving the employees notice, or holding a hearing, before withholding the benefits until the review had been completed in favor of the employees.

According to the Workers Compensation Research Institute, network providers not only save a lot of money when injured workers are treated there, but offer a quality of care comparable to non-network care. Based on a sample of claims in California, Connecticut, and Texas between 1995 and 1997, treatment of a back injury by a network provider cost an average of $884; non-network providers charged about 50% more ($1233). Treatment of miscellaneous injuries averaged $752 for network, $1012 for non-network providers. Non-network providers averaged 14.8 physical therapy visits to treat a back injury; network providers averaged only 9.7. However, in 1996 and 1997, the cost disparity between network and non-network treatment narrowed. (See Alisa Tang, "Bending the Cost Averages for Those Aching Backs," *New York Times*, 12/29/99, p. G1.)

Elliott A. Kellman & Laurence K. Flaccus, "Holding Costs at Bay," *HR Magazine*, 11/99, p. 81, explains how Baystate Health Systems cut Worker's Compensation costs as a percentage of payroll from 2.6% (1993) to 0.82% (1999), based on four concepts:

- Integrated, multidisciplinary approach
- Shared management accountability for managing WC function
- Nonadversarial approach to injured EEs
- Proactive management of safety and accident prevention

Before the program was instituted, no one had responsibility for following, managing, or cutting costs. Afterwards, it was acknowledged that everybody was responsible for reducing injuries and maintaining a safer workplace, and efforts were made to get injured employees back to work. The company fired its TPA and hired a full-time in-house Worker's Compensation consultant/manager and adopted software to track and report injury and cost data. Costs were allocated to each department by using injury rates for comparable operations, and managers are expected to meet or exceed those targets.

The subject of returning to work is discussed shortly after an injury, and the company has a relationship with a Preferred Provider Organization of specialists knowledgeable in rehabilitation after work-related injuries.

An article in CCH's Worker's Compensation newsletter gives some useful tips for spotting potentially fraudulent claims:

- Delayed reporting of injury
- Accidents of a type that might be staged
- The worker claiming injury is on probation or has been noted as performing poorly
- The alleged injury is not consistent with the injured person's work duties
- Injury is reported just after the employee returns from a weekend or holiday—showing that the injury might have occurred away from the workplace, or a non-work-related injury might have been exacerbated.

The article suggests asking the employee to sign a written statement explaining the incident as soon as possible—that way, the employee is locked into his or her version of the facts, and can't keep editing it to make it more favorable.

California employers can access a database of all WC claims sorted by claimant's Social Security number, so the employer can see if the employee has a history of claims, or if the current employer is being expected to compensate for an injury that occurred during earlier employment somewhere else. ["Tips on Discovering and Investigating Workers' Comp Fraud," CCH *Worker's Compensation Business and Management Guide* (BMG) 2/1/00 p. 19.]

20.2 [NEW] CLASSIFICATION OF BENEFITS

An injury that occurs at the worker's home can qualify for WC, if the employee was engaged in work-related tasks at the time: e.g., *A.E. Clevite, Inc. v. Tjas*, Utah App. No. 990218-CA; see BMG 4/4/00 p. 49. In this case, the employee was rendered paraplegic when he slipped while salting down his driveway so it would be safe for the expected delivery of a work-related package.

Widow's benefits are not available to a spouse who is living apart from the worker pursuant to a separation agreement (in this case, when the worker was murdered by a co-worker): *Pickrel v. D.C. Department Services*, No. 99-AA-712 (District of Columbia 10/5/00).]

According to the New York Supreme Court, suicide can be compensable, even if the worker suffered from pre-existing depression, as long as a work-related injury was at least a contributing cause of the suicide. [*Altes v. Petrocelli Electric Co.*, N.Y. Sup. No. 85588 (3/23/00); BMG 4/18/00 p. 60.]

A union dock worker did not act unreasonably when he turned down a non-union job offered by his employer once he was cleared to return to work. He would have lost seniority and other benefits by taking a non-union job. Even if the employer had provided equal health and other benefits for union and non-union workers, the Pennsylvania court said that union membership provides benefits such as collective bargaining and grievance mechanisms. [*ABF Freight Systems Inc. v. Worker's Compensation Appeals Board*, Pa. Sup. No. 52099 (1/11/00); see BMG 2/15/00 p. 30.]

20.3.1 Compensable Injuries

Schmidt v. Smith, 155 N.J. 44, 713 A.2d 1014 (1998), says that bodily injury caused by sexual harassment is covered by the employer liability section of the Worker's Compensation insurance policy, because this section of the policy is designed to make funds available to compensate employees for their work-related injuries, even those for which Worker's Compensation payments are not available.

In an Arkansas case, WC benefits were granted for a fractured spine sustained in a carpenter's fall from scaffolding, even though his medical record from the emergency room showed that he "reeked" of alcohol. The mere presence of alcohol was held not to trigger the statutory presumption that the accident was caused by substance abuse. However, the Arkansas Supreme Court reversed, saying that testimony about the smell of alcohol at the time of the injury, and about other workers seeing the injured carpenter with beer at job sites was enough to trigger the presumption of substance abuse causation, even though the hospital staff did not perform a blood alcohol test that could be introduced into the record. [*Flowers v. Norman Oaks Construction*, Ark. Sup. 6/1/00, discussed in BMG 7/18/00 p. 11.]

Benefits were denied for an at-work ankle injury suffered by an employee who hitched a ride on a forklift; the forklift operator accidentally drove over his foot. The Illinois court said the injury was not compensable because the injury was not work-related even though it occurred in the workplace: the employee was going to the break room to pick up his lunch. Furthermore, the employer had an adequately publicized policy against riding double on forklifts, because they are not designed to carry passengers and therefore passenger safety can't be guaranteed. [*Saunders v. The Industrial Commission*, Ill.Supp. No. 86969 (1/21/00), BMG 2/15/00 p. 28.]

20.5.1 [NEW] Psychological Injuries

In the past few years, Pennsylvania has decided a number of interesting comp cases relating to mental injuries that are manifested with mental rather than physical consequences. In early 1999, a mental injury award was upheld for an employee who was falsely blamed for theft by an inefficient employer whose records were in disarray. The plaintiff suffered so much stress that she was unable to work and was institutionalized in a mental hospital. [Danielle N. Rogers, "Mental Injury Wins Rare Comp," *National Law Journal* 3/1/99 p. B2.]

In May, 2000, the Pennsylvania Supreme Court ruled that the burden of proof is the same for mental/mental as for mental/physical claims. In other words, when an employee claims work-related psychological injuries, whether or not physical manifestations such as an ulcer or heart palpitations are alleged, the award of WC benefits depends on the claimant's proof that the injury arose out of abnormal working conditions.

In two cases from mid-2000, the Commonwealth Court of Pennsylvania ruled that oppressive behavior by a supervisor, if pressed far enough, can constitute abnormal working conditions. In one case, threats to the claimant (who also had objects thrown at her) were serious enough to aggravate her pre-existing depression. In the other case, accusations of falsifying time cards led to physical touching and pushing. After her dismissal, the clerk suffered major depression and was unable to work. [See Tracy Blitz Newman, "PA. High Court Raises Bar on Workers' Comp. Mental/Physical Claims," *The Legal Intelligencer* 5/22/00; Danielle N. Rodier, "Run-Ins With Screaming Supervisors Can Be Abnormal Working Conditions," *The Legal Intelligencer* 6/2/00, both available through law.com.]

20.4 WORKER'S COMPENSATION EXCLUSIVITY

For WC purposes, rape and robbery committed at a workplace by an unknown assailant are considered "accidental workplace injury." Therefore, according to *Melo v. Jewish Board of Family & Children's Services Inc., N.Y.L.J.*, 2/8/00, p. 29, col. 3 (N.Y. Sup. Court), WC exclusivity applies, and the victim does not have the right to bring tort claims against the employer.

Late in 2000, a trial jury awarded $500,000 in a negligence action brought by a retarded worker against the Goodwill sheltered workshop where she worked, and where she was raped by a fellow employee who had previously molested her.

There is a traditional exception to WC exclusivity for third-party attacks caused by personal animus and not directed against the victim on account of employment. The Pennsylvania Superior Court ruled that the employee doesn't have to show a past history of animosity by the attacker to recover against the employer in any case of personal attack. However, there is a presumption of work-relatedness whenever the attack occurs in the workplace rather than somewhere else. [Lori Litchman, "Employee Sexually Assaulted at Work May Recover Damages Against Employer," *The Legal Intelligencer* 11/20/00; see law.com.]

In a 2000 Florida case [*Turner v. PCR, Inc.*, Fla. Sup. No. SC 94468 (3/2/00); BMG 3/21/00 p. 44.], one worker died and one was seriously injured in an explosion that occurred while they were mixing chemicals. The plaintiffs asserted the intentional tort exception to WC exclusivity. Proving this requires either the employer's deliberate intent to injure (which was not asserted here) or conduct that a reasonable fact-finder would consider substantially certain to result in injury or death. The case was allowed to go to trial, because the employer did conceal the hazards of the mixing process, did not provide training or safety equipment, and was aware of the risks because there had been three similar explosions over the previous two years.

20.6 ALTERNATIVES FOR INSURING WORKER'S COMPENSATION

Employers have been rejoicing in much lower WC premiums in recent years, although rates may increase in the future if losses trend upward sharply. The reduction in rates has had a severe impact on insurers. The WC insurance industry expects to lose at least $1 billion in 1999. Business written through reinsurance pools may cost insurers as much as $2.5 billion. Some important reinsurance companies are bowing out.

Texas allows employers to self-insure for WC, but they must be careful to provide benefits at least roughly comparable to the benefits that would be available under an insured plan. In *Reyes v. Storage & Processors Inc.*, 995 S.W.2d 722 (Tex. App.

1999), the court said that employers cannot require arbitration of claims for work-related injuries if their benefits are substantially less generous than Comp benefits.

Strawn v. AFC Enterprises Inc., 68 LW 1302 (S.D. Tex. 11/4/99) builds on this by refusing to enforce an arbitration agreement imposed on all employees. Because the employer's plan offered only "miserly" benefits to injured employees, an employee was allowed to raise tort claims even after accepting an arbitration award of about $50,000 for work-related injuries. In the court's view, the arbitration award was completely void, not just voidable, and therefore was not ratified by the employee's acceptance of benefits.

American International Group Inc. has sued reinsurers Unicover and ReliaStar Life Insurance Co. in New York Supreme Court, charging them with repudiating reinsurance contracts with American International. American International wants the reinsurers to be ordered to abide by the contracts and to pay damages. See Deborah Lohse, "Decline in Workers' Compensation Rates Leaves Insurers With Billion-Dollar Tab," *WSJ*, 3/5/99, p. A4.

According to the Sixth Circuit, unpaid WC premiums owed by a bankruptcy debtor to its insurer are not entitled to priority status under the Bankruptcy Code. [*Travelers Property Casualty Corp. v. Birmingham-Nashville Express Inc.*, 69 LW 1100 (6th Cir. 8/1/00).]

20.8 BAN ON RETALIATION

The Washington State case of *Warnek v. ABB Combustion Engineering*, 67 LW 1558 (Wash. 3/4/99), permits an employer to refuse to rehire employees who made WC claims against the same employer in another state. In this reading, the antiretaliation statute applies only within a state, not outside it. The court also drew a distinction between refusing to rehire, on the one hand, and discrimination during employment or discharge, on the other. Only the latter would be unlawful.

An employee's retaliatory wrongful discharge claim survived summary judgment in *Newell v. Kmart Corp.*, 35 F.Supp. 2d 1312 (D. Kan. 1998). The plaintiff was fired, allegedly for excessive absenteeism, after she asked to take a vacation day and thought her request was approved. To prevail, the employee must be able to show a connection between filing a WC claim and the discharge. (However, ERISA claims were dismissed for lack of evidence, and the employer's conduct was not outrageous enough to support a claim for intentional infliction of mental distress.)

A terminated employee sued in West Virginia state court, alleging that she had suffered a retaliatory discharge because she filed a comp claim. The employer removed the case to federal court, but the federal court agreed with the plaintiff's argument and sent the case back to state court: *Thorne v. Wampler Foods Inc.*, D.W.V. Civil Action No. 3:00CV24 (8/29/00). Civil actions "arising under" state WC laws cannot be removed to federal court: see 28 U.S.C. §1445(c). However, there is an exception for suits alleging "deliberate injury" (which can be removed and heard in federal court). According to the District Court for the District of West Virginia, a retaliatory discharge case does arise under WC, and therefore belongs in state, not federal, court.

20.10 WORKER'S COMPENSATION IN RELATION TO LAWS ON OTHER SUBJECTS

A person injured on the job might take FMLA leave in addition to, or instead of, collecting WC benefits, and might be (or might claim to be) a qualified person with a disability for ADA benefits. "When Regs Collide: The ADA and Workers' Compensation," WestGroup *Employment Alert*, 11/25/98, p. 1, tackles the interface issues for these statutes.

The right to get WC benefits is considered a privilege of employment for ADA purposes [see, e.g., *Harding v. Winn-Dixie Stores, Inc.*, 907 F. Supp. 386 (M.D. Fla. 1995)], so an argument that a person suffered discrimination in this area can be litigated. WC statutes do not violate the ADA just because they cover physical disabilities but exclude mental disabilities [*Hensley v. Punta Gorda*, 686 So.2d 714 (Fla. App. 1997)].

But the ADA doesn't have the strong preemptive power that ERISA has to eliminate state-law claims. Recently, for instance, state-law claims were allowed to proceed, even though the ADA's standard of proof is higher for employees with preexisting conditions [*Baley v. Reynolds Metals*, 153 Ore. App. 498, 959 P.2d 84 (Ore. App. 1998)].

A person injured at work might be entitled to WC benefits yet able to work with reasonable accommodation. But a WC judge's determination that the individual could not work even on a reduced schedule is proof that the person was not a qualified individual with a disability [*Dush v. Appleton Electric Co.*, 124 F.3d 957 (8th Cir. 1997)]. An employee who enters into an agreement stating that he or she needs a stress-free work environment isn't qualified for a high-stress job like being a safety police officer [*Jackson v. County of Los Angeles*, 60 Cal. App. 4th 171, 70 Cal. Rptr.2d 96 (1998)].

Testimony or findings from an ADA case can have powerful evidentiary effect in a WC case. A person who sued under the ADA because of a past injury can't deny that the injury involved in the suit was a preexisting disability vis-à-vis the later injury that is the subject of a WC case [*Cobb v. Coyne Cylinder Co.*, 1998 Westlaw 45320 (Ala. App. 1998)].

When an injured person's "weekly wage" is being calculated, in order to determine the level of benefit to be paid to replace lost income, should the value of health insurance premiums paid by the employer be included? In 2000, the Georgia Court of Appeals said no, but early in 2001 the Washington Supreme Court said yes, because "wages" includes the reasonable value of any "consideration of like nature" extending to room and board that is received in conjunction with the employment relationship. [*Groover v. Johnson Controls World Wide Service*, No. A99A1792 (Ga.App. 1/12/00);*Cockle v. Dep't of Labor & Industries* No. 68539-8 (Wash.Sup. 1/18/01).]

An employee's answers to questions that the employer should not have asked (because the questions violated the ADA) can be legitimate evidence in a WC case—for instance, where a person lies about past medical history; see *Dureoun v. C&P Production Specialist*, 718 So. 2d 460 (La. App. 1998), and *Caldwell v. Aarlin/Holcombe Armature Co.*, 267 Ga. 613, 481 S.E. 2d 196 (1997).

An illegal alien who presented forged IRCA documentation, which the employer relied on, to get a job did not become an "employee" because no valid employment contract could have been formed. Therefore, when the alien was injured on the job, he was not eligible for Worker's Compensation because he was not a lawful employee: *Granados v. Windson Development Corp.*, 257 Va. 103, 509 S.E.2d 290 (1999).

One worker deliberately falsely claimed that another worker threatened "to bring a gun in here and kill someone." The employee who was supposed to have made the threat was taken to a mental hospital by the police, then released after an interview with a psychiatrist. She claimed severe emotional distress, and sued the employer for defamation.

The employer cited Worker's Compensation exclusivity because defamation is an intentional tort causing emotional distress. But the Pennsylvania Superior Court decision in 1999 [*Urban v. Dollar Bank*, 725 A.2d 815 (Pa.Super. 1999)] allowed the employee to maintain the defamation lawsuit, on the theory that Worker's Compensation deals with physical or mental injuries, whereas defamation deals with damage to reputation.

20.10.6 [NEW] Problems of Co-Employment

A laborer who worked for Southern Personnel died after incurring injuries at Compression Coat, a pipe coating facility. Compression Coat paid weekly invoices to Southern Personnel for staffing costs, including WC insurance. Because another Southern Personnel employee died in a similar accident, Southern's WC insurer refused to provide insurance at the Compression Coat facility. Southern transferred all its employees to C.L. Management, which leased them back to Southern; C.L. got lower WC rates than Southern could have.

After the laborer's death, his family sued Southern and CC for wrongful death and survivor benefits. CC said that it was his special employer, Southern said it was immune from tort suit because it was his general employer. The plaintiffs identified C.L. Management as his employer. The suit was dismissed by the Louisiana Court of Appeals against Southern, either because it was his employer and immune from tort suit, or was not his employer and therefore owed him no duty. CC was also exempt, as a borrowing employer.

In a less drastic case, a worker was injured when he fell into an uncovered floor drain. He received comp benefits from his employer, the Stanley Jones Corporation, which was a subcontractor of Haskell Co. He sued Haskell for personal injuries, based on a Kansas statute that relieves the principal contractor of responsibility for providing WC when the subcontractor obtains the coverage. The Kansas court hearing the case said that the contractor is still the statutory employer, and therefore immune from tort suits.

[*Pradia v. Southern Personnel of Louisiana, Inc.*, 2000 La. App. LEXIS 2308 and *Robinett v. The Haskell Co.*, 2000 Kan. LEXIS 825, discussed in "Shared Employees—Who Provides Coverage?" *Claims Magazine*, January 2001, http://www.claimsmag.com/Issues/Jan01/decisions.asp.]

Chapter 21

OSHA

21.1 INTRODUCTION

A visit to OSHA's Web site, http://www.osha-slc.gov, is worthwhile, especially for the smaller enterprise that is subject to OSHA jurisdictions but can't afford a full-time staffer who is specifically involved in occupational safety and health issues.

Three vital OSHA forms (Form 101, the Supplementary Record of Occupational Injuries & Illnesses; Form 200, the Log and Summary of Occupational Injuries & Illnesses; and Form 174, the Material Safety Data Sheet) are available online, through the OSHA publications server, http://www.osha-slc.gov/OshDoc/Additional.html. This is also the place to locate online versions of significant OSHA documents, such as

- All About OSHA (publication 2056)
- Assessing the Need for Personal Protective Equipment: A Guide for Small Business Employers (publication 3151)
- Concepts & Techniques of Machine Safeguarding (publication 3067)
- Consultation Services for the Employer (publication 3047)
- Employee Workplace Rights (publication 3021)
- Handbook for Small Business (publication 2209)
- How to Prepare for Workplace Emergencies (publication 3088)
- Industrial Hygiene (publication 3143)
- Materials Handling and Storing (publication 2236)
- Safety and Health Guide for the Microelectronics Industry (publication 3107)
- Small Entity Compliance Guide for Respiratory Protection Standard (no publication number)

- Training Requirements in OSHA Standards and Training Guidelines (publication 2254)

➟ TIP

Many of these documents use the Adobe PDF format; the software for reading PDFs can be downloaded free from many government and private sites.

OSHA's Partnership Page, http://www.osha-slc.gov/fso/vpp/partnership/index.html provides information about OSHA's Partnership program, described as "an extended, voluntary, cooperative relationship with groups of employers, employees, and employee representatives" to improve worker safety and health.

However, although you would expect to be able to download the poster that employers are required to display in the workplace, the latest version, Publication 3165, cannot be printed directly from the site. Instead, the poster can be accessed as a PDF file at http://www.osha.gov/oshpubs/poster.html, downloaded to your hard drive, opened as a PDF file from the hard drive, and then printed on a printer that can handle paper that is 8 1/2 x 14" (i.e., legal and not letter size). Other options are to download the file and have it printed by a professional printer, or ordering pre-printed copies from the online publications order form at the OSHA site.

The results of an OSHA poll appearing in the December 1999 issue of *HR Magazine* (p. 23) show that over half (56%) of respondents had had an OSHA inspection, and 42% have been cited by the agency. On the basis of lost workdays per 200,000 hours worked, 41% of respondents had an injury rate of 0–5, 17% a rate of 6–10, 11% a rate of 11–15, and 12% a rate over 16. Thirty percent had a positive experience using OSHA consulting services; 1% used and had negative experience; 18% don't even want to consider it; 38% haven't used but would consider; 13% don't know. Forty-nine percent voluntarily asked advice from an OSHA officer and had a positive experience; 3% had negative experience; 14% won't do it; and 16% might consider it.

The Occupational Safety and Health Review Commission (OSHRC) decided in 1998 that an employee leasing company was not subject to the OSH Act, because the workers in question were not their "employees" who worked in their "business" as defined by the OSH Act. The leased employees worked in a factory, and the leasing company failed to exercise significant control over them. However, OSHA released a draft of its multiemployer worksite policy, providing that the controlling employer (e.g., the general contractor) can become liable for site hazards if it has sufficient control over employees of the other companies working at the sites. The policy, which applies to both the general and construction standards, defines sufficient control as contractual authority to require subcontractors to prevent or correct violations; or as failure to exercise reasonable care, with the result that employees are placed at risk. [*Sec'y of Labor v. Team America Corp.*, 1998 Westlaw 733708 (OSHRC 1998); but see 67 LW 2249.]

Workplace Violence

According to a joint survey between members of the Risk and Insurance Management Society and the Risk Management/Insurance Division of the American Society of Safety Engineers, performed in the autumn of 1998 and released in December, 1999 [Joann M. Sullivan, Workplace Violence Survey and White Paper, http://www.rims.org/govt/work.shtml (12/99)] and data from the Department of Justice, there were 21,300 assaults and violent acts in the workplace serious enough to require days off. Harassment is the leading type of violent act (about 16,000 cases a year), although stalking, threats, trespass, and harassment by telephone and e-mail also occur.

About half of the organizations surveyed have programs to address workplace violence (e.g., in-plant security; screening of applicants; no-weapons policies). Most businesses had some insurance coverage that would cover violent workplace incidents, but few performed formal risk assessments.

21.2 OSHA POWERS

HR Magazine's William Atkinson reports on 1998–1999 OSHA enforcement in "When OSHA Comes Knocking," on page 35 of the October 1999 issue. Total OSHA penalties for 1998 were $79 million, and penalties as of July 1999 (two months before the end of the fiscal year) had already reached close to $75 million after about 34,000 inspections.

In fiscal 1998, the ten most frequent serious violations cited by OSHA were:

1. Scaffolding (5,537)
2. Fall protection (3,862)
3. Hazard communication (3,274)
4. Lockout/tagout (3,532)
5. Machine guarding (2,266)
6. Power presses (2,230)
7. Mechanical power (2,151)
8. Electrical (1,902)
9. Excavation (1,399)
10. Machine guarding/abrasive wheels (1,338)

For advice about how to sail through an inspection unharmed (or as close to unharmed as possible), see Robert J. Grossman, "Handling Inspections: Tips from Insiders," *HR Magazine,* 10/99, p. 40.

- Check the credentials of anyone claiming to be an OSHA inspector. (OSHA photo IDs have the Department of Labor seal on the back.) An environmental activist, labor organizer, or industrial spy could be pretending to be from OSHA.
- Ask if the inspection is programmed or from a complaint or follow-up after an accident.
- Find out if the complainant is a current employee. (The inspector won't give you the name, but will tell you if the complainant falls into this category.)
- Have your lawyer review all requests for documents and information, and review what you turn over.
- If documents submitted are complete and up to date, the inspector may quit after inspecting the records.
- At the opening conference, make sure that the inspector will take steps to make sure your trade secrets are protected.
- If the inspector takes photos or videos at the walk-around stage, take your own confirming photos and videos and keep them for comparison.
- Get duplicates of physical samples taken by the inspector, and ask for copies of OSHA's test results.
- Appoint someone in your organization with ongoing OSHA responsibility (this responsibility often goes to the HR department, if no one else takes it over). Train employees how to respond to questions from OSHA inspector.
- Take inspector to the area he or she asks to see by the shortest, most direct route, not the long way, in case they see something else they want to cite.
- Get to know the personnel in the OSHA area office, and develop a cooperative working relationship with them.

21.3 OSHA REGULATIONS

In November 1999, OSHA posted a notice on its Web site answering a request for information from CSC Credit Services. The agency responded that "ensuring safe and healthful working conditions for the employee should be a precondition for any home-based work assignments," and "the employer is responsible for correcting hazards of which it is aware or should be aware." This implies that employers would have an OSHA burden not only in the formal workplace, but in the homes of employees who telecommute or otherwise work at home. Employers might have to invest heavily in bringing employees' homes up to facility standards, and OSHA inspections of homes would trigger privacy concerns.

But in early January 2000, OSHA responded to significant opposition from industry by formally withdrawing the letter. (It was also noted that OSHA undertook to regulate home workplaces off its own bat; the agency received no complaints by injured or endangered at-home employees.)

For the history of the OSHA home-work notice, see Sarah Lueck, "Business Groups Attack OSHA Advisory," *WSJ,* 1/5/00, p. A3; "Home Work-Safety Letter is Rescinded," *WSJ,* 1/6/00, p. A2; and "Home Workers Didn't File Any OSHA Protests," *WSJ,* 1/10/00, p. A6. For more information on telecommuting, see ¶8.6.

OSHA doesn't regulate employees' exposure to their own tobacco smoke. Permissible exposure limits (PELs) apply only to a situation in which an employee is obligated to enter a contaminated area in order to perform work for the benefit of the employer. See *Employment Alert* 12/23/98 p.5.

21.3.1 Bathroom Breaks

Theoretically, both the OSH Act and state occupational health laws require employers to provide an adequate number of toilets for the size of the workforce. The OSHA general industry sanitation standard (29 CFR §1910.141) requires the presence of toilet facilities in the workplace.

However, until recently, there was little or no regulation of workplace practices that affect employees' access to bathroom breaks. This emerged as an issue of concern, and especially of union activism, in 1998. It's easy for management (who can take breaks anytime they want) to forget that access to restrooms is not just a matter of comfort or dignity, but of health. Employees who are denied bathroom access can suffer bladder or kidney infections or dysfunction. If they restrict their liquid consumption, they can suffer the ill effects of dehydration.

Although the average worker needs to use the restroom two to three times a day, female workers need more bathroom breaks than male workers (other than older male workers, who need to use the restroom more often because of prostate enlargement), and pregnant women need to use the restroom more often than nonpregnant women. If the employee's increased need for elimination is due to a health condition, the Americans with Disabilities Act may require reasonable accommodation. For instance, the worker might be allowed more breaks during the day, but short breaks suitable for bathroom visits, not longer breaks. Or the employee might be assigned to the workstation closest to the restroom, so he or she can return to work quickly.

An April 6, 1998 letter from OSHA forbids employers to impose unreasonable restrictions on bathroom use. OSHA inspectors who receive worker complaints on this issue are directed to investigate the reasonableness of the employer's policy, including the length of time that employees are expected to defer calls of nature.

Union activists point out that lack of bathroom breaks is associated with a speeded-up work schedule that deprives employees of all sorts of needed breaks. Activists also point out that uncomfortable, resentful, or exhausted workers are not only at risk of injury but also likely to experience declining productivity. See 66 LW 2579 (3/31/98) and 2636 (4/21/98).

Mary Williams Walsh's "Blue-Collar Urgency: Bathroom Rights," *NYT* 11/22/00 p. G1 discusses problems of restroom access to blue-collar workers, especially those on fast assembly lines. Women in blue-collar jobs, such as electrical line workers, may also find themselves in areas where there are no public or even private bathroom facilities to which they have access. According to the Seventh Circuit [*DeClue v. Central Illinois Light Co.*, 69 LW 1089 (7th Cir. 8/2/00).] the employer's failure to provide a toilet for a woman worker did not constitute hostile environment sex discrimination. The court said that the plaintiff pleaded improperly—it should have been raised as a disparate impact, not a hostile environment, claim. However, the employer is entitled to an undue burden defense in a disparate impact case—e.g., showing that it would not be feasible to install private toilet facilities on the truck used to drive to job sites.

21.4 [NEW] RECORD-KEEPING REQUIREMENTS

On January 18, 2001, OSHA revised the rules for reporting workplace injuries. [See http://www.osha-slc.gov/recordkeeping/index.html, 66 FR 5965, 6115 (1/19/01).] Effective January 1, 2002 (the year's grace was given to allow employers to phase in the new requirements), updated forms are issued for Form 300 (Log of Work-Related Injuries and Illnesses), Form 301 (Injury and Illness Incident Report; now more detailed than the earlier version) and Form 300A (Summary of Work-Related Injuries and Illnesses).

Approximately 1.3 million workplaces (those with 10 or more employees) will be subject to the new rule, although low-hazard industries such as retail, finance, insurance, real estate, and service businesses are generally exempt—although all employers must report any workplace incident that results in the hospitalization of three or more workers or that causes a death.

The regulation is drafted in a plain English, Q&A format, with checklists and flowcharts to make it easier to understand the reporting of restricted work and light duty cases. For the first time, employees are guaranteed privacy rights in information about them on the reporting logs. Pre-existing illnesses and injuries need only be reported if a current incident has significantly aggravated them; minor aggravations no longer need to be reported.

As discussed below, OSHA released a controversial ergonomics rule in November, 2000. OSHA's pre-2001 reporting requirements had a separate system for reporting musculo-skeletal disorders (MSDs); the new rule simply adds a column to the standard form for reporting MSDs. In light of the repeal of the ergonomics rule (see below), the status of this form is now unclear.

21.5 USE OF PERSONAL PROTECTIVE EQUIPMENT

A Proposed Rule, published at 64 FR 15401 (3/31/99), requires the employer not only to require personal protective equipment where appropriate, but also to pay for all such equipment, other than prescription eyeware, safety-toe shoes, and logging boots (i.e., items that employees can use in private life, away from the work-site—unlike things like gas masks that have no general usefulness).

21.5.1 Respiratory Protection

OSHA adopted a new respiratory protection rule, published in the *Federal Register* on January 8, 1998, that took effect October 5, 1998. The standard, known as 1910.134, covers respirator use in general industry, shipyards, longshore work, and construction—but not in agriculture. Nor does the standard deal with the issue of tuberculosis prevention (e.g., in health care workplaces).

For guidance to employers, OSHA issued compliance directive CPL 2-0.120, explaining how to select respirators and analyze workplace hazards, when to change the chemical cartridges in respirators, and how to make sure that respirators are properly fitted. Private-sector workers engaged in firefighting must be relieved from the fire site on a "two in-two out" schedule. The respiratory protection directive is explained in an OSHA news release dated 9/24/98; text of the directive can be found at http://www.osha.gov, Library/Reading Room, Directives.

21.8 ERGONOMICS

Background

The struggle to adopt OSHA ergonomics standards has been going on for many years. Congress' appropriations bills for OSHA between 1996 and 1998 forbade the agency to adopt ergonomics standards. As soon as it was free to do so, OSHA published a draft ergonomics regulation on January 6, 1999. A revised Working Draft of March 12, 1999, marked "do not cite or quote," was published on the OSHA Web site.

OSHA issued proposed regulations on ergonomics on November 22, 1999. If adopted in that form, the proposal would require about 1.6 million employers to set up a basic ergonomics program of education and reporting. A full program of prevention would be required if at least one musculo-skeletal disorder (MSD) occurred in the workplace at any time.

Originally, comments were due February 1, 2000, and informal public hearings were scheduled to begin on February 2, 2000. The rule was supposed to become effective 60 days after OSHA's publication of a final standard reflecting the comments. But on January 27, 2000, then-Secretary of Labor Alexis Herman extended the comment period to March 2 and re-scheduled the hearing date to March 13.

In June, 2000, the House of Representatives, by a narrow margin (220-203) voted to prevent the Department of Labor from implementing new ergonomics standards at least until October of 2001. [David Rogers, "House Approves Delay in Ergonomics Standards," *WSJ* 6/9/00).] OSHA published a huge rule in the November 14, 2000 Federal Register.

Ironically, because the ergonomic rules were published as Final Rules early in the wave of late-Clinton-era regulations, they are exempt from the moratorium (see Introduction). Therefore, the Bush Administration was not able to defer their effectiveness merely by invoking the moratorium.

However, the ink was barely dry on the regulations before challenges were filed in the federal courts (by, e.g., the Society for Human Resource Management, U.S. Chamber of Commerce, and National Association of Manufacturers)—and shots were fired from both directions. Business groups say that the regulations were promulgated too hastily. Labor groups say that they don't go far enough to protect worker safety. As of December, 2000, suits had been filed by business groups in the Fourth, Fifth, and D.C. Circuits, whereas the challenges came from labor organizations in the First, Second, Third, and Ninth Circuits. It was anticipated that the Judicial Panel on Multi-District Litigation would assign a single consolidated petition to one Circuit, by lottery, and that the decision would not be made before November 2001. [Yochi J. Dreazen, "Ergonomic Rules Are the First in a Wave of Late Regulations," *WSJ* 11/14/00 p. A4; Darryl Van Duch, "Ergonomics Rules Draw Attacks," *Nat'l L.J.* 12/5/00 (law.com); "OSHA's Final Ergonomics Rule Hits Federal Register: Lawsuit Filed," http://www.hrnext.com/news/inex.cfm?id=865.]

Provisions of the Rule

The ergonomics Final Rule is a general industry standard, so it covers approximately 6.1 million work sites and 102 million workers. It does not apply to construction, agriculture, or shipping (maritime or railroad) work.

The main focus of the rule is on musculo-skeletal disorders (MSDs). In the final rule, OSHA provides a two-page checklist of specific examples of MSD situations and risk factors, such as use of a computer keyboard or mouse for more than four hours a day, lifting heavy packages repeatedly during the workshift, kneeling or squatting for over two hours a day, and exposure to vibration and physical stress.

Whenever an employee experiences any work-related MSD, even an employer with no previous experience of such injuries must take action. The employer must implement a program for managing MSDs within seven calendar days. The employer also has to provide employee training, do a job hazard analysis, and create a program to reduce further MSDs in the workplace.

Employees who suffer work-related MSDs are entitled to receive paid leave (including sick leave and disability benefits) and benefits when they are off work or back at work on a light duty job. This is referred to as the Work Restriction Period (WRP). The WRP expires after 90 days, or earlier if the worker is cleared to go back to his or her job or, on the other hand, there is medical certification that the employee will never be able to return to work. This is a concession to employers: the 1999 proposal called for a WRP of up to six months. Employees are entitled to have the employer pay for an independent second and even third opinion as to whether an injury claimed by the employee actually is an MSD that requires paid leave or a light duty assignment.

The final rule contains a "grandfather clause" for employers who already have an adequate ergonomics program, but OSHA places demanding requirements on such programs, including reporting systems, hazard control mechanisms, and evaluation and follow-up of alleged MSDs.

Employers with a generally good record can use an informal "Quick Fix" program to return to ergonomics compliance on an informal basis.

. . . And Statistics

Proverbially, there are three levels: lies, damned lies, and statistics. Certainly, both sides in the ergonomics debate have provided a blizzard of statistics and projections for the cost and effect of ergonomics rules.

One rationale for imposing tough rules on MSDs is to protect workers. However, BLS data show that repetitive trauma cases became significant with widespread computer use. In 1980, 23,200 repetitive trauma cases were reported, peaking at 332,100 in 1994—but declining significantly since then, even though ergonomics rules have not been put into effect. Depending on whom you ask, that could show that employers are already handling the problem—or that employers are being kept in line and imposing self-regulation because of the threat of tough government regulation.

In 1992, the rate of work-related illnesses and injuries was 8.9 per 100 full-time equivalent (FTE) employees, which declined to 6.7/100 in 2000—much lower than the predicted rate of 10/100, with the result that the economy was at least $125 billion more productive because of reduction in injuries, and the number of injuries actually reported was about one million lower than the number that would be projected based on the unemployment rate. This reduction flouted an accepted principle of labor economics, that the lower the unemployment rate, the higher the injury rate (because presumably less unemployment means longer hours and more stress and therefore more risk for workers). [Alan B. Krueger, "Economic Scene," *NYT* 9/14/00 p. C2.]

In 1998, for instance, there were 49,100 injuries to nursing aides, orderlies and attendants, making these health care jobs the most dangerous in terms of occupational injury; 43,900 truck drivers were injured, as were 36,600 laborers in non-construction jobs, 19,700 assemblers, and 14,000 janitors and cleaners.

Focusing on repetitive task injuries causing lost workdays in 1998, 3,700 such injuries occurred in the mining industry, 8,000 in agriculture, forestry, and fishing, 12,000 in financial services (although this is not usually considered a physically risky injury, it is heavily computer-dependent), 44,400 in construction.

A report prepared by the National Academy of Sciences, released in January, 2001 by Congressional Democrats and union officials, "Musculo-skeletal Disorders and the Workplace," says that there are about a million occupational repetitive stress injuries each year, costing at least $20 million.

To its proponents, the report proves that U.S. workers are at heavy risk and need detailed ergonomics rules to make the workplace safer. OSHA critics, however, say that this report proves that the ergonomics rules are much too costly in comparison with the benefit they could be expected to provide. [Phil Kuntz, "Proposed OSHA Rules for Workplace Injuries Make Companies Ache," *WSJ* 9/18/00 p. A1; Steven Greenhouse, "Battle Lines Drawn Over Ergonomic Rules," *NYT* 11/18/00 p. C1, and "Ergonomics Report Cites Job Injuries," *NYT* 1/8/01 p. C6.]

Invocation of the CRA

In March, 2001, both Houses of Congress used a little-known federal statute called the Congressional Review Act of 1996 (CRA) to repeal the ergonomics regulations—the first time the CRA had actually been put into practice. Under the CRA, as long as 30 Senators agree, a vote can be taken directly on the floor of Congress without committee discussions to overturn regulations promulgated during the preceding 60 days. The matter is determined with debate limited to 10 hours in the Senate. Amendments to the original petition will not be heard—and, furthermore, if the CRA is successfully invoked, the administrative agency that promulgated the regulations struck down by Congress will never be allowed to enact "substantially similar" rules.

Senate Joint Resolution 6, dealing with the ergonomics rules, was introduced on March 1. The Senate voted 56-44 to overturn the ergonomics rules. On March 7, the House also voted to reject the OSHA regulation, by 223-206. Although some Congress members crossed the floor, generally speaking the Republicans voted to eliminate the rules, the Democrats to retain them.

In a way, the ergonomics battle has not ended, only shifted to the courts and to the statehouses. Some states have taken over occupational safety enforcement; they have the power—but not the obligation—to set their own ergonomics standards, and three states have already adopted their own ergonomics rules. [See Deirdre Davidson and Tatiana Boncompagni, "The Swift Demise of OSHA Rules," *Legal Times* 3/14/01 (law.com); David Espo, "Congress Repeals Workplace Rules," http://dailynews.yahoo.com/h/ap/2001/0308/ts/workplace_injuries_31.html; no www; Robert Gavin, "Ergonomics Rules Still Alive in Many States," *Wall Street Journal* 3/14/01 p. B15.]

21.9 DIVISION OF RESPONSIBILITY

Under the "peculiar risk" doctrine, someone who hires an independent contractor to perform inherently dangerous work is liable for damages for torts committed by the independent contractor against others in the course of doing the work. However, in California, this doctrine cannot be used by employees of a subcontractor, injured by the subcontractor's negligence, to sue the general contractor [*Toland v. Sunland Housing Group Inc.*, 18 Cal. 4th 253, 74 Cal. Rptr. 2d 504, 955 P.2d 504 (Cal. 1998)].

The Seventh Circuit found that an engineering firm, which consulted on a sewer project where a fatal accident occurred, did not become subject to the OSHA construction standard: *CH2M Hill Inc. v. Herman*, 68 LW 1207 (7th Cir. 9/23/99). OSHA uses a two-step test to see whether construction standards should be applied to nonconstruction companies: ability to direct or control trade contractors, and degree of involvement in the multiple activities that are necessary to complete a construction project. However, the Seventh Circuit preferred a simpler analysis: presence or absence of substantial supervision over actual construction, and found that the engineering firm did not have the necessary degree of control.

Also see *Universal Construction Co. Inc. v. OSHRC*, 1999 WL 430200 (10th Cir. 1999): A general contractor can be held liable for its subcontractors' OSHA violations, if the general contractor creates or controls the workplace hazard that endangers employees of other companies.

Sec'y of Labor v. Yandell, OSHRC No. 94-3080 (3/12/99) holds that an individual or corporate employer can still be cited for violating OSHA regulations after it has gone out of business. (In many instances, the OSHA problems would trigger business dissolution.)

OSHA's internal directive, CPL 2-0.214, explains how OSHA will issue citations to multi-employer workplaces. If a particular employer is in a position to create, control, or correct hazards, or if it exposes employees to danger, OSHA will check the employer's conduct to see if it has met all its OSH obligations; if not, citations can be issued. See WestGroup Employment Alert, 1/6/00, p. 9, for discussion; the text of the directive can be found at http://www.osha.gov.

21.10 OSHA ENFORCEMENT

It does not constitute double jeopardy to impose administrative penalties on an employer after it has been convicted of criminal OSHA violations, because the administrative penalties are clearly civil and cannot result in imprisonment [*S. A. Healy Co. v. OSHRC*, 138 F.3d 686 (7th Cir. 1998)].

The Fourth Circuit ruled that it does not violate the Fourth Amendment prohibition of unreasonable searches and seizures for OSHA to perform off-site videotaping of the worksite, showing that workers 80 feet above ground level did not have safety cables. (The inspector got permission to tape from a hotel rooftop across the street.) See *L. R. Willson & Sons Inc. v. OSHRC*, 134 F.3d 1235 (4th Cir. 1998), *cert. denied* 119 S.Ct. 404 (affirming the decision in the main volume).

29 USC §666(e) imposes penalties whenever a willful violation of an OSHA standard leads to the death of "any employee."

➠ TIP

An early 1999 decision permits the penalty to be assessed against the culpable employer on a multiemployer worksite, even though the deceased employee worked for one of the other employers [*U.S. v. Pitt-Des Moines Inc.*, 168 F.3d 976 (7th Cir. 1999)].

In mid-2000, OSHA formalized a policy discussed in earlier supplements: see 65 FR 46,498 (7/18/00). OSHA inspectors will not routinely request to see the employer's self-audit reports during an inspection. Nor will OSHA use audit reports to target hazards as a focus of the inspection. The existence of self-audits, combined with a good-faith effort to correct problems, will deter OSHA from imposing penalties.

OSHA Directive CPL 2.001, effective 12/2/99, replaces CPL 2.91. Under CPL 2.001, citations, and even penalties in willful and egregious cases, can be imposed on employers if their reporting of illness and injury information on OSHA annual survey forms is incorrect. In the year 2000, OSHA plans to audit 250 establishments and check these figures against records such as payroll figures and Worker's Compensation records. The text of the Directive can be found at http://www.osha-slc.gov/OshDoc/Directive_pdf/CPL_2-2000-1.pdf.

Once OSHA has inspected a workplace pursuant to a warrant, the company can no longer appeal the denial of its motion in federal court to quash the warrant. Instead, after the inspection, the employer has to exhaust its administrative remedies within OSHA and assert the challenges to the validity of the warrant in enforcement proceedings for any sanctions imposed because of the inspection. See *Sturm, Ruger & Co., Inc. v. OSHA*, 1999 WL 595353 (1st Cir. 1999).

In spring 1999, however, the D.C. Circuit ruled that the cooperative compliance program was improper, because OSHA should have promulgated it as a rule, subject to notice to affected parties and with an opportunity for them to comment. See *Chamber of Commerce of the U.S. v. OSHA*, 67 LW 1622 (D.C. Cir. 4/9/99), discussed in Glenn Burkins' article, "Court Rules OSHA Improperly Started Program for Dangerous Workplaces," *WSJ*, 4/12/99, p. A4.

An employee who is injured at work cannot sue OSHA inspectors for failure to detect the hazard at the inspection, because OSHA inspections are "discretionary functions" that are entitled to exemption from the Federal Tort Claims Act [*Irving v. U.S.*, 162 F.3d 154 (1st Cir. 1998)].

Roy G. Stoops, owner of a steel company in Indiana, was sentenced to four months' imprisonment for willful OSHA violations that resulted in the death of a worker. Stoops' company had already had a substantial history of violations. Many dangerous conditions were present at the site, and subcontractors had warned of the risks. Stoops was placed on one year of supervised release and was ordered to pay $6000 toward the funeral expenses of the deceased worker. The company was placed on probation and made jointly liable for the restitution. For more on the Stoops conviction, see WestGroup *Employment Alert,* 11/25/98, p. 10.

Prevention and Planning

In an October 16, 1998 interview with BNA, Marthe Kent, Director of OSHA's Office of Regulatory Analysis, said that OSHA intended to promulgate a regulation, not a standard, to govern workplace safety and health programs. The agency was willing to be held to the tougher standard of analysis that applies to standards. An OSHA standard must address a significant risk; be technologically and economically feasible; be cost effective; and substantially reduce the risk. A regulation is acceptable as long as it is not arbitrary or capricious. Standards can be more specific than regulations because standards are aimed at specific hazards; regulations are not. See 67 LW 2316.

Chapter 22

Privacy Issues

22.1 INTRODUCTION

Although many employers take advantage of the simplicity of using Social Security numbers as employment ID numbers, this is not always sound policy. Many people are concerned about the privacy implications of having too many computerized records tied to the same ID number (and vulnerable to unauthorized access). Legislation has been introduced in Congress (and has attracted significant support) to require organizations other than the Social Security Administration to get advance written consent before using Social Security numbers for any purpose. See Susan J. Wells, "You've Got Their Numbers—And They Want Them Back," *HR Magazine*, "Focus," 12/98, p. 3.

To an increasing extent, business is becoming internationalized, so a U.S. company may find that it has employees and contractors outside the United States. These people won't have Social Security numbers. Don't forget that the European Union's privacy requirements are much stricter than U.S. federal law and will become a factor in operations outside the United States.

Wells' article suggests adopting an identification system that does not use Social Security numbers. It's best not to use a nine-digit number (to avoid confusion with the Social Security number). Most companies will find a six-digit number perfectly adequate: After all, that allows 999,999 options, so even if a 5000-person workforce has a lot of turnover, the ID numbers won't run out for a while. Shorter numbers call for fewer keystrokes, so there's less risk of error—but a large company might need more numbers than a five-digit system will permit.

It's better to assign numbers at random rather than sequentially. If the numbers are assigned based on the order in which employees are hired, it's easy to breach security by getting one number and extrapolating from the hiring dates. Check the format requirements of your payroll and database programs; it may be necessary to start each ID number with a digit, not a zero, a blank space, or a character such as an asterisk or ampersand. Formatting needs also determine whether you can mix letters and numbers or include dots, dashes, or underscores.

Connecticut Gen. Stats. §31-51q make employers liable to employees for damages if the employer disciplines or discharges employees because they exercise their First Amendment rights, provided that the employee activity does not substantially or materially interfere with job performance or the working relationship between employer and employee.

Cotto v. United Technologies Corp., 68 LW 1221 (Conn. 10/12/99) clarifies that the statute applies to private as well as governmental employers. However, the plaintiff employee still lost his case. According to the court, it was not unlawful for the employer, a defense contractor, to fire the employee for refusing to display an American flag at his workstation. In this reading, refusal to display a flag is not a protected exercise of First Amendment rights.

22.3 DRUG USE IN THE WORKPLACE

According to the Pennsylvania Commonwealth Court (in a 2000 decision) it did not constitute disparate treatment to fire an employee for selling marijuana at the workplace, while the buyers of the marijuana were not fired even though they engaged in drug use on the premises. [See Danielle N. Rodier, "Retaining Pot-Smoking Employees While Firing Drug Dealer Not Disparate Treatment," *The Legal Intelligencer* 7/14/00; law.com.] The discharged employee applied for unemployment compensation which, not surprisingly, was denied. The denial was affirmed by the unemployment referee and the Unemployment Compensation Board of Review. The Commonwealth Court rejected the argument that the drug dealer was the victim of disparate treatment, because it was a business necessity for the employer to stop on-premises drug dealing.

A late-1999 Wyoming case, *Duncan v. Afton Inc.*, 68 LW 1350 (Wyo. 11/30/99)—like earlier cases in Illinois, Louisiana, and New York—holds that an employee who is fired because of a false-positive drug test can sue the testing firm for failing to meet its duty of due care in collecting, handling, and processing the specimens. However, the Fifth Circuit, and Texas and Pennsylvania courts, have held that testing firms do not have such a duty running to the employees; after all, the employer company is the one that hires the testing company.

In a variation on this theme, a job applicant who was not hired because he flunked the required drug test sued the laboratory and its doctor for negligence. He lost: the lab's duty of due care ran to the employer that hired it, not to the job applicant. Anyway, because the job was an at-will position, any injury resulting from the drug test was speculative, not determinable by the court: *Ney v. Axelrod*, 723 A.2d 719 (Pa. Sup. 1999).

An employee fired for testing positive on a urine test sued the employer for wrongful discharge, claiming that the employer violated public policy by submitting the sample to a lab that was not state-certified. (The North Carolina state statute dealing with drug tests requires the use of certified labs.) The ex-employee lost: *Garner v. Reutenbach Constructors Inc.*, 515 S.E.2d 438 (N.C. 1999). Not every violation of public policy carries a private right of action. Here, there was no evidence that the employer even knew the lab was not certified, much less that the employer flouted the law by deliberately choosing an uncertified lab.

According to the Fourth Circuit, neither imposing a drug testing requirement nor firing two workers for refusal to take the test violated the National Labor Relations Act. (The fired employees claimed that they were really fired because they were union activists.) Even though the testing program was implemented one week after a strike, all employees were required to take drug tests. Furthermore, since 6 out of 20 employees tested positive, the employer had a valid concern about drug use in the workforce. Drug testing policies are valid as long as they are not disparately enforced (e.g., based on race or union membership). This policy required all employees to take the test, and therefore passed muster [*Eldeco Inc. v. NLRB*, 132 F.3d 1007 (4th Cir. 1997)].

It was legitimate for a school board to fire a teacher who refused to take a drug test ordered after a local law-enforcement sweep found marijuana in her car, which was parked in the school parking lot. The demand did not violate the teachers' contract or a school board policy requiring either consent or a search warrant for search of teachers' personal property **in the school building**. Given the reasonable suspicion that the teacher had violated the school's drug and alcohol policy (which calls for testing within two hours of the incident giving rise to suspicion), the demand for testing was appropriate. [*Hearn v. Board of Public Education*, 191 F.3d 1329 (11th Cir. 10/6/99).

In a First Circuit case, an arbitrator said that an employee who failed a drug test should not be fired and should be reinstated if he passed a second drug test. The employer sued the union to get the arbitration award set aside. The First Circuit's decision was that the Collective Bargaining Agreement required just cause for disciplinary determinations. However, the arbitrator's decision couldn't be enforced because it violated the well-established public policy against letting drug users maintain safety-sensitive jobs [*Exxon Corp. v. Esso Workers' Union*, 118 F.3d 841 (1st Cir. 1997)].

But the court reached the opposite conclusion in a later case, where the arbitrator ruled for the employee in what might seem like an even stronger case for the employer: *Kennecott Utah Copper Corp. v. Becker*, 68 LW 1268 (10th Cir. 10/29/99). A truck driver was routinely tested for drugs after an accident. The result was positive, and he admitted smoking marijuana two days before the accident.

He was fired, but the arbitrator ordered his reinstatement. The arbitrator read the CBA, which protects against discharge other than for just cause, to mean that there must be proof of on-the-job drug use, drug dealing, or impairment (not just drug use outside working hours).

To the Tenth Circuit, arbitrators' rulings must be upheld if they "draw their essence" from the CBA. In this view, courts have very little power to police arbitration decisions that are plausible interpretations of the CBA. Utah, like Connecticut, has a public policy against drug use in safety-sensitive jobs, but the Tenth Circuit dismissed it as general and permissive, not specific and mandatory.

In *Atchison, Topeka & Santa Fe Railway v. United Transp. Union*, 1999 WL 288264 (5th Cir. 1999), an employee subjected to a random drug test tested positive for cocaine use. The employer had a policy of double-checking positive results of employees taking prescription medications, but this particular employee didn't ask for a confirming test.

The collective bargaining agreement required a hearing for employees with positive test results. At the hearing, the employee raised the issue of false positives caused by prescription drugs, and the arbitrator ordered his reinstatement. The Fifth Circuit upheld the arbitrator's decision despite the employer's claim that reinstatement would be contrary to public policy, which is anti-drug. The court did not accept the public policy argument, because the arbitrator's decision was based on the insufficiency of the evidence, rather than on reinstatement of a known drug user.

Connecticut's statute, §31-51x, prohibits urine testing for drugs unless the employer has a reasonable suspicion that the employee is using drugs or alcohol in a way that does or could adversely affect job performance. *Poulos v. Pfizer*, 711 A.2d 688 (Conn. 1998), is a suit brought by a discharged employee for violation of that statute. The employee was caught stealing from the factory where he worked, and a drug test was ordered because of his suspicious behavior. Cocaine use was detected. He consented to drug testing because he was trying to reduce the consequences of the workplace theft.

The trial court found that the employer did not have reasonable suspicion of drug use and therefore awarded damages to the terminated employee. The appellate court reversed and ordered a new trial, because §31-51x deals with tests required by the employer, not those to which the employee consents. In this reading, an employee's consent does not become invalid merely because he or she faces hard choices when confronted with a threat of termination. Thus, the case was remanded for a determination of the reasonableness of asking for a drug test in such circumstances.

Under California law, an employer can test job applicants even if there is no particular reason to suspect them of drug use, but suspicion is required to test active employees. In a 1998 case, a job offer was extended conditional on the applicant's passing a drug test. The applicant had to move in order to take the new job, and logistics kept him from actually taking the drug test (which he failed) until after he was actually on the payroll. The employer fired him; he claimed that a suspicionless drug test was improper because he was already an employee. The California Court of Appeals didn't buy the employee's argument. In the court's view, the distinction between job applicants and employees exists because employers have a chance to observe their active employees and detect signs of drug use. The plaintiff in this case had not yet given the employer a chance to observe his behavior, and therefore the employer could treat him as an applicant for drug testing purposes [*Pilkington Barnes Hind v. Superior Court*, 66 Cal. App. 4th 28, 77 Cal. Rptr. 2nd 596 (Cal. App. 1998)].

The employer's policy called for termination of any employee found with a detectable level of alcohol or illegal drugs. The plaintiff of *Smith v. Zero Defects Inc.*, 1999 WL 330163 (Ida. 1999) tested positive for amphetamines in a random test; he was not impaired at that particular time.

However, Idaho, like Nebraska, Nevada, Oklahoma, and Utah, but unlike Arizona, Kansas, Oregon, and Washington, considers violation of an employer's zero-tolerance policy to constitute misconduct serious enough to prevent receipt of unemployment insurance benefits, even if the employee was not currently impaired at the time of the test. In other words, off-duty drug use can be serious enough to prevent the user from receiving unemployment benefits.

Sherlock Holmes might have called it "The Case of the Pharmacist's Drugs." *Zenor v. El Paso Healthcare System, Limited*, 67 LW 1729 (5th Cir. 5/24/99), involves a hospital pharmacist who was also a marijuana user and cocaine addict. One night, he was unable to come to work because he was still dizzy from an earlier cocaine injection. He told his supervisor that he couldn't come into work because of drug side effects. His supervisor asked if he would use the EAP. The pharmacist agreed.

The pharmacist went to the hospital for emergency treatment and then spent nine days in an in-patient detox program; his employer didn't know where he was or why he missed work. The hospital's HR director told him he could take a twelve-week FMLA leave, and his job would be protected until he finished rehab. However, he was fired, in part because his job gave him access to pharmaceutical cocaine.

He sued, charging ADA and state human relations law violations, as well as fraud, breach of contract, promissory estoppel, and intentional infliction of emotional distress. At the trial court level, all of the claims were dismissed except the promissory estoppel claim. The plaintiff won and was awarded significant damages by the jury, but the trial court knocked out some of the grounds on which promissory estoppel was found.

The case got to the Fifth Circuit to challenge the dismissal of the ADA claims (as well as the breach of contract and promissory estoppel claims). As §12.2 in the main volume discusses, being a current drug user is not an ADA disability. The Fifth Circuit cited this provision and took the position that a cocaine user is not qualified for the job of hospital pharmacist, and so could not take advantage of the ADA.

What is the time frame for determining if someone is a "current user"—the date of firing, or the date of entering rehab? The Fifth Circuit's view is that the adverse employment action occurs when someone is told that he or she will be terminated, not the actual effective date of the termination. Otherwise, employers would be penalized if they allowed medical leaves of absence for substance abusers.

The *Zenor* case defines "current" drug use as use recent enough to make it reasonable for the employer to conclude that drug abuse is an ongoing problem. Drug use several weeks prior to termination can fit this definition: See, for example, *Shafer v. Preston Memorial Hospital*, 107 F.3d 274 (4th Cir. 1997); *Collings v. Longview Fibre Co.*, 63 F.3d 828 (9th Cir. 1975).

A brief rehab program is not enough to make it unreasonable for an employer to fear that an addict will resume the use of illegal drugs. Relapse is always a meaningful risk even after a treatment program has been completed.

The ADA has a safe harbor [42 USC §12114(b)] for people who have completed a rehab program, but just entering a rehab program is not enough—the safe harbor is intended for people with a history of staying clean. *Zenor* cites *Baustian v. Louisiana,* 901 F. Supp. 274 (E.D. La. 1996), for the proposition that it isn't enough for an employee to self-report a drug problem before being caught by the employer (although self-reporting is a factor in the employee's favor).

As for the breach of contract claim, the Fifth Circuit considered Zenor to be an at-will employee. There was no public policy reason not to fire him (in fact, public policy might well demand that drug abusers be kept out of hospital pharmacies!).

The hospital's formal policy against workplace drug and alcohol use did not alter Zenor's at-will status. The policy made rehabilitation a condition of continued employment. The policy did say that employees would be reinstated after completion of rehab. However, the employee handbook stressed that employees worked at will. The substance abuse policy itself placed stress on the employer's discretion to discipline employees, including terminating them, for violating the policy. Texas courts do not imply a contractual relationship on the basis of general assurance of job security: See, for example, *Montgomery County Hospital District v. Brown,* 965 S.W.2d 501 (Texas 1998).

Nor did the Fifth Circuit believe that promissory estoppel had occurred. The workplace substance abuse policy was not a promise of reinstatement, only a condition that rehabilitation was a prerequisite for reinstatement. The jury ordered types of damages that are not available under Texas law even if promissory estoppel occurred. So all of the pharmacist's claims were legally invalid.

The ACLU published a report, "Drug Testing: A Bad Investment," in the Fall of 1999. You probably won't be too surprised to find out that the organization does not consider drug testing cost-effective for employers, and believes that it can impair productivity in the workplace by reducing morale. The organization does not see off-duty drug use as a major problem, as long as performance is not affected, as far as employers are concerned, and therefore does not believe that large investments in testing are effective.

The SmithKline Beecham Drug Testing Index shows that in 1997, 5% of random drug tests produced a positive result, much lower than the 18.1% found in 1987. This could be interpreted to mean that drug testing is no longer required, or that employers' zero-tolerance policies have been very effective in cutting drug use!

The ACLU suggests that there are more economical alternatives that are also more protective of employees' privacy. For instance, testing could be limited to testing of workers in safety-sensitive jobs for actual impairment; or, employers could redirect their efforts from catching drug users to offering them rehabilitation. [See Simon J. Nadel, "Workplace Drug Testing is Bad Investment," 68 LW 2191 (10/5/99).]

22.5 GENETIC TESTING

A study published in the *Journal of Occupational and Environmental Medicine* suggests that in appropriate cases, genetic screening to determine which workers are at high risk of suffering ill effects of chemical exposure can be cost-effective. Genetic screening only works for conditions that are fairly common (say, 50 cases occurring for every 1000 workers exposed to the hazardous condition). Otherwise, it costs too much to prevent even one case of disease by identifying a susceptible worker. (See WestGroup Employment Alert, 8/19/99, p. 8.)

On February 8, 2000, President Clinton issued an Executive Order that prevents federal workplaces from subjecting their workers to genetic testing, and from using genetic information in any employment-related decision.

The Executive Order has no force on private employers, but the President advocates the passage of a federal law to forbid genetic testing in the private workplace. The Daschle-Slaughter Bill, already pending in Congress, would do so. It would also prevent insurers from using genetic predisposition to deny coverage or set premiums. (Insurers in the over-50-member EGHP market are already forbidden to discriminate based on genetic markers, but the ban does not apply to individual or small-group policies.) [Robert Pear, "Clinton Bans Use of Genetic Makeup in Federal Employment," *NYT,* 2/9/00, p. A16; news item, "Clinton Order Bars Discrimination Based on Genetic Testing," *WSJ,* 2/9/00, p. A6.]

Connecticut passed a statute in 1998 (P.A. 98-1890, effective 10/1/98), forbidding employers to request genetic information from employees or discriminate against employees or applicants on the basic of genetic information. The statute defines genetic information as information about genes, gene products, or inherited characteristics.

22.6 SEARCHES AND SURVEILLANCE

Theoretically, employees will spend their workplace computing and online time carrying out employment-related tasks. In the real world, it's inevitable that employees will waste a certain amount of time on benevolent tasks like personal e-mail, shopping, and playing computer games. This is not necessarily a problem, unless it is prolonged enough to impair productivity, or unless the employee goes to pay-per-view sites at the employer's expense. Many pay-per-view sites are pornographic, so moral issues arise.

Some employee computer use can be harmful to the employer. Employee e-mail can be used to prove that the work environment was sexually or racially harassing, for instance. Does the risk of wasted time or employer liability justify the employer in monitoring employees' e-mail messages or computer use?

A *National Law Journal* article by Cheryl Blackwell Bryson and Michelle Day, "Workplace Surveillance Poses Legal, Ethical Issues" (1/11/99, p. B8), sums up the practical issues and court responses. On the practical front, the American Management Association reports that in fact close to two-thirds of medium- to large-sized companies do in fact perform electronic surveillance, but over half of them limit it to simple nonintrusive measures such as video cameras in the lobby. Only about 15% reviewed the content of employees' e-mail, and 10.4% taped phone conversations (e.g., in order to monitor the quality of customer service). About one-seventh of respondents review computer files, but only a little over 5% reviewed voice mail messages. This report, which reflects 1997 practices, can be found at http://www.ama.org.

Employers might be guilty of torts, and required to pay damages to employees, if they violate employee rights of privacy. However, there are workplace contexts in which employees do not have a reasonable expectation of privacy, so monitoring in those situations is not tortious.

An example is the case of *Bohach v. City of Reno*, 932 F.Supp. 1232 (D. Nev. 1997). To investigate charges of misuse of the police paging system, Reno monitored pagers. The court considered that there was no search, and federal wiretap statutes were not violated, because the pager technology required centralized storage of the messages, defeating any reasonable expectation of privacy.

State and federal wiretap statutes typically include a "provider exception," under which it is permissible for the "provider" of communications to intercept messages on the system. An employer clearly counts as a provider if it owns the equipment on which the employees communicate.

In *Smyth v. Pillsbury Co.*, 914 F.Supp. 97 (E.D. Pa. 1996), an employer was held not to have invaded the privacy of an employee who was fired after sending hostile e-mail messages to a supervisor. The court applied the provider rule because the employer company owned the communications equipment—even though the employees were told that their e-mails were confidential and would not give rise to employee discipline.

TIP

The exception might not be available if an Internet service provider actually handles e-mail service.

In *Konop v. Hawaiian Airlines*, 236 F.3d 1035 (9th Cir. 2000), the Ninth Circuit ruled that the District Court improperly dismissed claims by pilot Robert Konop that Hawaiian Airlines illegally gained access to his Web site, which criticized airline management. The Ninth Circuit said that gaining access to a private Web site without the consent of the site's owner can violate the federal Wiretap Act or the Stored Communication Act (or both). The Ninth Circuit sent the case back to the District Court for a full hearing.

Surveillance programs are most likely to survive an invasion of privacy or other employment-tort-based challenge if

- They are created in response to a real problem or real threat (e.g., potential employer liability).
- Employees are accurately informed of the purposes and content of the program—it's definitely a bad idea to tell employees their communications are confidential and turn around and use them against the employees!
- Surveillance is restricted to the least intrusive methods that will get the job done.

In the view of the Seventh Circuit, an employer may have violated the Employee Polygraph Protection Act by asking for a taped voice sample from an employee, to be analyzed to see if the employee was the person who left a threatening voice mail for another employee. Therefore, the employee's suit survived the employer's motion for summary judgment (although the employer might still win after a full trial).

Because the sample was used for analysis of truthfulness (not a simple comparison between the employee's voice and the threatening message), it fell under the statutory definition of "lie detector." See *Veazey v. Communications & Cable of Chicago, Inc.*, 194 F.3d 850 (7th Cir. 10/20/99).

Job hunters and HR staffers usually agree on most workplace privacy issues, with two important exceptions: e-mail monitoring and searches of employees' desks. That's the conclusion of a poll done by the Wall Street Journal Interactive Edition and the Society for Human Resource Management. (You can read survey results at http://www.careers.wsj.com or http://www.shrm.org/issues/survey.)

For instance, over three-quarters of HR professionals, and close to two-thirds of job seekers, think it's okay for the company to monitor the way that employees connect to the Internet during working hours. Over two-thirds of the HR respondents thought that it was appropriate for employers to monitor employee e-mail, but 51% of job applicants object to this practice. Evidently, they think that e-mail is a personal communication, and therefore less within the employer's control than at-work Internet access.

Close to half (48%) of HR professionals surveyed thought that employers had a right to search employees' desks, whereas almost three-quarters of job seekers said that this was not appropriate.

22.7 [NEW] HHS REGULATIONS ON PRIVACY IN HEALTH RECORDS

When Congress passed the Health Insurance Portability and Accessibility Act (HIPAA), one of the requirements of this lengthy and wide-ranging statute was that Congress had an obligation to issue federal health care privacy standards no later than August, 1999. Congress failed to do so, which gave the Department of Health and Human Services the power to draft its own regulations.

HHS proposed regulations on this topic in November, 1999 and finalized them in December, 2000 (see 65 FR 82511 et.seq., 12/28/00). State health care laws are not preempted if they furnish even greater protection of patient confidentiality.

The direct impact of these rules is on EGHP insurers, although some employers are also affected because they sponsor self-insured health plans.

The privacy rules apply to medical records and other confidential health information (whether oral or written—and whether the written record is on paper or electronic) that identify a specific individual. In other words, a statistical study of the health history of steel industry workers would not count, but the medical records of U.S. Steel employee John Smith would be covered.

Of course the health plan (or other entity covered by the rule) is allowed to disclose health information to the individual to whom it applies. Other disclosures can be made based on the individual's consent. But covered entities have an obligation to limit disclosure to the minimum needed to perform the task at hand.

Employees have a right to inspect and copy their medical records and other confidential information. They can ask the health plan to amend what they believe to be incorrect information. The EGHP has to provide its enrollees with information about how they intend to use, disclose, and protect confidential information about individuals. If information is legitimately disclosed (e.g., to administer a health plan), the covered entity must take steps to make sure that the recipients of the disclosures do not abuse the information.

A covered entity that violates this rule can be subjected to civil penalties of up to $100/incident, up to a maximum of $25,000 per person per year for each standard violated. Criminal penalties can be imposed for improper access or disclosure of information, obtaining personal health information under false pretenses, or making malicious use of confidential information, especially with a profit motive.

Initially, the rules had an effective date as of publication, but because of the moratorium on regulations, the effective date was deferred until April 14, 2001 by a notice appearing in the February 26, 2001 Federal Register (page 12433), and which therefore also adds 60 days to the original compliance dates (general: 2/26/03; 2/26/04 for small plans with annual receipts below $5 million). It's safe to say that these rules are controversial, and have angered business and health care groups, so it is logical to assume that they will be tested in court and may be struck down.

Chapter 23
Title VII

23.1 INTRODUCTION

The EEOC has compiled charge statistics for its fiscal years 1992-2000. Over this time period, the number of charges began at 72,302 (for 1992), peaked at 91,189 (in 1994) and stands at 79,896 brought in 2000. In each year, more than a third of the charges involved racial discrimination. In FY 2000, 36.2% of charges involved race, versus 31.5% alleging sex discrimination, only 9.8% national origin discrimination, and 2.4% religious discrimination. Retaliation, under all statutes, was alleged in 27.1% of 2000 cases (versus only 15.3% in 1992, growing steadily). See http://www.eeoc.gov/stats/charges.html for the chart.

In FY 2000, the EEOC reduced its backlog of charges to the lowest level in 17 years, although even at that point the agency had a backlog of 34,297 cases. The EEOC focuses on what it calls the Comprehensive Enforcement Program (CEP), coordinating all agency resources to handle cases from outreach to resolution and increasing the use of mediation to achieve quicker resolution. The EEOC's long-range enforcement plan targets equal pay violations and sex-based pay discrimination; hostile work environments; barriers to promotion of women and minorities; and English-only rules. [See EEOC's press release at http://www.eeoc.gov/press/1-18-01.html.]

Also see EEOC's massive rewrite of Section 3 of the Compliance Manual, http://www.eeoc.gov/docs/benefits.html explaining the agency's view of the employer's burden in providing equal and non-discriminatory benefits to employees. Employers are not permitted to consider race, color, sex/pregnancy, national origin or religion in determining eligibility for, amount of, or charges for employee benefits. Increased cost of providing equal benefits is no defense. Employers are also required to use unisex rather than sex-based actuarial tables, even though there are statistically valid differences in life expectancy between men and women.

A March 1999 case (*McDonnell v. Illinois,* 725 A.2d 126 (N.J. Super. 3/15/99) allows a New Jersey resident who worked in the state of Illinois' New Jersey field office (the state had a field office in order to audit the tax records of multi-state corporations) to use the New Jersey court system to sue the state of Illinois for violating the New Jersey Law Against Discrimination (that state's counterpart of Title VII). The theory is that Illinois didn't have sovereign immunity, and it couldn't argue that it should have been sued in Illinois under its own antidiscrimination laws, because those laws only apply to conduct occurring within the state of Illinois.

Additional information about retaliation charges can be found at 67 LW 2259, where the EEOC noted that retaliation claims rose from under 8000 in 1991 to over 18,000 in 1998. The agency pointed out that sometimes juries will award damages on retaliation claims even if the underlying discrimination charges are dismissed.

The September 1998 case of *Gutner v. Cheyney University of Pennsylvania,* #94-7443 (E.D. Pa. 9/23/98), awarded $2.2 million to two white former college professors who claimed they were subjected to systematic reprisals and then forced out of their jobs because they complained about a black department chairman's manipulation of the hiring process.

Similarly, *Johnson v. University of Cincinnati,* 68 LW 1784 (6th Cir. 6/1/00) permits an affirmative action official who claims that he was dismissed because of his zealous advocacy for women and minorities to pursue discrimination and retaliation claims, even though he is a white male.

Certainly, the risks are substantial within the court system. In early 1999, United Parcel Service announced its agreement to pay $12.1 million to settle charges of racial discrimination raised in a 1997 class action. Of this amount, $8.2 million was allocated among 12,000 current and former part-time workers, plus $626,500 to 14 full-time and part-time workers who were original class plaintiffs. Attorneys' fees amounted to some $3.3 million. The class action charged that UPS disadvantaged black drivers when delivery routes were assigned and also deprived black part-time workers of the training necessary for promotion to better-paid full-time status. The UPS settlement is discussed in a news item, *Wall Street Journal,* 1/19/99, p. B8.

EEOC/DOJ Memorandum of Understanding

See 63 FR 5518 (2/3/98) for the Memorandum of Understanding (MOU) between the EEOC and the Department of Justice's Office of Special Counsel for Immigration Related Unfair Employment Practices. Under the MOU, each agency can act as the other's agents to receive complaints about immigration-related discrimination charges. The two agencies will coordinate to avoid duplication of effort.

In response to immigration-law changes, the two agencies will treat document abuse, intimidation, and retaliation as immigration-related unfair labor practices and will accept pattern or practice charges. The EEOC has agreed not to ask if the charging party is a U.S. citizen, national, or work-authorized alien as a condition for referring charges to the DOJ.

23.2 TITLE VII COVERAGE

In August 1998, the full Fourth Circuit reversed its earlier panel ruling. Now *Egbuna v. Time-Life Libraries, Inc.*, 153 F.3d 184 (4th Cir. 1998), holds that it is necessary to be a U.S. citizen, or an alien holding a valid work visa, to be a "qualified" individual. Therefore, an alien who does not have legal worker status in the United States cannot make out a Title VII prima facie case.

In late 1998, the Fourth Circuit joined the Third, Fifth, Seventh, Eighth, Tenth, Eleventh, and D.C. Circuits in ruling that individuals cannot be held liable under Title VII [*Lissau v. Southern Food Service*, 159 F.3d 177 (4th Cir. 1998)].

Under *Jones v. American Postal Workers Union*, 192 F.3d 417 (4th Cir. 9/10/99), a union of federal employees falls under the definition of "labor organization" and thus can be sued by its members for Title VII (or ADA) violations.

Union stewards are included in the count to see if an employer has the 15 employees necessary to Title VII coverage: *Daggitt v. United Food & Commercial Workers*, 59 F.Supp.2d 980 (D.S.D. 8/20/99).

It's always been clear that federal agencies can be sued under Title VII; in June 1999, the Supreme Court held that the EEOC can award compensatory damages (within the Civil Rights Act of 1991 limits) against them too: *West v. Gibson*, #98-238, 527 U.S. 212 (Sup.Ct. 6/14/99).

A person who is an independent contractor for tax purposes, and who is excluded from participation in the company's benefit plans, can still be an employee under state and local anti-discrimination laws. The crucial test is the extent of control by the hiring party, so the more routine and less creative the work, the more likely the worker is to be considered an employee and not an independent contractor. [*Eisenberg v. Advance Relocation and Storage Inc.*, #00-7216 (2nd Cir. 2000), discussed in Mark Hamblett, "Court Revives Contract Worker's Claim," *N.Y.L.J.* 12/28/00 (law.com).]

23.2.4 Race Discrimination

At-will employees can sue under 42 USC §1981 (the prohibition of racial discrimination in the making of contracts), according to four Circuits: *Fadeyi v. Planned Parenthood*, 160 F.3d 1048 (5th Cir. 1998); *Perry v. Woodward*, 199 F.3d 1126 (10th Cir. 1999), *cert. denied* 120 S.Ct 1964; *Spriggs v. Diamond Auto Glass*, 165 F.3d 1015 (4th Cir. 1999); *Lauture v. IBM*, 216 F.3d 258 (2nd Cir. 6/30/00).

The Tenth Circuit has applied the *Faragher/Burlington* test (see ¶23.3) to conduct that creates a racially hostile environment. That is, if the conduct is motivated by an intent to serve the employer, it is within the scope of employment. Thus, the employer will be liable for discriminatory conduct by a supervisor reflecting prejudice within the labor force [*Wright-Simmons v. City of Oklahoma City*, 155 F.3d 1264 (10th Cir. 1998)].

Even a single racial slur by a supervisor in the presence of another supervisor can be severe, thus creating a hostile work environment [*Taylor v. Metzger*, 706 A.2d 685 (N.J. 1998)].

In *Johnson v. Zema Systems Corp.*, 1999 WL 138716 (7th Cir. 1999), a black manager said he was fired because he spent much of time supervising white rather than black employees in a segregated and hostile environment. The employer said that, despite good evaluations, he had some performance problems. The employer relied on the "same actor" defense: i.e., if the manager responsible for hiring a plaintiff also fired him or her, presumably the manager could not have been motivated by racial bigotry. The Seventh Circuit did not accept the validity of the same-actor defense, noting that firing might occur because the hiree did not conform to the hirer's stereotypes about the class of person hired.

A black woman was hired to telemarket to black voters, then fired after the election. The employer in *Ferrill v. Parker Group, Inc.*, 1999 WL 98174 (11th Cir. 1999) was unsuccessful in its claim that being black is a BFOQ for appealing to black people contacted by telephone. In the Eleventh Circuit's view, Title VII was specifically drafted to rule out the possibility of using race as a BFOQ.

Although private social clubs (e.g., country clubs) are exempt from Title VII, the Eastern District of Virginia permits §1981 civil rights claims to be brought by their employees and ex-employees (here, a black chef asserting that he was fired for racial reasons). In this reading, the purpose of the Title VII exclusion is to protect freedom of association, a purpose that is not served by forbidding §1981 actions by employees. [*Crawford v. Willow Oaks Country Club*, 68 LW 1256 (E.D. Va. 9/29/99).]

In January 2000, the EEOC targeted companies that allow racial harassment in the form of hostile and threatening racist graffiti that the employer does nothing to prevent and that are not removed in a timely fashion. The EEOC settled one case (for $1.3 million, to be shared among about 100 employees) and filed a lawsuit in another case. The complaint in the second case asks for compensatory and punitive damages, a mandatory injunction requiring the company to take steps to prevent further graffiti offenses, and a permanent injunction against discrimination in the future. ["Chicago EEOC Makes Second Move Against On-the-Job Racist Graffiti," Employment Law Weekly (online) 1/20/00.]

23.2.5 Sex Discrimination

A male social worker's sex-discrimination claims, challenging the employer's subjective interview practices, failed in *Scott v. Parkview Memorial Hospital*, 67 LW 1720 (7th Cir. 4/23/99). The plaintiff claimed that the interview process unfairly favored women because it favored traditionally feminine qualities such as warmth and empathy. However, the Seventh Circuit viewed subjective interviews as a necessary part of professional recruitment and, furthermore, found that the qualities that were useful in the interview were also useful in performing the job, so the interview practice was valid and job-related.

A 2000 Ninth Circuit decision holds that it is illegal sex discrimination for an airline to set its weight limits for female flight attendants based on tables for persons with a medium frame, while using tables for a large frame to set limits for male flight attendants. The court treated this as disparate impact discrimination not qualifying for a BFOQ defense. The airline asserted that it was a grooming standard (which can permissibly differ by sex) but the court said that requiring woman flight attendants to be thinner than males of the same height did not improve their ability to do their jobs. [*Frank v. United Airlines,* 216 F.3d 845 (9th Cir. 2000).]

23.2.6 The Pregnancy Discrimination Act (PDA)

The plaintiff in *Piraino v. International Orientation Resources,* 137 F.3d 987 (7th Cir. 1998), lost her case under the PDA. She applied for a leave of absence around the time of delivery. This was approved. Two months later, the company changed its policy and refused to guarantee the reinstatement of employees who took leave when they had worked for the company for less than one year. The plaintiff was unsuccessful because the court did not find proof that pregnant employees who had worked for the company for less than a year were treated differently from their nonpregnant peers.

In September, 2000 the Ninth Circuit refused to award back pay to a prevailing PDA plaintiff for the period of time after she decided to stay at home with her newborn, on the theory that her loss of income was voluntary and thus not compensable by the court system. (The plaintiff was fired when she was eight months pregnant; she looked for work once the baby was born, didn't get any job offers, and decided after six months to take some childrearing time off from paid work. [Michael Joe, "Stay-at-Home Mom Can't Collect," *The Recorder* 9/18/00 (law.com)]).

Peralta v. Chromium Plating & Polishing Corp., N.Y.L.J. 10/18/00 p. 38 col. 4 (S.D.N.Y.) makes it clear that it was improper to fire a pregnant employee whose doctor said she should be placed on light duty. The employer said that she was placed on unpaid leave, but in either case she was treated differently from nonpregnant employees, which is why the Southern District granted summary judgment to her against the employer.

According to the Southern District, the employer could not say that protecting the unborn baby was a BFOQ (even though the employee had miscarried an earlier pregnancy when she was working there), because the BFOQ exception only comes into play when the employer seeks to protect third parties whose safety is part of the company's central mission. Customers fall into that category, but employees' fetuses don't.

In this analysis, potential tort liability isn't a BFOQ either. The way to handle potential liability risk is to get a waiver from an employee who wants to keep working, instead of terminating her employment.

The *Wall Street Journal's* Sue Shellenbarger took up the topic of light-duty assignments for pregnant workers. ("Pregnant Workers Clash With Employers Over

Job Inflexibility," *WSJ*, 2/10/99, p. B1). She noted that pregnant workers may need limitations on the weight they lift or the length of time they must stand—but are otherwise able to work. It's easy to imagine a case in which a pregnant woman can't perform all of the tasks associated with her job but is still healthy and fit enough so that she can't be described as "disabled."

Many mothers-to-be experience problems, because employers seldom make an effort to find light-duty assignments for pregnant workers. Each year, close to 2 million employed women become pregnant, and about 640,000 of those workers have jobs that involve at least some physical exertion. A lot of companies only have a few light-duty slots, and they often prefer to assign them to Worker's Compensation recipients who were injured at work and therefore must be kept on the payroll with or without work assignments.

The Fifth Circuit, in *Urbano v. Continental Airlines*, 138 F.3d 204 (5th Cir. 1998), upholds an employer's policy of limiting light duty assignments to workers injured on the job. In this reading, as long as pregnancy-related disability is treated on a par with other nonoccupational disability, the PDA has not been violated, even if the result is that pregnant workers have to leave work earlier than they would have preferred.

23.3 SEXUAL HARASSMENT

In 1998, the Supreme Court settled the conflict as to whether or not same-sex harassment is actionable under Title VII. *Oncale v. Sundowner Offshore Services Inc.*, 523 U.S. 45 (Sup.Ct. 1998), reached the unsurprising conclusion that same-sex harassment (which can be even more upsetting to the recipient than opposite-sex harassment) is indeed a violation of Title VII.

So it's surprising that, in 2000, the Seventh Circuit ruled that neither male nor female state-government employees could bring suit for sexual harassment, on the grounds that the supervisor could not have been discriminating on account of sex because he propositioned both male and female subordinates. [*Holman v. State of Indiana*, 211 F.3d 399 (7th Cir. 2000).]

Two major decisions, *Burlington Industries, Inc. v. Ellerth*, 524 U.S. 742 (Sup.Ct. 1998), and *Faragher v. City of Boca Raton*, 524 U.S. 735 (Sup. Ct. 1998), changed the standard for assessing the employer's burden in providing a harassment-free workplace. The new test, under *Faragher/Burlington*, is whether the action had adverse employment effect on the victim. If so, the employer is absolutely liable. In the absence of adverse employment effect, the employer is still liable—unless it maintained proper antiharassment and grievance policies.

In the *Ellerth* case, a sales representative felt threatened by repeated remarks and gestures from a manager (who was not her immediate supervisor), although she was not deprived of job benefits. She quit her job but did not attribute her resignation to harassment. Three weeks later, she sent a letter to the company explaining that her resignation was due to harassment. She did not report the harassment while it was occurring, although she knew Burlington had an antiharassment policy.

The Supreme Court's decision was that the supervisor's threats of adverse job action created a hostile work environment. The employer becomes vicariously liable for the supervisor's conduct if the employer failed to stop harassment after knowing about it; if the supervisor was able to harass because of apparent authority over the harassment victim; or if adverse job action was actually taken by the supervisor.

The other side of the coin is that the employer can be free of liability if it took reasonable care to maintain a workable complaint procedure, and if the plaintiff failed to use the procedure.

The *Faragher* case involves a lifeguard who sued her municipal employer and two supervisors for a hostile environment (including lewd touching of female employees). The employer did have an antiharassment policy but didn't inform employees of it, didn't supervise supervisors' conduct, and didn't create a procedure for reporting harassment by supervisors to someone other than the supervisors themselves. The Supreme Court's ruling was that the employer was liable for the hostile environment, because it had failed to communicate the antiharassment policy and didn't track the conduct of supervisors.

What's the bottom line? The employer has to make sure that the environment does not become hostile, intimidating, or offensive, so severe and pervasive unwelcome physical and verbal conduct must be prevented. Employees must understand that their complaints will be taken seriously and that there is a chain of command that can bypass the person who is alleged to have committed harassment. Top management should be involved in the process, to signal that the company treats these complaints as serious, and supervisors and managers should be trained to observe and report harassment.

Because the Supreme Court decisions revolve around agency law concepts such as the apparent authority of the supervisor, the employer should not only limit the extent to which supervisors can punish subordinates for not yielding to sexual pressures, but should make it clear that supervisors can only impose workplace discipline for legitimate reasons. It's important to look behind supervisors' write-ups and to check to see not only that the subordinate really did do poor work, come in late, have excessive absences, etc., but that the subordinate was not singled out for sanctions of conduct that was tolerated in other employees who were not sexual targets.

Of course, actual complaints should be given careful investigation, not shrugged off. (See ¶23.3.2 for a discussion of what constitutes appropriate investigation of a complaint.)

Naturally, most companies are aware of the potential risk of sexual harassment litigation, and 97% of survey respondents told the Society for Human Resource Management (SHRM) that they have written anti-harassment policies. Nearly all (86%) have a formal complaint investigation procedure, and close to two-thirds (62%) have formal training so employees can recognize, avoid, and prevent harassment. Nevertheless, respondents indicated that the number of sexual harassment complaints made by employees has increased in every year between 1995 and 1999. The problem is not just excessive sensitivity on the part of complaining employees: Investigation shows that two-thirds of the complaints can be substantiated. Copies of the SHRM Sexual Harassment Survey cost $49.95, and can be ordered from the SHRMStore, (800) 444-5006.

Defining Harassment and Hostile Environment

To the First Circuit, a gay man who was fired after complaining about a decade-long sequence of anti-gay harassment from co-employees did not state a Title VII claim against the employer. Harassment on the basis of sexual orientation is not covered by Title VII. [*Higgins v. New Balance Athletic Shoe Inc.*, 68 LW 1288 (1st Cir. 10/22/99).

Similarly, *Hamner v. St. Vincent Hospital and Health Care Center Inc.*, 224 F.3d 701 (7th Cir. 2000), holds that sexual orientation discrimination and harassment by a supervisor premised on the plaintiff's perceived effeminacy is not covered by Title VII, because it is not "specifically intimidating to men and their manhood" or premised on "general hostility to men." However, according to the Human Rights Campaign, there are 11 states and 116 cities and counties that have their own laws forbidding employment discrimination on the basis of sexual orientation. [See Jess Bravin, "Courts Open Alternate Route to Extend Job-Bias Laws to Homosexuals," *WSJ* 9/22/00 p. B1.]

It can be hard to predict what conduct will or will not be considered sufficiently outrageous to create a hostile environment; courts have reached very different answers. For instance, according to *Howley v. Town of Stratford*, 217 F.3d 141 (2nd Cir. 2000), one incident of verbal harassment of a female fire lieutenant by a male subordinate, at a union meeting, can be considered an intolerable alteration of the work environment. The theory is that it diminishes subordinates' respect for a commanding officer, which in turn impairs the fire department's basic mission of safeguarding lives and property.

In contrast, one incident in which a male employee touched a female co-worker's breast and stomach was held not to create a hostile environment. No physical injury occurred, and the employer promptly removed him from the workplace, so the Ninth Circuit did not believe a reasonable employee would have deemed the terms and conditions of employment to be altered for the worse. The male employee had already created at least two similar incidents, but they were not reported. Furthermore, the Ninth Circuit said that ostracism suffered by the female employee from her co-workers, because she reported the incident, cannot be considered adverse employment action. *[Brooks v. San Mateo, California,* 69 LW 1265 (9th Cir. 10/23/00).]

Suggestive male nude pictures posted on an office bulletin board by a male employee did not constitute sexual harassment of the female plaintiff: *Brennan v. Metropolitan Opera Association Inc.*, 68 LW 1224 (2nd Cir. 9/21/99), in that, according to the court, no rational jury could find that the terms of the plaintiff's employment were altered to create a pervasive atmosphere of intimidation, ridicule, and insult.

A male employee failed to prove sexual harassment by his female boss; the various cards, e-mails, and conversations introduced into evidence were personal, although not sexual (e.g., holiday greetings to him and his family; hopes that he would have a good vacation). The nature of the allegations, and the absence of complaint by the employee, showed that the conduct was not severe enough to constitute harassment. [*Opp v. Source One Management Inc.*, 1999 WL 144911 (N.D. 1999).]

An employer refused to reinstate a worker returning from medical leave. The employer said that she was totally disabled by paranoid schizophrenia, whereas the employee charged that the employer was retaliating against her for complaining about on-the-job sexual harassment. During the leave, the employee had applied for, and received, Social Security Disability (SSDI) benefits.

The Seventh Circuit ruled, in *Wilson v. Chrysler Corp.*, 172 F.3d 500 (7th Cir. 1999) that applying for disability benefits rules out a sexual harassment claim. This is not necessarily true of an ADA claim: The Seventh Circuit view is that in ADA cases, a qualified disabled person may be able to work if reasonable accommodations are provided, but in Title VII cases (including sexual harassment cases), the issue of reasonable accommodation does not arise.

Although hostile work environment charges are usually made in the sexual context, the employer might be liable in a racially or religiously hostile workplace. One way to cope is a "mutual respect" policy, which reminds employees not to taunt or insult others or speak slightingly of their culture or religion.

Although by and large employer companies and not individuals will be liable under Title VII and related statutes, *Speight v. Albano Cleaners,* 21 F.Supp. 2d 560 (E.D. Va. 1998), does permit a Title VII suit against an individual supervisor who had significant degree of control over the plaintiff (and the conduct in question was not plainly delegable). However, in this case, the employer was found not to be liable for quid pro quo harassment in a situation in which the plaintiff was denied a promotion allegedly promised to her. The employer was not aware of the harassment, and the supervisor who committed the harassment did not have authority to promote the plaintiff. Because the employee failed to take advantage of an existing antiharassment policy, the employer could not be held liable for hostile environment harassment either.

But see yet another case finding that individuals are not personally liable for discrimination: *Carrisales v. Dep't of Corrections,* 68 LW 1399 (Cal. 12/9/99) says that the California Fair Employment and Housing Act cannot be used to sue a co-employee for sexual harassment because the purpose of the statute is to impel employers to maintain a harassment-free workplace.

In *Corcoran v. Shoney's Colonial Inc.*, 24 F.Supp.2d 601 (W.D. Va. 1998), the employer was held vicariously liable on the plaintiff's hostile environment claim, notwithstanding the employer's prompt investigation followed by separation of harasser and victim. The Western District reads *Faragher/Burlington* to impose vicarious liability, even if prompt remedial action is taken, unless the employee failed to take advantage of the employer's corrective mechanism.

In *Corcoran,* the plaintiff did in fact delay in reporting the harassment, but the court did not find this to be fatal to her case because she did not act unreasonably. Harassment began in June, tapered off, then escalated the following February, at which time the employee complained. The case of *NLRB v. Wehr Constructors Inc.,* 159 F.3d 946 (6th Cir. 1998), imposes vicarious liability on the employer, despite prompt action to separate harasser and victim and despite a reporting delay (which the court deemed to be reasonable under the circumstances).

The Eleventh Circuit held in 2000 that an employer was on notice as soon as an employee complained of alleged harassment to her manager, the person designated by the employer to receive such complaints. This was true even though the employee did not observe the suggested policy of contacting the HR department in case of dissatisfaction with the manager's response. Notice to the manager was the only compulsory part of the process, and the employee did take this step. [*Breda v. Wolf Camera & Video,* 222 F.3d 886 (11th Cir. 2000).]

The Fifth Circuit took up timing issues in *Williamson v. City of Houston,* 148 F.3d 462 (8th Cir. 1998). In that case, a woman police officer reported harassment by a male officer in her squad to her supervising sergeant. After about a dozen unproductive meetings, the sergeant told the woman to report the case to the Internal Affairs Division (IAD). She did so. The City of Houston took the position that it was not on notice of the harassment until she went to the IAD. To Houston, the sergeant was not a member of "upper management," and therefore his knowledge of harassment could not be imputed to the city. The Fifth Circuit disagreed, finding the sergeant to be the plaintiff's supervisor. Therefore, the employer was on notice of the harassment as soon as the plaintiff-employee triggered the complaint mechanism by reporting to her supervisor.

In a quid pro quo case, a series of minor detriments that would not be actionable by themselves can be aggregated to demonstrate tangible job detriment and make out the prima facie case [*Reinhold v. Virginia,* 151 F.3d 920 (4th Cir. 1998)]. If the harassment is committed by customers, the Tenth Circuit analyzes the situation as if the harassers were coemployees (not supervisors). The employer will be held liable if its negligence permitted the harassment to continue but will not be held strictly liable for the actions of customers [*Lockard v. Pizza Hut Inc.,* 162 F.3d 1062 (10th Cir. 1998)].

In Maryland, an employee discharged for refusing to have sexual intercourse with a harasser can pursue a tort claim for abusive discharge in addition to the sexual harassment charges. The independent tort claim for abusive discharge can be pursued, because the state has a public policy against prostitution—and having sex to keep a job is, in effect, prostitution: *Insignia Residential Corp. v. Ashton, Maryland,* 755 A.2d 1080 (Md. 2000).

Summary judgment is not appropriate in a hostile environment case where the plaintiff alleges that the sexual comments made in her presence were commonplace, ongoing, and continuing [*Abeita v. Transamerica Mailings Inc.*, 159 F.3d 246 (6th Cir. 1998)].

The Seventh Circuit allows a sexual harassment plaintiff to get punitive damages in cases in which there were no compensatory damages: See *Timm v. Progressive Steel Treating Inc.,* 137 F.3d 1008 (7th Cir. 1998). This might occur, for instance, where a company fails to establish a complaint procedure and then blames the plaintiff for failure to complain. In this case, the plaintiff mitigated damages so effectively that she got a higher-paying job, and therefore could not collect a back pay award.

Interpreting California rather than federal law (FEHA, the state's Fair Employment and Housing Act), the California Court of Appeals ruled that a law firm is directly, not vicariously, liable for failing to protect a staffer against harassment by a partner. The ruling of *Weeks v. Baker & McKenzie,* 74 Cal. Rptr. 2d 510 (Cal. App. 1998), is that the firm employed the partner in conscious disregard of the safety and rights of vulnerable employees. Therefore, $3.5 million in punitive damages could be assessed against the firm. The firm's liability was not limited to the $225,000 punitive damage award against the harassing partner.

Reno v. Baird, 957 P.2d 1333 (Cal. 1998), holds that an individual manager, although potentially liable for harassment, is not an "employer" under the Fair Employment and Housing Act. Nor can the individual manager be sued for wrongful discharge in violation of the public policy expressed in FEHA. The FEHA definition of "employer" includes "any person acting as an agent of an employer, directly or indirectly," but the *Baird* court interpreted this language to have been included in the statute to make employers liable for the actions of their agents, not to subject the agents to personal liability.

According to *Lai v. Prudential Insurance Co.*, 72 Cal. Rptr. 2d 551 (Cal. App. 1998), California's rule is even tougher than the federal rule: The employer remains strictly liable whether the harassment was of the quid pro quo or hostile environment variety.

The Eleventh Circuit did not permit a "reverse-discrimination" sexual harassment suit, brought by a plaintiff who was denied the promotion that went to the employee who had a consensual sexual relationship with the boss. The holding of *Womack v. Runyon,* 147 F.3d 1298 (11th Cir. 1998), is that an isolated instance of favoring a sexual partner cannot constitute sex discrimination, because the plaintiff class would consist of all of the company's employees (male and female), because they were all equally disadvantaged by such favoritism.

As Chapter 30 shows, it can be difficult to get insurance coverage in sexual harassment cases. The 1998 Fifth Circuit case of *American States Insurance Co. v. Natchez Steam Laundry,* 131 F.3d 551 (5th Cir. 1998), agrees with the insurer that there was no duty to defend, under a commercial general liability (CGL) or umbrella policy, against the EEOC's suit for intentional sexual harassment.

Therefore, the insurance company did not act in bad faith by not providing a defense or insurance benefits. The agency's allegations fit well within the intentional-acts exception of the policy, and the insurer made an adequate investigation before denying the claim. Whether or not there is a duty to defend depends on the language of the complaint, and the EEOC clearly charged intentional acts excluded by the policies.

23.3.2 Required Employer Response

According to the Eleventh Circuit, if the appropriate response to a minor act of harassment is to admonish the harasser, it's permissible for the HR manager to delegate the task of admonition to a co-worker instead of doing it personally, as long as it's clear that the harasser gets the message and the harassed person is satisfied with the outcome of his or her complaint [*Coates v. Sundor Brands, Inc.*, 164 F.3d 1361 (11th Cir. 1998)].

The issue of harassment moved to another arena in *Blakey v. Continental Airlines* [#A-5-99, N.J. Sup. 6/1/00; see Mary P. Gallagher, "Worker Slurred by Peers Online May Sue Employer," *New Jersey Law Journal,* on law.com.], which holds that the employer has a duty to remedy harassment once it is placed on notice that a work-related online forum is being used as part of a pattern of retaliatory harassment.

Tammy Blakey, a Continental Airlines pilot (who won a 1997 harassment suit, but did not collect damages because of Continental's bankruptcy) was permitted to pursue state-court claims (business libel; sexual harassment and hostile work environment; intentional infliction of mental distress) based on derogatory comments posted by co-workers on an official company electronic bulletin board that was used to post scheduling and assignment information.

Because of the pervasive influence of electronic communications on the workplace, the employer may have a duty to correct harassment that occurs on an electronic forum. The case was remanded to see whether the electronic bulletin board was closely enough connected to Continental operations to make the company liable for its contents, and to see whether Continental was on notice of the nature of the postings. In this reading, employers do not have a duty to monitor communications posted by employees, but once employers are on notice of offensive communications, obligations are triggered.

The employer must also consider how it will respond to the employee who is charged with harassment. A 2000 Minnesota case says that a male supervisor who successfully defends himself against a female employee's harassment charges is entitled to be indemnified by his employer (a Delaware corporation) because, at that time, Delaware law required corporations to indemnify anyone who was sued by reason of serving as a corporate director, officer, employee, or agent, and who was vindicated in court. [*Rudebeck v. Paulson,* 612 N.W.2d 450 (Minn. 2000).]

EEOC Enforcement Guidance

The EEOC's position on how employers must respond is summarized in its 20-page "Enforcement Guidance: Vicarious Employer Liability for Unlawful Harassment by Supervisors," Number 915.002 (6/18/99), which can be downloaded at http://www.eeoc.gov/docs/harassment.html.

The EEOC interprets *Faragher* and *Burlington* to mean that harassment by a supervisor—that does not subject the employee to tangible disadvantages—will not make the employer liable as long as the employer uses reasonable care to prevent harassment, or uses reasonable care to correct harassment that has occurred, provided that the employee is also at fault by failing to take advantage of the employer's anti-harassment policies and procedures. Sometimes the employer is unable to completely avoid liability, but can show that damages should be reduced because of its anti-harassment efforts.

The Guidance requires employers to prevent harassment of all kinds: harassment based on sex (including derogation of women or men because they are women or men, even if the harasser's motive is not his or her own sexual gratification), race, color, religion, national origin, protected activity (i.e., complaining to the EEOC), age, or disability.

Because the employer faces potential liability because of the action of "supervisors," and because Title VII doesn't include a statutory definition of "supervisor," it becomes crucial to determine the relative corporate status of the alleged harasser and the person charging harassment. The key test is whether, based on the real facts of the workplace, the alleged harasser had authority over the alleged victim of harassment, to an extent that the authority made it easier to harass and harder for the victim to resist.

The EEOC uses a two-part test. A supervisor either has authority to direct someone else's daily work activities, OR has authority to implement or recommend tangible employment decisions affecting another employee (e.g., firing or promoting the employee; awarding a raise or bonus). The EEOC says that some workers are NOT supervisors: for instance, those who only communicate someone else's instructions about work assignments, or someone who coordinates or directs only limited tasks or assignments. However, the EEOC position is that the employer can be liable for harassment even by someone who was not a supervisor, as long as the harassed employee reasonably believed that the harasser actually had supervisory status.

The EEOC's position is that the employer is **always** liable when the harassing supervisor subjects the employee to tangible employment action, so it becomes crucial to define this concept. The EEOC says that a tangible employment action is a significant change in employment status (e.g., firing, denial of a promotion, an undesirable work assignment or reassignment), not just an unfulfilled threat, a trivial effect, or a "bruised ego." Tangible actions are official acts of the business enterprise, and are usually documented in the company's records; approval of the supervisor's own superiors may be required (thus further implicating the company).

The agency's definition of a **minimum** acceptable anti-harassment policy comprises:

- Clear explanation of what constitutes prohibited harassment.

- Assurances that employees who report harassment will not suffer retaliation.
- A feasible (i.e., employees should not be required to report harassment to a supervisor who is alleged to have committed the harassment!), clearly disclosed complaint procedure that investigates allegations promptly, thoroughly, and impartially.
- Confidentiality of complaints.
- Assurance of fast, appropriate response whenever an investigation shows that harassment has occurred.

Merely having a policy isn't enough; it must really be carried out. Furthermore, the EEOC encourages employers to stamp out harassment even before it reaches the severe, protracted level that would justify a lawsuit. The Guidelines include sample questions to ask complaining employees and witnesses, and standards for assessing the credibility of complaints.

EEOC's suggestions for adequate responses to harassment include:

- A warning or reprimand (oral or written) to the harasser
- Training and counseling the harasser about why the conduct violated the employer's anti-harassment policy
- Transferring, reassigning, demoting, suspending, or, in appropriate cases, firing, the harasser
- Monitoring the harasser to make sure such conduct has ended
- Giving the harassed employee credit for leave time taken to get out of the range of harassment
- Correcting the harassed employee's file to remove unfair evaluations
- Having the harasser apologize to the harassed employee
- Checking to make sure that there is no retaliation against the harassed employee for using the complaint procedure

The mere fact that an employer adequately investigates sexual harassment claims is not necessarily enough to get the employer off the hook under *Faragher/Burlington.* But an adequate investigation is certainly a valuable first step.

A May 1999 article by attorneys Susan Schenkel-Savitt and Jill H. Turner, of the firm of Winston & Strawn, available at http://www.lawnewsnetwork.com/practice/employmentlaw/papers/lawfirm/A1058-1999Apr30.html, gives some insights into appropriate investigative efforts.

The investigation has further implications. If an employer simply dismisses all accused harassers, this could constitute wrongful termination, in that efforts were not made to determine the validity of the charges. To balance between the interests of accused persons and accusers, the employer must maintain a mechanism for unbiased internal investigations.

The person who conducts the investigation may have to testify later on, so an in-house or outside attorney who normally represents the corporation could be a poor choice. Attorneys are not allowed to serve as witnesses in cases where they are also representing a party. However, choosing an attorney rather than someone else can be a good choice, because communications between an attorney and a client are privileged (opposing parties in litigation can't get hold of them). An attorney's "work product" (materials drafted by the attorney while preparing the case)is also protected. Similar privileges are not extended to nonattorney professionals.

In order to assert confidentiality at the pretrial and trial level, the company must be sure to keep the materials confidential. They must not be given general distribution, and access must be limited to persons involved in the investigation.

The person conducting the investigation must determine the following:

- Person(s) accused of committing harassment, including those contributing to a hostile work environment or participating in a cover-up
- Person(s) who are described as witnesses; the degree to which their recollection tallies with the complainant's
- Any other person(s) who also claim to be harassment victims
- Detailed information about the alleged acts of harassment or the duration and nature of the hostile environment
- Did the acts occur on company property, at company functions, or elsewhere?
- Did the employee make a prompt report of the alleged harassing incident? To whom was it made? If there was no report, was there any justification for failing to report at the time of the incident?

Naturally, the investigator should follow up by contacting witnesses and checking matters of fact. If an incident of harassment was alleged to have occurred on a particular date, for instance, it should be ascertained if the alleged harasser was in the office on that date or was elsewhere.

Interviewing the alleged harasser is very important. It's up to the employer's discretion whether or not to reveal the name of the person making the allegation. To protect the employer against claims by the alleged harasser, the investigator should make it clear that an investigation is being made and that no conclusions have yet been reached as to the validity of the accusations. The accused person should be given a full, fair chance to get his or her own story on the record.

Additional rounds of interviews may be necessary to follow new lines of investigation or confirm disputed facts. The product of the investigation should be a confidential written report rendered to the person with corporate HR responsibility. It's important to indicate whether a particular statement in the report is factual or whether it represents opinion, gossip, or rumor.

The company has an obligation to take at least some action whenever it is determined that a harassment allegation is well-founded. Appropriate action is proportionate to the seriousness of the conduct and has the effect of discouraging future harassment. The action should also be proportionate to actions the employer has taken in similar cases in the past. The harasser's employment record may provide either mitigating (long history of good performance) or aggravating factors (past instances of discipline, especially prior instances of harassment).

If the employer determines that a sanction short of dismissal is appropriate, steps should be taken to keep the harasser and victim apart—but without making it seem that the complainant is being penalized for making a well-founded complaint. The employer should also follow up (and make a written record of the follow-up) to make sure that the disciplinary action has served to prevent future harassment incidents.

For an example of how an employer succeeded in meeting its burden, see *Montero v. AGCO Corp.*, 68 LW 1239 (9th Cir. 9/28/99), where the employee's claim was dismissed because the employer promptly investigated and resolved an allegation of sexual harassment. (The claim was resolved within 11 days.) Furthermore, because the employee had taken two years to complain, she was also at fault for failing to make use of the employer's complaint mechanism.

Punitive damages were **not** awarded against the employer in the sexual harassment case of *Scott v. Ameritex Yarn Co.*, 68 LW 1384 (D.S.C. 11/19/99). In this case, a former employee alleged that frequent suggestive comments and gestures from her supervisor caused emotional distress, affected her family relationships, and eventually caused her to quit her job. The District Court found no evidence that the employer had authorized the harassment, or had recklessly employed an unfit individual. The District Court's interpretation of *Kolstad* is that mere lack of good-faith effort to comply with Title VII is not enough to impose punitive damages on an employer.

Savino v. C.P.Hall Co., 1999 WL 1172892 (7th Cir. 1999) is a case of alleged non–quid-pro-quo harassment by a supervisor. The jury agreed with the employer that the employee had taken too long to complain about the alleged harassment, and the employer responded adequately. The plaintiff said that her delay in reporting was the equivalent of failing to mitigate damages: in other words, it should reduce but not eliminate her right to recover. But the Seventh Circuit ruled that the delay was enough to insulate the employer against liability.

A company with a no-tolerance policy fired an employee after investigation showed that he had sexually harassed another worker. The discharged employee went to arbitration, and the arbitrator held that discharge was too severe a punishment and ordered his reinstatement, although without back pay. The practical effect was a nine-month unpaid suspension.

The employer brought suit under Labor-Management Relations Act §301, claiming that reinstating the harasser would violate public policy. The Fourth Circuit disagreed, agreeing with the arbitrator that losing nine months' pay was adequate punishment. [*Westvaco Corp. v. United Paperworkers Int'l Union*, 171 F.3d 971 (4th Cir. 1999).] In other words, public policy requires that employer companies must investigate harassment charges, and punish the harasser appropriately, but discharge is not the appropriate sanction in every case of harassment.

Several recent cases make the employer's worst nightmare real: a suit by the alleged harasser, brought in the wake of an employer investigation. In *Ribando v. United Airlines Inc.*, 68 LW 1448 (7th Cir. 12/23/99), a male worker accused a female co-worker of making a harassing or derogatory remark about him. The employer engaged in union-management mediation, questioned several people, and put a "letter of concern" in the female worker's file, but didn't take any other action. The Seventh Circuit held that the woman could not maintain that the employer had engaged in severe or pervasive gender-based harassment against her; in fact, it had fulfilled its obligation to investigate harassment charges.

The District Court awarded $120,000 to an alleged harasser for the employer's negligent infliction of emotional distress on him. However, the Second Circuit reversed, once again pointing out that the employer had merely satisfied its duty to investigate: *Malik v. Carrier Corp.*, 68 LW 1462 (2nd Cir. 1/26/00).

FCRA Implications

In April 1999, the Federal Trade Commission (FTC) raised an explosive issue that few people had ever considered. As ¶1.11 of the main volume explains, employers are limited in the way they can use employees' and job applicants' credit reports, especially under September 1997 amendments to the Fair Credit Reporting Act (FCRA).

The FTC staff answered an inquiry from a lawyer and took the surprising position that an attorney who is paid by a corporation to investigate sexual harassment charges is thereby acting as a "credit reporting agency"—and therefore must conform to FCRA requirements. Failure to satisfy the FCRA can be penalized by a fine of up to $1000, plus punitive damages and the obligation to pay the opponent's attorneys' fees. Another risk is that reports prepared by attorneys in this "credit investigation" role might be denied protection under the attorney-client privilege. This issue is discussed in a May 17, 1999 article by Kevin Livingston, available at http://www.lawnewsnet.com/stories/A1499-1999May14.html. The letter itself can be found at http://www.ftc.gov/os/statutes/fcra/vail.htm.

23.4 RELIGIOUS DISCRIMINATION AND THE ISSUE OF REASONABLE ACCOMMODATION

According to the EEOC, charges of religious discrimination, although still few in number, are increasing: The 1709 charges filed in 1997 were 43% higher than the level prevailing in the early 1990s, for instance. In 2000, about one out of every 40 charges alleged religious discrimination. According to the Society for Human Resource Management's 1997 survey, about two-thirds of managers say that their company offers flexible schedules that can be used for religious holidays. However, only 19% included religious issues in diversity training; 18% trained their managers in accommodating religious preference; 15% provided space or time for prayer, study, or discussion; and only 13% accommodated religious attire.

It can be especially difficult to accommodate Muslim employees in a production line environment, because devout Muslims are required to pray five times daily, with several of the obligatory prayers occurring during the work day. Furthermore, part of the prayer obligation is keyed to sunset, so it does not occur at the same time each day, making it even harder to schedule prayers. The need for Muslims to wash their hands and feet before prayer can cause hazardous wet conditions in the washrooms (or hallways, if water is tracked). One simple solution is to install a special self-draining basin, or arrange to have the floors mopped more often.

If possible, flexible scheduling should be permitted—for instance, an employee who wants to leave early on Friday for the Jewish Sabbath or the Muslim prayer service can simply work later on Thursday or start earlier on Friday morning.

Although it is often impossible to provide food in employee cafeterias that fully complies with all religious dietary restrictions, it is a reasonable gesture to provide some vegetarian alternatives (for employees whose religion forbids meat eating) as well as some alternatives to pork and beef dishes (which are shunned by various religious groups). Low-fat vegetarian alternatives can also appeal to health-conscious employees who do not have religious limitations on their food consumption.

Not all religious discrimination claims involve non-Christians. In March 1999, the Eastern District of New York allowed a suit to proceed on a claim that a born-again Christian employee was fired because of "speaking in tongues" at work. The judge found that born-again Christians are entitled to treatment as a protected class.

In *Shelton v. University of Medicine & Dentistry of New Jersey* [(3rd Cir. 2000), discussed in Shannon P. Duffy, "Religious Employee Must Cooperate in Accommodation, 3rd Circuit Rules," *The Legal Intelligencer* 8/11/00 (law.com).] a nurse said she was not offered reasonable accommodation to her religious objection to performing tasks that would allow infants to die. The hospital didn't perform elective abortions, but sometimes labor and delivery staff had to assist in abortions performed for reasons of the mother's health. Therefore, the hospital offered her a transfer from the labor ward to the neonatal ICU. She refused to discuss open nursing positions with the hospital's HR department.

In the Third Circuit view, the plaintiff satisfied her prima facie case of religious discrimination, in that she did hold sincere religious views, and she did lose her job. However, the Third Circuit still ruled for the employer, on the theory that the employer's duty is satisfied by offering any reasonable accommodation, even if it is distasteful to the employee. In this case, even if the suggested accommodation had not been reasonable, the plaintiff would have forfeited her cause of action by refusing to discuss other possible job assignments.

Easy steps toward religious accommodation include the following:

- Extend the same toleration to religious dress as you accord to "fashion statements".
- If there is a genuine safety risk (such as flowing robes getting caught in machinery), document the risk.
- Discuss the issue with religious leaders: For instance, if the objective is modesty, a female worker could wear a long dress that is not tight, but is narrow enough not to present a hazard; long sleeves might be gathered into bands or gloves to reduce hazards. Such consultation also allows you to find out which holidays merely require believers to attend a religious service or pray and which require days off.
- Workers might exchange their lunch hours for departing early on or before their religious holidays.
- Use bulletin board posting (or your corporate intranet) to get volunteers to cover for workers who need time off for religious observance.
- Diversity can really help everyone in this context: Muslim or Jewish workers can cover the Christmas holidays, for instance, while Christian employees cover the holidays of other religions.
- If you allow optional or floating personal days, these can be used for religious observance.

According to *Weber v. Roadway Express Inc.*, 68 LW 1464 (5th Cir. 1/7/00), the employer had no obligation to accommodate a Jehovah's Witness truck driver who wanted to be assigned only male driving partners, because his religion forbade him to take overnight trips with any woman other than his wife. The employer would have to encounter more than a de minimis burden to reconfigure the schedules. Although the employer had accommodated secular requests from employees, it did so only consistent with its business needs, and did not have to encounter undue hardship to accommodate the truck driver.

In the case of *Hernandez-Torres v. Intercontinental Trading Co.*, 158 F.3d 43 (1st Cir. 1998), the plaintiff's claim of a religiously hostile workplace was rejected. Although he received a number of e-mails urging greater productivity, he was not singled out (nonreligious employees got similar messages), and he continued to receive favorable assessments, so he did not suffer job detriment. Since the claim of religious discrimination failed, so did his claim of retaliation.

23.5 THE EQUAL PAY ACT

President Clinton's 1999 State of the Union Address noted that full-time female workers earned an average of 74 cents for every dollar earned by a full-time male worker. The President proposed a $14 million equal pay initiative to be undertaken by the EEOC and Department of Labor; no details of the plan were given. See 67 LW 2567.

An EPA suit by female professors against a state university was vacated and remanded by the Supreme Court; on remand, the Seventh Circuit upheld the EPA as a valid exercise of Congressional authority, which meant that it was also legitimate for Congress to take away the state's Eleventh Amendment immunity from being sued. [*Varner v. Illinois State U.*, 226 F.3d 927 (7th Cir. 2000).]

In the spring of 1999, the Bureau of Labor Statistics (BLS) released 1998 figures (*Highlights of Women's Earnings in 1998*, Report 928, discussed in a news item, "Women's Earnings Difference Higher After Age 45," *Compensation and Benefits Update*, 5/19/99, p. 5). For 1998, median female earnings for full-time work, $456, were 76% of median male earnings, $598 (up from 63% in 1979). Pay disparities increased with age. Women under age 25 have virtually achieved wage parity, at an average of 91% of the male wage for the same age bracket. But in the 45–54 bracket, women earned only 70.5% of the male median. For women with college degrees, inflation-adjusted income went up 21.7% since 1979, versus only 7.7% for male college graduates for the same period.

Data on job classification of female workers is only available since 1983. In that year, 34.2% of full-time women workers held executive/managerial/administrative positions (i.e., had the potential for high earnings). In 1998, 46.4% of women employed full time held such positions. However, in both 1983 and 1998, about three-quarters of administrative support (e.g., secretarial) positions were held by women. In other words, the "pink collar" sector remains a largely female domain.

In 1998, about one-quarter of women in the paid workforce were part-time workers, earning a median of about one-third the full-time wage for women. The median wage for female part-time workers was actually higher than that for male part-timers, so this is an area in which women have not only reached but surpassed wage parity.

For full-time female workers, median wage increased with age (although parity with male wages declined), as you would expect with enhanced experience and seniority. But wages stayed fairly stable over time for female part-time workers, indicating a lack of mobility and promotion opportunity.

The Office of Federal Contract Compliance Programs (OFCCP) announced in late 1998 that it would target EPA compliance. Bernard E. Anderson, head of the Employment Standards Administration, the Department of Labor agency that enforces wage and hour laws, cited major 1998 EPA settlements. In April, Philadelphia's Corestates Bank agreed to pay $1.5 million. In October, Chicago's R. R. Donnelly agreed to pay $425,000. In December, a proposal was made that the OFCCP and EEOC enter into a Memorandum of Understanding that would permit the OFCCP to seek Title VII damages on behalf of employees deprived of equal pay.

The OFCCP's largest EPA case in its entire four-year "glass ceiling" program was settled when Texaco agreed to pay $3.1 million to 186 women executives and professionals who worked in its corporate office between 1993 and 1996. The back pay awards ranged from $1700 to $51,000; the average award was $12,000. The OFCCP performs 30 to 40 "glass ceiling" reviews a year; it checks to see if the company under investigation imposes subtle barriers to the advancement of women and members of minority groups. See 67 LW 2405, 2428. Since 1992, government contractors have ponied up an average of $32 million a year in DOL settlements, usually back pay ordered as a result of routine audits.

Marc Adams' article, "Fair and Square," *HR Magazine*, 5/99, p. 39, suggests some useful resources for auditing your compensation policies for equal pay compliance. The Web site for the DOL's Women's Bureau, http://www2.dol.gov/wb/10step71.htm, suggests ten steps for promoting pay equality. The Equal Employment Advisory Council's site is http://www.eeac.org, and it can be reached by telephone at (202) 789-8650.

Federal contractors can access the audit manual for OFCCP compliance at http://www.dol.gov/dol/esa/public/regs/compliance/ofccp/compdata.htm.

Even satisfying the audit requirements may not be enough to stave off EPA challenges. Your compensation system may have to pass the test of "regression analysis": That is, raw figures may have to be adjusted to reflect differing work experience and performance. It helps to maintain an objective grading system (i.e., Mr. X is at Grade 11; Ms. Y is at Grade 12)—but it also helps to have an objective outside opinion. Pay grades can reflect unspoken assumptions that jobs typically performed by women take less skill than those typically performed by men, even if there is no objective support for such prejudices.

23.6 DISCRIMINATION SUIT PROCEDURAL ISSUES

The EEOC's investigative powers generally end as soon as a Right to Sue letter has been issued [*EEOC v. Federal Home Loan Mortgage Co.*, 37 F.Supp.2d 769 (E.D. Va. 3/10/99)]. The exception is the case where the EEOC thinks its investigation goes beyond the litigation, in which case it can intervene in the employee's private suit or file its own charges.

Although employers can benefit from situations in which employees delay too long in filing charges, employees may be given additional time to file EEOC charges if the employer actually misleads the employees as to the existence of an investigation by the employer. The doctrine of "equitable estoppel" is applied if, for instance, the employee is afraid to approach the EEOC and imperil the internal grievance proceeding. See *Currier v. Radio Free Europe*, 159 F.3d 1363 (D.C. Cir. 1998).

In a recent California case, *Ramirez v. Circuit City Stores Inc.*, 68 LW 1376 (Cal.App. 12/10/99), the court refused to enforce the ADR policy in an employer's standard employment contract, finding that it was oppressive to employees; was a contract of adhesion; and imposed obligations on employees but not the employer.

On the propriety of class certification in Title VII cases, see *Jefferson v. Ingersoll Int'l Inc.*, 68 LW 1265 (7th Cir. 10/25/99), further discussed in ¶27.7.

23.7 AFFIRMATIVE ACTION

An affirmative action program that preferentially hires minority applicants over equally qualified non-minority applicants can be harmonized with Title VII only if the plan was adopted as a remedy for present or past discrimination in a traditionally segregated job category. An affirmative action program that does not have this remedial justification is invalid. [*Schurr v. Resorts Int'l Hotel*, 68 LW 1296 (3rd Cir. 11/12/99).]

A white male plaintiff said that he was denied a promotion because he was the victim of reverse discrimination, and that the woman who got the promotion was less qualified. Because a white male is not a member of a protected class, the Seventh Circuit defined the prima facie as showing "background circumstances" evidencing reverse discrimination.

For instance, a pattern of not promoting white males, or the choice of a significantly weaker candidate, would suffice. Here, it was held that the plaintiff succeeded in presenting a prima facie case by showing that most of the promotions were given to women. However, he did not win at trial because the issue was the employer's intent to discriminate. The plaintiff did not show that the employer's contention, that it believed the woman was actually better qualified for the promotion, was false or pretextual. [*Mills v. Health Care Service Corp.*, 1999 WL 144274 (7th Cir. 1999).

Even the EEOC sometimes concedes that affirmative action is inappropriate. On January 31, 2000, the agency issued an opinion letter saying that an employer should use a vacant position to provide reasonable accommodation to a disabled current employee, instead of hiring a black female candidate for the job, or promoting a black female employee to the position. In fact, the EEOC views disability accommodation as so important that a qualified disabled employee should be reassigned to the vacant position, even if there is another, **more** qualified candidate. ["EEOC Says Accommodation Takes Priority Over Affirmative Action," http://www.lawnewsnetwork.com/practice/employmentlaw/news/A15911-2000Feb10.html.]

See 63 FR 59,629 and 59,657 (11/4/98) for a Department of Labor Final Rule as to federal contractors' affirmative action obligations for hiring and promoting Vietnam veterans and disabled veterans (irrespective of which war disabled them).

The Institute for Women's Policy Research, on behalf of the AFL-CIO, calculated the lifetime earnings lost by women workers who do not receive equal pay for equal work. The lifetime earnings loss is the difference between expected lifetime earnings between the sexes, assuming that women work an average of 47 years. The figures are corrected for actual work experience and education.

If current wage patterns continue, after 40 years in the workforce, an average 25-year-old woman will earn $523,000 less than the average 25-year-old man. (See http://www.aflcio.org/women/about.htm.) Although in a sense underpaying women is beneficial to business, if women workers had an additional $500,000 over the length of a career, they would use most or all of it to invest or purchase goods and services for themselves and their families—so business as a whole would benefit.

23.8 RETALIATION

EEOC Compliance Manual

The first step that the EEOC took in its issuance of a revised Compliance Manual (used by EEOC offices) was to issue Section 8, dealing with Retaliation. Volume 2, Section 614 of the earlier Compliance Manual has become obsolete. New Section 8 is found in EEOC Directives Transmittal 915.003, dated 5/20/98.

Under Section 8, there are three essential elements in a retaliation claim that the EEOC will pursue:

- Protected activity by the charging party—opposing discrimination, or participating in the Title VII complaint process
- Adverse action taken by the employer
- A causal connection between the protected activity and the employer's adverse action

If the charging party reasonably and in good faith believed that the employer committed discrimination (even if this belief was incorrect), and if the charging party protested this discrimination to the employer, using a reasonable means of protest, then there is a possible retaliation complaint.

Charging parties are legally protected against retaliation if the charging party, or someone "closely associated" with him or her, participated in any statutory enforcement proceeding. That includes any investigation, proceeding, hearing, or suit under either Title VII or any other statute enforced by the EEOC. It is unlawful for one employer to retaliate on the basis of a complaint against another employer.

Trivial adverse actions are not covered by the compliance manual, but "more significant retaliatory treatment that is reasonably likely to deter protected activity" is banned. The adverse action need not materially affect the terms, conditions, or privileges of employment. Ex-employees have the right to complain of retaliation (e.g., bad references).

The EEOC might seek temporary or preliminary relief (e.g., injunctions) if retaliation places the charging party at risk of irreparable injury and if there is a substantial likelihood that the retaliation claim will succeed. The compliance manual notes that all of the statutes enforced by the EEOC make both compensatory and punitive damages available to victims of retaliation.

Although Title VII retaliation damages are subject to the statutory cap, there is no cap on ADEA or EPA damages. The manual says that punitive damages are "often" appropriate in retaliation cases. For discussion, see "EEOC Issues Retaliation Guidelines," *Employment Alert*, 7/9/98, p. 6.

Retaliation Case Law

➠ TIP

An employee who gives a deposition in another person's sex discrimination case is protected against retaliation for the testimony; the employer is not permitted to impose a requirement that the testimony be "reasonable" [*Glover v. South Carolina Law Enforcement Division*, 170 F.3d 411 (4th Cir. 1999)].

In a 2000 case from the Eleventh Circuit, however, it was held that it is not unlawful retaliation to discharge an employee based on the employer's good-faith belief that she lied during an internal investigation of a sexual harassment charge. According to *EEOC v. Total System Services Inc.*, 221 F.3d 1171 (11th Cir. 2000), Title VII's retaliation provision does not come into play until an EEOC filing has been made.

Morris v. Oldham County, Kentucky Fiscal Court, 68 LW 1438 (6th Cir. 1/20/00) applies more or less the same analysis as *Faragher/Burlington* to severe or pervasive retaliation committed by a supervisor against an employee who has complained of prior sexual harassment. That is to say, retaliatory harassment is not considered a tangible employment action in and of itself, so the employer is entitled to assert the affirmative defense of adequate response and employee failure to make use of the complaint mechanism.

The Southern District of New York permitted two black employees to maintain a Title VII case alleging retaliation (professional isolation and lack of opportunities for advancement) after they complained about racist jokes in an e-mail on the corporate system. However, the S.D.N.Y. did not permit a class action to be maintained based on those charges [*Owens v. Morgan Stanley & Co.*, 66 LW 1432 (S.D.N.Y. 12/24/97)].

A lateral transfer requiring the employee to perform tasks that the employer knew the employee would be unable to handle (because of phobia), in retaliation for complaining about harassment by a supervisor, is actionable under Title VII. The transfer involved the same pay, benefits, and status, but the employer knew that the alleged transfer was really a constructive discharge. See *DiIenno v. Goodwill Industries*, 162 F.3d 235 (3rd Cir. 1998).

According to the Eleventh Circuit, protection against retaliation for participation in an investigation is limited to the EEOC investigation. An employer is not liable for retaliation on the basis of participation in the employer's own internal investigation [*Clover v. Total Systems Services Inc.*, 157 F.3d 824 (11th Cir. 1998)].

Chapter 24

THE AMERICANS WITH DISABILITIES ACT (ADA)

24.1 INTRODUCTION

During the supplement period, the ADA was one of the main focuses of litigation (including Supreme Court decisions and cases accepted for hearing) and EEOC guidance.

At press time, the Supreme Court had just handed down its decision in *Board of Trustees of the University of Alabama v. Garrett*, #99-1240 (2/21/01). Like the 1999 *Kimel* decision (see ¶26.2) it holds that states are entitled to immunity from suits by state employees—in *Kimel*, from ADEA suits, in *Garrett*, from ADA suits seeking money damages (as distinct from injunctive relief).

In each case, the Supreme Court's rationale is that Congress did not properly abrogate Eleventh Amendment immunity by providing adequate evidence that the states in the role of employer had actually perpetrated a pattern of discrimination that required redress.

Under *Bragdon v. Abbott*, 524 U.S. 624 (Sup. Ct. 1998), ADA cases are subject to a three-step test:

- Does the plaintiff have an impairment? (As you'll see, this can be a very difficult question to answer.)
- Is the major life activity that is impaired covered by the ADA?
- Does the plaintiff's impairment substantially limit that major life activity?

Bragdon is not an employment case. It arose when a dentist refused to treat an HIV positive but asymptomatic patient in his office, telling her that she would have to be treated at a hospital. The Supreme Court refused to accept the dentist's argument that treating HIV positive patients in the office posed a direct threat, because the medical consensus is that treatment can be safe for patient, dentist, and other patients as long as precautions are followed.

Although this is not an employment case, the court did treat asymptomatic HIV infection as a disability, because it is a physical impairment that substantially limits major life activities such as reproduction. To the extent that reproduction is considered a major life activity, coverage of infertility treatment under health plans might be mandated.

An EEOC Administrative Decision—not a full-scale rule promulgated after an opportunity for notice and comment—says that denying a female employee coverage for infertility treatments and related medical expenses violates Title VII and the ADA, because the plan covered medically necessary treatments of other kinds of ailments that had a comparable effect on bodily functioning. See 64 FR 22769 (4/27/99).

The Northern District of Illinois ruled, in September 1997, that female infertility is a disability as defined by the ADA, because reproduction can be a major life activity even if it doesn't affect work [*Erickson v. Board of Governors, Northeastern Illinois University*, 66 LW 1304 (N.D. Ill. 9/29/97)]. This contradicts *Krauel v. Iowa Methodist Medical Center*, 95 F.3d 674 (8th Cir. 1996), which holds that reproduction is *not* a major life activity.

In the post-*Bragdon* environment, the Southern District of New York has ruled [*Saks v. Franklin Covey Co.*, 117 F.Supp.2d 318 (S.D.N.Y. 2000)] that infertility cannot be ruled out as a disability, because of the interference with the major life activity of reproduction. But that didn't mean victory for the plaintiff, who was covered by a self-insured health plan that excluded "surgical impregnation procedures."

She brought claims under Title VII, the ADA, and the PDA. But the ADA claim was dismissed because the same coverage was offered to all employees—the infertile did not receive inferior coverage for reproduction-related services. The plan was also a bona fide employee benefit plan qualifying for the ADA safe harbor. The Title VII claim failed because both male and female infertility were excluded, and the female-only surgical procedures were excluded for both female employees and wives of male employees. The PDA claim failed because infertility treatments were equally unavailable to pregnant and non-pregnant employees and beneficiaries.

According to the Northern District of Illinois, a plan's refusal to pay for infertility treatment for an employee's spouse did not violate the ADA (because that law doesn't extend to dependents of an employee who do not perform services for the employer). Furthermore, non-employees do not have standing to sue under Title VII or the PDA. The employee himself had standing to raise the PDA claim, but the claim itself was invalid because, although the plan covered normal pregnancy and excluded infertility treatment, it did not cover fertility treatment for either sex. [*Niemeier v. Tri-State Fire Protection District*, 2000 U.S. Dist. LEXIS 12621 (N.D. Ill. 2000).]

One of several major Supreme Court ADA cases in the supplement period was decided in late 1998. *Wright v. Universal Maritime Service Corp.*, #97-889 67 523 U.S. 70 Sup.Ct. 11/16/98, involves an injured stevedore who was denied employment because companies deemed him to be permanently disabled. The plaintiff sued under the ADA without first filing a grievance or going through arbitration under the collective bargaining agreement.

Although the District Court and Fourth Circuit dismissed the stevedore's case, because of his failure to exhaust grievance remedies, the Supreme Court unanimously reversed. *Gilmer* does permit compulsory arbitration of an ADA claim (under the U-4), but to the Supreme Court, this case is different because the employee's claim derived from a statute, not a contract. Although contract claims are presumed arbitrable, that presumption does not apply to statutory claims. For a collective bargaining agreement to preclude litigation of a statutory claim, it must be very clear on that point. A generalized arbitration clause that fails to discuss antidiscrimination statutes will not be enough to keep disgruntled employees out of the court system.

At least in the Northern District of Washington, ADA suits can be brought for disability-based harassment and hostile work environment: *Fox v. General Motors*, 94 F.Supp.2d 723 (N.D. Wash. 2000).

In an ADA case (or an ADEA case), *Papa v. Katy Industries Inc.* 67 LW 1485 (7th Cir. 2/8/99) says that several small affiliates of a larger corporation can have their workforces aggregated when determining the application of the antidiscrimination statute, as long as they are closely related. Aggregation is proper if the corporate veil can be pierced (i.e., the formal organization can be disregarded in favor of practical realities) and the parent company is liable for its subsidiaries' debts, torts, and breaches of contract; if the enterprise was divided with the objective of avoiding employment laws; or if the parent company directed the discriminatory act or policy.

Carson v. Giant Food Inc., 1999 WL 254438 (4th Cir. 4/29/99) says that there has been a clear and unmistakeable waiver of the right to litigate if a collective bargaining agreement (CBA) arbitration clause either specifically says that statutory discrimination claims are arbitrable, or fully incorporates the antidiscrimination statutes into the contract.

However, *Brown v. ABF Freight Systems Inc.*, 183 F.3d 319 (4th Cir. 7/13/99) finds that the CBA at issue in that particular case, although it referred to the ADA, did not fully incorporate it, and thus litigation could proceed.

Under *EEOC v. Wal-Mart Stores*, 187 F.3d 1241 (10th Cir. 8/23/99), a written antidiscrimination policy, taken by itself, is not the equivalent of a good-faith effort to comply with the ADA. Thus, the employer is vicariously liable and can be subjected to punitive damages, where a supervisor discriminated against a hearing-impaired employee. The employer didn't provide ADA training for supervisors, and thus didn't really implement the antidiscrimination rules. The jury's punitive damage award of $75,000 was upheld; the Eighth Circuit did not find it large enough to shock the conscience.

According to the American Bar Association, based on a study of 1200 reported and unreported cases between 1992 and 1998, the employer wins 92% of the ADA cases that are pursued to a final decision (this survey is discussed at 67 LW 2005).

In that sample, 440 cases were not yet final; of the 750 decided, the employer won 92.1%. There were some striking differences based on the location of the case. In the Fifth Circuit, employers won 98.1% of the time, versus a comparatively small 83.3% rate of employer victory in the Ninth Circuit.

It should be noted, however, that very few charges ever proceed to litigation. The EEOC's own statistics show that, between FY 1992 (the first year of EEOC enforcement of the ADA; the statute did not take effect until July 26, 1992) and FY 1997, 91,133 ADA charges were filed. The agency reports resolution of 83,664 of the charges, 13.5% of which were merit resolutions. 4.5% of the cases were settled; 6.0% were withdrawn by the complainant after receipt of benefits. About half of the charges (49.6%) were deemed by the EEOC to have been made without reasonable cause, and about one-third (36.9%) were closed administratively.

Good-cause determinations were made in 3.1% of the cases. Conciliation succeeded in about one-third of the good-cause cases and failed in the other two-thirds. In the five years studied, employers were required to pay $162 million with respect to ADA claims.

The most common impairment cited by ADA charging parties was back injury (15,954 cases between 1992 and 1997; 17.5% of the total). The next most common was emotional or psychiatric impairment: 13.2% of the total, or 12,028 charges, followed by neurological impairment (11.0%; 10,004 charges) and injuries to the extremities (9.3%; 8,497 charges). The various other complaints each represented less than 5% of the total.

About half of all ADA charges (52.2%; 47,535 charges) alleged inappropriate dismissal, and more than a quarter (28.9%; 26,319 charges) alleged failure to make reasonable accommodations to a worker's disability. About one-eighth of the claims (12.5%; 11,410 charges) alleged harassment of disabled persons. (The EEOC ADA figures are from *Employment Alert*, 9/3/98, p. 4.)

Several Circuits are in conflict as to whether employees of state and local government agencies can use Title II of the ADA (which forbids disability discrimination in the services, programs, and activities of public entities) to assert job discrimination claims. The Ninth Circuit says yes [*Zimmerman v. Oregon*, 170 F.3d 1169 (9th Cir. 3/18/99)]. The Eleventh Circuit says no [*Bledsoe v. Palm Beach County Soil & Water Conservation District*, 133 F.3d 816 (11th Cir. 1998)].

Alsbrook v. Maumelle, 68 LW 1060 (8th Cir. 7/23/99) says that Congress exceeded its authority under the Fourteenth Amendment when it allowed ADA Title II suits against state government, because states can be penalized even for activities that should be exempt because they serve a rational state interest. (The plaintiff was a would-be police officer who was rejected for failure to meet vision standards.)

A union of federal employees is a "labor organization," and therefore can be sued by its members for ADA (and Title VII) violations: *Jones v. American Postal Workers Union*, 192 F.3d 417 (4th Cir. 9/10/99).

Although individuals are nearly always exempt from being sued under Title VII and other employment statutes, *Alberte v. Anew Health Care Services*, 588 N.W.2d 298 (Wis. App. 1998), does permit an ADA suit against an individual who was president, administrator, and 47.5% shareholder in a company accused of disability discrimination. In this reading, the president was the company's agent and can be held personally liable for both compensatory and punitive damages.

In January 1999, the Clinton Administration proposed initiatives to help disabled people return to work which were enacted on December 17, 1999 as P.L. 106-170, the "Ticket to Work and Work Incentives Improvement Act of 1999."

See Robert Pear, "Proposal Aims at Returning Disabled Workers to Jobs," *NYT* 1/13/99, p. A12, and Laurie McGinley and Bob Davis, "Disabled Workers to Gain Health Care, Tax Benefits Under Bipartisan Plan," *WSJ*, 1/13/99, p. A6. Under the new law, disabled people retain Medicare and/or Medicaid coverage for their health needs after returning to the workforce. The Administration also called for devoting $35 million in the FY 2000 budget (twice the 1999 level) for research into the development of additional assistive technology. The estimated cost of the proposals over a five-year period would be about $2 billion.

24.2 UNDERSTANDING THE DEFINITION OF DISABILITY

At first glance, it might seem obvious who is, or is not, disabled, but the questions are numerous, subtle, and often give rise to opposing interpretations by different courts.

1999 Case Law

The holding of *Todd v. Academy Corp.*, 57 F.Supp.2d 448 (S.D.Tex. 8/5/99) is that epilepsy, controlled by medication but nevertheless causing light seizures lasting under fifteen seconds each, about once a week, was not an ADA disability, because it had only a very limited impact on major life activities.

The plaintiff could recognize the onset of a seizure and lie down, so he was not dangerous to himself or others. The fact pattern in this case was that the employer claimed that the employee was fired for taking unauthorized sick days when he had the flu; the plaintiff charged that he was fired because of his epilepsy.

Under *McAlindin v. San Diego*, 68 LW 1207 (9th Cir. 9/16/99), a factual issue remains as to whether a person who takes medication for panic disorder is limited in major life activities (sleep; social and sexual interaction). The medication doesn't necessarily eliminate disability, and medication side effects can create disability.

The co-president of a company was demoted, and his salary cut in half, after he returned from work after cancer treatment. His doctor said that he was healthy enough to return to work, although he would require ongoing chemotherapy. In the view of the Fifth Circuit, the executive was not "disabled" because he could still maintain a full workload (*EEOC v. R.J. Gallagher*, 181 F.3d 645 (5th Cir. 7/15/99)).

His ability to work was somewhat affected, but not to the point of substantial limitation. However, summary judgment could not be granted for the employer on the question of whether he was regarded as disabled, so the case was remanded for trial on that issue.

The D.C. Circuit reversed a $250,000 jury verdict obtained by an unskilled laborer with back problems. According to *Duncan v. Washington Metropolitan Area Transit Authority*, 68 LW 1455 (D.C. Cir. 1/28/00), he failed to demonstrate the availability of unskilled jobs in his geographic area, and therefore didn't show the impact of his impairment (inability to lift over 20 pounds; his previous jobs had required heavy lifting) on his ability to work.

A woman who used a prosthetic device to replace four lost fingers worked in a hospital as a paramedic. Her job was eliminated, and she started training as an operating room technician. However, after one day, she was dismissed from the training class for inability to carry out the essential functions of the technician's job.

The hospital moved to have her ADA claim dismissed, on the grounds that her prosthesis permitted her normal functioning and therefore moved her out of the "disabled" category. Motion to dismiss was denied by the New York Supreme Court, which found that New York State and City antidiscrimination laws work like the ADA. In this reading, not every person who uses a corrective device is not disabled; fact questions about actual ability to perform life activities must be resolved by the court. The case is *Shine v. Roosevelt Hospital*, discussed in Cerisse Anderson, "Hospital Loses Bid to Dismiss Bias Suit," http://www.lawnewsnetwork.com/stories/A12642-2000Jan3.html.

Substance Abuse as a Disability

The 1999 Fifth Circuit case of *Zenor v. El Paso Healthcare System Ltd.*, 67 LW 1729 (5th Cir. 5/24/99), discussed in more detail in ¶22.3, takes the position that even though a hospital pharmacist voluntarily reported his cocaine addiction and entered a rehab program, the hospital did not violate the ADA by firing him. He was considered to be a "current user" of an illegal substance, not qualified for the "rehab" safe harbor, because of the risk of relapse. Furthermore, his job gave him access to pharmaceutical cocaine, greatly increasing the risk of future drug abuse.

Nor could a substance abuser be considered a "qualified person" under the ADA for the specific job of hospital pharmacist (although he might have been qualified for many other jobs that required professional skills but did not involve daily contact with controlled substances).

An employee who abuses illegal drugs is breaking the law—an element that is not present when employees encounter alcohol-related disabilities. An article by John P. Furfaro and Maury B. Josephson, "Alcoholism as a Disability," *New York Law Journal* 2/5/99, p. 3, sums up the case law, with an emphasis on New York cases.

Some cases take the view that, once an employee goes through rehab, it constitutes discrimination against the disability of alcoholism to fire or otherwise discipline the employee for pretreatment absenteeism—for instance, *McEniry v. Landi*, 84 N.Y.2d 554 (1994). But even this case points out that employees who flunk rehab, or who are likely to relapse, are not protected from the consequences of a lapse. *Myszczenko v. City of Poughkeepsie*, 239 A.D.2d 584 (2nd Dept. 1997), says that it's OK to fire an employee for misconduct that occurred after a postrehab relapse.

More recently, in *Mercado v. NYC Housing Authority*, 1998 Westlaw 151039 (S.D.N.Y. 3/31/98), the Southern District dismissed a termination case, pointing out that the ADA allows employers to apply the same standards of conduct to all employees, whether or not they have a substance abuse problem. Similar results were reached in other courts [*Williams v. Widnall*, 79 F.3d 1003 (10th Cir. 1996) and *Rollison v. Gwinnett County*, 865 F.Supp. 1564 (N.D.Ga. 1994)].

The Fifth Circuit decided a case challenging Exxon's policy of permanently removing employees who had been treated for substance abuse from safety-sensitive positions where there was little supervision. [*EEOC v. Exxon*, 203 F.3d 871 (5th Cir. 2000)]. The Fifth Circuit allowed the employer to defend such practices by showing business necessity for the standard. As long as the standard is applied equally to all employees within a class, the employer does not have to prove that former substance abusers constitute a direct threat to safety.

➠ TIP

Several courts have upheld "last-chance" agreements, under which the substance abuser acknowledges that job-related misconduct occurred in the past and that the employee's reinstatement after rehab is only conditional, based on continued good performance (and perhaps dependent on giving consent for drug/alcohol testing and passing periodic tests). *Marrari v. WCI Steel Inc.*, 130 F.3d 1180 (6th Cir. 1997), treats the last-chance agreement as a reasonable accommodation to the disability of alcoholism. Does someone have to be given more than one last chance? *Evans v. Federal Express*, 133 F.3d 137 (1st Cir. 1998), upholds the termination of an employee who sought a leave of absence to go to an alcohol rehab program; he had already taken leave for drug rehab. He was discharged for absenteeism. The First Circuit's view is that employers are entitled to be skeptical about the success of a second rehab effort after one has failed.

Employers can't penalize rehabilitated individuals based on the mere fact that they are alcoholics or have been addicted to drugs—but it's perfectly legitimate to punish misconduct that happens to be the result of alcoholism [*Brennan v. NYC Police Department*, 1997 Westlaw 811543 (S.D.N.Y. 5/27/97)].

24.2.1 "Regarded As" Liability

Not only does the ADA cover qualified individuals who indeed have a disability, it also covers qualified individuals who do **not** have a disability, but are discriminated against because of employer perception that they have a disability.

TIP

Don't forget that a substance abuser entering rehab (at least an in-patient program) may be entitled to FMLA leave. Additional leave, after the 12 weeks of FMLA leave have been used up, may be required by the ADA as a reasonable accommodation. There are technical legal questions involved, but it's probably true that the employee has to request accommodation in advance. It probably isn't good enough for a person who has already been terminated or disciplined to make a retroactive request for leave.

This issue is discussed in "Disability Discrimination: Trends in 'Regarded As' Cases," WestGroup Employment Alert, 1/20/00, p. 4, which notes that the issue in *EEOC v. R.J. Gallagher Co.*, 181 F.3d 645 (5th Cir. 1999) is whether the employer perceived that the employee had an impairment that caused substantial limitation in a major life activity. In other words, relevant evidence is what the employer believed, not medical evidence about the employee's health condition and abilities.

In *Heyman v. Queens Village Committee for Mental Health*, 68 LW 1341 (2nd Cir. 11/30/99), a dismissed medical clinic administrator's ADA suit survived the employer's summary judgment motion. The plaintiff had been diagnosed as having lymphoma (a disease from which another clinic employee had recently died) but was still asymptomatic. The Second Circuit allowed him to pursue his claim that he was regarded as disabled, based on a memo expressing concern about his continued ability to work once he became symptomatic. The employer claimed that the discharge occurred for poor performance, but it also occurred shortly after the plaintiff took some time off for medical care. The employer had never given the employee a written evaluation, and so was unable to document its allegations of poor performance and negative behavior.

As Dorothy Parker might have said, courts don't give passes to troopers with glasses. A group of would-be Pennsylvania state troopers were not hired because of poor vision. Of course, *Sutton* disposes of the argument that people with poor vision that can be corrected with glasses are disabled. What about the argument that eyeglass wearers are "regarded" as disabled even though they really are not? *Sutton* says that being turned down for a particular job doesn't show the employer's perception that the applicant is limited in the major life activity of working, only that he or she isn't appropriate for the job in question.

The Pennsylvania plaintiffs sought leave to amend their complaint, to say that they were regarded as being limited in the major life activities of "running, seeing, operating a motor vehicle, and/or working in a class of jobs."

They were allowed to amend their complaint, except for naming driving as a major life activity; the court didn't consider it important enough to rank with working, seeing, hearing, breathing, and other recognized major life activities. The court considered it proper to allow the amendment, because there was at least some chance that they could prove their claims [*Wilson v. Pennsylvania State Police Department*, discussed in Claudia Ginanni, "'Regarded As' Provision of ADA Saves Claim by Plaintiffs With Glasses," *The Legal Intelligencer*, 1/19/00.]

An employer can be liable on a "regarded as disabled" claim based on an innocent misunderstanding (or adherence to stereotypes) about the employee's capacity, unless the employee himself or herself is responsible for the error, or unreasonably failed to correct the employer's misconceptions: *Taylor v. Pathmark*, 177 F.3d 180 (3rd Cir. 5/15/99).

In *Hilburn v. Murata Electronics*, 181 F.3d 1220 (11th Cir. 7/20/99), the employee had two problems: her own health (coronary heart disease culminating in a heart attack) and serious illness of family members, requiring substantial time off. After the heart attack, she had some limitations in lifting, but could walk, run, and carry out all other normal activities. Her "regarded-as" claim failed, because the Eleventh Circuit ruled that "a perceived impairment must be believed to substantially limit a major life activity of the individual." Here, the major life activity of working was substantially unimpaired.

The employer's refusal to reinstate a firefighter after an injury-related absence was caused by belief that the employee was no longer able to perform the specific job, not the employer's perception of an overall limitation in the life activity of working: *Shipley v. City of University City*, 195 F.3d 1020 (8th Cir. 1999).

What about absenteeism caused by the need for frequent doctors' appointments? The Seventh Circuit view, as expressed in *Gorbitz v. Corvilla*, 196 F.3d 879 (7th Cir. 1999), is that a discharge for absenteeism does not support a "regarded as" claim, because it is not necessary that a person have a substantial limitation in major life activities to need frequent medical appointments.

Employers have a duty of reasonable accommodation only in the case of actual, not perceived, disability: *Weber v. Strippit, Inc.*, 186 F.3d 907 (8th Cir. 1999). Of course, that raises the question of how far the employer must go to provide reasonable accommodation when it is required.

24.3 PREEMPLOYMENT INQUIRIES

A job applicant who is not hired because the employer was not satisfied with the applicant's answers to impermissible inquiries has an ADA cause of action—even if the applicant is not disabled. See *Griffin v. Steeltek Inc.*, 160 F.3d 591 (10th Cir. 1998).

Questions can be asked about prior Worker's Compensation claims once a conditional job offer is extended, as long as all potential new hires are asked the same question. But the EEOC's position is that it is inappropriate to refuse to hire because of past occupational injury or potential for filing future WC claims.

In October, 2000, the Western District of Missouri decided that it was not an ADA violation for a factory to reject job applicants whose pre-employment tests showed a proclivity to develop carpal tunnel syndrome: *EEOC v. Woodbridge Corp.*, 69 LW 1231 (W.D. Mo. 10/2/00). The applicants were not qualified to do high-speed assembly-line work. The court said that they were not entitled to relief as "regarded as disabled" because they were not kept out of a broad range of jobs, only the ones where they were at risk of carpal tunnel syndrome.

24.4 REASONABLE ACCOMMODATIONS

Some recent cases say that the employer has no duty to attempt reasonable accommodations (or additional accommodations for a person who has already received some) until and unless the employee takes the first step and requests accommodation. See *Gaston v. Bellingrath Gardens & Home Inc.* 167 F.3d 1361 (11th Cir. 2/12/99) and *More v. Buckhorn Rubber Products Inc.*, 67 LW 1528 (8th Cir. 2/1/99).

Taylor v. Phoenixville School District, 174 F.3d 142 (3rd Cir. 1999) adopts the EEOC position that, as soon as an employee asks for reasonable accommodation, the employer has a duty to engage in an interactive process with the employee to find the appropriate accommodation.

Some employees who ask for accommodation don't fit the definition of qualified individuals with disabilities. But *Taylor* suggests that employers lose the ability to get summary judgment on ADA claims if they don't at least cooperate with the employee to the extent of discovering whether the employee really fits the ADA definition of disability; finding out what accommodations the employee wants; and seeing if they are practical.

Fjellestad v. Pizza Hut of America, Inc., 1999 WL 391911 (8th Cir. 1999) also rules out summary judgment for the employer if the employer refused to participate in good faith in the interactive process.

In contrast, the 2000 Third Circuit case of *Donahue v. Consolidated Rail Corp.*, [discussed in Shannon P. Duffy, "When No Jobs Available, Employer's Duty Eliminated," The Legal Intelligencer 8/22/00 (law.com).] holds that the employer can not only win an ADA case but get summary judgment (i.e., prevent the case from being fully tried) without engaging in the interactive process—if the plaintiff fails to show that there were any jobs available that he or she could have done.

In this reading, failure to engage in the interactive process does not create a separate cause of action for the plaintiff. In a case like this one, where the plaintiff alleges failure to transfer to a job he could have done, the plaintiff has the burden of proving that there was a vacant, funded job at or below the level of the former job, that the plaintiff could perform given reasonable accommodation. The employer has no obligation to create a new job to accommodate disability.

Furthermore, both parties must participate in the interactive process; a $1.5 million plaintiff's verdict was vacated because the jury should never have found for a plaintiff who rejected the proposed accommodation without discussion or counter-offer, and applied for long-term disability instead. [*Davis v. Guardian Life Ins. Co. of America*, discussed in Shannon P. Duffy, "Judge Vacates $1.5 Million Verdict in ADA Case," The Legal Intelligencer 12/20/00 (law.com).] In this reading, an employee's subjective, untested belief (here, that she would not be able to comply with the work schedule proposed by the employer, and would be discharged for excessive absences) cannot prevent a proposed accommodation from being treated as reasonable for legal purposes.

The employer can select which reasonable accommodation to offer [in the case of *Keever v. City of Middletown*, 145 F.3d 809 (6th Cir. 1998), a desk job at the same pay for a police officer previously assigned to a beat]. It is not obligated to accept the employee's suggestions (e.g., a shift change or promotion to detective).

Similarly, *Rehling v. City of Chicago*, 207 F.3d 1009 (7th Cir. 2000) does not require the employer to provide the accommodation preferred by the employee, merely one that is reasonable; where there are no positions available, the employee is not entitled to demand to be transferred back to the district where he or she formerly worked.

➠ TIP

Finding a job free of stress caused by fellow-employees is not a "reasonable accommodation" to which a clinically depressed employee is entitled [*Gaul v. Lucent Technologies, Inc.*, 134 F.3d 576 (3rd Cir. 1998)].

Restructuring the job of a psychologist in a mental institution to avoid contact with violent and/or infectious patients is not a reasonable accommodation to his asthma and weakened immune system, because the requested accommodations go to the very heart of the job: *Webb v. Choate Mental Health Center*, 69 LW 1320 (7th Cir. 10/25/00). However, the First Circuit found that a supermarket acted unreasonably by requiring a wheelchair-using employee to cover the cash register during busy times. Although this was required of all employees, it was considered unreasonable in her case because she had to transfer from her wheelchair to a special stool to use the cash register: *Marcano-Rivera v. Pueblo Int'l Inc.*, 69 LW 1336 (1st Cir. 10/25/00).

Smith v. Midland Brake Inc., 138 F.3d 1304 (10th Cir. 3/13/98), says that, if an employee is unable to handle his or her current job, the employer is not obligated to assign him to another job that he or she *can* handle, because the employee is not "qualified" for the existing job.

Malabarba v. Chicago Tribune Co., 149 F.3d 690 (7th Cir. 1998), involved a plaintiff whose multiple physical problems prevented him from returning to his old job as packager (which required several kinds of strenuous physical labor). The company tried to retrain him for the sedentary job of customer service representative, but he failed the exam. The company didn't have any other jobs he could do, so he was terminated.

The Seventh Circuit's position is that the employer was not liable: The plaintiff couldn't do his old job even with accommodation, and whether a person is a "qualified" individual with a disability depends on the job for which he or she was initially hired, not a temporary light-duty reassignment. If an employer's policy is to offer only temporary light-duty assignments for recuperating employees, the ADA does not require creation of permanent light-duty jobs as an accommodation. The employer need only offer a reasonable accommodation, not the accommodation preferred by the employee. When a job involves multiple duties, the employer is not obligated to separate out the duties that the employee can handle after an illness or injury.

In contrast, however, the EEOC position, echoed by several appellate cases, is that reassignment to a job that the employee can handle constitutes a reasonable accommodation: See 29 CFR §1630.2(o). Cases of this type include *Dalton v. Subaru-Isuzu Automotive, Inc.*, 141 F.3d 667 (7th Cir. 1998), *Cravens v. Blue Cross/Blue Shield*, 214 F.3d 1011 (8th Cir. 2000) and *Aka v. Washington Hospital Center*, 156 F.3d 1284 (D.C. Cir. 1998) (disabled person who cannot do the current job is entitled to ADA relief such as reassignment, with or without accommodation, to a job he or she can perform). The disabled employee in search of accommodation must be able to prove his or her ability to handle the new job [*DePaoli v. Abbott Laboratories*, 140 F.3d 668 (7th Cir. 1998)].

In September, 2000, the Seventh Circuit held that, as long as the employer maintains a consistent policy of selecting the best-qualified employee, it will not be necessary to reassign a disabled employee to a vacant position that a better-qualified, non-disabled person also wants. In other words, it is not necessary to give preference to the disabled applicant. [*EEOC v. Humiston-Keeling Inc.*, 227 F.3d 1024 (7th Cir. 2000).] Furthermore, according to the Eleventh Circuit, the employee must show that reasonable accommodation is possible before the employer has to show undue hardship from the requested accommodation [*Earl v. Mervyns Inc.*, 207 F.3d 1361 (11th Cir. 2000); punctuality was a core task of the job of area coordinator, so it was legitimate to fire the plaintiff for persistent lateness.]

In the view of the Second Circuit, as long as a comparable job is available, it is not a reasonable accommodation to offer an ADA plaintiff reassignment to a part-time job (which would result in much lower compensation and benefits) or to another location (which would result in loss of seniority). See *Norville v. Staten Island University Hospital*, 68 LW 1336 (2nd Cir. 11/2/99).

The ADA does not require the employer to discard its existing, nondiscriminatory policies or work rules. (It is settled law, expressed recently in *Pond v. Michelin North America Inc.*, 68 LW 1080 (7th Cir. 6/28/99), that it is not necessary to bump an employee with greater seniority to accommodate a less senior employee with a disability.) But contrast this with *Barnett v. U.S. Air*, 228 F.3d 1105 (9th Cir. 2000), which treats the seniority system as merely one factor in the reasonableness analysis, not complete exoneration for the employer. There was no collective bargaining agreement in this case, so the seniority system was unilaterally imposed by the employer—which probably affected the court's analysis. If the employer maintains a rule against demotions, it is not necessary to demote a disabled employee to a position that he or she can handle [*Duckett v. Dunlop Tire Corp.*, 120 F.3d 1222 (11th

Cir. 1997)]. If the employer's policy is to give full-time employees greater access to transfers than part-time employees, the policy can be enforced in the ADA context [*Daugherty v. City of El Paso,* 56 F.3d 695 (5th Cir. 1995)]. The *Dalton* case discussed previously says that if the employer had light-duty positions, but wants to reserve them for employees returning to work after a work-related injury, this can be done without violating the ADA.

Employers can lawfully stipulate that light-duty positions are temporary; but if no end date is specified, a court might treat the light-duty job as a permanent accommodation that cannot be terminated without violating the ADA [*Hendricks-Robinson v. Excel Corp.,* 154 F.3d 685 (7th Cir. 1998)]. Furthermore, the employer must volunteer information about potential transfers for which the disabled employee might be suited; it cannot wait for the employee to do research. For a discussion of the reassignment issue, see "Reassignment as a Reasonable Accommodation: How Far Must an Employer Go?" (no byline), WestGroup Employment Alert, 10/1/98, p. 1.

According to *Barnett v. U.S. Air,* 157 F.3d 744 (9th Cir. 1998), the ADA plaintiff's prima facie case includes proof of the existence of an available job he or she could perform with reasonable accommodation. Although the EEOC says that employers are supposed to engage in an interactive process with employees to evolve reasonable accommodations, *Barnett* says that failure to do so is not a separate cause of action under the ADA.

Another case that deals with the ADA prima facie case is *Community Hospital v. Fail,* 969 F.3d 667 (Colo. Sup. 1998). Under *Fail,* once the disabled employee makes the prima facie case, the burden then shifts to the employer to prove, by a preponderance of the evidence, that it either offered the plaintiff reasonable accommodation or was unable to do so because of undue hardship. In this analysis, the employer has greater access to information about the availability of accommodation and therefore should be required to prove this issue.

Even the EEOC sometimes concedes that affirmative action is inappropriate. On January 31, 2000, the agency issued an opinion letter saying that an employer should use a vacant position to provide reasonable accommodation to a disabled current employee, instead of hiring a black female candidate for the job, or promoting a black female employee to the position. In fact, the EEOC views disability accommodation as so important that a qualified disabled employee should be reassigned to the vacant position, even if there is another, **more** qualified candidate. ["EEOC Says Accommodation Takes Priority Over Affirmative Action," http://www.lawnewsnetwork.com/practice/employmentlaw/news/A15911-2000Feb10.html.]

24.4.3 1999 EEOC Enforcement Guidance

On March 2, 1999, the EEOC released a major document, the 39-page "Enforcement Guidance: Reasonable Accommodation and Undue Hardship

Under the Americans With Disabilities Act." This paper, which contains many practical examples of situations and EEOC responses, can be found at the EEOC Web site, at http://www.eeoc.gov/docs/accommodation.html. The document contains a checklist for the use of EEOC investigators assessing ADA charges. For a practice-oriented interpretation, see John P. Furfaro and Maury B. Josephson's article, "New Enforcement Guidance on Reasonable Accommodation Under the ADA," http://www.lawnewsnetwork.com/practice/employmentlaw/papers/lawfirm/A1163-1999May4.html.

A corporation that complies with these guidelines should be free from EEOC enforcement worries. However, since the courts have seldom required corporations to adopt the EEOC viewpoint in every respect, not satisfying all of the EEOC guidelines would not necessarily result in legal liability.

As the document notes, an employer may have to make various kinds of reasonable accommodations to disability (e.g., restructuring jobs; making work facilities and equipment handicap accessible; modifying work schedules; reassigning a disabled worker to a vacant job) but does not have to eliminate essential job functions. Employers do not have to provide items used for both work and nonwork tasks. For instance, employees are responsible for furnishing their own prostheses, eyeglasses, and hearing aids, because these are needed for nonwork functions as well.

Employers are not required to undergo undue hardship, defined by the document as financial difficulty or reasonable accommodations that are unduly extensive, substantial, or disruptive or that would fundamentally alter the nature or operation of the business.

Employees who feel the need for reasonable accommodation must make a clear request but need not use the term "reasonable accommodation"—they can, for instance, ask for time off or adaptive equipment. The request can be made by a representative (family member friend, health professional) on behalf of the disabled individual. Employers must act on reasonable verbal requests but can ask to have them confirmed by a written memorandum, and can demand reasonable documentation of the need for accommodation (e.g., nature, severity, duration of the impairment; which activities are impaired; extent of limitation in employee's functional ability). But documentation cannot be required if the disability and accommodation are obvious or the employee has already provided sufficient substantiating information.

As long as the employer provides an effective accommodation, it can choose its preferred (e.g., most cost-effective) accommodation and need not furnish the one suggested by the employee. Employers can't force an accommodation on an unwilling employee—but someone who rejects an accommodation that would remove a direct threat, or that is necessary to performance of an essential job function, might not be ADA qualified.

Employers must make sure that disabled employees receive equal access to information communicated in the workplace to other employees—(e.g., notices and training). The EEOC regards the obligation of reasonable accommodation as ongoing. Merely making one accommodation doesn't mean that no further accommodations need be made in the future.

The EEOC's position is that an employer can legitimately reallocate essential job functions to accommodate disability but is not obligated to do so. Altering marginal functions is a reasonable accommodation. Using accrued paid leave, or unpaid leave, is a reasonable accommodation, but employers do not have to offer additional paid leave to employees who have a disability.

Employees should be allowed to exhaust their paid leave before going on unpaid leave. The employer must keep the job open during leave, unless this operates as an undue hardship on the employer. In undue-hardship situations, the employer should consider whether the employee with a disability can be transferred to an equivalent vacant position for which he or she is qualified. Furthermore, a leave request need not be granted if the employer can provide an alternative reasonable accommodation that would keep the employee at work.

In the disputed territory where the ADA and FMLA overlap, the EEOC's position is that "An employer should determine an employee's rights under each statute separately, and then consider whether the two statutes overlap regarding the appropriate actions to take."

One example the EEOC gives is an ADA-disabled person who needs 13 weeks of leave. Under the FMLA, only 12 weeks of leave are required, but the ADA does not allow the employer to deny the thirteenth week of leave unless that would be an undue hardship (bearing in mind the impact of the 12 weeks of FMLA leave on the employer's operations). When an ADA-disabled employee returns from leave, the ADA requires reinstatement in the original position (absent undue hardship, or unless the employee has ceased to be qualified for the original position), whereas the FMLA permits reinstatement to any equivalent position.

Offering a modified or part-time schedule is a required reasonable accommodation, unless this would work an undue hardship on the employer. The EEOC's example is an HIV positive employee who has to take medication that induces nausea and wants a 45-minute break to cope with nausea. Employers must consider reassignment to another, vacant position if the requested schedule modifications would be an undue hardship. In "overlap" situations between FMLA and ADA, modified schedules must be offered if mandated by the FMLA, even if the result is undue hardship for the employer that would not be required by the ADA.

Employees need not be offered the chance to work at home unless this would be effective (would not impair essential job functions that have to be performed at the employer's location) and would not cause undue hardship.

If there is a vacant position available for transfer, the employer need not provide training to assist the employee to become qualified, but if training would be offered to a nondisabled employee, it must be offered to the disabled transferee employee. The EEOC's position is that transfer to a vacant position is a reasonable accommodation and therefore must be offered to qualified disabled employees even if the employer does not normally offer transfers. It's not enough that the employee be permitted to compete for a vacant position—the job must go to any qualified disabled employee seeking reasonable accommodation who wants the transfer.

The determination of undue hardship is based on net cost, after accessing potential third-party sources of funds (e.g., state grants). The EEOC does not support the use of cost-benefit analysis in assessing hardship, stating that the cost of the accommodation should be compared to the employer's resources and not to the worker's salary, position, or status. Employers can and should ask employees to contribute to the cost of accommodations that would otherwise not be required because they are too costly.

24.5 WHAT CONSTITUTES DISABILITY?

In June 1999, the Supreme Court decided three major employment-related ADA cases holding that an individual is not "disabled" if his or her condition has been corrected, e.g., by medication or an assistive device.

The first employment-related case was *Murphy v. United Parcel Service*, #97-1992 527 U.S. 516, involving the question of whether a person whose hypertension is controlled by medication is disabled and therefore able to sue under the ADA. *Sutton v. United Air Lines*, #97-1943 527 U.S. 471, copes with the common situation of a person with defective vision whose vision can be corrected with eyeglasses. For both *Murphy* and *Sutton*, then, the critical issue is whether disability is measured before or after corrective measures are taken. *Albertsons v. Kirkingburg*, #98-591 527 U.S. 555, is the case of a one-eyed truck driver whose brain has adapted to provide functional but "different" vision. All three were decided 6/25/99.

The Third Circuit decided in April 1998 [*Deane v. Pocono Medical Center*, 142 F.3d 138 (3rd Cir. 1998)], that a person who can perform the *essential* functions of the job without accommodation is qualified, whether or not that person is able to perform other functions of the job (with or without accommodation).

EEOC Rules

Of course, the EEOC had to adjust its policies to comply with *Murphy/Sutton/Albertsons*. The agency issued a Final Rule on June 8, 2000 (65 FR 36327), providing interpretive guidance on ADA Title I. The EEOC rescinded the language that required evaluation of an alleged disability without mitigating measures.

See http://www.eeoc.gov/docs/902sum.html, an Addendum to §902 of the EEOC Compliance Manual. The EEOC's current definition of impairment is a physiological disorder affecting at least one body system, or a mental or psychological disorder. But the manual states explicitly that sexual orientation, environmental, cultural, and economic disadvantages; pregnancy; physical characteristics; common personality traits; and normal variations in height, weight, and strength are **not** impairments.

According to the manual, an impairment is substantially limiting if it prohibits or significantly restricts the individual's ability to perform one or more major life activities, in comparison to an average person in the general population. A temporary impairment can be a disability if it is severe and takes significantly longer than normal to heal, or if its duration is long or indefinite. Multiple impairments that are not very serious individually can create a disability if their joint effect is substantial limitation of one or more major life activities.

The EEOC's re-drafted Compliance Manual Section 3 (10/3/00), http://www.eeoc.gov/docs/benefits.html, explores the employer's obligations to provide "equal" benefits (including health insurance, life insurance, and retirement benefits). A plan can be lawful and provide "equal" benefits even if it makes certain distinctions on the basis of disability. The employer is entitled to use practices that reflect sound actuarial principles or are related to actual or reasonably anticipated experiences.

In assessing a charge of disability discrimination in benefits, the EEOC's first question is whether a qualified employee with a disability has benefits equal to other employees—i.e., the same types of benefits, same payment options, and same coverage for the same costs. If the benefits are unequal, the question is whether the difference is based on the disability. There is no violation if the disputed provision is applied equally to all employees. But if the benefits are unequal, and the inequality is based on disability, the employer has violated the ADA unless it can show that the distinction is not a subterfuge to avoid the purposes of the ADA. However, the EEOC takes the position that a practice can be a subterfuge even if it was adopted before the ADA was enacted. Nor does there have to be intent to discriminate for a practice to be treated as a subterfuge.

The "same coverage" for all employees means the same as to premiums, deductibles, waiting periods, and coverage caps. A distinction is based on disability if it singles out a particular disability (e.g., major depression), a discrete group of disabilities, or disability in general. A distinction is not disability-based if it applies to many dissimilar conditions, and imposes limitations on both individuals with and without disabilities.

The EEOC permits distinctions in benefits between mental and physical disabilities because in the health insurance context mental conditions covers not only ADA impairments such as schizophrenia and major depression, but also personal issues such as marriage and grief counseling that do not constitute ADA impairments.

The employer can also rebut charges of disability discrimination by proving that disability-based disparate treatment is necessary to maintain the solvency of the plan: covering the disability(ies) at issue would cost so much that it would threaten the fiscal soundness of the plan under commonly accepted or legally required standards and there is no way to change the plan without affecting disabilities.

The EEOC's position is that, because employers are not required to have any kind of retirement plan at all, it does not violate the ADA to offer benefits for service retirement (i.e., conventional plans tying the benefit to the length of service for the employer) but not for retirement before normal retirement age due to disability. However, if the employer offers both types of retirement plan, disability discrimination is forbidden.

In the EEOC view, it violates the ADA to:

- Exclude an employee from participation in a service or disability retirement plan because of his or her disabilities
- Have a different length of employment participation requirements within the same plan based on disability
- Provide different levels or types of coverage within a plan—but it's acceptable for a disability retirement plan to have lower levels of coverage than the same employer's service retirement plan. It is not an ADA violation to deny service retirement benefits to any employee who voluntarily took disability retirement.

Case Law

An employee suffering from neuropathy had trouble walking. She asked for permission to park near the loading dock, take shortcuts inside the store, and eat lunch in the stockroom; these requests were denied. The employer's litigating position was that, because the employee could walk with a cane, she was not disabled.

But the Seventh Circuit treated this argument as oversimplified; it is significant whether a particular impairment's effect on a major life activity is short-term or long-term. According to the opinion in *EEOC v. Sears, Roebuck & Co.*, 2000 Westlaw 1672612 (7th Cir. 2000), there were triable issues as to how far the employee could walk with a cane as of the time she requested accommodation, versus the distance a person without an impairment could walk.

Ross v. Indiana State Teacher's Ass'n Trust, 159 F.3d 1001 (7th Cir. 1998), raises some interesting questions. The plaintiff had been on disability for a while, after a hip operation. The plan questioned his continuing need for benefits, so he applied for reinstatement, with a list of requested accommodations. The employer was willing to adopt most, but not all, of them and asked for documentation of the plaintiff's needs. The plaintiff's doctor showed doubt about the plaintiff's ability to work. The employer withdrew the reinstatement offer, and the plaintiff ended up in a bind. Although the Seventh Circuit agreed with the employer that not reinstating a person whose ability to work was dubious was not a denial of reasonable accommodation, the plaintiff was unable to get continued disability benefits. The disability plan's contention was that he was now able to work—he just wasn't able to return to the old job even with reasonable accommodation.

Urinary incontinence was not deemed to be a disability, because it would not debar the plaintiff from holding jobs that permitted her to control her own access to the restroom, even though her teaching position did not allow her to leave the classroom during class periods [*Swain v. Hillsborough County School Board*, 146 F.3d 855 (11th Cir. 1998)].

Somewhat similarly, a person whose physical or mental condition precludes working over 40 hours a week was held not to be ADA disabled by [*Tardie v. Rehab. Hospital of Rhode Island*, 168 F.3d 538 (1st Cir. 2/24/99)], given that there are many jobs available that do not require a commitment of over 40 hours a week. Jonathan L. Israel review the question of disciplining employees whose condition prevents regular attendance at work in "When an Employee's Absence From Work is Disability-Related," *New York Law Journal*, 2/8/99, p. S5.

But see *Davis v. Florida Power & Light*, 205 F.3d 1301 (11th Cir. 2000), finding that mandatory overtime was an essential function of the job, and it would violate the collective bargaining agreement to provide a no-overtime or selective-overtime arrangement for a disabled worker. The ADA does not require employers to violate CBAs as part of the process of reasonable accommodation.

In the view of the Fifth Circuit, not all seizures limit major life activities; the court declined to define "awareness" as a major life activity [*Deas v. River West LP*, 152 F.3d 471 (5th Cir. 1998)]. Also see *LaChance v. Duffy's Draft House Inc.*, 146 F.3d 832 (11th Cir. 1998), holding that a cook's epilepsy made him a direct threat to others (if he had a seizure while using the stove or other kitchen equipment),and therefore not a qualified employee. In this reading, the employee always has the burden of showing that he or she does not offer a direct threat and therefore can perform essential job functions, or that reasonable accommodation is possible. However, the employee did not have to pay the employer's attorneys' fees, because the employee's appeal, although unsuccessful, was not frivolous or unreasonable.

The Sixth Circuit agreed that a grocery store was justified in firing a produce clerk who said that he was HIV positive but neither verified his condition nor took the medical examination requested by the employer. The examination was job related and consistent with business necessity, because minor injuries at work could endanger an HIV positive employee or others [*EEOC v. Prevo's Family Market Inc.*, 135 F.3d 1089 (6th Cir. 2/4/98)].

For more about workplace HIV issues, including a sample business case and sample workplace policies and training materials, see the HIV/AIDS Workplace Toolkit, http://www.shrm.org/diversity/aidsguide/brta.htm, explaining Business Responds to AIDS (BRTA), a joint venture between business groups and the Centers for Disease Control.

In a somewhat similar Seventh Circuit case, an employee took time off from work because of a claimed back injury. The supervisor thought she was malingering and had an investigation done—revealing that she really was malingering and not disabled. Therefore, firing her did not violate the ADA, because her firing was not related to disability but to deception [*Jasmantas v. Subaru-Isuzu Automotive, Inc.*, 139 F.3d 1155 (7th Cir. 1998)].

An employee with chronic obstructive pulmonary disease was not qualified, because even on a flex-time schedule he could not arrive at work early enough to perform essential job functions; the employer had no duty to offer work at home as an accommodation. The Fifth Circuit ruled, in *Hypes v. First Commerce Corp.*, 134 F.3d 721 (5th Cir. 1998), that he was fired on the basis of absenteeism, not age or disability.

The Eighth Circuit accepted an employer's argument that a diabetic sales representative was terminated for cause, not for disability, in that his bad driving record, including a drunk driving conviction, prevented him from holding a valid driver's license, which in turn prevented him from being covered under the employer's automobile insurance policy, which was a requirement of the job [*Mathews v. Trilogy Communications, Inc.*, 143 F.3d 1160 (8th Cir. 1998)].

Four Circuits have ruled that the employer must prove the availability of equivalent jobs in the same geographic area, in order to limit the back pay award of a successful plaintiff who failed to seek other work. Most recently, the First Circuit joined the three other Circuits in saying that it's up to the employee to show that the equivalent jobs were unavailable. In this reading [see, e.g., *Quint v. A. E. Staley Mfg. Co.*, 170 F.3d 641 (1st Cir. 3/15/99)], the employee knows why he or she failed to seek other work and thus is the best person to explain it.

The Tenth Circuit requires ADA plaintiffs to articulate, with particularity, the alleged impairment from which they suffer and the major life activity affected [*Poindexter v. Atchison, Topeka & Santa Fe Railroad*, 168 F.3d 1228 (10th Cir. 1999)].

24.6 DISABILITY AND THE BENEFIT PLAN

Three Circuit Courts (the Sixth, Seventh, and Eleventh) have ruled that a totally disabled retiree or ex-employee is not "qualified" (because he or she is unable to perform job functions) and therefore cannot sue for fringe-benefit discrimination [*EEOC v. CAN Ins. Companies*, 96 F.3d 1038 (7th Cir. 1997); *Parker v. Metropolitan Life Ins. Co.*, 99 F.3d 181, aff'd 121 F.3d 1006 (6th Cir. 1997), *cert. denied* 1998 Westlaw 15861; and *Gonzales v. Garner Food Services, Inc.*, 89 F.3d 1523 (11th Cir. 1996), *cert. denied* 117 S.Ct. 1822].

But that only covers ADA Title I, the employment discrimination portion of the statute. Another front on which employers may have to fight is Title III, the public accommodations title. If an employee benefits plan is considered a public accommodation (and this is far from a settled legal principle!), then excluding a disabled person from it could violate the ADA, even if the disabled person is no longer a qualified employee. See "Post-Employment Fringe Benefits and the ADA: Suing for Differential Disability Coverage," WestGroup Employment Alert, 7/9/98, p. 1.

The argument for bringing disability insurance under Title III is pretty far fetched. The definition of "public accommodation," which is found in 42 USC §12181(7)(F), includes insurance offices, so a few cases say that the policies sold in an insurance office must also be public accommodations—for instance, *Carparts Distribution Center, Inc. v. Automotive Wholesalers' Association of New England, Inc.*, 37 F.3d 12 (1st Cir. 1994), which deals with a cap on AIDS-related insurance coverage.

Most courts do not think Title III is applicable to employment-related disability plans, because they think that all employment-related issues should fall under Title I, or because they limit "place of public accommodation" to mean a physical place like an office or shopping mall that the plaintiff has to attempt to visit physically, or because, as discussed later, they think that Title III requires physical accessibility but doesn't govern the content of services offered to the public. The most significant cases on these issues are *Ford v. Schering-Plough Corp.*, 145 F.3d 601 (3rd Cir. 1998), and *Parker v. Metropolitan Life Ins. Co.*, 121 F.3d 1006 (6th Cir. 1997).

According to "Two New ADA Rules Emerge From Recent Cases," WestGroup Employment Alert, 9/17/98, p. 1, the ADA is being interpreted to prevent employers favoring nondisabled over disabled employees (and job applicants). However, employees who feel that one group of disabled persons is being given an unfair advantage over other groups of disabled persons will probably not be able to use the ADA to sue the employer—(e.g., if physical disabilities are treated more leniently than mental disabilities, or if AIDS is disadvantaged vis-à-vis other diseases). Cases of this type include *Parker v. Metropolitan Life Ins. Co.*, 121 F.3d 1006 (6th Cir. 1997), *cert. denied* 1998 Westlaw 15861, and *Rogers v. Dep't of Health & Environmental Control*, 985 F.Supp. 635 (D.S.C., 1997). However, *Lewis v. Aetna Life Ins. Co.*, 982 F.Supp. 1158 (E.D. Va. 1997), does permit suits for discrimination between classes of disabled people.

Doe v. Mutual of Omaha, #98-4112, (Sup. Ct. 1/25/00) affirms the Seventh Circuit (without opinion). ADA Title II (the public accommodations title) is not violated by a health insurance policy or self-funded health plan that places a much lower limitation on AIDS-related health problems than other illnesses. The Seventh Circuit's rationale was that the insurer didn't refuse to sell insurance to people with AIDS, although the policy was certainly less valuable to them than to people with other types of health problems.

Another "cap" issue—distinctions in the level of disability benefits provided for physical and mental ailments—is the subject of several decisions. *Kimber v. Thiokol Corp.*, 68 LW 1335 (10th Cir. 11/10/99) holds that the ADA is not violated by the differential. *Rogers v. Dept of Health & Environmental Control*, 67 LW 1671 (4th Cir. 4/8/99) says that neither the ADA nor Title VII requires plans for state employees to furnish the same level of benefits for physical and mental ailments.

Morrill v. Lorillard Tobacco Co., 2000 U.S. Dist. LEXIS 18810 (D.N.H.2000) finds that ADA Title I was not violated by imposing a 50% co-payment and 20-visit limit on mental health benefits versus a 15-20% co-payment and no limit on number of visits for other claims.

The Ninth Circuit found that the plaintiff in *Weyer v. Twentieth Century Fox Film Corp.*, 68 LW 1432 (9th Cir. 1/3/00) was totally disabled and could not perform the essential functions of the job even with accommodation, so ADA Title I was not violated by the differential. Nor was Title III violated, because there was no public accommodation involved, and insurance underwriting decisions are entitled to safe-harbor protection.

ADA Title IV, 42 USC §12201(c) et. seq., provides a safe harbor for insurers and employee benefit plans. They are allowed to underwrite, classify, and administer "risks" as long as they do not violate state law and as long as the risk classifications are not adopted as a way to evade the ADA. It's not too clear how far the safe harbor extends, but *Lewis v. Aetna Life Ins. Co.*, 7 F.Supp.2d 743 (E.D. Va. 1998), says that the ADA is violated by a plan's distinction between physical and mental disabilities unless the distinction has actuarial support that Aetna was unable to produce. [The Mental Health Parity Act, 42 USC §300gg, discussed in ¶9.2.1, is limited to health insurance and does not extend to disability benefit plans; see *Brewster v. Cooley Associates*, 1997 Westlaw 823634 (D.N.M. 1997).]

24.7 EMPLOYEE DISCIPLINE

It was not a violation of the ADA for a school district to demand that a teacher, who had been verbally abusive and otherwise disruptive, undergo physical and mental testing. [The plaintiff in *Sullivan v. River Valley School District*, 68 LW 1328 (6th Cir. 11/29/99) refused to be tested, and was suspended for insubordination.]

The plaintiff's theory in his lawsuit was that the ADA was involved because the school district regarded him as disabled. To the Sixth Circuit, tests can be demanded even absent perception of disability, although post-hiring demands for examinations must be job-related and consistent with business necessity. In other words, a reasonable person would have been dubious of the employee's continued ability to perform job functions. A valid request for testing must be limited in scope, not a wild goose chase, but the employer is not required to show direct risk to justify the demand.

24.8 "DIRECT RISK" AS AN ADA DEFENSE

It was not a violation of the ADA for the Wyoming Board of Medicine to revoke the license of a doctor suffering from bipolar disorder, even without granting him the treatment options offered to substance-abusing doctors. In this analysis, although he unquestionably suffered from a disability, he was not a "qualified individual" because of the severe health and safety risk he posed to others; he had performed unnecessary and inappropriate surgery, and at least one patient had died. [*Kirbens v. Wyoming State Bd. of Medicine*, 68 LW 1361 (Wyo. 12/6/99).]

24.9 INTERACTION WITH OTHER STATUTES

The mere fact of applying for Social Security or employer-based disability benefits will not preclude an ADA suit: *Cleveland v. Policy Management Systems Corp.*, #97-1008,

526 U.S. 795 (Sup.Ct. 1999). The SSDI application focuses on disability, whereas the ADA deals with **ability** to work, with accommodations, so the two are not necessarily contradictory. According to *EEOC v. Stowe-Pharr Mills Inc.*, 216 F.3d 373 (4th Cir. 2000), the employer doesn't get automatic summary judgment because the ADA plaintiff also applied for SSDI; the employee must be given a chance to explain the apparent contradictions. Also see *Parker v. Columbia Pictures Industries,* 204 F.3d 326 (2nd Cir. 2000) (statements as to total disability in long-term disability and SSDI applications do not preclude ADA suit because of the potential for working with appropriate accommodation). However, information provided in the applications for such benefits is admissible as evidence in the ADA case, because it is probative on the question of whether the plaintiff previously requested accommodation [*Whitbeck v. Vital Signs Inc.*, 159 F.3d 1369 (D.C. Cir. 1998)]. Also see *King v. Herbert J. Thomas Memorial Hospital,* 159 F.3d 192 (4th Cir. 1998), which holds that receipt of disability benefits (as distinct from the mere application) estops an age discrimination plaintiff from claiming she was able to perform the job at the time of her discharge.

A one-time state trooper who alleged total disability on his application for disability benefits stemming from an on-duty injury cannot bring an ADA claim for denial of promotion [*Motley v. New Jersey State Police,* 68 LW 1320 (3rd Cir. 11/1/99)]. His disability application did not refer to his ability to work, even with accommodation. [*Vassallo v. N.Y., N.Y.L.J.* 10/13/00 p. 33 col. 5 (E.D.N.Y.)]

A group of state troopers injured at work received full pay plus benefits, based on their asserted inability to work. When the benefits were exhausted, the Police Department submitted disability retirement applications on their behalf. When the applications were denied, the plaintiffs changed their assertion, now claiming to be able to handle light duty positions with reasonable accommodation, and the unavailability of accommodation violated the ADA and the Rehabilitation Act.

However, the Eastern District of New York treated their claims as time-barred, because the discriminatory act was putting them on unpaid leave, not terminating them. Nor did they provide evidence of a continuing violation that would justify extending the statute of limitations.

A slightly different formulation is found in *Flowers v. Komatsu Mining Systems,* 165 F.3d 554 (7th Cir. 1999), which holds that evidence of the Social Security disability determination can affect the plaintiff's damages, by proving the periods of time during which the plaintiff would not have been able to perform the essential job functions even with accommodation.

"Employee Leave and the Law," WestGroup Employment Alert, 9/17/98, p. 4, discusses the interface between the FMLA and the ADA. FMLA leave, although unpaid, is easier to obtain than medical leave as a reasonable ADA accommodation, because the FMLA requires that employers with 50 or more employees grant up to 12 weeks' unpaid leave to any employee who needs the leave because of his or her own illness or the serious illness of a close family member. Reinstatement after

FMLA leave is also automatic, but ADA reinstatement requires a showing of ability to perform essential work tasks (with or without reasonable accommodation).

This article also discusses the need for predictable, regular attendance as a fundamental part of job qualification. The article suggests that as long as the employer has a neutral, uniformly applied policy that is actually communicated to employees and enforced, it is in a better position to assert that regular attendance is essential. This argument was raised, for instance, in *Carlson v. Inacom Corp.*, 885 F.Supp. 1314 (D. Neb. 1995); *Fritz v. Mascotech Automotive Sys. Group Inc.*, 914 F.Supp. 1481 (E.D. Mich. 1996); and *Vorhies v. Pioneer Mfg.*, 906 F.Supp. 578 (D. Colo. 1995).

However, *Cehrs v. Northeast Ohio Alzheimer's Research Center*, 155 F. 3d 775 (6th Cir. 1998), does not permit employers to rely on a presumption that regular, predictable attendance is an essential job function. Employers facing this argument should be prepared with additional evidence relating to the need for predictability in this particular job rather than as an everyday part of the working world.

In the view of the Ninth Circuit, the ADEA may be violated by calculating disability retirement benefits using the age at the time of hiring. The plan calculated the benefit on the basis of years of service lost due to disability, based on the length of service between age 55 (presumed retirement date) and the age at which the disabled individual became a public employee. Under *Hazen*, calculations based on actual years of service are acceptable because a younger person might have more years of service, and vice versa.

However, this is a slightly different question because the age at hire had a strong effect on the potential disability benefit. The Ninth Circuit remanded the case to the District Court for disposition: *Arnett v. California Public Employees Retirement System*, 67 LW 1742 (9th Cir. 6/2/99).

In the case of *Hiler v. Brown*, 177 F.3d 542 (6th Cir. 1999) a brain-injured Vietnam veteran claimed he was denied a promotion because he was unable to communicate quickly in writing, which he could not do because of his war injuries. He brought a case under the Rehabilitation Act, and sued his supervisors as individuals. The District Court agreed with his interpretation, that 29 USC §794(a) forbids discrimination by a "person." But the Sixth Circuit reversed it, finding that the Rehabilitation Act language tracks Title VII language, and only the employer company—not individuals—can be sued under Title VII.

The FMLA, the ADA, and Worker's Compensation have been described as the "Bermuda triangle" for employers. "When Regs Collide: The ADA and Workers' Compensation," WestGroup Employment Alert, 11/25/98, p. 1, discussed in more detail in ¶20.10, explains the interaction among these, especially the ADA and Worker's Compensation.

Chapter 25

FAMILY AND MEDICAL LEAVE ACT (FMLA)

25.1 INTRODUCTION

Most of this chapter deals with FMLA Title I, which covers private employers. There is a Title II, covering federal employees. However, Title II doesn't provide a private right of action (i.e., federal workers can't sue if they claim their FMLA rights were violated), and the federal government never expressly waived sovereign immunity. See *Russell v. Department of the Army*, 191 F.3d 1016 (9th Cir. 9/14/99).

According to the Second Circuit, government agencies have to offer the other FMLA benefits, but are not required to grant FMLA leave to their employees on the basis of the employees' own illnesses, because when it passed the FMLA, Congress did not think that government employees had been disadvantaged by lack of access to "own-illness" leave. [*Hale v. Mann*, #99-7326 (2nd Cir.); see Michael A. Riccardi, "No Leave Required for Agency Employee's Illness," *N.Y.L.J.* 5/26/00; on law.com.]

A disabled person's claims based on denial of a handicapped parking spot at work cannot be brought under both ADA Title I (employment) and Title III (public accommodations): according to *DeWyer v. Temple University* [see Shannon P. Duffy, "Federal Judge Throws Out Double ADA Claim," *The Legal Intelligencer* 2/8/01; on law.com], because the ADA was drafted so that **all** employment-related claims must be brought under Title I; Title III claims are limited to claims by non-employees who have been denied their right to accessible public spaces.

A group of automobile service companies that shared the same majority shareholder, and that had some interrelated operations, were nevertheless not a single integrated employer because they lacked common management. Therefore, because the particular unit where the employee worked had fewer than 50 employees, and aggregation with the other units was denied, his FMLA claim had to be dismissed: *Hukill v. Auto Care Inc.*, 68 LW 1240 (4th Cir. 9/22/99).

See Eric Paltell, "FMLA: After Six Years, a Bit More Clarity," *HR Magazine*, 9/99, p. 144, for a good discussion of which conditions are serious enough to trigger FMLA protection.

According to the Department of Labor's 2000 Family and Medical Leave Survey [http://www.dol.gov/dol/asp/public/fmal/factsheet.htm], more than 35 million workers have taken FMLA leave since 1993. Two-thirds of covered employers said that FMLA compliance was very easy or somewhat easy (although this is a smaller proportion than in the previous survey, taken in 1995). Few employers reported adverse effects of the FMLA on their productivity, profitability, or growth.

To qualify for FMLA leave, the employee must have worked at least 1250 hours for the employer in the previous year. An employee had so much leave that he worked only 1037 hours in the relevant time period. Therefore, in the view of the Eastern District of Pennsylvania, he didn't qualify for FMLA leave—vacation and personal days, suspensions, sick days, and holidays don't count toward the required 1250 hours [*Clark v. Allegheny University Hospital*, 1998 Westlaw 94803 (E.D. Pa. 1998)].

The requirement of working 1250 hours is calculated by counting back from the time the employee went on FMLA leave, and not from the time the employer took adverse action (such as firing the employee for excessive absences). Therefore, a plaintiff who did not work 1250 hours during the year before her discharge (because she took three leaves that she claimed satisfied FMLA requirements) was still entitled to sue under the FMLA: *Butler v. Owens-Brockway Plastic Products Inc.*, 68 LW 1399 (6th Cir. 12/9/99).

A person who has not yet worked for the employer for 12 months is not eligible for FMLA leave [*Dolese v. Office Depot Inc.*, 69 LW 1352 (5th Cir. 11/7/00).] This is true even though the employer's own policies are more generous than the FMLA actually requires. Although DOL regulations require employers to live up to their own policies, the regulation doesn't apply to eligibility criteria, only to extended family/medical leave rights.

The Eleventh Circuit says that employees are not required to use up their paid sick leave before taking FMLA leave. [*Strickland v. Water Works*, No. 99-14103 (11th Cir. 1/22/01).]

The FMLA does not preempt a Wisconsin law that allows an employee to substitute any type of paid or unpaid leave for FMLA leave, because this is a protective state law of the type deliberately exempted from federal preemption. [*Aurora Medical Group v. Dep't of Workforce Development*, 612 N.W.2d 646 (Wis. 2000).]

25.2 NOTICE REQUIREMENTS

The DOL's FMLA regulations have been understandably unpopular with employers, and have given rise to litigation throughout the United States.

29 CFR §825.208 provides that, where the employer fails to notify employees that FMLA leave will run concurrently with other leave (e.g., paid sick leave), the

employee is entitled to additional leave, because the two leave periods must be permitted to run consecutively.

This Regulation was found invalid and unenforceable by the Eleventh Circuit [*McGregor v. AutoZone Inc.*, 180 F.3d 1305 (11th Cir. 1999) and the Eighth Circuit [*Ragsdale v. Wolverine Worldwide Inc.*, 218 F.3d 933 (8th Cir. 7/11/00)].

However, the Sixth Circuit reached the opposite conclusion in 2000 [*Plant v. Morton International Inc.*, 212 F.3d 929 (6th Cir. 2000). When such "Circuit conflicts" occur, the Supreme Court often agrees to hear a case to impose a single, uniform national rule.

Another Regulation, 29 CFR §825.1100(d) was held to be invalid by the Seventh Circuit: *Dormeyer v. Comerica Bank-Illinois,* 223 F.3d 579 (7th Cir. 2000). The Regulation says that an employer that fails to respond promptly to a request for FMLA leave may be forced to provide leave that would otherwise be unavailable. The Seventh Circuit said that the DOL was not authorized to promulgate this Regulation, and the Regulation is unreasonable because it imposes FMLA benefits to which the employee would not otherwise be entitled. *Brungart v. Bell South Telecommunications Inc.,* 69 LW 1267 (11th Cir. 10/24/00) says that this Regulation is invalid because it alters the terms of the statute as passed by Congress.

Yet the District Court for the District of New Hampshire upheld yet another DOL regulation, 29 CFR §825.219(a), which requires the employer to reinstate a highly paid employee returning from FMLA leave, even if the job has been eliminated and the company undergoes substantial and grievous economic injury, if the employer failed to inform the employee of his key-employee status and discuss the implications of this status when he requested FMLA leave: *Panza v. Grappone Co.,* 69 LW 1272 (D.N.H. 10/20/00).

An employee who didn't have a telephone sent a note to her employer saying that she couldn't come in that day because of a pain in her side. She didn't communicate with the employer at all for 12 days, after she had been operated on. This was her fourth unexcused absence in three weeks, so she was fired. The ruling of *Satterfield v. Wal-Mart Stores, Inc.*, 135 F.3d 973 (5th Cir. 1998), is that she did not even give the employer enough notice to trigger a duty to investigate her need for FMLA leave, and her prior unexcused absences made it reasonable for the employer to conclude that she was merely being irresponsible, not in need of medical leave.

If the employee's doctor reports that there is no need for leave, the employer is entitled to rely on that report and deny an FMLA leave request; the plaintiff can't claim that circumstances changed since the medical consultation [*Stoops v. One Call Communications, Inc.*, 1998 Westlaw 142297 (7th Cir. 1997)]. (He or she should have gotten an updated medical certification in such a case.)

However, an employer can't demand certification or recertification without giving the employee the amount of time provided by the FMLA (15 days for an initial certification; recertification no more often than every 30 days) and then fire the employee for failure to provide adequate certification. As *LeGrand v. Village of McCook,* 1998 Westlaw 182462 (N.D. Ill. 1998), points out, reducing the time frame makes it impossible to determine whether the employee didn't have valid evidence—or could have assembled the necessary proof given enough time.

> **TIP**
>
> If an employee provides medical certification of a serious health condition, but you are dubious about its accuracy (or whether the need for leave continues as long as the employee says it does), be sure to ask for a second opinion right away. Failure to do so might make it impossible for you to challenge the medical findings if the case ever comes to court. See *Sims v. Alameda-Contra Costa Transit District*, 2 F.Supp.2d 1253 (N.D. Cal, 1998).

Summary judgment was granted for the employer in *Enright v. CGH Medical Center*, 1999 WL 24683 (N.D. Ill. 1999). The plaintiff was reduced to part-time status, and eventually fired, after she took 49 days off (33 of them FMLA leave). Even before the leave, the employee had been warned about excessive absenteeism, so the employer's actions seemed related to legitimate concerns about attendance and did not seem to be motivated by hostility to exercise of FMLA rights.

An employee told the company nurse and his manager that he suffered from a heart condition requiring occasional time off. Later, following company practice, he left a message with the company security guard that he had chest pains and trouble breathing, and was taking time off from work. After being fired for excessive absences, he brought FMLA suit. Under *Barnett v. Revere Smelting & Refining Co.*, 1999 WL 965429 (S.D.N.Y. 1999), the employer was not entitled to summary judgment; there was a triable issue of fact as to whether the employee had provided adequate notice.

An employee mentioned that he might have bipolar disorder, and might need to get medical care. However, such remarks were not specific enough to constitute a request for leave or put the employer on notice. Therefore, the FMLA was not violated by firing the employee during an argument with his supervisor when he asked for vacation time, after being suspended for unexcused absences from work. [*Seaman v. CSPH, Inc.*, 179 F.3d 297 (5th Cir. 1999).]

According to 29 CFR §825.114(c), the flu is ordinarily not a "serious" illness, unless complications occur. But that doesn't mean that an employee's doctor can't certify that the flu is a serious illness, in the appropriate case. Therefore, it was improper for an employer to fire an employee who got a doctor's certification that she had suffered from severe flu and dehydration, but was now fit to return to work. The employer couldn't complain that the certification was inadequate, because the DOL WH-380 form was completed in full. If the employer really had doubts about the seriousness of the illness, the correct response would have been to reinstate the employee and demand a second opinion. [*Miller v. AT&T*, 60 F.Supp.2d 574 (S.D.W.V. 1999).

A UPS driver fired because of poor attendance did not prevail in his FMLA claim [*Haefling v. UPS*, 67 LW 1592 (7th Cir. 3/4/99)]. Although he saw a doctor and got physical therapy for a neck injury, he did not prove that he had a period of incapacity lasting at least three days, or even that medical treatment was really necessary. Therefore, he did not prove that he had suffered a "serious medical condition" as defined by the FMLA.

Effect of Leave

If an employee returns to work after FMLA leave and has been pronounced fit to work by his or her doctor, the employer can require the employee to take another medical examination only if the employee's behavior justifies an inference of ongoing limitations that interfere with the ability to work [*Albert v. Runyon,* 6 F.Supp.2d 57 (D. Mass. 1998)].

An employer unsure about the employee's ability to return to work after FMLA leave, based on reasonable doubt, can require the employee to get an independent fitness-for-duty exam (i.e., independent of the doctor's certification submitted by the employee). However, according to *Underhill v. Willamina Lumber Co.*, 1999 WL 421596 (D. Ore. 1999), the employer's duty is to reinstate the worker first, then ask for the examination. Reinstatement can't be delayed until the examination is completed to the satisfaction of the employer.

According to *Tardie v. Rehab. Hospital of Rhode Island,* 168 F.3d 538 (1st Cir. 1999), the FMLA is not violated by firing an employee who is on medical leave, because the FMLA (unlike the ADA) does not require reasonable accommodation. If an employer is carrying out a Reduction in Force, employees who are on FMLA leave can lawfully be laid off, if they would have been laid off if they had not been on leave. In other words, *O'Connor v. PLA Family Health Plan Inc.*, 68 LW 1442 (11th Cir. 1/18/00) says that the right to reinstatement after FMLA leave is not absolute. Reinstatement is not required if the employee is no longer able to perform the essential job functions. And if an employee's work performance is poor enough to justify termination anyway, it's not a FMLA violation to fire the employee while he or she is on leave [*Hubbard v. Blue Cross/Blue Shield Ass'n*, 1 F.Supp.2d 867 (N.D. Ill. 1998)].

In the view of the Eighth Circuit, the FMLA was not violated by the dismissal of an employee who was injured in an automobile accident. (The employer's contention was that the dismissal occurred because of the employee's violation of the rule that an employee who failed to appear at work for three days, without notifying the employer of a reason, was subject to firing.) *Reynolds v. Phillips & Temro Industries Inc.*, 68 LW 1320 (8th Cir. 10/29/99) holds that the employee was not protected by the FMLA because there was reason to believe that he would not be able to return to work, and perform the essential functions of the job, within the 12-week FMLA leave period. This conclusion was based on his application for no-fault insurance economic loss benefits, which included a doctor's certification of continuing disability that would preclude his return to his normal occupation.

An employee suffering from multiple sclerosis was able to work only a four-day week after returning from leave. The employer said that she would be placed as a payroll clerk, and not reinstated to her old job as purchasing agent, until her intermittent leave allowance was used up; then she would be placed on unpaid leave until a suitable job became open. The plaintiff quit and sued under the FMLA, alleging that she was entitled to reinstatement in her former position.

The court in *Covey v. Methodist Hospital of Dyersburg,* 56 F.Supp.2d 965 (W.D.Tenn. 1999) disagreed. The court read 29 CFR §825.204(a) to mean that reinstatement is required if the returning employee is able to work a full normal schedule. For employees on intermittent leave, it's permissible for the employer to transfer the employee to any available position that satisfies the employee's need for time off.

Covey also raises another important issue. The plaintiff said that putting her on unpaid leave, while not inconsistent with the FMLA, violated the employer's own, more generous, leave policy. The employer prevailed on this issue too: The court says that the FMLA doesn't give employees the right to bring lawsuits based on employer's failure to live up to their own policies. The remedy, if any, is a suit for breach of contract.

25.5 FMLA LITIGATION AND REMEDIES

The FMLA became effective August 5, 1993; between then and the end of the DOL's 1998 fiscal year, the DOL served as plaintiff in 29 FMLA suits. As of January 1999, seven of the suits were still pending. The DOL brought most of those cases based on termination of employees who took FMLA leave or refusal to reinstate employees subsequent to FMLA leave.

As in all employment-related contexts, lawsuits were just the tip of the iceberg. DOL received 13,597 FMLA-related employee complaints during that time period. A total of 8364 complaints were resolved by conciliation; 5233 were resolved through investigation. DOL claims successful resolution in 87% of completed cases. Violations were found in 8067 cases, and damages of about $13.2 million were assessed. Back pay recoveries ranged from $1000 to $40,000; the employee who received the $40,000 also got an equal amount of liquidated damages and was reinstated.

At the end of 1997, the Seventh Circuit held that the *McDonnell-Douglas* burden-shifting analysis does not apply in FMLA cases [*Diaz v. Fort Wayne Foundry Corp.,* 131 F.3d 711 (7th Cir. 1997)]. Instead, the FMLA plaintiff's obligation is to prove, by preponderance of the evidence, that his or her discharge violated FMLA rights.

The Courts of Appeals have not resolved the validity of DOL's notification requirements (see §25.2, preceding), but the Fourth Circuit applied the requirement in the case of *Cline v. Wal-Mart Stores, Inc.*, 144 F.3d 294 (4th Cir. 1998), without a lengthy discussion that could serve as explanation and precedent.

Also in 1998, the First Circuit decided that an ex-employee (in this case, a laid-off worker who charges that his previous use of FMLA leave induced his employer to refuse to rehire him) is entitled to sue under the FMLA [*Duckworth v. Pratt & Whitney*, 152 F.3d 1 (1st Cir. 1998)]. That is, the right to bring an FMLA case does not depend on current employment witht he defendant employer.

A company's litigation position was that a decision had been made to fire a plant manager for poor performance, effective May 31. On May 29, before he had been notified, he had a heart attack. He returned to work in mid-July and was offered a choice between a permanent demotion and 90 days at full salary in the lesser job, giving him time to look for another job.

The employee's contention was that he was fired for taking medical leave, and that the company violated ERISA, the ADEA, and the ADA as well as the FMLA. The jury found for him on the FMLA and ERISA claims, but for the employer on age and disability discrimination. The jury verdict was for approximately $41,000 for lost wages and benefits, $11,000 for mental anguish, and $5,000 for out-of-pocket expenses. The District Court added an approximately equivalent amount as FMLA liquidated damages.

The Fifth Circuit found that the jury had evidence to support its findings that the employer violated the FMLA (the employee's written evaluations were fairly good, casting doubt on the employer's stated reason for discharging the employee) and also ERISA §510 (reprisal for accessing employee benefits).

Under 29 USC §2617(a)(iii), liquidated damages "shall" be awarded, although a trial court can reduce the damages based on the employer's showing of good faith. But once the case gets to the Court of Appeals, the Court of Appeals can only reverse the District Court's finding on the good-faith issue if the lower court's decision was clearly erroneous, which was not true in this case.

However, the Fifth Circuit didn't completely rubber-stamp the District Court decision. The Court of Appeals pointed out that the FMLA doesn't allow awards of out-of-pocket expenses such as job-hunting and moving expenses, because they do not represent the "lost compensation" covered by the statute. The expenses are also ruled out by ERISA §510, which does not allow extracontractual damages. Damages for mental anguish are also extracontractual, so awarding them was a plain error subject to reversal by the appellate court.

The employee in *Hite v. Biomet Inc.*, 38 F.Supp.2d 720 (N.D. Ind. 1999) asserted that, when she returned from FMLA leave, she was subjected to retaliation when she was given an inferior office, the hardest work assignments, and rude treatment from supervisors and co-workers. The employer asked for summary judgment, which was denied, because the employer offered no legitimate explanation for treating the employee that way. In other words, working conditions—not just demotion or pay cuts—can be actionable retaliation that violates the FMLA.

The Sixth Circuit allowed FMLA jury trials [*Frizzell v. Southwest Motor Freight,* 154 F.3d 641 (6th Cir. 1998)] on the grounds that, since damages are available, a jury should set them. An additional rationale was the resemblance between the statutory schemes of the FMLA and the Fair Labor Standards Act; FLSA jury trials are well accepted.

At the District Court level, the District of Maryland found that 29 CFR §110(d) (employer is not allowed to challenge eligibility once it has confirmed that the employee is eligible to take FMLA leave) is invalid. To the court in *Seaman v. Downtown Partnership of Baltimore Inc.*, 991 F.Supp. 751 (D. Md. 1998), the regulation goes too far because it usurps Congress's authority to set policy. For discussion of DOL FMLA enforcement, see Deborah Billings, "DOL Rule on Employer Notification Duty to Employees on FMLA Leave Under Attack," 67 LW 2419 (1/26/99).

In late 1998, the Middle District of Florida decided that the Eleventh Amendment precludes FMLA suits in federal court against a state-agency employer [*Driesse v. Florida Board of Regents,* 26 F.Supp.2d 1078 (M.D. Fla. 1998)]. *Garrett v. Board of Trustees of University of Alabama,* 989 F.Supp. 1409 (N.D. Ala. 1998), says that state employers are free of FMLA liability.

The statute of limitations is three years for "willful" FMLA violations—a year longer than the normal two-year rule. The Eastern District of Virginia says that, because willfulness is a matter of state of mind, the three-year statute of limitations is triggered whenever the plaintiff alleges willfulness; it is not necessary (at the pleading stage) to support the claim [*Settle v. S.W. Rogers Co.*, 998 F.Supp. 657 (E.D. Va. 1998)].

FMLA damages are defined by 29 USC §2612 as lost compensation; or, if no compensation was lost, the cost of purchasing care for the person requiring care. The Eastern District of Louisiana ruled, in *Barrilleaux v. Thayer Lodging Groups Inc.*, 1998 Westlaw 614181 (E.D. La. 1998), that a person who sues for lost wages is not entitled to be compensated for care costs as well.

Wright v. Universal Maritime Service Corp., 525 U.S. 70 (Sup. Ct. 11/16/98), says that a collective bargaining agreement arbitration clause can effectively bar litigation of statutory claims (such as FMLA claims) only if it is quite specific. A generalized ban on litigation is not sufficient.

The holding of *Albertson's v. United Food & Commercial Workers,* 157 F.3d 758 (9th Cir. 1998), is that a private single-employee employment contract can mandate arbitration of FMLA claims, but a collective bargaining agreement covering an entire bargaining unit cannot.

A (male) state trooper was awarded $375,000 by a Maryland jury because he was denied FMLA leave for the birth of his first child. At that time, Maryland had a law (since changed) that made 30 days of paid leave available to "primary caregivers," but only 10 days available for "secondary caregivers." (Current law has abolished this distinction; all new birth and adoptive parents are entitled to 30 days' paid leave.) The plaintiff's supervisor told him that he could not be a primary caregiver because he could not breast feed his new baby. The case, relating to events in December 1994, was filed in April 1995. By the time it was decided in February 1999, the trooper and his wife had a second child. The second time around, he got his 12 weeks' FMLA leave with no problems. This case is discussed by Tamar Lewin, "Father Awarded $375,000 In a Parental Leave Case," *NYT*, 2/3/99, p. A9.

A determination by a state human rights agency that an employer had a valid business reason for eliminating the employee's job while she was on medical leave collaterally estops FMLA claims that the job was eliminated for discriminatory reasons: *Kosakow v. New Rochelle Radiology Associates,* 88 F.Supp.2d 199 (S.D.N.Y. 2000).

25.7 FMLA INTERFACE WITH OTHER LAWS

Some tough questions of reconciling FMLA and COBRA were settled by an IRS Final Rule published on February 3, 1999, at 64 FR 5160. The Final Rule provides that merely taking FMLA leave is not a COBRA qualifying event. However, a qualifying event does occur with respect to an employee (and any dependents of the employee who are at risk of losing health coverage) who fails to return to work at the end of the FMLA leave. The typical example is a new mother who does not return to work after her maternity leave has ended.

Under the Final Rule, the COBRA qualifying event occurs on the last day of the FMLA leave. The employer is not allowed to condition the COBRA election on the employee's reimbursement of EGHP premiums paid on his or her behalf during the leave. However, if the employer has actually terminated coverage under the group plan for the class of employees that the employee belonged to before the FMLA leave, it is not necessary to offer continuation coverage to employees who do not return from leave.

Although the two statutes were designed to accomplish different goals, workers sometimes find that FMLA leave is more accessible than taking time off as an ADA "reasonable accommodation." These issues are raised by "Employee Leave and the Law," *Employment Alert*, 9/17/98, p. 4. Remember, FMLA leave is available in the case of the employee's own illness, not just the illness of a family member who needs care.

Furthermore, if the employer company has at least 50 employees and the employee has worked there for at least 12 months, entitlement to FMLA leave is automatic. The employer's discretion as to what constitutes a reasonable accommodation is not a factor. The right to reinstatement is also automatic, and employers are not allowed to raise a defense of unreasonable hardship in the FMLA context, although it is available under the ADA.

An Opinion Letter from the Department of Labor (#89; see *Employment Alert*, 3/5/98, p. 11) takes the position that salaried workers who are exempt from the Fair Labor Standards Act (FLSA) are not brought under FLSA coverage merely because their employer docks their paychecks to reflect unpaid leave under the

FMLA. (Normally, pay deductions for absence are characteristic of FLSA-covered wage workers, not exempt salaried workers.) However, the exclusion is limited to FMLA leave taken by employees of companies covered by the FMLA (e.g., those with 50 or more employees).

Chapter 26

THE AGE DISCRIMINATION IN EMPLOYMENT ACT

26.1 INTRODUCTION

Late in 2000, a jury in Youngstown, Ohio awarded one of the largest employment discrimination verdicts ever given to a single plaintiff: over $30 million, to a 68-year-old branch manager of a home health care agency. [Margaret Cronin Fisk, "Ohio Jury Awards $30 Million Age Discrimination Verdict," *Nat.L.J.* 12/6/00; on law.com.] Her litigation theory was that discrimination was not terminating her, but refusing to give her another job within the company when two offices were merged. Ironically, the plaintiff would have settled the case for $300,000. Of course, the bulk of the damages were punitive—and, because this was a state court case, the CRA '91 cap does not apply.

The Eastern District of Michigan ruled in late 2000 that tort-based compensatory damages are not available in federal ADEA cases, and did not permit a widow to sue for wrongful death when her husband killed himself in the wake of a layoff. [*Kulling v. Grinders for Industry Inc.*, 69 LW 1304 (E.D. Mich. 10/1/00).]

In the view of the Second Circuit, the ADEA applies to employees of the U.S. branch of a foreign corporation that has 20 or more employees throughout the world—it's not necessary that there be 20 employees at the U.S. location [*Morelli v. Cedel*, 141 F.3d 39 (2nd Cir. 1998)].

In the domestic context, the Seventh Circuit allowed employees at several small affiliates of a larger corporation to be aggregated to determine the number of employees (and therefore ADEA coverage) if

- The "corporate veil" can be pierced, and the parent corporation would be liable for its subsidiaries' debts, torts, and breaches of contract.
- An original larger enterprise was split up to avoid employment-related liability.
- The parent company directed the discriminatory act or policy.

This new test replaces an earlier requirement of interrelated operations, common management, common ownership, or centralized control of personnel and labor relations. See *Papa v. Katy Industries Inc.,* 166 F.3d 937 (7th Cir. 1999).

Reallocation of duties to several younger workers can be treated as a "replacement" of the demoted employee for ADEA purposes. See *Hindman v. Transkrit Corp.,* 145 F.3d 986 (8th Cir. 1998).

In late 1998, the Eighth Circuit joined the Fifth, Sixth, and Seventh Circuits in ruling that it does not constitute age discrimination for an employer to make reasonable inquiries about an older person's retirement plans [*Watkins v. J&S Oil Co.,* 164 F.3d 55 (8th Cir. 12/30/98)].

Although the nominal range of the ADEA is persons aged 40 and over, in late February 1999, the Supreme Court of New Jersey permitted a 25-year-old to maintain an age discrimination suit and found the New Jersey age discrimination statute to be broad enough to encompass reverse age discrimination (i.e., firing a qualified person who is perceived to be too young for a particular job). This case, *Bergen Commercial Bank v. Sisler,* 67 LW 1560 (N.J. 2/24/99), is discussed in a news item, "State's High Court Lets Man, 25, Sue on Age Discrimination," *NYT,* 2/26/99, p. B8.

The Michigan Court of Appeals reached a similar conclusion in 2000. When "discrimination because of age" is forbidden, a 30-year-old fired for sounding too young, and replaced by a presumably more authoritative older person, is entitled to sue. [*Zanni v. Medaphis Physician Services Corp.*, 2000 Westlaw 381503 (Mich.App. 2000).]

Because of *Wright v. Universal Maritime Service Corp.*, #97-889, 525 U.S. 70 (Sup. Ct. 11/16/98), a general arbitration clause in a collective bargaining agreement will not preclude litigation of ADEA and other statutory claims. Only a specific clause enumerating the claims can compel arbitration.

See ¶27.3 for a discussion of pre-dispute arbitration clauses.

Conversion of defined benefit plans to cash balance plans can have negative practical effects on the pensions of older workers. See ¶12.4.6 for a discussion of the controversy over these conversions.

Front and back pay awarded to a job applicant who was not hired because of age bias does not constitute "wages" and is not subject to tax withholding [*Newhouse v. McCormick & Co.*, 157 F.3d 582 (8th Cir. 1998)].

26.2 ADEA EXCEPTIONS

On January 11, 1999, the Supreme Court announced its decision in *Kimel v. Florida Board of Regents,* #98-796, 528 U.S. 62. On a basic level, *Kimel* deals with the ADEA, holding that Congress had no right to subject state governments to federal regulation of their age-related hiring practices.

The court's majority opinion gave two main arguments for allowing states to practice age discrimination in hiring (as long as there is a rational state interest behind the age-based classification). First, Congress had no evidence that states were guilty of age discrimination before drafting the ADEA to include them. Second, almost all of the states have themselves passed laws prohibiting age discrimination (including age discrimination in state employment), so state employees are protected even if the federal statute does not apply to them.

The broader implications of *Kimel* are that the Supreme Court is likely to advance its states-rights agenda in the context of other laws.

The Higher Education Amendments of 1998, H.R. 6, signed 10/7/98, reinstate a traditional ADEA exception. Under the Amendments, it is lawful to require tenured faculty members to retire solely on the basis of age. Although this act affects a small group of individuals—and almost certainly does not include any employees of any of the readers of this book!—it is significant as a possible trend toward cutting back the scope of the ADEA (and other civil rights legislation).

26.3 THE ADEA PLAINTIFF'S BURDEN OF PROOF

The Supreme Court seldom takes employment discrimination cases. Its June, 2000 decision in *Reeves v. Sanderson Plumbing Products Inc.*, #99-356, 530 U.S. 33 (Sup.Ct. 6/12/00) is a narrow procedural one. This case holds that an ADEA plaintiff can defeat a motion for judgment as a matter of law (a procedural technique for terminating a lawsuit without a full trial) by establishing a prima facie case plus enough evidence for a reasonable court or jury to find that the employer's defense is merely pretextual. It is not required that the plaintiff introduce any further evidence at this stage, unless a rational finder of fact would not be able to find the defendant's conduct discriminatory.

But *Reeves* does not mean that all ADEA plaintiffs will prevail—very far from it. In fact, employment lawyers report that *Reeves* has had little practical impact on the litigation climate. [See "Reeves So Far Is Having Little Impact on ADEA Judgments," 69 LW 2185 (10/3/00).]

Late in 2000, the Second Circuit found that if there is enough evidence of the plaintiff's poor work performance, then the jury cannot accept the plaintiff's pretextuality argument. Therefore, summary judgment can validly be granted for the employer. [*Schnabel v. Abramson*, 69 LW 1313 (2nd Cir. 11/8/00).]

For instance, in an October, 2000 case, summary judgment was granted for the employer because the plaintiff failed to refute testimony that he was not hired because of his poor interview performance (he didn't ask any questions about the position; he didn't give a good reason for having had so many jobs; he rambled instead of giving concise answers to the interviewer's questions): *Chapman v. AI Transport Inc.*, 69 LW 1271 (11th Cir. 10/21/00).

A 60-year-old employee was terminated when his employer lost government contracts. At his exit interview, he asked if he was being fired for poor performance, and was told "absolutely not." When he filed an ADEA suit, the employer claimed that he was terminated because he was impossible to get along with. The jury didn't believe this, and the Seventh Circuit upheld, particularly since there was no documentation of the alleged personality problems in his generally good evaluations. [*Wilson v. AMGen Corp.*, 1999 WL 50271 (7th Cir. 1999).]

The jury's verdict for the plaintiff was upheld in *Morse v. Southern Union Co.*, 1999 WL 212844 (8th Cir. 1999) despite the employer's contention that statements by the company president about getting a "young, fresh, new look" for the company, where no one should expect to stay long enough to retire, did not affect supervisors' decision-making. The court agreed with the jury that statements like that from top management would influence personnel decisions.

The New Jersey Law Against Discrimination makes employers liable for punitive damages based on actions of their "upper management." In *Cavuoti v. New Jersey Transit Corp.*, 735 A.2d 548 (N.J. 8/10/99), involving an alleged age-based refusal to promote, the court held that the class of upper management is not limited to top officers. Instead, it includes all managers with broad supervisory powers over the plaintiff-employee—**and** all managers to whom the employer company has delegated the responsibility for maintaining a nondiscriminatory workplace.

An early 1999 ruling by the First Circuit denies the availability of disparate impact analysis in ADEA cases. *Mullin v. Raytheon Co.*, 164 F.3d 696 (1st Cir. 1999), says that age-related discrimination does not reflect a legacy of past discrimination (as, for instance, racial discrimination does), so disparate impact analysis is inappropriate.

The ADEA case of *Norton v. Sam's Club*, 145 F.3d 114 *cert. denied* 119 S.Ct. 511 (2nd Cir. 1998), was dismissed. The evidence showed that the plaintiff was already under suspicion before he was terminated for taking a long lunch hour but claiming only a 30-minute meal break on his time card. The plaintiff lost despite a significant mitigating circumstance: The long lunch was taken in the company of colleagues condoling the employee over his father's terminal illness.

An over-40 store manager was demoted after receiving a warning that, although her personal sales were acceptable, the overall performance of the store was below par. A younger store manager was not demoted despite a similar failure to meet quota—but the employer prevailed, by showing that 35 other managers (34 of whom were under 40) were demoted for failure to meet overall store production standards [*Simpson v. Kay Jewelers*, 142 F.3d 639 (3rd Cir. 1998)].

According to the Fourth Circuit, disparaging comments about age are weaker evidence of discrimination than similar comments about race or sex. Racist or sexist remarks can be made by "outsiders," whereas everyone ages [*Dockins v. Benchmark Communications*, 176 F.3d 745 (4th Cir. 1999)].

EEOC Rules on ADEA Waivers

On June 5, 1998, the EEOC published a Final Rule on ADEA waivers, effective July 6, 1998. The rule, affecting 29 CFR §1625.22, appeared at 63 *Federal Register* 30624. The purpose of the rule is to set standards, pursuant to the Older Workers Benefit Protection Act (OWBPA) §7(f)(1), for determining when a waiver is knowing and voluntary, and therefore adequate and entitled to enforcement. All private- and public-sector (including federal) workers are covered.

The June 1998 rule reflects an interesting trend in administrative agency policy: negotiated rulemaking. Instead of an agency promulgating a rule without consulting industry—and very likely having the rule challenged in court by companies that find it unfair or unworkable—negotiated rulemaking involves industry input from the very beginning.

A valid ADEA waiver must

- Be written, and the entire agreement must be in the document (not partially oral, partially written)
- Be written in plain English and be appropriate to the signer's educational level; information about exit incentives must also be understandable
- Be honest and accurate, not misleading
- Specify that it relates to ADEA claims
- Advise the signer to consult an attorney before signing

In general, waivers can release existing claims but not those that might arise in the future. However, the Final Rule allows a waiver that is otherwise valid to include the signer's agreement to retire, or otherwise terminate employment, at a specified future date.

For the waiver to be valid, the person signing must receive valuable consideration specific to the waiver, and more than he or she would receive absent the waiver—(i.e., normal severance pay doesn't count). Nor does it constitute valuable consideration if the employer restores a benefit that was wrongfully terminated. However, it is not necessary to give greater consideration to over-40 employees who sign releases than to under-40 employees, even though younger employees waive non-ADEA claims (e.g., Title VII and Equal Pay Act claims) and older employees waive ADEA claims in addition to such other claims.

If exit incentives are offered to a group or class of employees, the Final Rule contains rules for notifying group members and drafting valid waivers once they have received the mandated notification.

The Supreme Court tackled the controversial issue of "tender-back" in *Oubre v. Entergy Operations Inc.*, 522 U.S. 422 (1998). If a person signs a purported release that is not in fact valid as a "knowing and voluntary" waiver as required by the OWBPA, then he or she can bring suit under the ADEA even without tendering back the severance pay received under the agreement that includes the invalid waiver. The theory is that a defective waiver doesn't qualify for ratification under any circumstances, so it is not necessary to give back the consideration to prevent ratification.

The Regulations proposed at 64 FR 19952 (4/23/99), discussed in the previous Supplement, implementing *Oubre*, dealing with tender-back of consideration received in exchange for a waiver, were finalized by the EEOC at 65 FR 77438-77447 (12/11/00). The rule amends 29 CFR Part 1625, with an effective date of January 1, 2001.

The EEOC's position is that Congress' intent in passing the OWBPA was to make a valid waiver an affirmative defense for the employer. The employer has the burden of proving that the waiver is valid, but the employee can produce evidence that the waiver was not knowing and voluntary.

According to the EEOC, ordinary contract principles of ratification and tender-back do not apply to employment waivers, because ex-employees might not be able to afford to give back the consideration even if they have a valid claim against the former employer. But the trial court may have to determine the employer's entitlement to restitution, recoupment, or set-off once the case is finally resolved (but the employer can only recover the amount of consideration paid for the waiver, or the amount the plaintiff is awarded for winning the case—whichever is lower). If the employee brings suit in bad faith, the employer is entitled to get an attorneys' fee award from the employee.

Under the Final Rule, tender-back is not required before filing discrimination charges with the EEOC or a state or local anti-discrimination agency. A clause in a waiver requiring tender-back is therefore invalid. The employee does not ratify the waiver, or rule out a challenge to its validity, by accepting the consideration. Tender-back is not required even if the waiver seems to be lawful, and even if the employee does not allege fraud or duress.

The EEOC treats covenants not to sue in the same way as waivers, and in fact believes they may be even more damaging to employee rights because employees might be deterred from bringing suit with respect to wrongdoing occurring after the covenant was signed.

Although the EEOC Final Rule was not popular with employers, as of January, 2001, no formal challenges had been filed in federal court. [Darryl Van Duch, "Employers Gripe at EEOC Rule," *Nat.Law.J.* 1/4/01, on law.com.]

Note that, although the OWBPA requires employers to give employees 21 days to think over an early retirement offer, the offer does not become irrevocable for this 21-day period; the employer can still withdraw it [*Ellison v. Premier Salons Int'l Inc.*, 164 F.3d 111 (8th Cir. 1999)].

In the post-OWBPA world, can employers enforce pre-dispute arbitration agreements and prevent employees from bringing ADEA suits? *Rosenberg v. Merrill Lynch*, 170 F.3d 1 (1st Cir. 1999) says yes; *Thiele v. Merrill Lynch*, 68 LW 1087 (S.D. Cal. 7/23/99) says no.

The key question is OWBPA compliance, which in turn depends on the way the waiver is drafted and the circumstances surrounding its signing. The Seventh Circuit gave effect to a clear, unambiguous waiver signed by a lawyer (!) employed by a corporation. Presumably, he was able to understand the document. Even though he believed he was given the choice of resigning and being terminated because of his age, he was still bound by the waiver he signed: *Lloyd v. Brunswick Corp.*, 180 F.3d 893 (7th Cir. 1999).

However, given the possibility of fraud that the company used to induce employees to sign waivers, the Tenth Circuit refused to give effect to the waivers: *Bennett v. Coors Brewing Co.*, 189 F.3d 1221 (10th Cir. 1999).

The District Court, upheld by the Ninth Circuit, granted summary judgment for the employer in a suit brought by a group of over-40 Quaker Oats workers who alleged that tests of analytical skill, used to select employees to be RIFed during a corporate reorganization, had a disparate impact on older workers. [*Coleman v. Quaker Oats*, #99-15885 (9th Cir. 2000); see Jason Hoppin, "Age Bias Theory Must be Pleaded to Proceed," *The Recorder* 11/21/00, on law.com.] The Ninth Circuit did not find their statistical evidence (showing twice as many over-40 as under-40 employees were selected for RIF) to be persuasive. The Ninth Circuit accepted the employer's argument that the tests results were not random, but reflected non-discriminatory factors such as educational levels.

Furthermore, the plaintiffs did not plead their disparate impact theory correctly; they did not raise this claim in the original complaint, only in response to the defense motion for summary judgment.

The theory of "virtual representation" is sometimes used to prevent a second class action once issues have already been raised in another class action. The Seventh Circuit, however, decided that a group of airline pilots challenging an airline's policies for over-60 pilots were not adequately represented by the earlier class action.

The earlier class action dealt with pilots and copilots, who are subject to an Federal Aviation Administration (FAA) policy that requires them to retire at 60. This action dealt with the position of first officer. First officers can be over 60 without violating FAA rules, but the airline refused to employ anyone in that job who could not be promoted to captain status.

Tice v. American Airlines, 162 F.3d 966 (7th Cir. 1998), says that the earlier class action was not res judicata (did not resolve) the current case. ADEA class actions are on an "opt-in" rather than "opt-out" basis (i.e., no one is covered without making a choice of being included). The earlier case dealt with potential employees denied employment because of age; *Tice* dealt with current employees seeking to remain employed by accepting a demotion.

The question of timing in class actions is also addressed in *Armstrong v. Martin Marietta Corp.*, 138 F.3d 1374 (11th Cir. 1998). In this case, some employees were dismissed as plaintiffs from a pending ADEA class action. They brought their own suits. According to the Eleventh Circuit, the statute of limitations is tolled (suspended) while a class action is pending, but the statute of limitations starts all over again as soon as the District Court issues an order denying the certification of the class.

When would-be plaintiffs are thrown out of a class action because they are not similarly situated to the proper class-action plaintiffs, they must file their own suits within 90 days of being removed from the class. Equitable tolling (i.e., permitting an action to continue on the grounds of fairness, although it would otherwise be too late) can be granted only if the EEOC actually misinformed the plaintiffs about the statute of limitations, not if they simply failed to consider this issue or made an incorrect determination of how long they had to sue.

26.5 PENSION AND BENEFIT ISSUES

In the view of the Ninth Circuit, the ADEA may be violated by calculating disability retirement benefits using the age at the time of hiring. The plan calculated the benefit on the basis of years of service lost due to disability, based on the length of service between age 55 (presumed retirement date) and the age at which the disabled individual became a public employee.

Under *Hazen*, calculations based on actual years of service are acceptable because a younger person might have more years of service, and vice versa. However, this is a slightly different question because the age at hire had a strong effect on the potential disability benefit. The Ninth Circuit remanded the case to the District Court for disposition: *Arnett v. California Public Employees Retirement System*, 67 LW 1742 (9th Cir. 6/2/99).

Receiving disability benefits prevents an ADEA plaintiff from claiming she was able to perform the job from which she was discharged [*King v. Herbert J. Thomas Memorial Hospital*, 159 F.3d 192 (4th Cir. 1998)]. Unlike the ADA, the ADEA does not embody a concept of reasonable accommodation.

In October, 2000, the EEOC published Transmittal Number 915.003 (10/3/00), Compliance Manual Section 3, "Employee Benefits," which is available online as http://www.eeoc.gov/docs/benefits.html. The Transmittal addresses all kinds of pension and benefit issues and explains the employer's duty to avoid age and disability discrimination.

TIP

In the EEOC view, ERISA compliance is no defense to a charge of age discrimination.

Where the benefits are the same for older and younger workers, clearly no ADEA issue is raised. And furthermore, even certain differentials are acceptable under the ADEA, including differences in benefits where the employer spends the same amount, or incurs the same cost, for all employees irrespective of age, and legitimate early retirement incentives.

The purpose of allowing offsets under the ADEA is to make sure that the older employee receives, from all sources, a total benefit that is no less favorable than that received by younger employees.

An "equal" benefit means that older and younger workers must have access to the same payment options (e.g., lump sum or annuity for both). They must have access to the same types of benefits, in the same amount. (It is acceptable to provide the same monthly benefit, even though it is likely that the older worker will die sooner and collect fewer payments.) Benefits are not equal if an age-based cutoff is imposed, or where benefits are reduced or eliminated on the basis of a criterion that is partially or wholly explicitly defined by age.

The analysis must be performed using similarly situated older and younger workers (e.g., those who have worked for the employer for a similar length of time and thus have equal seniority).

TIP

The EEOC does not require its investigators to find a specific younger employee who has better benefits than an older employee; comparisons based on hypothetical employees are allowed.

It is even acceptable, in the EEOC view, for benefits to be better for older than younger employees, as long as the employer does this to redress past age discrimination. If the benefits are unequal and favor younger rather than older employees, the employer has violated the ADEA unless a justification such as the "equal cost" rule is available.

The equal cost rule is limited to life insurance benefits, health insurance benefits, and disability benefits, because the actual cost of providing such benefits increases with the age of the employee. It cannot be used to justify refusal to hire or involuntary retirement. An employer asserting an equal cost defense may reduce benefits only enough to provide equivalency. It's acceptable to premise the defense based on the entire package of benefits whose cost rises with age, so it can be permissible to reduce one benefit more than cost justifies as long as other benefits are increased to compensate.

In plans wholly or partially funded by employee contributions, the employer may not force the older employee to pay more for the benefit as a condition of employment. Older employees faced with a premium increase must be given the option of withdrawing from the plan or maintaining reduced coverage at the original premium.

The ADEA, and therefore the EEOC manual, permits certain offsets to avoid duplication of benefits. Therefore, certain pension benefits can be offset by long-term disability (LTD) payments. Certain retiree health benefits and extra pension benefits can be deducted from severance pay.

The EEOC position is that all similarly situated employees must be given parity in severance benefits, irrespective of age, and severance benefits cannot be denied on the grounds that the employee is eligible for a pension. Older workers must be granted recall rights—otherwise, they would be subjected to illegal forced retirement. But there are circumstances under which retiree health benefits can be used to offset severance pay.

The EEOC recognizes that it is legitimate and lawful for employers to set a normal and/or early retirement age for receipt of pension benefits. They can require a certain number of years of service or a time period before the employee will be eligible for retirement. They can even limit the total amount of benefits that will be provided to an individual or limit the number of years of service that will be credited toward defined benefit plan benefits—as long as those limits are not linked to age.

The EEOC view is that, with three exceptions discussed below, the ADEA is violated by excluding an employee from plan participation because he or she was close to NRA at the time of hiring. Nor may employers stop or reduce their rate of accruals or contributions because of the employee's age. No equal cost defense is available.

However, if the employer actuarially increases the value of the pension for work after the NRA, it's lawful to offset this extra amount from pension accruals. If the employee continues to work after beginning to draw pension benefits, the actuarial value of payments actually made can be used to offset further pension accruals, and plans can be integrated with Social Security (i.e., Social Security benefits offset the pension).

See ¶11.1 for a discussion of Compliance Manual provisions dealing with ADEA implications of early retirement incentive programs.

Chapter 27

PROCEDURE FOR DISCRIMINATION SUITS

27.2 [NEW] POTENTIAL CAUSES OF ACTION

In the Second Circuit view, an employer is not liable for the employee's emotional distress if there is disagreement as to the adequacy of the employee's job performance, the employer followed its chain of command in taking adverse action against the employee, and there was no intentional, malicious falsehood or egregious overreaching. Employers are obligated to investigate harassment complaints, and doing so does not constitute intentional infliction of distress on the person charged with harassment. [*Malik v. Carrier Corp.*, 202 F.3d 97 (2nd Cir. 2000).]

In mid-2000, the Second Circuit joined three other circuits in permitting at-will employees to bring suit under 42 USC §1981 (the statute guaranteeing all citizens the same right to make contracts as "white citizens") for racially discriminatory termination, even though there was no written contract of employment: *Lauture v. IBM,* 216 F.3d 258 (2nd Cir. 2000); the other cases are *Perry v. Woodward,* 199 F.3d 1126 (10th Cir. 1999), *cert.denied* 120 S.Ct. 1964; *Spriggs v. Diamond Auto Glass,* 165 F.3d 1015 (4th Cir. 1999), and *Fadeyi v. Planned Parenthood,* 160 F.3d 1048 (5th Cir. 1998).

Although the general statute of limitations for civil actions brought under statutes passed since 1990—a category which includes CRA '91—is four years, *Zubi v. AT&T Corp.,* 219 F.3d 220 (3rd Cir. 2000) says that the right statute of limitations for a §1981 wrongful discharge case is whatever the statute of limitations would be for a state-court wrongful discharge suit in the state where the federal court is located.

By analogy with the housing context, the Seventh Circuit decided that employment testers (minority group members who apply for a job to see if they are not hired, whereas non-minority applicants with inferior qualifications are offered jobs) play a valuable role in combating employment discrimination. Therefore, they have standing to sue under Title VII even though they don't really want the job. But they do not have standing under 42 USC §1981, which would require actual intent to form a contract which is prevented because of race.

However, when the case was sent back to the District Court, the jury found for the employer, not the tester-plaintiffs. [*Kyles v. J.K. Guardian Security Services Inc.,* 69 LW 1038 and 2170 (2000).]

Denial of an employee's FMLA claim based on being fired while on maternity leave is res judicata to Title VII, ADEA, and Florida Civil Rights Act claims. That is, such claims are considered already determined by the negative FMLA ruling, because all the claims involve the same facts, which have already been litigated. [*O'Connor v. PCA Family Health Plan,* 81 FEP Cases 1112 (11th Cir. 1/18/00).]

However, the Third Circuit allowed a Title VII suit to proceed even though the employee was denied unemployment benefits on the grounds that she had been fired for willful misconduct. The court held that unemployment proceedings are substantially different in their economic effects, and are subject to such different procedural standards, that the finding should not be permitted to preclude a Title VII suit. [*Torres v. EAFCO Inc.,* discussed in Shannon P. Duffy, "Following 'Rue,' Worker Sees Title VII Claim Advance," *The Legal Intelligencer* 1/24/01 (law.com).]

27.3 ARBITRATION AND ALTERNATIVE DISPUTE RESOLUTION (ADR)

Late in 2000, the Supreme Court decided a case that arose when a truck driver was fired, after his second positive random test for marijuana use. The arbitrator said that a 90-day unpaid suspension would have been adequate punishment: firing him was excessive. The employer didn't want to reinstate him, citing the public policy against drug use by transportation workers.

The Supreme Court required enforcement of the arbitrator's award, because in a unionized workplace, the court system has to enforce arbitration awards that draw their essence from the Collective Bargaining Agreement. Therefore, the arbitrator's decision must be enforced unless it violates a statute or regulation; violating public policy isn't enough to prevent enforcement. [*Eastern Associated Coal Corp. v. UMW,* #99-1038, 121 S.Ct. 462 (Sup.Ct. 11/28/00).] Also see ¶18.9.

The difficult question of the extent to which employees who allege discrimination can be compelled to arbitrate their claims was resolved by *Wright v. Universal Maritime Service Corp., #97-889,* 525 U.S. 70 (Sup.Ct. 1998). In this case, an injured stevedore was denied employment because potential employer companies deemed him to be permanently disabled. The plaintiff sued under the ADA without filing a grievance or going through arbitration under the collective bargaining agreement. Although the District Court and Fourth Circuit dismissed his case, because of his failure to exhaust grievance remedies, the Supreme Court unanimously reversed. *Gilmer* does permit compulsory arbitration of an ADA claim (under the U-4, the securities industry agreement), but to the Supreme Court, this case is different because the employee's claim derived from a statute, not a contract.

Although contract claims are presumed arbitrable, that presumption does not apply to statutory claims. For a collective bargaining agreement to preclude litigation of a statutory claim, it must be very clear on that point. A generalized arbitration clause that fails to discuss antidiscrimination statutes will not be enough to keep disgruntled employees out of the court system. However, as you can see, numerous cases have arisen involving extremely specific collective bargaining act provisions.

For example, in *Rogers v. New York University*, 220 F.3d 73 (2nd Cir. 2000), a university employee was permitted to sue the university for ADA, FMLA, state and city human rights law violations despite a broad, general arbitration provision which was deemed not to clearly and unmistakably substitute arbitration for litigation in all instances.

Carson v. Giant Food Inc., 1999 WL 254438 (4th Cir. 4/29/99) says that there has been a clear and unmistakable waiver of the right to litigate if a CBA arbitration clause either specifically says that statutory discrimination claims are arbitrable, or fully incorporates the antidiscrimination statutes into the contract. However, *Brown v. ABF Freight Systems Inc.*, 183 F.3d 319 (4th Cir. 7/13/99) finds that the CBA at issue in that particular case, although it referred to the ADA, did not fully incorporate it, and thus litigation could proceed.

At the very end of 1999, *ALPA v. Northwest Airlines Inc.*, 1999 WL 256118 (D.C. Cir. 12/28/99) made life much easier for unionized employers to mandate pre-dispute arbitration agreements from their employees. In this analysis, unions can't agree to substitute arbitration for litigation for all of their members' statutory discrimination claims. That takes arbitration out of the category of mandatory bargaining subjects. That, in turn, means that employers are free to require arbitration agreements as a condition of employment, without negotiating with the union first. [Samuel Estreicher and Sam S. Shaulson give a good explanation of these issues in "Bypass Unions to Negotiate Individual Agreements," *N.Y.L.J.*, 1/25/00, p. 1.]

According to the Fourth Circuit, it is a material breach of the collective bargaining agreement for an employer to adopt arbitration rules that are grossly in its own favor and excessively stringent on the employee. If arbitration rules are unfair, the FAA will not require their enforcement, and therefore the employee will be able to bring suit under Title VII despite the purported arbitration requirement [*Hooters of America Inc. v. Phillips*, 173 F.3d 933 (4th Cir. 1999)]. *Gonzalez v. Hughes Aircraft Employees Federal Credit Union*, 67 LW 1543 (Cal. App. 2/23/99), also strikes down an unfair and one-sided arbitration agreement.

The Ninth Circuit has been quite resistant to claims that employees can be compelled to arbitrate employment claims that they prefer to litigate. At the end of 1998, the Ninth Circuit decided that labor and employment contracts do not fall under the scope of the Federal Arbitration Act. Therefore, an employee can't be forced to arbitrate the portion of a grievance alleging Title VII violations [*Craft v. Campbell Soup Co.*, 161 F.3d 1199 (9th Cir. 1998).]

The California Court of Appeals refused to enforce the ADR policy expressed in employment contracts with rank-and-file workers. The policy mandates arbitration; imposes a one-year statute of limitations on employee claims; limits back pay and discovery; eliminates front pay; caps punitive damages at $5000; and requires employees to pay part of the costs of arbitration. The court found the agreement to be unenforceable because it is oppressive to employees; places obligations on them, but not on the employer; and because potential new hires did not have a meaningful opportunity to negotiate terms or reject the agreement. [*Ramirez v. Circuit City Stores Inc.*, 68 LW 1376 (Cal. App. 12/10/99).]

A mandatory arbitration provision was held not to bind employees as to state-law sex discrimination claims, because the agreement included provisions that violate public policy. The unconscionably unilateral agreement allowed the employer (but not the employees) to use the court system and ruled out remedies (such as injunction and compensatory and punitive damages) otherwise available under state law. Furthermore, an employer who compels arbitration must assume all the costs of arbitration. The California court found so many defects in the contract that it had to be discarded entirely rather than merely having the invalid sections removed. [*Armendariz v. Foundation Health Psycare Services Inc.,* 99 Cal.Rptr.2d 745 (Cal. 2000).]

Yet earlier in 1999, the California Court of Appeals ruled that it is not wrongful discharge to fire an employee for refusal to sign a pre-dispute arbitration agreement, covering all employment-related claims, as a condition of employment. According to *Lagatree v. Luce, Forward, Hamilton & Scripps*, 88 Cal.Rptr.2d 664 (Cal. App. 9/13/99), California law allows contractual waiver of the right to jury trial, or any court trial at all. The court didn't accept the plaintiff's argument that public policy forbids compulsory arbitration clauses, finding instead that public policy favors arbitration. (However, current California law requires employers to pay the full cost of arbitration.)

The Ninth Circuit had already decided, in *Duffield v. Robertson Stephens & Co.*, 144 F.3d 1182 (9th Cir. 1998), *cert. denied* 119 S.Ct. 445, that the U-4 (securities industry form agreement) did not preclude litigation of a Title VII sex discrimination claim, because it is improper to require waiver of the right to sue under Title VII as a condition of employment.

In contrast, the Third Circuit decided that the U-4 arbitration clause is enforceable and precludes Title VII and ADEA suits [*Seus v. John Nuveen & Co.*, 146 F.3d 175 (3rd Cir. 1998), *cert. denied* 119 S.Ct. 1028 (3rd Cir. 6/8/98)]. Indeed, according to *Kovalevskie v. SBC Capital Markets Inc.*, 167 F.3d 361 (7th Cir. 1999) (7th Cir. 2/4/99), all of the Circuits except the Ninth Circuit have affirmed the validity of the U-4 arbitration clause.

The Second Circuit joined those other Circuits in September 1999, ruling that the U-4 arbitration clause is valid and enforceable: *Desiderio v. NASD*, 68 LW 1256 (2nd Cir. 9/22/99).

For the Sixth Circuit, see *Haskins v. Prudential Ins. of America,* 69 LW 1150 (6th Cir. 8/28/00)—even though the employee never received a copy of the NASD arbitration rules referred to in the U-4; ignorance of related issues won't make a contract invalid.

NASD has changed its policy, so that for claims filed on or after 1/1/99, arbitration will not be mandated. Nevertheless, the Second Circuit held that the case was not moot because the NASD could change policy again and reinstate the arbitration requirement.

The District of Massachusetts agrees with the Ninth Circuit position. It has ruled, in *Rosenberg v. Merrill Lynch,* 66 LW 1471 (D. Mass. 1/28/98), that the Civil Rights Act of 1991 bars enforcement of U-4 Title VII claims. Because the D. Mass decided that the New York Stock Exchange arbitration system is "structurally imbalanced" in favor of employers, it could not be imposed on employees who preferred to litigate their age discrimination claims.

You should also be warned that, in the view of the Sixth Circuit, even if an employee's agreement to arbitrate rather than litigate statutory discrimination claims is valid and enforceable, the EEOC can still sue the employer for money damages and injunctive relief on the employee's behalf. See *EEOC v. Frank's Nursery & Crafts Inc.*, 177 F.3d 448 (6th Cir. 1999).

According to the Fourth Circuit, *EEOC v. Waffle House Inc.*, 68 LW 1215 (4th Cir. 10/6/99), the employees' arbitration agreement with the employer doesn't prevent the EEOC from suing the employer for injunctive relief, but it does rule out an EEOC suit for back pay, compensatory or punitive damages, or reinstatement. The ruling in *EEOC v. Kidder, Peabody & Co.*, 156 F.3d 298 (2nd Cir. 1998) is similar.

The Ninth Circuit's holding in *Albertson's v. United Food & Commercial Workers,* 157 F.3d 758 (9th Cir. 1998), is that litigation of FMLA claims can be restricted by employment contracts negotiated for an individual worker, but not for an entire collective bargaining agreement.

With respect to yet another employment statute, see *EEOC v. Kidder Peabody,* 156 F.3d 298 (2nd Cir. 1998): An employment contract between the employer and one employee, calling for arbitration of ADEA claims, prevents the EEOC from bringing ADEA claims that seek monetary relief but does not prevent the agency from seeking classwide injunctive relief.

According to *Thiele v. Merrill Lynch,* 68 LW 1087 (S.D.Cal. 7/23/99), a pre-dispute arbitration agreement signed after the effective date of the OWBPA is not enforceable with respect to ADEA claims. However, another case also involving Merrill Lynch, *Rosenberg v. Merrill Lynch,* 170 F.3d 1 (1st Cir. 1999) reaches the opposite conclusion.

The Fourth Circuit did not accept the argument that an arbitration clause in an employment contract was unenforceable for lack of consideration. The *Johnson v. Circuit City Stores Inc.*, 148 F.3d 373 (4th Cir. 1998), court found that the employer's agreement to be bound by the arbitrator's ruling supplies the necessary consideration.

In *Strawn v. AFC Enterprises Inc.*, 68 LW 1302 (S.D. Tex. 11/4/99), all employees had to sign a "Value Deal Agreement" mandating arbitration of all injury claims. Texas allows employers to opt out of the Worker's Compensation system, as this employer did. It had its own benefit plan, providing much less for injured workers than the Compensation system. This case arose when an injured worker went through arbitration, receiving about $50,000 in benefits, and subsequently sued for additional tort damages.

The employer moved to compel arbitration. The employee countered that the arbitration agreement was unenforceable, relying on *Reyes v. Storage & Processors Inc.*, 995 S.W.2d 722 (Tex. App. 1999). *Reyes* says that a waiver of common-law causes of action is void as against public policy if the employer provides benefits substantially less generous than the Worker's Comp system. The court agreed with the employee that the "miserly" benefits provided by AFC Enterprises were not good enough. The arbitration agreement was merely voidable, not void. Therefore, the employee did not ratify the agreement by accepting benefits under the arbitration award.

The Fifth Circuit ruled on a case in which the collective bargaining agreement called for a 30-minute unpaid meal break in each shift. The employer wanted the time to be treated as personal time, but the jury deemed it to be overtime. The employer then challenged the litigation (rather than arbitration) of the claim. The Fifth Circuit said that the Fair Labor Standards Act cause of action was distinct from the collective bargaining act claims. In this context, arbitration is inadequate because it does not grant access to FLSA remedies such as liquidated damages and attorneys' fees [*Bernard v. IBP, Inc. of Nebraska*, 154 F.3d 259 (5th Cir. 1998)].

The National Association of Securities Dealers (NASD) form signed by new employees stipulates arbitration of employment disputes, other than those concerned with "the business of insurance." An employee of an insurance company was fired after he said that he lost some records that were critical to a suit against the employer. He sued the insurer for wrongful discharge and defamation. His position was that the suit involved the business of insurance, and therefore litigation—not arbitration—was appropriate.

The New Jersey Court of Appeals disagreed. The dispute was really about whether the employee violated the employer's document retention policy by disposing of the controversial documents. The dispute could have happened in any workplace—it had nothing in particular to do with insurance. Therefore, any claims brought by the employee would have to go through arbitration [*Fastenberg v. Prudential Insurance Co. of America*, 1998 Westlaw 158826 (N.J. App. 1998)].

The settlement proposal in *Martens v. Smith Barney Inc.*, #96-3779, submitted to the Southern District of New York on November 18, 1997, called for settlement of sex discrimination claims by creating a workplace diversity program; eliminating mandatory arbitration; and establishing an alternative ADR process. The ADR process would involve three steps. First, the claim would be submitted to the Duke Private Adjudication Center. The company would have 60 days to make a settlement offer. Offers rejected by the complaining employee would go to a neutral mediator, paid by Smith Barney. If single-mediator mediation failed, the final step would be a three-member mediation panel. See 66 LW 2355.

A plaintiff sought arbitration to get overtime pay from her ex-employer. The employer characterized her as an executive or administrator and thus an exempt employee not entitled to overtime pay. The Eleventh Circuit enforced an arbitration clause, even though she signed it during her first job with the company, but not during her second when she transferred to another office [*Montes v. Shearson Lehman Brothers*, 128 F.3d 1456 (11th Cir. 1997)].

However, the actual arbitration award was vacated, and the case was sent back for a new arbitration panel. The employer's lawyer urged the arbitrators to ignore the Fair Labor Standards Act, and apparently they gave in to this urging. Although arbitration is supposed to be somewhat less formal than litigation, it should not deprive participants of legal principles and protections available through the court system. Furthermore, arbitration awards can't be reversed based on misinterpretation of law, but can be if the applicable law is actually disregarded. In this case, the facts showed that she was exempt in her first job, but nonexempt and entitled to overtime in her second job.

If an employee loses sex and disability discrimination claims at trial, it is improper for the District Court to issue an injunction forbidding her to arbitrate the claims that have already been struck down. Injunctions can only be granted in situations in which there is no adequate remedy at law. In this situation, the employer could simply appear at the arbitration and get the case dismissed because the issues had already been decided by the court system [*Weaver v. Florida Power & Light Co.*, 172 F.3d 771 (11th Cir. 1999)].

27.3.3 EEOC ADR

The EEOC is stressing mediation and other forms of ADR as a means of speeding up resolution of charges. The agency's backlog peaked at 111,451 unresolved charges in June 1995. As of February 1999, the backlog had been approximately 52,000 charges pending. Newly appointed EEOC chair Ida Castro set a goal of 120 days to resolve a charge, but as of February 1999 the average complaint took 276 days to adjudicate. In a December 3, 1998 interview with BNA, Castro said that the EEOC will both use staffers as mediators and will also outsource some ADR functions under contracts with private mediators and mediation associations.

EEOC ADR began in 1997, when 780 cases were settled for a total of $10.8 million; in 1998, there were 1500 settlements aggregating $17 million. The EEOC's goal for FY 2000 is 8000 settlements, according to Steven A. Holmes, "Jobs Discrimination Agency Lightening Its Load," *New York Times*, 2/22/99, p. A1; also see 67 LW 2342.

As of the end of 1999, EEOC officials acclaimed the nationwide mediation effort as a major success. Since February 1999, almost 4000 successful mediations had been conducted. The EEOC considered mediation an integral part of its enforcement efforts.

Mediation led to $56 million in settlements (i.e., about 30% of the $188 million total discrimination settlements for FY 1999). When the project began, one-quarter of employers accepted the offer to mediate; over one-third did so by the end of 1999. Mediation takes an average of 87 days to complete, versus nine months to resolve a discrimination claim, so speedy resolution is promoted. [Bill Leonard, "HR Update," *HR Magazine,* 11/99, p. 32.]

With respect to using mediation later in the discrimination suit process, at a September, 2000 seminar, mediator Hunter R. Hughes said that mediating class actions before or just after filing reduces defense costs and gives plaintiffs the chance to make systemic changes in their employer's practices. He said that the earlier mediation begins, the better—because litigating positions haven't hardened yet, and there will be less unfavorable publicity and bad feeling. However, plaintiff attorneys are less supportive of this option because they believe that it gives class representatives more than a fair share of the settlement since the class hasn't really come together by the time the matter is resolved. ["Early Mediation of Class Actions Provides Advantages for Defendants and Plaintiffs," (no by-line), 69 LW 2207 (10/10/00).]

27.4 THE EEOC CHARGE PROCESS

On December 14, 1998, the EEOC and the Department of Labor (DOL) proposed a new plan for work sharing between the two agencies, giving 30 days for public comment (see Glenn Burkins, "EEOC Gives Labor Department Power to Seek Damages in Worker Bias Cases," *WSJ,* 4/9/99, p. A20). Few comments were received because of the holiday season.

The work-sharing agreement lets the DOL sue federal contractors for remedies, including punitive damages, if the contractors are guilty of race, sex, or religious discrimination. Employees of federal contractors have the option of filing discrimination charges either with the EEOC or with DOL. (About 200,000 companies have federal contracts and thus fall into this category.)

Under prior law, the DOL could review the employment practices of federal contractors (even if no charges were filed), under the Office of Federal Contract Compliance Programs. However, the OFCCP did not have the power to sue employers for damages. The proposal calls for information sharing as well as work sharing, so the EEOC's investigation of a complaint can be supplemented by DOL information about pay and promotion practices in the company.

According to the Fifth Circuit, procedural failures required that a judgment in favor of an employee had to be vacated, and his age discrimination case had to be dismissed. He filed a complaint with the EEOC and did NOT check the box on the form indicating that he wanted the charge filed with both the EEOC and the Texas Commission on Human Rights. Therefore, he failed to go through the mandatory step of filing a state charge—and his federal lawsuit was invalid.

Texas has a work-sharing arrangement, but that just means that a single filing can apply to both state and federal procedures—not that the state procedure can be ignored (even though he raised only federal, and not state, law claims against the employer.) [*Jones v. Grinnell Corp.,* (5th Cir. 1/4/01), discussed in Stephanie Hoops, "5th Circuit Tosses Case Because "X" Didn't Mark the Spot," *Texas Lawyer* 1/19/01 (law.com).]

Another Fifth Circuit case, *Villma v. Eureka Co.,* 218 F.3d 458 (5th Cir. 2000), says that because Texas is a deferral state, the EEOC has to hold off on its charge processing for at least 60 days to permit the state investigation to be done. Although the only way to trigger the 90-day period for bringing a federal suit is to get an EEOC Right-to-Sue letter, the EEOC letter does not start the 60-day period for a state-court suit under the Texas Human Rights Act. Only a civil action letter from the Texas Commission on Human Rights will trigger the state time period.

Although the EEOC has reduced its backlog, it's nevertheless clear that the heavily burdened agency is not going to complete its investigation of every charge within 180 days. That creates a question—resolved in different ways in different courts—as to whether it is proper for the EEOC to issue Right-to-Sue letters based on simple inability to resolve the charge in time. [This issue is discussed in Helen D. Irvin, "Courts Differ on 'Early' Right-to-Sue Letters," 69 LW 2259 (11/7/00).]

The EEOC's own regulations, 29 CFR §1601.28(a)(2) say that an early letter can be issued if the EEOC determines that it probably won't be able to complete the investigation within 180 days, and various District Courts have agreed. However some courts say that the EEOC is not permitted to issue a Right-to-Sue letter before the 180 days have elapsed, because that would allow the agency to avoid meeting its obligation to investigate charges. *Martini v. FNMA,* 179 F.3d 1336 (D.C. Cir. 1999) says that Title VII requires complainants to wait the full 180 days, to encourage informal resolution of as many charges as possible.

According to the Ninth Circuit, the "continuing violation" theory allows the plaintiff to seek damages for years' worth of discriminatory conduct that would otherwise be ruled out by the statute of limitations: *Morgan v. National Railroad Passenger Corp.,* 69 LW 1296 (9th Cir. 11/8/00). There were numerous incidents of discord during the employee's tenure with the employer that the employee interpreted as racial. The question was whether he should have gone to the EEOC as soon as the problems began, rather than waiting for his final suspension to file a charge.

An earlier case, *Galloway v. General Motors Service Parts Operation,* 190 F.3d 930 (7th Cir. 1996) said that the continuing violation doctrine can only be applied to cases where the plaintiff could not reasonably have been expected to sue before the statute of limitations expired—whereas the Ninth Circuit's own position, as explained in *Fielder v. UAL Corp.,* 218 F.3d 973 (9th Cir. 2000) is that two kinds of continuing violations can legitimately be asserted in a lawsuit.

A serial violation is a group of related acts, with at least one of them taking place during the limitations period; a systemic violation is a discriminatory policy or practice occurring during the limitations period. In the Morgan case, the Ninth Circuit held that there was a close enough connection between the conduct before and after the statute of limitations expired to justify invocation of the continuing violation doctrine.

27.5 ADEA PROCEDURE

See ¶26.3 for a discussion of 1998 and 1999 rules on ADEA waivers.

27.7 LITIGATION

The basic case on the use of after-acquired evidence is *McKennon v. Nashville Banner Pub. Co.*, 513 U.S. 352 (Sup. Ct. 1995). *O'Day v. McDonnell-Douglas Helicopter Co.*, 191 Ariz. 535, 959 P.2d 792 (Ariz. 1998), provides guidance on how to apply *McKennon* in state courts. If the employee sues for breach of the employment contract, seeking lost wages and benefits, the after-acquired evidence can provide a complete defense for the employer as long as the employer can prove that the after-acquired evidence was serious enough to justify firing the employee if the employer had known about it earlier. In a tort suit for wrongful termination, the after-acquired evidence is not a complete defense, but it does have the effect of limiting the remedies available to the plaintiff.

The Fourth Circuit decertified the employee class in a racial discrimination pattern or practice case [*Lowery v. Circuit City Stores Inc.*, 158 F.3d 742 (4th Cir. 1998)]. Individual employees who were once members of the class cannot maintain the pattern or practice case. Each must satisfy the *McDonnell-Douglas* burden-shifting analysis individually. The Fourth Circuit vacated most of the District Court's $4.2 million judgment (of which $3.9 million was attorney's fees). Most of the injunctive relief (e.g., establishment of a department of diversity management; career paths for black employees) was also eliminated, on the grounds of overbreadth.

The Michigan Court of Appeals applied the after-acquired evidence doctrine to a case in which the plaintiff was not hired, rather than one in which a person was hired, fired, sued for discrimination, at which point the defendant employer discovered resume fabrication or other misconduct. *Smith v. Charter Township of Union*, 1998 Westlaw 17798 (Mich. App. 1998), holds that, in failure-to-hire cases, the damage period can extend only from the date of the wrongful denial of hiring until the inevitable point at which the employer would have fired the plaintiff based on the plaintiff's lack of the minimum qualifications that were falsely stated on the fabricated resume.

A defense expert witness should not have been allowed to testify as to the plaintiff's psychiatric credibility. This was not a proper subject for testimony under

Federal Rules of Evidence 702, in that it invaded the jury's role of assessing the credibility of testimony. Nor should the defendant have been allowed to introduce evidence of the plaintiff's decade-earlier abortion, because such evidence is prejudicial and not probative. A new trial was ordered in *Nichols v. American National Insurance Co.*, 154 F.3d 875 (8th Cir. 1998), because of the evidentiary improprieties.

As for other evidence questions, the Second Circuit ruled that racist comments by a white employee can be used to show that the work environment was hostile to black people, even if the remarks were made after the black plaintiffs resigned: *Whidbee v. Garzarelli Food Specialties,* 223 F.3d 62 (2nd Cir. 2000). But testimony by four of the plaintiff's co-workers (that a supervisor's treatment of the demoted black employee was racially motivated) should not have been admitted: *Hester v. BIC Corp.*, 225 F.3d 178 (2nd Cir. 2000). The witnesses could testify about their observations, but because they didn't know how good or bad the plaintiff's work performance actually was, they couldn't testify about the supervisor's motivation.

The plaintiff's prima facie case in a Title VII failure-to-promote case requires the employee to identify specific positions that he or she applied for but was denied; saying that he or she was qualified for numerous promotions is not sufficient [*Brown v. Coach Stores Inc.*, 163 F.3d 706 (2nd Cir. 1998)].

In the Seventh and Tenth Circuits, the 90-day period for bringing Title VII suits starts when the employee actually receives the EEOC's right-to-sue notice, not the day on which the Post Office issues its first notice that it has a certified letter for the postal patron: *Houston v. Sidley & Austin,* (7th Cir. 7/26/99 both 68 LW 1112); *Jackson v. Continental Cargo-Denver,* (10th Cir. 6/24/99). However, the earlier case of *Watts-Means v. Prince George's Family Crisis Center,* 7 F.3d 40 (4th Cir. 1993) starts the clock running with the Post Office attempt to deliver the certified letter.

A white male plaintiff said that he was denied a promotion because he was the victim of reverse discrimination, and that the woman who got the promotion was less qualified. Because a white male is not a member of a protected class, the Seventh Circuit defined the prima facie as showing "background circumstances" evidencing reverse discrimination. For instance, a pattern of not promoting white males, or the choice of a significantly weaker candidate, would suffice.

Here, it was held that the plaintiff did present a prima facie case by showing that most of the promotions were given to women. However, he did not win at trial because the issue was the employer's intent to discriminate. The plaintiff did not show that the employer's contention—that it believed the woman was actually better qualified for the promotion—was false or pretextual. [*Mills v. Health Care Service Corp.*, 1999 WL 144274 (7th Cir. 1999).]

Two sexual harassment cases a few months apart reach different conclusions as to whether the 90-day filing period should have been tolled. The D.C. Circuit refused to grant equitable tolling to an employee who claimed that severe, continuing harassment rendered her non compos mentis and unable to protect her own interests by filing in time. To the court in *Smith-Haynie v. District of Columbia,* 155 F.3d 575 (D.C. Cir. 1998), the only evidence of the plaintiff's distraction was her own statement. But the Ninth Circuit did permit equitable tolling in *Stoll v. Runyon*, 165 F.3d 1238 (9th Cir. 1999), where the plaintiff suffered psychiatric disability after repeated sexual abuse, assault, and rape.

On one level, a class action might seem the obvious way for employees who seek damages and injunctive relief to raise charges of company-wide Title VII violations in hiring. However, the Seventh Circuit vacated class certification of a Rule 23(b)(2) class action, finding that although a (b)(2) class action is not always unavailable in a case calling for money damages (as long as they are only incidental to equitable relief), the possibility of receiving Title VII compensatory and punitive damages limits the appropriateness of this type of class action.

A (b)(3) class action, which requires the plaintiff class to notify all potential plaintiffs and give them a chance to opt out, is probably more appropriate. Another possibility is for the court to certify a (b)(2) class as to injunctive relief, and a (b)(3) class as to money damages, then try the damages part of the case first so that a jury trial can be obtained. A third possibility: to certify a (b)(2) class but impose additional requirements about notice and opt-out. [*Jefferson v. Ingersoll Int'l Inc.*, 195 F.3d 894 (7th Cir. 1999).]

In many cases, attorneys for the defense can prevent class certification, because of the individual nature of most claims of discrimination (especially those involving sexual harassment). Furthermore, discrimination cases focusing on monetary damages can be hard to certify as class actions, because Rule 23(b)(2) requires not only a common injury but uniform remedies for the whole class. For instance, the Southern District of New York decided in 2000 (*Robinson v. Metro-North Commuter Railroad Co.*, 69 LW 1287 (S.D.N.Y. 9/28/00).] that a class action can't be certified for a group of black employees seeking compensatory damages and injunctive relief, because there are more issues of individualized damages than claims for injunctive relief for the whole class.

Would-be plaintiffs who can't use 23(b)(2) may have to fall back on 23(b)(3), which requires them to prove that class-wide issues are more important in the case than individual issues, and also to prove that a class action is better than other methods of resolving the dispute. However, in some cases, a hybrid class action will be allowed, where a class is certified under 23(b)(2) to decide if the employer is liable and, if it is, damages are determined under 23(b)(3). [Shannon P. Duffy, "Class Dismissed: Judge Denies Class Status for Race Bias Suit," *The Legal Intelligencer* 2/1/01 (law.com); "Defense Attorneys Describe Strategies for Blocking Class Action Certification," (no by-line), 69 LW 2206 (10/10/00).]

The EEOC's jurisdiction and power to investigate a Title VII charge ends when a right-to-sue notice is issued. The EEOC must cease investigating, unless it determines that its enforcement interests extend past the claim of that particular individual employees. If so, the EEOC can either bring its own lawsuit, or intervene in the pending lawsuit brought by the employee who received the Right-to-Sue letter: *EEOC v. Federal Home Loan Mortgage Corp.*, 67 LW 1608 (E.D. Va. 3/10/99).

The EEOC was not allowed to introduce a report prepared by the employer's attorneys, evidencing their investigation into a charge of sexual harassment. The

EEOC claimed that, by failing to object to the EEOC's subpoena for this report within five days, the employer had waived attorney-client privilege and deprived the report of status as attorney work product. The D.C. Circuit disagreed: *EEOC v. Lutheran Social Services*, 68 LW 1120 (D.C. Cir. 8/24/99). As the court pointed out, the subpoena itself didn't include the five-day requirement; and courts still have jurisdiction over objections to EEOC subpoenas after the five-day period has elapsed.

Trial lawyer Gilmore F. Diekmann, Jr. tackles the mistakes that employer defendants make in a May 1999 article, "The Top Three Mistakes Employers Make At Trial," posted at http://www.lawnewsnetwork.com/practice/employmentlaw/papers/lawfirm/A1489-1999May14.html. Although the vast majority of claims of employment discrimination wash out (see ¶23.1) and employers can get summary judgment (i.e., dismissal of poorly supported claims without a full trial), the fact remains that of the cases that actually go to a jury, the employee-plaintiff wins about two out of three.

Some of these are cases in which the employer got caught doing something obviously wrong and has to take its medicine. But others are cases that the employer could have won with better trial tactics and a better job of showing its side of the story to the jury.

Diekmann suggests that some cases go to trial because the employer's lawyer got involved too late and failed to identify a losing case that should have been settled. Sometimes the wrong lawyer handles the case: Someone who is essentially business oriented rather than an experienced litigator who is fully cognizant of employment law developments and has handled the case from the very outset.

It's especially important for the trial lawyer to be completely familiar with all the depositions in the case. Depositions not only reflect testimony that was given at a particular time (and can be used to challenge inconsistent trial testimony) but give insight into the witness's character and thought processes (and thus the best way to challenge the testimony).

Juries are usually predisposed to like and sympathize with employee plaintiffs, so it's usually counterproductive for the defense lawyer to seem arrogant, hostile, or bullying. In Diekmann's analysis, the defense lawyer's job is to present a simple story that the jury can understand and accept. Juries have to learn to look at the facts and the legal strategies rather than maintaining their initial sympathy for the plaintiff in situations where, in fact, the employer has the stronger legal arguments and the facts on its side.

Employers and their counsel can also take a more proactive role. For example, when faced by a potential EEOC complaint of age and sex discrimination, Bessemer Trust sued the potential complainant in the District Court for the District of Maryland, seeking a declaratory judgment that it had **not** discriminated. The suit was settled, under a confidentiality agreement (so no one knows the exact outcome).

According to EEOC attorney Susan Oxford, employers bring three kinds of preemptive suits: to defend the internal arbitration procedure; to make sure that the company is freed of charges of wrongdoing; and charging employees with wrongdoing such as fraud, defamation, or theft of trade secrets. Of course, any such charges must truly reflect hard evidence, not a smokescreen for unlawful retaliation against employees who assert their legal rights.

Employment defense lawyers suggest that companies can protect themselves by doing a thorough exit interview to inform employees about confidentiality and trade secrets; by making sure that employees return laptop computers (and do not copy files that are corporate property before they leave), and by getting a properly drafted and signed waiver and agreement not to sue as part of the process of negotiating termination or resignation. [Sana Siwolop, "Recourse or Retribution? Employers Are Taking on Disgruntled Workers in Court," *NYT* 6/7/00 p. C1.]

27.9 REMEDIES

The employer's conduct doesn't have to be "egregious" for punitive damages to be available: *Kolstad v. American Dental Ass'n*, #98-208, 527 U.S. 526 (Sup.Ct. 1999).

The Tenth Circuit's test for awarding Title VII punitive damages is the preponderance of the evidence, not proof beyond a reasonable doubt of the employer's willful conduct [*Karnes v. SCI Colorado Funeral Services*, 162 F.3d 1077 (10th Cir. 1998)].

The Eleventh Circuit declined to impose punitive damages on a large retail company because a low-level manager at one store demoted the plaintiff for discriminatory reasons. *Dudley v. Wal-Mart Stores*, 166 F.3d 1317 (11th Cir. 1999), holds that imposition of punitive damages requires discrimination by a person high up in the hierarchy or at least knowledge of discrimination by persons in authority. However, you should note that *Deffenbaugh-Williams v. Wal-Mart*, 156 F.3d 581 (5th Cir. 1998), uses a lower standard for imposing punitive damages on corporate hierarchy.

Punitive damages were **not** awarded against the employer in the sexual harassment case of *Scott v. Ameritex Yarn Co.*, 68 LW 1384 (D.S.C. 11/19/99). In this case, a former employee alleged that frequent suggestive comments and gestures from her supervisor caused emotional distress, affected her family relationships, and eventually caused her to quit her job. The District Court found no evidence that the employer had authorized the harassment, or had recklessly employed an unfit individual. The District Court's interpretation of *Kolstad* is that mere lack of good-faith effort to comply with Title VII is not enough to impose punitive damages on an employer.

But the First Circuit permitted imposition on both a parent and a subsidiary company that fired a female employee on the basis of sex. Although the employer published an anti-discrimination policy, it could not show that the materials were updated and re-distributed as necessary, that supervisors were trained to prevent discrimination, or that the company's nominal policies were effectively carried out. [*Romano v. U-Haul Int'l*, 69 LW 1383 (1st Cir. 12/7/00).]

On the other side of the coin, a successful employer-defendant was awarded costs (transcription, copying, and videotaping) in a sexual harassment case that was weak enough for summary judgment to be granted to the employer. See *Cherry v.*

Champion Int'l Inc., 68 LW 1069 (4th Cir. 7/27/99). In fact, the Fourth Circuit said that the District Court abused its discretion by **not** awarding the costs, and it should **not** have considered factors such as the plaintiff's good faith, lack of economic power as compared with the defendant, or the public interest in courts being used to bring Title VII claims.

In fact, a Florida court went further, requiring the plaintiff whose frivolous suit was dismissed at the summary judgment stage to pay $160,000 of the employer's attorneys' fees and costs. [*Bernard v. Air Express International USA Inc.,* discussed in Susan R. Miller, "Judges Reversing Tide, Making Some Plaintiffs Pay Attorney Fees, Costs," *Miami Daily Business Review* 12/7/00 (law.com)].

In the Seventh Circuit, a Title VII plaintiff can get both front pay and lost future earnings [*Williams v. Pharmacia Inc.*, 137 F.3d 944 (7th Cir. 1998)]. The court found that the two remedies are not duplicative, because front pay substitutes for reinstatement and is ordered for a limited period. It is an equitable remedy, and the judge sets its amount. In contrast, lost future earnings, as authorized by the Civil Rights Act of 1991 (CRA '91), constitute the future pecuniary loss attributable to the effects of discrimination.

Front and back pay awarded under the ADEA to a job applicant who was not hired was not treated as "wages" subject to tax withholding [*Newhouse v. McCormick & Co.*, 157 F.3d 582 (8th Cir. 1998)].

In early 1998, Astra USA Inc. agreed to pay close to $10 million to settle EEOC claims of widespread sexual harassment. In 1999, a special master determined how the funds should be allocated among the 120 employees whose harassment claims were deemed to be valid.

The special master created a hierarchy of harassment injuries, awarding anywhere from $12,000 to $300,000, depending on the seriousness of the conduct. Seriousness was assessed along two axes: not only the nature of the conduct, but whether it was committed by a co-employee, a low-level manager, or a high-level manager.

For instance, isolated verbal harassment by low-ranking perpetrators gave rise to a $25,000 award; persistent verbal harassment by a direct supervisor was penalized by a $75,000 award; and repeated sexual solicitation or actual unwanted sexual touching by high-level managers was evaluated at $250,000. [Mark Maremont, "A Case Puts a Value on Touching and Fondling," *Wall Street Journal,* 5/25/99, p. B1.]

27.9.1 Title VII and the CRA

In mid-1999, the Supreme Court decided that, in a Title VII case against a federal agency, the EEOC has the power to award compensatory damages as defined by CRA '91: *West v. Gibson*, #98-238, 527 U.S. 212 (Sup.Ct. 6/14/99).

Because of the Second Circuit decision in *Morelli v. Cedel,* 141 F.3d 39 (2nd Cir. 1998), the Southern District of New York reversed an earlier ruling and held that the damage cap on foreign employers who violate Title VII is based on their total number of employees throughout the world, not just those in the United States

[*Greenbaum v. Svenska Handelsbanken,* 26 F. Supp. 2d 649 (S.D.N.Y. 1998)]. Since more employees means a higher damage cap, this decision increases the damage exposure of foreign corporations.

In the Sixth Circuit, front pay is included in the cap: *Pollard v. DuPont,* 69 LW 1768 (6th Cir. 5/26/00). In contrast, however, the Seventh Circuit held that the CRA '91 cap does not prevent an ADA plaintiff from recovering over $1 million in ADA damages, because that award might have been calculated to included back pay and front pay which are not capped: *Pals v. Schepel Buick & GMC Truck,* 220 F.3d 495 (7th Cir. 2000).

The Eleventh Circuit says that every employee who is represented by the EEOC in a Title VII action is entitled to recover the full cap amount without filing a separate action or even intervening in the EEOC-s action—they are not required to divide a single cap amount among them: *EEOC v. W&O Inc.,* 213 F.3d 600 (11th Cir. 2000).

An attorney who wins a mixed-motive Title VII case, proving the role of discrimination in the adverse job action against the plaintiff, performs an important public function (discouraging employment discrimination). In the view of the Tenth Circuit, this function justifies a fee award under 42 USC §2000e-5(g)(2)(B), even if the actual damages awarded to the plaintiff are limited or even nonexistent. See *Gudenkauf v. Stauffer Communications Inc.*, 158 F.3d 1074 (10th Cir. 1998). The Southern District of New York reached a similar conclusion in *Rodriguez v. McLoughlin,* 20 F. Supp. 2d 597 (S.D.N.Y. 1998), and so did the Tenth Circuit in *Brandau v. Kansas,* 168 F.3d 1179 (10th Cir. 1999).

The District Court's jurisdiction to hear suits "brought under" Title VII doesn't extend to a suit in federal court brought purely to recover attorneys' fees after winning an administrative claim, because no substantive rights under the statute are involved. [*Chris v. Tenet,* 69 LW 1069 (4th Cir. 7/27/00).]

Chapter 28

Wrongful Termination

28.1 INTRODUCTION

Charles J. Muhl's article, "The Employment-at-Will Doctrine: Three Major Exceptions," in the January 2001 issue of the Monthly Labor Review (http://www.bls.gov/opub/mlr/2001/01/art1full.pdf) sums up the state of at-will employment nationwide as of October 1, 2000. Mr. Muhl notes that nearly all the states recognized a public policy exception—all of them, in fact, except Alabama, Florida, Georgia, Louisiana, Maine, Nebraska, New York, and Rhode Island.

The vast majority of states (38 of them) allowed employees to enforce the terms of implied contracts (e.g., created by employee handbooks; see Chapter 3 of the main volume). However, Delaware, Florida, Georgia, Indiana, Louisiana, Massachusetts, Missouri, Montana, North Carolina, Pennsylvania, Rhode Island, Texas, and Virginia do not accept the implied-contract theory.

Only a minority of states (eleven of them: Alabama, Alaska, Arizona, California, Delaware, Idaho, Massachusetts, Montana, Nevada, Utah, and Wyoming) believe that employers should be treated as if they were subject to a covenant of good faith and fair dealing with respect to employees.

In late 1998, the Fifth Circuit permitted at-will employees to sue under 42 USC §1981 (which forbids racial discrimination in the making of contracts) [*Fadeyi v. Planned Parenthood*, 160 F.3d 1048 (5th Cir. 1998)]. The court's position was that Congress planned a §1981 remedy for at-will employees of companies that are too small to be covered by Title VII.

Such suits have also been permitted by several other courts, because the "contract" that black persons have the right to form on equal terms with white persons is defined to include an at-will employment relationship even though there is no written employment contract: *Perry v. Woodward*, 199 F.3d 1126 (10th Cir. 1999), *cert. denied* 120 S.Ct 1964; *Spriggs v. Diamond Auto Glass*, 165 F.3d 1015 (4th Cir. 1999); *Lauture v. IBM*, 216 F.3d 258 (2nd Cir. 6/30/00).

A Virginia man lost his job in a reduction in force. He claimed that the employer told him that a white male had to be RIFed to prevent an inference of discrimination against the many female and minority employees who also lost their jobs. In his wrongful discrimination suit against the employer, the employer requested a jury instruction that would have made it liable only if its sole reason for RIFing the employee was his age, race, and sex. The trial court, upheld by the state's highest court, refused to grant this instruction. The courts held that the proper instruction would be whether the plaintiff was fired *because* of any combination of age, race, and sex [*Shaw v. Titan Corp.*, 1998 Westlaw 190860 (Virginia 1998)]. See *Employment Alert*, 6/25/98, p. 11.

Although Illinois precludes in-house attorneys from suing their employers for wrongful discharge (because of the risk that confidential client matters will be disclosed in the litigation), the rule was not applied to a law firm attorney who was fired for pointing out the firm's practice of filing collection suits in the wrong county, contrary to the state's venue laws. If the discharged attorney works for a law firm rather than a single corporation, a wrongful discharge suit is a possibility, under *Jacobson v. Knepper & Moga, P.C.*, 228 Ill. Dec. 115, 688 N.E.2d 813 (App. 1997).

28.3 EMPLOYEE TENURE

A church employee was fired when the priest observed him receiving illegal anabolic steroids at the church. The employee brought suit, alleging breach of his written contract, which called for 30 days' notice of termination. (Obviously his nerve, as well as his muscles, was pumped up.) Understandably, he lost. The New Jersey court deemed both employer and employee to work subject to a duty of good faith and fair dealing. The employee's serious violation of his obligation relieved the church of its obligation to give him 30 days' notice of termination. See *McGarry v. Saint Anthony of Padua Roman Catholic Church*, 307 N.J. Super. 525, 704 A.2d 1353 (1998).

28.4 PROMISSORY ESTOPPEL

The May 1999 Fifth Circuit case of *Zenor v. El Paso Healthcare Sys. Ltd.* 67 LW 1729 (5th Cir. 5/24/99) involves a hospital pharmacist who entered a rehab program when his cocaine addiction got out of control. In federal District Court, the jury awarded him promissory estoppel damages, but the federal judge threw out most of the award. The appeal to the Fifth Circuit eliminated his promissory estoppel claims altogether. (ADA aspects of this case are discussed at ¶24.2.)

In the Fifth Circuit view, the employee handbook made it clear that the plaintiff was an at-will employee. The Texas rule, as expressed in *Montgomery County*

Hospital District v. Brown, 965 S.W. 2d 501 (Tex. 1998), is that at-will employees remain such, even if they have been promised that they can only be fired for "good cause."

The hospital's substance abuse policy made it a necessary condition of reinstatement that a drug or alcohol abuser complete a rehab program—but gave the hospital discretion to reinstate or not reinstate the employee after treatment. The existence of this policy did not change the plaintiff's status as an at-will employee, nor did it entitle him to get his job back postrehab.

Furthermore, promissory estoppel requires detrimental reliance (doing something against the plaintiff's interests). The plaintiff's argument was that the substance abuse policy caused him to disclose his cocaine addiction and seek treatment. But, in fact, he sought treatment after a drug-induced medical emergency, and entering rehab was beneficial and not harmful to him.

The trial court also misunderstood the damages available even if promissory estoppel is demonstrated. Texas law limits damages to "reliance" damages, putting the plaintiff in the same position he would have been if he or she had never relied on the promise. The jury awarded him mental anguish damages and damages for past and future lost earnings, and these are not available in Texas in promissory estoppel cases [*Central Texas Micrographics v. Leal,* 908 S. W. 2d 292 (Tex. App. 1995)].

The plaintiff in *Chieffalo v. Norden Systems, Inc.,* 49 Conn. App. 474, 714 A.2d 1261 (Conn. App. 1998), was previously employed by Norden; quit his job; and was rehired. Five years later, he didn't get a promotion he wanted, and his working relationship with the person who did get the job was poor. The plaintiff refused to participate in a team project and was told that he would be fired if he didn't participate. He continued to hold out, and was fired.

His suit was premised on an implied employment contract. He alleged that one of the company's managers told him at the time of rehiring that he would be employed indefinitely, as long as he returned to prior performance levels. The appellate court ruled that evidence about this statement should not have been admitted. Just because the person who made it was a manager did not give him the power to bind the employer, without proof that the statement was authorized by the employer.

Without that statement in the record, there was no proof that the plaintiff was not an at-will employee subject to discharge at any time, so the employer prevailed.

28.5 PUBLIC POLICY

Where a wrongful discharge violates public policy, California's Fair Employment and Housing Act (FEHA) is violated. However, the individual manager who fired the employee who refused to provide sexual favors is not personally liable under the FEHA. A 1998 California decision holds that, although the FEHA defines "employer" to include "any person acting as an agent of an employer, directly or indirectly," the purpose of this statutory provision is to make employer companies liable for the actions of their managers—not to create personal FEHA liability for the manager [*Reno v. Baird*, 957 P.2d 1333 (Cal. 1998)].

The First Amendment free speech right of a welfare department investigator was not violated when she was fired for making a racist joke at an off-duty political dinner. According to the Massachusetts court, she was not making a speech on a matter of public concern (which would have been protected), and racism can undermine the agency's mission. [*Pereira v. Comm'r of Social Services*, 733 N.E.2d 112 (Mass. 2000).]

In Maryland, an employee fired for refusing to have sex with a harasser can add a tort claim for abusive discharge to the sexual harassment suit. The independent tort of abusive discharge can be pursued, because the harasser's action violates the public policy against prostitution (in effect, an employee who has sexual relations to keep a job is unlawfully engaging in sex for pay): *Insignia Residential Corp. v. Ashton, Maryland*, 755 A.2d 1080 (Md. 2000).

The Pennsylvania worker's compensation statute doesn't say in so many words that it is illegal for employers to retaliate against employees who file Worker's Compensation claims. Nevertheless, employees in this situation are allowed to bring wrongful discharge claims, on the grounds that the legislature didn't rule out a retaliation action—it merely failed to make explicit provisions for one [*Shick v. Shirey*, 716 A.2d 1231 (Pa. 1998)].

Worker's Compensation was also involved in the case of *Lins v. Children's Discovery Center of America, Inc.*, No. 22424-1-II (Washington App. 4/7/99), http://www.lawnewsnetwork.com/practice/employmentlaw/authority/cases/G1431-1999May13.html. The plaintiff was a manager with responsibility for six day care centers. She and five other employees (directors of day care centers) were hurt in a work-related automobile accident. All six filed Worker's Compensation claims. The plaintiff was ordered by her supervisor to fire the other five employees because the supervisor expected the employees to sue the employer.

The plaintiff refused to do so because she knew that Worker's Compensation retaliation was illegal. Unlike Pennsylvania's law, the Washington statute (RCW §51.48.025) does prohibit employers from firing or otherwise discriminating against a person who has filed or announced an intention to file a WC claim.

The plaintiff, who previously had received good performance ratings, got a bad performance rating and was put on probation, then was fired for neglect of duty and poor performance. She sued for wrongful discharge in violation of public policy, because she refused to perform an illegal retaliatory act. The employer's contention was that although directly firing employees because they file WC claims is illegal, firing an insubordinate employee (even if the disobeyed order was illegal) is not illegal.

The Washington Court of Appeals extended the public policy argument to protect employees who refuse to violate the law. After all, it's in the public interest to provide disincentives for illegal acts, and employees who are not afraid of losing their jobs will be more likely to refuse illegal orders.

The plaintiff in *Lagatree v. Luce, Forward, Hamilton & Scripps*, 88 Cal.Rptr.2d 664 (Cal. App. 9/13/99) was fired for refusing to sign a mandatory pre-dispute arbitration agreement covering all job-related claims. He alleged that imposing an arbitration requirement on unwilling employees violates public policy. The California Court of Appeals did not accept this argument, holding that, in fact, public policy favors arbitration.

Even if the plaintiff in *Daley v. Aetna Life & Casualty*, 249 Conn. 766 (1999) could prove that she was fired for asking for a family-friendly work schedule (according to the employer, she was fired for incompetence), she would not be able to assert a wrongful termination claim. Although it is meritorious for employers to offer flexible work schedules, they are not obligated to do so, and not doing so is not a violation of public policy.

An employee fired for testing positive on a urine test sued the employer for wrongful discharge, claiming that the employer violated public policy by submitting the sample to a lab that was not state-certified. (North Carolina state law requires the use of certified labs.) The ex-employee lost: *Garner v. Reutenbach Constructors Inc.*, 515 S.E.2d 438 (N.C. 1999).

Not every violation of public policy carries a private right of action. Here, there was no evidence that the employer even knew the lab was not certified, much less that the employer flouted the law by deliberately choosing an uncertified lab.

28.5.1 Whistleblowers

At the end of 1998, the Supreme Court decided a whistleblower case, holding that an action under 42 USC §1985 (damage to person or property) can be maintained by an at-will employee who alleges that he was fired for assisting a federal criminal investigation of the employer company [*Haddle v. Garrison*, #97-1472, 525 U.S. 121 (Sup. Ct. 12/14/98)].

A Texas nurse reported a coemployee's apparent drug use at work and mishandling of prescription drugs. But it wasn't the drug user who got fired—it was the reporting nurse. The nurse lost her whistleblower action in state court. Although the Texas Supreme Court agreed that protection of the safety of hospital patients is part of public policy, it also held that Texas legislators have enacted whistleblower protection in some specific context—but there is no generalized state-law protection for employees discharged for reporting workplace wrongdoing [*Austin v. Healthtrust, Inc.*, 1998 Westlaw 181950 (Texas 1998)]. See *Employment Alert*, 6/25/98, p. 11.

In general, Wisconsin is not hospitable to whistleblower claims. In fact, it permits employers to fire employees for complying with a law (but not for refusing to break one). That precludes whistleblower cases brought by most employees who abide by a legal obligation to report employer wrongdoing. However, in 1997, the state's Supreme Court created a special exemption, allowing wrongful discharge suits only by nursing home whistleblowers [*Hausman v. St. Croix Care Center*, 571 N.W.2d 393 (Wis. 1997)].

The whistleblower provisions of the federal OSHA statute don't prevent state actions for wrongful termination by angry former employees. The OSHA provisions are limited to administrative proceedings and federal suits brought by the Secretary of Labor, not private suits in federal court (which might yield substantial damages). Therefore, according to a Kansas court, the OSH Act doesn't provide an adequate remedy that rules out state-law suits [*Flenker v. Willamette Industries Inc.*, 1998 Westlaw 271624 (Kansas 1998)].

According to the plaintiff in *Group Dekko Services LLC v. Miller*, 717 N.E.2d 967 (Ind. App. 1999), she was fired because she protested the mishandling of an employee's benefit claim. (The plaintiff was a benefits administrator, afraid that she would be considered an ERISA fiduciary and held liable for the claim handling.) The court held that state wrongful discharge claims were preempted by ERISA because determining her status as a fiduciary requires interpretation of the plan.

Another alleged whistleblowing employee, a quality control inspector, said that she informed management about tainted meat, but was ignored. She contacted government inspectors, who found deficiencies in the plant. She was ordered not to contact the inspectors again. She was fired when the employer suspected her of "leaking" information to the inspectors. She brought a wrongful termination suit, asserting protected whistleblower status, but lost. The court said that it was legitimate to fire her for disobeying an order to avoid further contact with inspectors: *Dray v. New Market Poultry Products, Inc.*, 518 S.E.2d 312 (Va. 1999).

In *Ragsdale v. Rubbermaid Inc.*, 68 LW 1271 (11th Cir. 10/27/99), a whistleblower was fired; brought a False Claims Act qui tam action against the ex-employer; and settled the qui tam action. The Eleventh Circuit ruled that he could not bring a later False Claims Act retaliation action. The qui tam and retaliation claims have a common nucleus of operative facts, and the firing had already occurred, so the employee could—and should have—resolved both claims at the same time. The legal doctrine of *res judicata* ("matter already decided") prevented him from pursuing the retaliation claim.

Peggy Farrior, a one-time secretary for a Connecticut school board, brought a 42 USC §1983 case against her ex-employer, charging harassment and retaliation for blowing the whistle on irregularities in purchasing and accounting. The ex-employer said that it had legitimate reasons to fire her for being rude and disruptive. In 1998, a federal jury awarded her $442,534 for lost wages and $118,940 for emotional harm. However, in 1999, District Judge Alvin W. Thompson, considering evidence about the plaintiff's angry and rude behavior, including taking two weeks off after an argument, threw out the jury verdict as against the weight of the evidence.

He granted a new trial, which resulted in a verdict for the employer, in December 2000. So, no conclusions should be drawn about the progress of a case until the case has been carried through to a complete resolution. See Thomas Sheffey's article (available on law.com), "$561,000 Whistleblower Verdict Cut to $0," originally appearing in the *Connecticut Law Tribune* for 1/8/01.

28.7 EMPLOYMENT CONTRACT TERMS

A California case from mid-2000 [*Asmus v. Pacific Bell*, 00 C.D.O.S. 4247 (Cal.Sup. 6/1/00); see Kevin Livingston, "Employers Win Right to Rescind Job Promises," *The Recorder* 6/5/00; available through law.com] allows a company to alter its established employment policies, as long as vested benefits are preserved, and employees get reasonable notice of the change, which occurs over a reasonable phase-in period. The employer does not have to provide additional consideration to employees to justify the change.

The case arose when Pacific Bell established a policy in 1986, under which managers who satisfied the company's business expectations would have job security. The company said it would maintain the policy as long as "there is no change that will materially alter Pacific Bell's business plan achievement." The job security policy was canceled in 1992, in a memo saying that the company needed greater flexibility in order to stay competitive against a background of economic changes. Sixty ex-managers sued for an injunction against implementation of the changes, and for damages under ERISA and for breach of contract, breach of fiduciary duty, and fraud. However, the California Supreme Court held that the managers accepted the changed policy by continuing to work for the company, which had a right to change its own employment policies.

In contrast, another California case, *Guz v. Bechtel National Inc.*, 69 LW 1272 (Cal. 10/5/00) finds that there was an implied contract, creating triable issues as to whether the employee still worked at-will, because of contradictory statements in the employer's personnel policies, stating that employees worked at-will but also that they could only be terminated for cause.

The Statute of Frauds says that a contract that lasts more than a year is only enforceable if it is in writing. In a Washington State case, the employee had an oral five-year contract, allowing either party to end the contract on six months' notice. The employee was fired after he'd spent about eleven months with the company. When he sued for breach of contract, his argument was that the Statute of Frauds shouldn't apply because the contract not only could have been wrapped up in less than a year, that is in fact what happened. But he lost his case. The Washington court said that the Statute of Frauds applies only to employment contracts whose duration is indefinite, not one with a specific term such as five years. Therefore, because he had no written agreement, he also had no case against the employer. [*French v. Sabey Corp.*, 134 Wash.2d 547, 951 P.2d 260 (1998)].

Oral promises to a relocating employee, that she would be fired only for good cause, didn't add up to a contract. Therefore, as an at-will employee, she could be fired even absent cause. Here, the problem for the employee wasn't the Statute of Frauds, but the failure to form an enforceable contract at all [*Montgomery County Hospital District v. Brown*, 1998 Westlaw 107922 (Texas 1998)].

In contrast, a very similar fact pattern in the same state (Texas) resulted in victory for the employee. A newly recruited employee, concerned about job security, was told on at least two occasions that she would not be fired as long as she performed her job well. After her discharge, she was permitted to sue for wrongful discharge under an oral contract theory. In this case, there was an employee handbook (issued after she was hired) that informed the employees that they were employed at will. However, the handbook also stated that it did not create a contract, so the court did not give effect to the at-will provision [*Doctors' Hospital of Laredo Ltd. Partnership v. Dromgoole*, 1998 Westlaw 75554 (Tex. App. 1998)].

An employee was orally promised a bonus equal to a percentage of the employer's profits. Of course, the year would have to end in order to figure out the bonus. The employer said that the Statute of Frauds precluded enforcement of the contract, in that calculation required a period of more than one year. The employee's argument was that he worked at will and certainly could be fired in less than one year. This argument prevailed with a New York court, which allowed enforcement of the oral contract. [*Cron v. Hargo Fabrics, Inc.*, 91 N.Y.2d 362 (N.Y. 1998)].

28.7.1 [NEW] Covenants Not to Compete

Contract terms also become significant after the termination of the employment relationship (for instance, if a terminated, retiring, or resigning employee previously agreed to a covenant not to compete with the initial employer).

An accounting firm's employment contract, requiring ex-employees to compensate the firm if they worked for any of the firm's clients during the 18 months following termination of employment, was unenforceable because it was overbroad: *BDO Seidman v. Hirshberg*, 93 N.Y.2d 382 (N.Y. App. 5/13/99). The court viewed it as inappropriate to bar ex-employees from working for clients they had not had contact with during their employment tenure, or for their own personal clients, whom they had brought to the ex-employer firm.

According to Marcia Semmes' article ["Rising Employee Turnover Puts Spotlight on Agreements to Protect Trade Secrets," 69 LW 2211 (10/17/00).] in 1999, one-seventh of all employees with permanent jobs changed jobs—much higher than the 8% figure from 1992 or 11% from 1994. Non-compete agreements are like ante-nuptial agreements in terms of protecting the company. However, she warns that to be enforceable, the agreement must really reflect market realities. It must be narrowly tailored to protect the employer's interests, so if the objective is protecting trade secrets, only employees who really have contact with trade secrets should be required to sign. Furthermore, an employer that gets a stack of agreements from low-level employees but never enforces them may find it hard to take steps against a higher-level ex-employee who really might harm corporate interests.

In a fast-moving business such as information technology, for instance, a one-year term might be unreasonable and unenforceable, even though that might be acceptable in a conventional retail environment. [See, e.g., *EarthWeb v. Schlack*, 71 F.Supp.2d 299 (S.D.N.Y. 1999), aff'd without opinion #99-9302 (2nd Cir. 5/18/00).]

California law actually forbids non-compete agreements, although, in the right case, California courts might agree with the 20 states that accept the "inevitable disclosure" doctrine—i.e., that an ex-employee can be enjoined from going to work for a competitor of the former employer, if the inevitable result would be disclosure of the ex-employer's trade secrets, even if the ex-employee does not intend to do so.

In general employees who are not bound by employment agreements or termination agreements containing noncompete clauses are free to compete with the employer after they leave. A top executive may be considered a fiduciary as to the employer, and a corporate-law principle called the corporate opportunity doctrine says that a current employee has a duty to disclose to the employer whenever a business opportunity arises that is appropriate for the corporation.

It's improper for the executive to take advantage of the opportunity personally. See *Hanover Ins. Co. v. Sutton,* 46 Mass. App. 153, 705 N.E.2d 279 (1999). In this analysis, the opportunity is an asset of the corporation, so the executive can no more take advantage of it without the corporation's knowledge than he could help himself to one of the computers from the office.

It may be deemed improper to contact the employer's customers while still employed, especially if the employee worked in a position of special confidence that provided contact with the customers and access to information about them: *Dalton v. Camp,* 519 S.E.2d 82 (N.C. App. 1999).

It might seem obvious that an employee with a good memory is no more allowed to memorize the employer's customer list and use it after leaving employment, than an employee with a bad memory is allowed to write the information down or photocopy it. However, a Washington State trial court refused to treat a memorized list as a protectable trade secret, but the state's Supreme Court granted protection to the information itself: *Ed Nowogroski Ins. Inc. v. Rucker,* 137 Wash.2d 427, 971 P.2d 736 (Wash. 1999).

In a 1998 Minnesota case, a company that hired a person away from a direct competitor was found liable for tortious interference with the covenant not to compete. Furthermore, it was ordered to reimburse the first employer for the $90,000 in attorney's fees it encountered when suing the employee to enforce the covenant. The cite is *Kallok v. Medtronic, Inc.,* 1998 Westlaw 10568 (Minn. 1998).

When the recruited employee got the job offer, he informed the recruiting company about the covenant, which barred employment in a field in which he had worked or had access to confidential information in the preceding year. The term of the agreement was two years. The recruiting company asked its outside attorney if hiring the competitor's employee would create legal problems; the lawyer said that it would be acceptable because the employee worked in a different field and didn't have confidential information.

Once the employee changed companies, the initial employer got a court order forbidding the employee to work for the new company. The competitor was also penalized for interfering with the employment contract. A "tortious interference" case requires proof of five elements:

- Existence of a contract that could be breached
- The defendant's knowledge that the contract existed

- Intentional action breaching or promoting breach of the contract
- Lack of justification for the action
- Damages to the injured contracting party

The Minnesota court decided that the competitor didn't do enough investigation; simple inquiries would have uncovered the real provisions of the noncompete agreement. Therefore, the company was not justified in its actions. Furthermore, the competitor's actions forced the first employer to sue its ex-employee, so the competitor should have to reimburse the first employer for legal fees directly resulting from this wrongdoing.

Cameco Inc. v. Gedicke, 157 N.S. 504, 724 A.2d 783 (N.J. Sup. 1999), holds that an employee can be liable for breach of the duty of loyalty for assisting the employer's competitors, even without directly competing with the employer. It depends on the nature of the employer/employee relationship and how inappropriate the employee's conduct (i.e., the level of assistance provided to competitors) was. Under this analysis, an employee has a duty to inform the employer of his or her plans before establishing a moonlighting business that could conflict with the employer's business. Damages for breach of the employee's duty of loyalty could include the injury to the employer's business plus the profits the employee earned from inappropriately competitive moonlighting.

28.10.5 EEOC Final Rule on ADEA Waivers

On June 5, 1998, the EEOC published a Final Rule on ADEA waivers, effective July 6, 1998. The rule, affecting 29 CFR Part 1625, appeared at 63 *Federal Register* 30624. The purpose of the rule is to set standards, pursuant to Older Workers Benefit Protection Act (OWBPA) §7(f)(1), for determining when a waiver is knowing and voluntary, and therefore adequate and entitled to enforcement. All private- and public-sector (including federal) workers are covered.

The June 1998 rule reflects an interesting trend in administrative agency policy: negotiated rulemaking. Instead of an agency promulgating a rule without consulting industry—and very likely having the rule challenged in court by companies that find it unfair or unworkable—negotiated rulemaking involves industry input from the very beginning.

A valid ADEA waiver must

- Be written, and the entire agreement must be in the document (not partially oral, partially written)
- Be written in plain English and be appropriate to the signer's educational level; information about exit incentives must also be understandable
- Be honest and accurate, not misleading
- Specify that it relates to ADEA claims
- Advise the signer to consult an attorney before signing

In general, waivers can release existing claims but not those that might arise in the future. However, the Final Rule allows a waiver that is otherwise valid to include the signer's agreement to retire, or otherwise terminate employment, at a specified future date.

For the waiver to be valid, the person signing must receive valuable consideration specific to the waiver, and more than he or she would receive absent the waiver—(i.e., normal severance pay doesn't count). Nor does it constitute valuable consideration if the employer restores a benefit that was wrongfully terminated. However, it is not necessary to give greater consideration to over-40 employees who sign releases than to under-40 employees, even though younger employees waive non-ADEA claims (e.g., Title VII and Equal Pay Act claims) and older employees waive ADEA claims in addition to such other claims.

If exit incentives are offered to a group or class of employees, the Final Rule contains rules for notifying group members and drafting valid waivers once they have received the mandated notification.

28.10.6 Tender-Back

The Supreme Court tackled the controversial issue of "tender-back" in *Oubre v. Entergy Operations Inc.*, 522 U.S. 422 (1/26/98). If a person signs a purported release that is not in fact valid as a "knowing and voluntary" waiver as required by the OWBPA, then he or she can bring suit under the ADEA even without tendering back the severance pay received under the agreement that includes the invalid waiver. The theory is that a defective waiver doesn't qualify for ratification under any circumstances, so it is not necessary to give back the consideration to prevent ratification.

See the EEOC Final Rule, 65 FR 77438 (12/11/00) that gives additional guidance for drafting a waiver that will *not* be deemed invalid and will *not* permit repudiation of the waiver without tender-back.

28.13 HANDLING A DISCHARGE FOR CAUSE

According to the Minnesota Court of Appeals, an employee who was justifiably discharged (for getting into an argument with one of the residents of a homeless shelter where he worked as an engineer) could not sue the ex-employer on a theory of "compelled self-publication." That doctrine can be used by wrongfully accused employees, not by those who were appropriately dismissed under circumstances justifying the employer's action [*Techam v. People Serving People, Inc.*, 1998 Westlaw 2431 (Minn. App. 1998); see *Employment Alert*, 3/19/98, p. 11].

A California employee could only be fired with just cause. The employer received two sexual harassment complaints about him, investigated and believed the complainants, and fired the employee. He sued, taking the position that he did not in fact harass the complainants.

The California Supreme Court, agreeing with Oregon, Nevada, and Washington courts (but disagreeing with the Michigan Supreme Court), decided that an employer has just cause to fire based on a reasonable inquiry that was appropriately conducted, as long as the inquiry is not used as a pretext for discriminatory or arbitrary discharge. It doesn't matter if the inquiry actually reached the wrong factual conclusion, as long as the employer acted reasonably [*Cotran v. Rollins Hudig Hall International, Inc.*, 17 Cal. 4th 93, 69 Cal. Rptr. 2d 900 (1998)].

A New Jersey casino's hair length policy, requiring pony-tail-wearing male employees to choose between cutting their hair and covering the pony tail with a wig, was upheld by the New Jersey Superior Court. Neither Title VII nor state law forbade a neutrally applied grooming policy that permitted female, but not male, employees to wear pony tails [*Rivera v. Resorts International/Trump Plaza Hotel & Casino*, 702 A.2d 1359 (N.J. Sup. 1997)].

Chapter 29

Corporate Communications

29.2 DEFAMATION

A law firm associate was fired subsequent to receiving a poor performance evaluation. She asked to have that evaluation reviewed, but the results were just as negative. After she was fired, the firm's attorneys merely confirmed her dates of employment and did not give any other information about her tenure at the defendant firm. The ex-associate sued, alleging professional defamation.

The law firm sought summary judgment, which was denied. The firm's theory was that any law firm associate agrees to be evaluated by the employer and that the results of the evaluation are entitled to absolute privilege. The District of Columbia Court of Appeals rejected the claim that evaluations are absolutely privileged, so the case had to go to trial. The law firm was held entitled to a qualified privilege for communications remaining within the firm. The privilege could be forfeited by revealing the information outside the firm, communicating too much information, or having a malicious motivation for communicating information about the former associate—all factual issues that would have to be resolved at the trial. For discussion of privilege re law firm evaluations, see *Wallace v. Skadden, Arps, Slate, Meagher & Flom*, 1998 Westlaw 12571 (D.C. App. 1998); analyzed in *Employment Alert*, 3/19/98, p. 11.

According to the Minnesota Court of Appeals, an employee who was justifiably discharged (for getting into an argument with one of the residents of a homeless shelter where he worked as an engineer) could not sue the ex-employer on a theory of "compelled self-publication." That doctrine can be used by wrongfully accused employees, not by those who were appropriately dismissed under circumstances justifying the employer's action [*Techam v. People Serving People, Inc.*, 1998 Westlaw 2431 (Minn. App. 1998); see *Employment Alert*, 3/19/98, p. 11].

Employees are even less likely to confront and cope with their substance abuse problems if they fear that they will lose their jobs if the employer finds out. Therefore, some employers pledge confidentiality to encourage employees to get treatment.

A Nevada employee claimed that his employer violated his confidentiality with respect to an alcohol treatment program; that other employees jeered at him; and that he was fired when he complained about the employer's indiscretion. He sued the employer, alleging that the employer's breach of confidentiality modified his status as an at-will employee, thus increasing the employer's obligation. But the court disagreed, holding that his at-will status continued. If an employer obligates itself not to fire employees in recovery without just cause, it can be held to that commitment—but this employer didn't make that kind of promise [*Barmettler v. Reno Air, Inc.*, 1998 Westlaw 178459 (Nevada 1998)]. See *Employment Alert*, 6/25/98, p. 11.

The music director of a church claimed that the pastor defamed her by spreading negative and untruthful explanations of the firing. The church had an insurance policy that covered defamation, but excluded employment-related liability of all kinds. Under *Parish of Christ Church v. Church Insurance Co.*, 166 F.3d 419 (1st Cir. 1999), there was no coverage, because whatever the pastor said related to the rationale for the discharge, and thus fell under the employment exclusion.

Information about a teacher's dismissal for sexually harassing students, and his subsequent reinstatement after arbitration, was newsworthy and of public interest. Therefore, comments by school district officials to the local newspaper were privileged and were not defamatory: *Corbally v. Kennewick School District*, 973 P.2d 1074 (Wash. App. 1999).

In another case involving allegations of sexual harassment, a co-worker of the plaintiff told a corporate manager that the plaintiff had committed sexual harassment, but the co-worker didn't want to make a formal complaint. Because there was no formal complaint, the manager didn't make a full investigation, but did sum up the charges in a memo to the personnel department. Later on, it was proved that the plaintiff was on vacation on one of the days when he was charged with committing harassment in the workplace.

Once this became known, the plaintiff sued the employer for defamation, but lost. There is a qualified privilege for reports of workplace harassment, so their dissemination can be defamatory only if the manager acted with malice. Here, the manager acted reasonably and without improper motive, so the employer was not liable: *Bierbower v. FHP, Inc.*, 70 Cal. App. 4th 1, 82 Cal.Rptr.2d 393 (1999).

"Malice" involves more than unquestioning acceptance of a statement that turns out to be false. *Sanderson v. Bellevue Maternity Hospital*, 1999 Westlaw 130451 (N.Y. A.D. 1999) draws a line between accepting a statement without really knowing it is true, and passing along a statement whose truth the communicator finds extremely doubtful. The latter case displays reckless disregard for the truth; the former does not, so it does not create defamation liability for the communicator or the employer company.

One worker deliberately falsely claimed that another worker threatened "to bring a gun in here and kill someone." The employee who was supposed to have made the threat was taken to a mental hospital by the police, then released after an interview with a psychiatrist. She claimed severe emotional distress, and sued the employer for defamation. The employer cited Worker's Compensation exclusivity because defamation is an intentional tort causing emotional distress. But the Pennsylvania Superior Court decided in 1999 [*Urban v. Dollar Bank*, 725 A.2d 815 (Pa. Super. 1999)] to allow the employee to maintain the defamation lawsuit, on the theory that Worker's Compensation deals with physical or mental injuries, whereas defamation deals with damage to reputation.

An employee with an injured back was out on disability leave. His supervisor saw him playing baseball, and suspended him, then contacted the employee's doctor. The doctor said the employee had not been given permission to play baseball, so the supervisor fired the employee and sent a memo to management explaining the firing by saying the employee "stole" from the company by making a false disability claim. The employee sued for defamation, on the grounds that playing baseball didn't violate his work restrictions. Therefore, he claimed that the supervisor's accusation of theft was false.

The court, in *Dominguez v. Davidson*, 974 P.2d 112 (Kan. 1999) absolved both supervisor and employer of defamation liability. The supervisor's report was entitled to qualified privilege (because it was work-related information) and, because it was based on investigation, malice was absent.

In *Hatch v. Fred Meyer, Inc.*, 1999 Westlaw 106923 (Wash. App. 1999), as a prank, a harassing e-mail that was supposed to have come from the plaintiff was sent to the plaintiff's supervisor. The supervisor realized that it was a prank and simply deleted it. The plaintiff sued, claiming that the e-mail was defamatory, but lost the case: no one had been deceived, so no one thought that the plaintiff had engaged in improper conduct.

29.3 PRIVILEGED STATEMENTS

The EEOC was not allowed to introduce a report prepared by the employer's attorneys, evidencing their investigation into a charge of sexual harassment. The EEOC claimed that, by failing to object to the EEOC's subpoena for this report within five days, the employer had waived attorney–client privilege and deprived the report of status as attorney work product. The D.C. Circuit disagreed: *EEOC v. Lutheran Social Services*, 68 LW 1120 (D.C. Cir. 8/24/99). As the court pointed out, the subpoena itself didn't include the five-day requirement; and courts still have jurisdiction over objections to EEOC subpoenas after the five-day period has elapsed.

29.5 RESPONSES TO REFERENCE CHECKS

Most companies are very circumspect about what they'll say when another company calls to check references. The Society for Human Resources Management (SHRM) reports that only 19% of about 850 HR staffers surveyed explain why an ex-employee had left, and only 13% gave any information about the work performance of the former employee. See Jeffrey L. Seglin, "Too Much Ado About Giving References," *NYT*, 2/21/99, Business, p. 4.

But that's only what goes on the record, in a formal contact such as a call from a lawyer. HR professionals often develop more effective off-the-record communications with people on their own level in other companies.

Of course, the reason for the guardedness is the fear of defamation suits. But Seglin's article cites business school professor C. Patrick Fleener's study of court records for the periods 1965–1970 and 1985–1990. He found reports of a mere 16 defamation cases (covering both federal and state courts)—and 12 of those were wins for the employer. Four plaintiff wins in ten years doesn't seem like a good reason to disrupt the entire practice of using references in hiring. Don't forget that truthful statements are not defamatory, so sticking to the facts, without embroidery, should be a defense in any event.

Chapter 30

Insurance Coverage for Claims Against the Employer

30.2 THE CGL

The music director of a church claimed that the pastor defamed her by spreading negative and untruthful explanations of the firing. The church had an insurance policy that covered defamation, but excluded employment-related liability of all kinds. Under *Parish of Christ Church v. Church Insurance Co.*, 166 F.3d 419 (1st Cir. 1999), there was no coverage, because whatever the pastor said related to the rationale for the discharge, and thus fell under the employment exclusion.

The CGL exclusion for "employment-related practices" does exclude direct coverage for sexual harassment liability. However, it did not exclude coverage of a sexually harassed employee's claim against the employer for negligent retention of the harassing employee. As the Florida Court of Appeals interpreted the case, charging a company with negligent retention charges it with negligence, not with an excluded claim of intentional injury [*Mactown, Inc. v. Continental Insurance Co.*, 1998 Westlaw 390612 (Fla. App. 1998)].

According to *SCI Liquidating Corp. v. Hartford Fire Insurance Co.*, 181 F.3d 1210 (11th Cir. 1999), the CGL does not have to cover the claims made by an employee who alleged sexual harassment (including assault and battery), retaliation, intentional infliction of emotional distress, and negligent hiring and retention of the perpetrator. In this reading, there was no CGL "occurrence," because intentional harassment is not an accident. Injury arising out of negligent hiring and retention didn't fit the definition of "occurrence" either, because of its close relationship with the harassment. The CGL did include discrimination in the category of covered personal injury, but it also excluded employment-related claims.

The employer also had an umbrella policy covering personal injury, specifically including discrimination-related injury. The Eleventh Circuit sent the case back to the Georgia Supreme Court for determination of whether sexual harassment by a co-employee "arises out of and in the course of employment"; at least in the Worker's Compensation context, Georgia law provides that co-employee harassment does **not** arise out of employment. If this is so, the employer would be entitled to coverage under the umbrella policy because its exclusion of employment-related claims would not come into play.

The CGL exclusion of bodily injury "arising out of and in the course of employment" barred coverage of an age discrimination wrongful termination claim, brought under state (New Jersey) law. The ex-employee alleged that emotional distress resulting from the termination caused physical consequences such as loss of libido, headaches, stomach pains, and eventually a stroke.

Litigation, like politics, makes strange bedfellows, and this time the ex-employee and the employer took the same position: that the bodily injury arose out of the wrongful termination, not out of employment, and therefore should come under the CGL. (The ex-employee, of course, wanted the insurer to be involved so that there would be an additional source of payment of potential damages.) However, the court was not persuaded and did not require the CGL insurer to defend or indemnify [*American Motorists Ins. Co. v. L-C-A Sales Co.*, 155 N.J. 29, 713 A.2d 1007 (N.J. 1998)]. (*Schmidt*, discussed later in this chapter, deals with another kind of policy, not the CGL.)

30.3 NON-CGL POLICIES

In 1997, 1998, and 1999, Employment Practices Liability Insurance (EPLI) attracted significant attention in the HR and legal press.

In 1994, there were only 10 carriers offering EPLI coverage; by 1997, at least 30, and probably about 50 companies, had this coverage for sale. By 1999, over 100 insurers were in the EPLI market, and the Insurance Services Organization (ISO) had at last developed a standard EPLI form. More competition led to increasing comprehensiveness of available EPLI policies, but in most cases, punitive damages and retaliation will *not* be covered, according to Daniel C. Skinner, William T. Edwards, and Gregory L. Gravlee ("Selecting Employment Practices Liability Insurance," *HR Magazine*, 9/98, p. 146).

However, greater availability of policies did not impel the majority of companies or executives to purchase. Aon Risk Services, Inc.'s 1997 survey of 2200 executives found that only about one-third had EPLI coverage; of that small sample, about two-thirds had the coverage as an endorsement to a CGL or directors & officers (D&O) policies, and only 26% owned stand-alone EPLI policies. What did EPLI cost in 1997? Anywhere from $15,000 to $70,000 for $1 million coverage, depending on geographic location and litigation history.

EPLI owners can benefit from the coverage even if they are never sued, because insurers require their insureds to audit their HR functions, improve their procedures, and add new procedures to minimize the risk of suit (e.g., better reporting and investigation procedures for sexual harassment claims). In a sense, this is a counterpart of security measures undertaken to reduce casualty and fire insurance premiums. (This information comes from Simon J. Nadel, "Employment Practices Liability Insurance Makes Some Headway With Employers," 66 LW 2275.)

Insurers are still treating stand-alone EPLI products with caution. Although these policies usually do not cover punitive damages (so the "wild card" multi-million-dollar claims are not covered), it is still difficult to predict what will happen in an employment case. Employers may be driven to settle even a fairly weak case, to resolve the uncertainty and avoid bad publicity and even a small risk of being subjected to a very large judgment.

Furthermore, employers are likely to insist that the insurer having a duty to defend provide them with top-flight, experienced employment defense attorneys. Compensating these skillful attorneys can be a painful task for the EPLI insurer! The insurer's outlook is addressed in Jennifer L. Cox and Bernard E. Jacques, "Risks of EPLI Coverage Prove Difficult to Assess," *National Law Journal*, 12/21/98, p. B14.

The ISO EPLI form modifies the basic claims-made structure in a way that helps employers. A claims-made policy is one that provides coverage when claims are made while the insured still has coverage. But the ISO EPLI form also covers claims made during the 30 days right after the policy expired, unless another insurer is already in the picture. If the same employee makes multiple claims, they are all considered to have arisen on the date of the first claim, so there will be no gap in coverage and it will not be necessary to figure out whether the initial or the later insurer is responsible.

Liability insurance is not very popular among HR professionals. SHRM's 1997 *Employment Litigation Survey* showed that 85% of HR professionals responding to the survey didn't have liability insurance, because they did not feel that they were at high personal risk of being sued. In the small number of cases in which an HR professional might be named as defendant, the employer's CGL would probably cover the HR professional. However, if the employer and the HR professional might find themselves at odds (if the HR professional objects to improper corporate policies, for instance), personal coverage might be worthwhile. See 66 LW 2276.

Employment Law Letter, an online newsletter (see http://www.ulmer.com/events/newsletters/sp99_shop.html), provides valuable guidance in its spring 1999 issue. Stephanie E. Trudeau and William D. Edwards suggest the following questions for evaluating an EPLI policy:

- Does it cover all employees? What about the actions of leased employees and independent contractors?
- Are former employees covered?
- Are claims for breach of explicit or implied employment contract excluded from the policy?

- What coverage (if any) is available for employment-related claims such as infliction of emotional distress or defamation?
- If you are aware of a high-quality employment defense firm, can you require your insurer to select that firm as your counsel, or are you stuck with the insurer's choice of counsel? How much control can you impose on the defense of your cases?
- Does the insurer have to provide you with a defense in adminstrative (e.g., EEOC) proceedings, or only at trial? Remember, very few employment cases actually get to trial—but the employer's life can be made very unpleasant before trial!
- Are you covered for retaliation claims (a growing area of employment litigation), including retaliation against Worker's Compensation claimants?
- Are you covered for injunctive and declaratory relief as well as money damages?
- Is the deductible imposed for each claimant? This is not a desirable provision for the employer, because it could result in having to satisfy the deductible several times a year.
- Does your state forbid insurance against punitive damages? If not, does the policy cover punitive damages?

Schmidt v. Smith, 155 N.J. 44, 713 A.2d 1014 (1998), says that bodily injury caused by sexual harassment is covered by the employer liability section of the Worker's Compensation insurance policy, which is a "gap-filler" designed to come into play when a person suffers job-related injuries, even if that person is not covered by Worker's Compensation.

Providing $1 million in general coverage under a social worker's professional liability policy, but capping coverage of damages for sexual abuse of clients at $25,000, does not violate insurance law or public policy. See *American Home Assurance Co. v. Levy*, Suffolk County Supreme Court, discussed in Bill Alden, "Judge Upholds Insurance Limits for Sex Claims," *N.Y.L.J.*, 2/11/99, p. 1.

In this analysis, therapists are not required to have malpractice insurance, so there is no public policy involved. To the extent that they choose to have the coverage, it is legitimate for the carriers to control the terms of coverage. The social workers argued that such a low cap would deter reporting of sexual abuse, but the court rejected the argument, pointing out that clients seldom know how much insurance their health care providers carry.

30.5 QUESTIONS OF TIMING

An employer faced with an ADEA suit was covered by a claims-made EPLI policy. That is, the employer was covered for claims that were first made while the policy was in force, and reported to the company not later than 60 days after expiration of the policy. The EEOC notified the employer of an ADEA charge on November 7. The employee brought suit on December 22, and the employer notified the insurer on January 21.

The Eastern District of Louisiana found that the employer did not give timely notice: *Specialty Food Systems Inc. v. Reliance Insurance Co.*, 1999 WL 20934 (E.D. La. 1999). Under the policy, the EEOC charge satisfied the definition of a "written demand or notice" received by the insured from any "person or administrative agency," so notice was due within 60 days of November 7.

Chapter 31

EFFECT OF CORPORATE TRANSITIONS ON LIABILITY

31.1 INTRODUCTION

A qualified plan can change its form for several reasons. As §12.12 (main volume) explains, plans can be amended; see Chapter 16 (main volume) for a discussion of what happens when a plan is terminated. Changes in form also occur as part of a corporate change in form (e.g., when the corporation that sponsors the plan merges with or is acquired by another company, with some or all of the first plan's employees becoming employees of the new or surviving corporation). Sometimes the transition involves the corporation, with its plans trailing behind as an accessory; sometimes the real purpose of the transition is to change the form or operation of the plan (for example, if an employer wants to combine several of its own existing plans for ease of administration or to reduce costs).

TIP

Even if a transition occurs, basic fiduciary principles continue to apply, and plans must be maintained for the sole benefit of participants and beneficiaries. Hence, in 1996 the Supreme Court decided that plan participants and beneficiaries could sue under ERISA §502(a)(3), to get equitable relief for themselves, when a company spun off its money-losing divisions to a new, financially unstable corporation and lied to employees about the safety of their benefits if they transferred to the new corporation.

In contrast, however, given that pension benefits vest but welfare benefits (including retiree health and insurance benefits) do not, ERISA fiduciary duty is not violated by transferring the obligation to pay nonpension retiree benefits to a new company spun off from the former employer. Nor is an ERISA contract claim cognizable. The Sixth Circuit's analysis in *Sengpiel v. B.F. Goodrich Co.*, 156 F.3d 660 (6th Cir. 1998), is that ERISA requires prefunding of pensions, but not of welfare benefits. The spun-off entity retained the right to reduce benefits in the plan documents, so reducing the benefits had to be analyzed as a plan termination, modification, or amendment (i.e., a business decision, not a discretionary administrative discretion by a fiduciary).

Certainly, part of the due diligence that must be undertaken prior to purchasing another business, or selling a business, is the effect of the change on each corporation's employee benefit plans. For example, if it is discovered that the seller's plan is underfunded, the sales documents might be redrafted so that the seller covenants to correct the underfunding, or the sales price might simply be reduced accordingly. At times, the deciding factor in structuring the deal will be which form offers the desired treatment of the plans.

The actuarial and consulting firm Milliman & Robertson has an online newsletter, "Benefits Perspectives." The Winter 2000 issue [available at http://www.milliman.com.] contains three excellent articles on HR and benefits issues in corporate M&A.

Changes in corporate structure can have unintended effects on plans, which may violate nondiscrimination, minimum participation, and anticutback rules. The buyer must be particularly careful to find out if defined contribution plans are unfunded or defined benefit plans are underfunded. The presence or absence of golden parachutes, retiree health benefit obligations, and COBRA obligations must be determined. WARN Act notification [see §18.11 (main volume)] may also be required if there is a significant reduction in the workforce after the corporate transition. Last but not least, the tests that establish whether a plan is discriminatory must be repeated after a change of corporate organization.

The test of whether two companies are alter egos (and therefore required to make up for delinquent contributions to a pension plan) comes from basic corporate law. The question is whether one company controls the other so closely that the second corporation has no independent existence, and the second corporation is just a sham used for fraudulent purposes.

Also see Ellen E. Schultz' reporting, "Raw Deals: Companies Quietly Use Mergers and Spinoffs to Cut Worker Benefits," *WSJ* 12/27/00 p. A1 explaining how a company can make a division that is up for sale seem more attractive to potential buyers by reducing liability for employee medical coverage; making the pension plan less generous; or freezing pension benefits while retaining control over plan investments. However, if the seller is a government contractor, it may have an obligation to return some plan surpluses to the government agencies with whom the seller does business—this is the assertion of several lawsuits against General Electric brought by the Department of Defense and other agencies.

In addition to questions involving pension plans, a corporate transition can have other implications: for labor law; for unemployment insurance; and for taxes, for example.

31.2 CHOICE OF FORM

Although the variations are almost infinite, there are several basic ways to structure a corporate transition. Two companies could merge, creating a new successor company or with one company absorbed into the other. One company could buy all of the other company's assets; or one company could buy all of the other company's stock. The consequences of stock and asset purchases are different.

If the deal is structured as either a merger or a sale of stock, the buyer acquires the seller's liabilities as an automatic part of the deal. The buyer will become the sponsor of the seller's employee benefit plans unless

- Action is taken to terminate or freeze the plan. Both corporate action (resolution of the Board of Directors; perhaps affirmation by the stockholders) and pension plan action (plan amendment) will be required.
- The plan is transferred away from the acquired entity (e.g., to a parent corporation that is selling one of its subsidiaries).
- The transaction is set up so the seller retains plan sponsorship.

In this situation, if the plan is *not* assumed, employees might end up forfeiting benefits that had not vested as of the time of the sale. However, if the transaction has the effect of a partial termination of the plan, vesting will be required.

In contrast, in an asset sale, the buyer is traditionally deemed to assume only the specific liabilities it agrees to assume. Thus, the buyer becomes a successor plan sponsor only if it takes action to become one, such as adopting the existing plan or a plan that is a spin-off of the existing plan. (A spin-off divides one plan into two or more; for instance, if a company assigns a spun-off plan to each of several divisions.) There are several reasons why the asset buyer might prefer not to adopt the seller's plan. It might be underfunded, or be associated with other liabilities, or might be inconsistent with the buyer's existing deferred compensation plans.

Nevertheless, companies planning asset purchases should beware: Some recent court cases make them liable for pension liabilities such as the asset seller's unpaid pension contributions and termination liability—even if the asset buyer did not expressly assume them, and even if it is not a successor under general principles governing corporate transitions, if there is continuity of operations and the seller bought the assets knowing that the liabilities existed.

T.D. 8928, 66 FR 1843 (1/10/01) provides that, when a corporation makes an asset sale (e.g., of substantially all the assets of a trade or business, or an asset as substantial as a factory or a corporate division) it is treated as the successor employer if the seller entirely ceases to provide group health plans, and the buyer maintains business operations using the assets. A transfer (e.g., in bankruptcy) is considered an asset sale if it has the same effect as a sale would have.

The plans that the seller maintained prior to the transaction could be retained, frozen, or terminated. A buyer who adopts an existing plan could agree to assume liability only going forward, with the seller retaining liability for violations of the plan rules that occurred before the sale. As for plans maintained by the buyer prior to the transaction, there might be a merger between the buyer's and seller's plans. (See ¶31.3 for a discussion of the anticutback rules and the requirement of crediting prior service to the new plan.)

There are exceptions to this rule. If the transaction is in effect a merger rather than an asset sale, liabilities will be characterized as they would be in a merger. If the buying corporation is a mere continuation of the selling corporation, or if the transaction is a fraud intended to escape liability, the transaction will be disregarded.

If only plan assets, and not the operating terms of the two plans, are merged, then the transaction is not considered a plan amendment that has the effect of reducing plan accruals. However, if the plans merge and one adopts the other's formulas and definitions, the original plan is deemed to have been amended, so if benefits are reduced notice must be given under ERISA §204.

31.3 THE ANTICUTBACK RULE

Code §411(d)(6) forbids amendments that reduce accrued benefits, including early retirement benefits and the availability of additional payout options in addition to the required QPSA and QJSA. If a plan is spun off, the spin-off plan is required to maintain the old plan's payment options as to benefits accrued before the spin-off. In a merger, employees are permitted to retain their premerger payout options. The practical effect is that, if the merged plan wants to have a single payout structure, it must improve the less-favorable plan to equal the options offered under the more-favorable plan.

Section 411(a)(10)(B) requires that individuals who had three years of service before the corporate transition are entitled to keep the old vesting schedule, if it is more favorable to them than the newly adopted one. Employers have an obligation to inform employees of this choice.

Also see §414(l): If plans (even plans maintained by the same employer) merge or consolidate, or a plan's assets and liabilities are transferred to another plan, each participant's benefit immediately after the transition, calculated on a termination basis, must be at least as great as his or her benefit would have been if the plan had terminated immediately before the transition. The regulations for this section say that a transfer of assets and liabilities from one plan to another will be treated as a spin-off followed by a merger. (Therefore, Form 5310-A will probably have to be filed at least 30 days before the merger, spin-off, or asset transfer.)

> **➠ TIP**
>
> Code §414 has separate rules for merging two defined contribution plans; two defined benefit plans; and one plan of each type, to make sure that participants' entitlement to benefits is not reduced by the transaction. There are further requirements to be observed if one of the plans is underfunded and the other one is fully funded.

31.4 THE MINIMUM PARTICIPATION RULE

Initially, minimum participation rules were applied to both defined contribution and defined benefit plans. However, the Small Business Job Protection Act of 1996 provides that, as of January 1, 1997, only defined benefit plans are required to have a minimum number or percentage of participants.

In the transition context, this is significant because it's common for asset buyers to decline to adopt the seller's plan. If the plan is not adopted, there is a risk that the new plan will not cover the mandated 50 employees or 40% of the workforce.

Some relief is available under Code §410(b)(6)(C), which allows one year after an acquisition or the disposition of a corporation to satisfy the minimum participation requirement. After that, however, the plan is likely to become disqualified (unless it has been terminated in the interim).

A possible strategy is to freeze the plan—but that creates difficulties if too many participants choose to cash out. Another option is to merge both (or all) the plans into a larger plan, no later than the fifteenth day of the tenth month after the end of the plan year. The new plan must offer a benefit structure at least as favorable as the most favorable of the merged plans.

31.5 OTHER PENSION ISSUES

If Employer #2 maintains the plan of its predecessor, Employer #1, then service with Employer #1 is credited as service with Employer #2: See Code §414(a)(1). The "same desk" rule provides that separation from service does not occur [with respect to 401(k) in-service distributions or §402(e) lump sums] if the employee holds the same job after the former employer goes through a liquidation, merger, consolidation, or sale of assets.

One fairly common plan provision permits plan participants who have not yet reached retirement age to take plan distributions upon "termination of employment." Courts are split as to whether a change in control of the employer corporation serves as termination of employment for this purpose. It might be worthwhile to draft or amend your company's plan to specify that sale of the business does not operate as termination of employment as long as the employee continues to work for the buyer of the business.

Because the underlying purpose of pension plans is providing postretirement financial security, "in-service distributions" (distributions from the plan while the individual is still working) are severely discouraged by the Internal Revenue Code. There are some special rules governing taxation of in-service distributions when a plan is undergoing transition. Regulation §1.401-1(b)(1)(i) provides that defined benefit plans are forbidden to make in-service distributions to employees before their retirement or termination of employment—unless the plan itself is terminated.

On the other hand, a defined contribution plan other than a 401(k) plan can use the "2 year/5 year" rule: that is, contributions can be withdrawn from the plan after the contributions have been in the plan for two years or the participant has five years of plan participation.

Revenue Procedure 2000-27, 2000-21 IRB 1016 alters the prior rules. The Revenue Procedure permits distribution of a participant's 401(k) asset balance for "separation from service" whenever substantially all the assets of a trade or business are sold to an unrelated buyer—even if, in fact, most of the employees continue to work for the successor corporation.

Private Letter Ruling (PLR) 200101037 (10/11/00) [Discussed in http://www.ebia.com/weekly/articles/401k010111AssetSales.html] follows the lead of Revenue Ruling 2000-27, but it limits the application of the "same desk" rule after some asset sales (but not after stock transactions or instances of outsourcing of business functions). The PLR addresses distributions from two successive corporate transactions. In the first, Company A merges with Company B, and A and its subsidiaries survive as wholly-owned subsidiaries of B. Less than 85% of the assets of A and its subsidiaries were sold to C, which hired many people who had been A employees. The 401(k) plans of A had already been merged into the B 401(k) plans. In this situation, the PLR says that Revenue Procedure 2000-27 still applies to the sale to C.

In *Dycus v. PBGC*, 133 F.3d 1367 (10th Cir. 1998), a plant closed and then was reopened by a new owner, who required employees to reapply for their jobs, cut wages, reduced benefits, and changed the seniority schedule. Notwithstanding these changes, employees were not entitled to early retirement benefits under the company's forced termination provision, because the Tenth Circuit ruled that there had not been a permanent shutdown triggering the entitlement to early retirement benefits.

In the view of the Sixth Circuit, a firm's dissolution that makes it impossible for an ex-employee to be reemployed before a five-year break in service elapses does not make the former employee an "affected participant." Therefore, the trustees can lawfully accelerate the forfeiture of his or her non-vested account balance; immediate vesting of the nonvested portion is not required [*Borda v. Hardy, Lewis, Pollard & Page PC*, 138 F.3d 1062 (6th Cir. 1998)]. *Borda* concerns a profit-sharing plan to which the plaintiff contributed salary reductions; employer contributions were made.

The vesting schedule for the profit-sharing plan extends over six or seven years. When Borda ceased to be employed by Hardy et al., he was 40% vested in his profit-sharing account. He could have withdrawn that portion, but he elected to leave the funds within the plan. The 60% of the balance that had not yet vested was placed in a suspense account, so if he went back to work for the Hardy PC within five years, he would have been able to earn additional profit-sharing credits.

However, before the five years were up, the firm dissolved. Borda's viewpoint was that dissolution of the firm made him fully vested—but the Sixth Circuit disagreed. He couldn't have been reemployed by a firm that no longer existed, so he could not be characterized as an "affected participant."

Notification

63 FR 68678 (12/14/98), in question-and-answer form, contains rules for giving ERISA §204(h) notice to plan participants. Question 15 says that whether 204(h) notice is required in connection with the sale of a business depends on whether any plan amendment reducing future benefit accruals is adopted.

However, as the four examples given in the Final Rule show, there are circumstances in which the corporation's (or surviving corporation's) obligation to pay pension benefits decreases for practical purposes, even though there has been no amendment adopted that is subject to ERISA 204(h), and therefore there is no obligation to give notice.

Example 4 in the Final Rule concerns a corporation that maintains several plans, including a plan covering employees of a particular division. The plan states that further benefit accruals cease if the employees cease to be employees of the parent corporation. The parent sells all of the assets of the division to another corporation, which also maintains the pension plan, but one with a much lower rate of future benefit accruals than the division's original plan. Then the division's plan is merged into the plan maintained by the corporation that purchases the division. 204(h) notice to the division's employees is not required, because they are no longer employees of the original parent corporation. They are now employees of the purchaser corporation, and future benefit accruals will be calculated under the less generous formula of the purchaser corporation.

The Pension and Welfare Benefits Administration (PWBA) has its own provision for informing employees of the effect of a transition on their pension and welfare benefits. The DOL agency has published a 32-page booklet, "Pension and Health Care Coverage: Questions and Answers for Dislocated Workers." It explains HIPAA and COBRA rights as well as ERISA pension rights. You may wish to add this booklet to your intranet or make copies available in the wake of a layoff or corporate transition. You can suggest that employees call (800) 998-7542 (the PWBA hotline) for free single copies; the text can be downloaded from http://www.dol.gov/dol/pwba.

PBGC's Technical Update 00-3 [see "PBGC Issues Guidance on Business Transactions Early Warning Program," *Deloitte & Touche Human Capital I.Q.*, http://www.us.deloitte.com/pub/iq/vol17/iq04.htm.] explains PBGC's Early

Warning Program, under which plan sponsors engaged in a merger, acquisition, spin-off, or other transaction that affects a defined benefit plan can report to the PBGC if there are factors that could weaken the pension plan (e.g., breaking up a controlled group; transferring liabilities out of a plan that is substantially underfunded).

31.5.1 Tax Aspects of the Transition

Assuming that, after a merger, liquidation, or reorganization, the surviving company maintains the qualified plan of the predecessor corporation, the general rule (under Code §381) is that the original plan's tax attributes are passed on to the successor plan. If two qualified plans consolidate, the deductions taken by each employer before the consolidation will not be retroactively disqualified by the consolidation. Furthermore, the surviving corporation will be able to carry over the predecessor plan's excess contributions and deduct it in its own operation of the plan.

The acquiring corporation can keep up the plan for the benefit of those covered by it under the old ownership—and with no obligation to extend the plan to cover the people who were its own employees before the acquisition.

If the acquirer maintains an existing profit-sharing or stock bonus plan, adds an existing profit-sharing or stock bonus plan to its own preexisting plan, or substitutes a comparable plan for the plan formerly maintained by the acquired corporation, the acquirer can make and deduct "catch-up" contributions equal to the difference between the maximum contribution to the plan (15% of aggregate employee compensation) and the amount the original employer actually contributed.

➡ TIP

If the buyer makes severance payments to employees of the seller, as part of the transaction, it may have to capitalize those payments instead of deducting them currently. In contrast, severance payments that a company makes in the course of downsizing do *not* have to be capitalized.

Revenue Procedure 99-50, 1999-52 IRB 757 explains both a standard and a separate elective procedure for preparing 1099s and some other tax forms, after a successor business acquires substantially all of the property used in the predecessor's company's trade or business, or a separate unit of the predecessor company's trade or business, in a merger or acquisition.

The procedure also applies to withholding, under IRC §3405, on certain periodic, nonperiodic, and rollover distributions from pension plans, and to the use of Form 5498 to report contributions to Medical Savings Accounts, IRAs, Roth IRAs, and small companies' simplified employee pension plans.

Applicability of Rev.Proc. 99-50 is limited to situations in which the predecessor corporation has the obligation to file the documents during the part of the year before the acquisition, and the predecessor doesn't make any payments or withhold or collect any taxes after the acquisition.

The standard procedure, under Rev.Proc. 99-50, is that **both** predecessor and successor companies must file 1099, 5498, and other relevant forms for the year of the acquisition. Obviously, this could be burdensome, so the alternative procedure allows the predecessor and successor to agree that the successor company will undertake the entire reporting burden for the year of the acquisition.

Rev.Proc. 99-45, 1999-49 IRB 603 (12/6/99) provides that, for certain mergers between defined benefit plans, one of which is much larger than the other (i.e., the smaller plan's liabilities are less than 3% of the larger plan's **assets**), the IRS will automatically approve merger-related changes in the surviving plan's funding method. Even in other mergers, the IRS will automatically approve valuation method changes for plans that have the same plan year, if the merger occurs on the first or last day of the plan year, and if the valuation date is either the first or last day of the plan year.

> **TIP**
>
> If a company acquires a second company that was liable for Federal Unemployment Act (FUTA) tax (and nearly all employers are), the acquiring company can claim a credit against its own FUTA tax for the state unemployment taxes paid by the predecessor.

At the employee level, *LTV Steel Co. v. U.S.*, 42 Fed.Cl. 65 (Fed. Cl. 1998), provides that FICA and FUTA taxes do not apply to payments from a separate trust set up to replace benefits lost because of termination or insolvency of plans. This case arose when the PBGC terminated four LTV defined benefit plans. The PBGC benefits were much lower than the amount that the company promised its workers. LTV entered into a settlement with the United Steelworkers, agreeing to establish a trust to make up the difference.

31.6 REPORTING REQUIREMENTS

In many cases, IRS Form 5310-A will have to be filed 30 days or more before a merger, consolidation, or transfer of plan assets or liabilities, if the transition involves transfer of assets from one qualified retirement plan to another. The exceptions include transactions that come under Regulation §1.414(1)-1(d): defined contribution plan mergers and spin-offs; de minimis mergers and spin-off transactions involving defined benefit plans.

Changes in the ownership or form of ownership of the corporation sponsoring the plan will frequently be "reportable events" that must be reported to the PBGC, as part of the agency's oversight of plans that might be or become unable to pay their benefits. [See §13.12 (main volume).]

Also see ERISA §§4062(f) and 4069(b). The reorganization of a plan's contributing sponsor renders the successor corporation responsible for certain plan liabilities (e.g., the plan's accumulated funding deficiencies, including those previously waived by the IRS).

A party who engages in a transaction within five years before a plan termination, if the intention of the transaction was to evade liability in connection with the plan, thereby becomes a contributing sponsor who is liable for such amounts. (In other words, the transaction has precisely the opposite effect of what was intended.)

An employer who terminates operations at a facility, leading to separation from service of 20% or more of the plan participants, must either fund the plan's guaranteed benefits immediately or make provisions for the funding. [This is also likely to be a WARN Act event; see ¶18.11 (main volume).]

FASB tackles the treatment of stock options post-acquisition in "Stock Compensation: Interpretation of Opinion 25," http://www.rutgers.edu/Accounting/raw/fasb/project/stockcom.html.

Question 17, which says that when one business purchases another, and the acquiror corporation grants stock options in exchange for outstanding vested options of the acquired corporation (or options that vest precisely because a change of control has occurred), the fair market value of the options in the acquiring corporation's stock is part of the purchase price for the acquired corporation.

Therefore, accounting treatment is determined by APB Opinion 16, "Business Combinations," not Opinion 25, which usually disposes of stock option issues. But nonvested options granted by the acquiring corporation in exchange for nonvested options in the acquired corporation's stock fall under Opinion 25.

31.7 TREATMENT OF EARLY RETIREMENT SUBSIDIES

Defined benefit plan early retirement subsidies typically call for two forms of qualification: a minimum age, and a minimum amount of service with the employer. What happens in a corporate transition for those who have not met the requirements for the subsidy at the time of the transition but continue to work for the successor employer?

Two cases from 1993 deal with this issue. The Third Circuit case says that if the new employer purchases the old employer's assets and assumes its liabilities, promising to maintain the former benefit package, plan participants can aggregate service with both employers and claim the subsidy as soon as they reach the minimum service.

On the other hand, the Eighth Circuit case involves the sale of a corporate division where the sale agreement made it clear that service with the first employer counted for vesting only, not for any other purposes. Thus, pre- and postsale service could not be aggregated to determine eligibility for the early retirement subsidy.

31.8 TRANSITIONS IN LABOR LAW

At one end of the spectrum, some transitions are clearly legitimate: A firm is failing until someone from outside takes it over, hoping to turn around; a corporation's founder wants to retire and sells the business to someone else; two companies with common interests form a merger. At the other end of the spectrum are paper transactions that have no real practical consequences but are merely a sham to prevent the operation of otherwise-applicable laws or to get rid of an unwanted obligation.

As Chapter 18 in the main volume discusses, it is significant who counts as an "employer" for labor law purposes. "Employees" are entitled to organize and take concerted action to protect their rights against their "employers." Furthermore, if a transaction lacks real substance, the successor may be required to assume the labor-law obligations of its predecessor. The main test is whether there has been a significant practical change, or whether operations in effect continue other than a nominal change in ownership.

31.8.1 Labor Law Implications of Choice of Form

Labor law follows the basic rule that a merger or sale of stock obligates the acquiring company to assume the liabilities of the acquired or selling company, and this includes Collective Bargaining Agreement (CBAs). But in an asset sale, the CBA is not assumed unless the purchaser voluntarily takes it on, or unless there is another reason to view the buyer as a successor or surrogate of the seller. Yet even if a company is not fully bound by its predecessor's CBA, it may still have a duty to bargain with the existing union in good faith—if there is continuity linking the old and new enterprises.

In addition to situations in which one entity replaces another, two or more enterprises can be viewed as a "single employer" for labor law purposes, or one might be treated as an alter ego (surrogate) of the other. If a parent company and its subsidiary engage in the same line of business, the NLRB will probably treat them as only a single enterprise, not two. Furthermore, "joint employers" that are separate entities that share decision making about labor issues may be treated together by the NLRB.

To summarize, it is important either to be prepared to undertake the predecessor's union contracts and other labor law obligations or to structure the transition in a way that leaves the surviving or successor operation free of these obligations. Also note that a change in corporate ownership (even if corporate structure remains the same) may lead to revocation of state-granted privilege to self-insure for Worker's Compensation claims.

Note that a new company that adopts an existing operation can unilaterally change the wage scale, unless it's "perfectly clear" that the new owner will hire all of the old employees. In a "perfectly clear" case where the new owner does not consult with the union and there is no evidence of what would have emerged if there had been negotiations, the employees are given the benefit of the doubt: It's assumed that the former wage rate would have continued, without diminution. Thus, new ownership in a "perfectly clear" case cannot lead to wage cuts without union acquiescence.

In late 1999, the Third Circuit held that a bankrupt company remained liable for retroactive wage payments under a collective bargaining agreement, even though the collective bargaining agreement was supposedly assigned in conjunction with the sale of the company's assets.

Under Bankruptcy Code §365(k), a debtor can avoid liability for contract obligations only if there has been a complete assignment of both rights and duties under those contracts. In this case, the purchaser specifically disavowed responsibility for those retroactive payments. The effect of the transaction was an attempt to unilaterally amend the collective bargaining agreement, which is forbidden by Bankruptcy Code §1133(f): *American Flint Glass Workers Union v. Anchor Resolution Corp.*, 68 LW 1324 (3rd Cir. 11/24/99).

31.8.2 CBA Bars

Generally speaking, the existence of a valid, ongoing collective bargaining agreement will constitute a bar to holding another representation election (although a petition can be filed during a "window" period before the existing contract expires). A CBA bars a new election in a merger or acquisition if the new operation carries on the old business; it is not a bar if the result is an entirely new operation that makes major personnel changes. A CBA is not a bar when a successor employer comes in and the successor does not issue a written assumption of the existing agreement.

31.9 TRANSITIONS AND UNEMPLOYMENT INSURANCE

Although it is a comparatively minor cost, the acquiror of a business may wish to take advantage of amounts of FUTA tax already paid by the transferor of the business during the portion of the year prior to the transfer to the new owner. [See ¶18.15 (main volume) for a more detailed discussion of FUTA compliance.] The successor employer can rely on wages paid by the predecessor employer (and thus on FUTA payments made by the predecessor) if either one of two circumstances exists. The first is that the transferee acquires substantially all the property used in the transferor's entire trade or business (or in a separate unit of the trade or business). The other is that, whether or not the property was acquired, at least one employee from the old business remains employed immediately after the transfer.

The IRS's view (for FICA and tax withholding as well as FUTA) is that, in a statutory merger or consolidation, the surviving corporation is the same taxpayer and the same corporation as the predecessor corporation(s). Of course, that means that the successor will have to pay any taxes due but unpaid by the predecessor—unless the successor gives the local administrative agency adequate written notice. (The form should be available from the agency.)

However, state unemployment laws usually provide that companies remain subject to unemployment insurance laws for at least two years once they have acquired an experience rating—with the result that the transferor may remain liable in a year after it ceases operations, unless it applies to the local administrative agency for a determination that it is no longer an employer.

TIP

Usually, in a multistate operation, wages paid in the various states can be combined for FUTA purposes.

If the predecessor has acquired a good experience rating, the successor will probably be able to acquire the experience rating with the rest of the operation, as long as operations remain more or less the same, at the original business location, and the workforce remains stable. (Altering these important factors in effect means that there is a new enterprise, which must acquire its own experience rating.)

31.10 CORPORATE CULTURE AND HR'S ROLE IN TRANSITION PLANNING

In 1998 alone, there were almost 11,500 merger or acquisition transactions, with an aggregate value over $1.6 trillion. Unfortunately, however, many of these transactions must be "unwound," or remain in force but disappoint one or more participants. According to Mark Herndon of Watson Wyatt Worldwide, 70% of mergers and acquisitions fall short of the financial goals for the deal. Almost half of the executives of acquired companies leave within a year, and by three years posttransaction, 75% of the former managers are gone. The deal can reduce productivity within the target company by 50%, and it can take up to three years to reconcile the corporate cultures.

For instance, the acquired company might have had a highly automated expense processing system, and a low-level manager might be able to spend up to $5000 without approval. Chaos ensues if the acquiring company relies on advance approval, using a paper form, and demands that the paperwork be completed for every purchase over $500.

Sometimes the business logic for the combination is faulty; in many cases, the problem is irreconcilability of corporate cultures. Earlier and deeper involvement of both companies' HR departments could have smoothed the transition. HR also plays a part in transactions that are contemplated but not consummated, by pointing out potential problems.

Transactions that can affect a corporation's continued existence or can change its form require "due diligence": It's the duty of the corporation's board of directors to study the transaction thoroughly, and recommend it only if it is in the best interests of the stockholders (and perhaps of other constituencies, such as employees, retirees, and the community as a whole). So it's important to determine if a potential merger partner is guilty of discrimination, labor law violations (e.g., unlawful union busting), or wage and hour violations. Even if the potential partner has behaved lawfully in every respect, it may have a more generous pension or benefit structure, which may have to be maintained as to current employees. The plan's investment performance could be poor (requiring additional funding from the employer to maintain promised levels); its actuarial assumptions could be defective.

Corporate culture issues are discussed in *HR Magazine*'s April 1999 issue, especially Bill Leonard's "Will This Marriage Work?" (p. 35) and Robert J. Grossman's "Irreconcilable Differences," (p. 42).

A later *HR Magazine* article, Paul L. Gilles' "Gaining Control During Changes in Control," (6/99, p. 98) looks at the impact of the risk of acquisition or merger on corporate recruitment. The risk makes it hard to attract top candidates, because they realistically fear losing their new jobs in a corporate shake-up. Therefore, employment agreements with sought-after candidates often include "golden parachutes" (offering generous compensation if the employee loses his or her job because of an acquisition or merger) and "golden handcuffs" (retention bonuses that are lost if the employee quits shortly after being hired).

Most such programs have a double rather than a single trigger. That is, they do not take effect when employees voluntarily quit, only when they suffer involuntary job loss.

Gilles advises the corporation to assess its objectives in drafting one of these "gold" plans. For instance, the objective might be to preserve employees' job rights; to deter unwanted takeover attempts; or to make top management concentrate on maximizing shareholder value.

A modified double trigger plan contains a window period, during which payments will be made even if the employee quits voluntarily. The window is often located in the thirteenth month of the agreement, when the 20% excise tax on excess parachute payments can be minimized. Companies that are extremely eager to acquire the services of a particular top executive may even agree to "gross up" the payment: i.e., to take over payment of the excise tax on excess parachute payments.

Parachute payments deal with the risk that current top management will be fired if there's a change in control. The acquiror may face the opposite problem: that managers whose skills are needed for success will quit because of the transition.

A "stay bonus" (a tool for retaining the management team after a transition) is a fixed benefit (and therefore is a fixed incremental cost for the buyer of the business). The bonus is paid if the employee remains for a certain period of time. It could also be combined with a golden parachute: for instance, the executive could be offered two months' salary as a bonus for staying a year, or given a severance package of three months' salary and outplacement assistance if terminated without good cause within 18 months of the transition.

The employer probably wants to pay severance as a lump sum and get it over with, but there are some advantages to a payment stream. For one thing, later payments can be contingent on the ex-employee not doing anything to hassle the ex-employer; keeping people on the payroll can also lower unemployment insurance costs. However, it is harder to keep track of and requires accruing a liability in the financial statements.

In the case of *Noorily v. Thomas & Betts Corp.*, 1999 WL 643363 (3rd Cir. 1999), Thomas & Betts bought a New Jersey company, then announced relocation of core functions to Memphis. Thomas & Betts' President announced that engineers refusing reassignment to Memphis had voluntarily resigned and therefore were not eligible for severance pay. The engineers sued, and prevailed at the District Court level. However, the Third Circuit viewed the characterization of the engineers as essential to the relocated company as a valid business decision, so severance benefits could legitimately be denied.

Chapter 32

FORMS

SPD NOTICE OF PBGC COVERAGE [SOURCE: 63 FR 48386 (9/9/98)]

Your pension benefits under this plan are insured by the Pension Benefit Guaranty Corporation (PBGC), a federal insurance agency. If the plan terminates (ends) without enough money to pay all benefits, the PBGC will step in to pay pension benefits. Most people receive all of the pension benefits they would have received under their plan, but some people may lose certain benefits.

The PBGC guarantee generally covers (1) normal and early retirement benefits; (2) disability benefits if you become disabled before the plan terminates; and (3) certain benefits for your survivors.

The PBGC guarantee generally does not cover (1) benefits greater than the maximum guaranteed amount set by law for the year in which the plan terminates; (2) some or all of benefit increases and new benefits based on plan provisions that have been in place for fewer than five years at the time the plan terminates; (3) benefits that are not vested because you have not worked long enough for the company; (4) benefits for which you have not met all of the requirements at the time the plan terminates; (5) certain early retirement payments (such as supplemental payments that stop when you become eligible for Social Security) that result in an early retirement monthly benefit greater than your monthly benefit at the plan's normal retirement age; and (6) nonpension benefits, such as health insurance, life insurance, certain death benefits, vacation pay, and severance pay.

Even if certain of your benefits are not guaranteed, you still may receive some of those benefits from the PBGC depending on how much money your plan has and on how much the PBGC collects from employers.

For more information about the PBGC and the benefits it guarantees, ask your plan administrator or contact the PBGC's Technical Assistance Division, 1200

K Street NW Suite 930, Washington, DC 20005-4026, or call 202-326-4000 (not a toll-free number). TTY/TDD users may call the federal relay service toll-free at 1-800-877-8339 and ask to be connected to 202-326-4000. Additional information about the PBGC's pension insurance program is available through the PBGC's Web site at http://www.pbgc.gov.

SPD NOTICE OF ERISA RIGHTS [SOURCE: 63 FR 48386 (9/9/98); DELETE ITEMS OF INFORMATION THAT ARE NOT APPLICABLE TO YOUR PLAN]

As a participant in (name of plan) you are entitled to certain rights and protections under the Employee Retirement Income Security Act of 1974 (ERISA). ERISA provides that all plan participants shall be entitled to

> Examine, without charge, at the plan administrator's office and at other specified locations, such as worksites and union halls, all documents governing the plan, including insurance contracts and collective bargaining agreements, and a copy of the latest annual report (Form 5500 Series) filed by the plan with the U.S. Department of Labor.
>
> Obtain, upon written request to the plan administrator, copies of documents governing the operation of the plan, including insurance contracts and collective bargaining agreements, and copies of the latest annual report (Form 5500 Series) and updated summary plan description. The administrator may make a reasonable charge for the copies.
>
> Receive a summary of the plan's annual financial report. The plan administrator is required by law to furnish each participant with a copy of this summary annual report.
>
> Obtain a statement telling you whether you have a right to receive a pension at normal retirement age (age * * *) and, if so, what your benefits would be at normal retirement age if you stop working under the plan now. If you do not have a right to a pension, the statement will tell you how many more years you have to work to get a right to a pension. This statement must be requested in writing and is not required to be given more than once every twelve (12) months. The plan must provide the statement free of charge.
>
> Continue health care coverage for yourself, spouse, or dependents if there is a loss of coverage under the plan as a result of a qualifying event. You or your dependents may have to pay for such coverage. Review this summary plan description and the documents governing the plan on the rules governing your COBRA continuation coverage rights.

Reduction or elimination of exclusionary periods of coverage for preexisting conditions under your group health plan, if you have creditable coverage from another plan. You should be provided a certificate of creditable coverage, free of charge, from your group health plan or health insurance issuer when you lose coverage under the plan, when you become entitled to elect COBRA continuation coverage, when your COBRA continuation coverage ceases, if you request it before losing coverage, or if you request it up to 24 months after losing coverage. Without evidence of creditable coverage, you may be subject to a preexisting condition exclusion for 12 months (18 months for late enrollees) after your enrollment date in your coverage.

In addition to creating rights for plan participants, ERISA imposes duties upon the people who are responsible for the operation of the employee benefit plan. The people who operate your plan, called "fiduciaries" of the plan, have a duty to do so prudently and in the interest of you and other plan participants and beneficiaries. No one, including your employer, your union, or any other person, may fire you or otherwise discriminate against you in any way to prevent you from obtaining a (pension, welfare) benefit or exercising your rights under ERISA. If your claim for a (pension, welfare) benefit is denied in whole or in part, you must receive a written explanation of the reason for the denial. You have the right to have the plan review and reconsider your claim. Under ERISA, there are steps you can take to enforce the above rights. For instance, if you request materials from the plan and do not receive them within 30 days, you may file suit in a federal court. In such a case, the court may require the plan administrator to provide the materials and pay you up to $110 a day until you receive the materials, unless the materials were not sent because of reasons beyond the control of the administrator. If you have a claim for benefits which is denied or ignored, in whole or in part, you may file suit in a state or federal court. In addition, if you disagree with the plan's decision or lack thereof concerning the qualified status of a domestic relations order or medical child support order, you may file suit in federal court. If it should happen that plan fiduciaries misuse the plan's money, or if you are discriminated against for asserting your rights, you may seek assistance from the U.S. Department of Labor, or you may file suit in a federal court. The court will decide who should pay court costs and legal fees. If you are successful the court may order the person you have sued to pay these costs and fees. If you lose, the court may order you to pay these costs and fees: for example, if it finds your claim is frivolous.

If you should have any questions about your plan, you should contact the plan administrator. If you have any questions about this statement or about your rights under ERISA, you should contact the nearest office of the Pension and Welfare Benefits Administration, U.S. Department of Labor, listed in your telephone directory, or the Division of Technical Assistance and Inquiries, Pension and Welfare Benefits Administration, U.S. Department of Labor, 200 Constitution Avenue N.W., Washington, DC 20210.

Federal Register / Vol. 65, No. 249 / Wednesday, December 27, 2000 / Rules and Regulations 82167

APPENDIX

NATIONAL MEDICAL SUPPORT NOTICE

PART A

NOTICE TO WITHHOLD FOR HEALTH CARE COVERAGE

This Notice is issued under section 466(a)(19) of the Social Security Act, section 609(a)(5)(C) of the Employee Retirement Income Security Act of 1974 (ERISA), and for State and local government and church plans, sections 401(e) and (f) of the Child Support Performance and Incentive Act of 1998.

Issuing Agency: ______ Issuing Agency Address: ______ ______ Date of Notice: ______ Case Number: ______ Telephone Number: ______ FAX Number:	Court or Administrative Authority: ______ Date of Support Order: ______ Support Order Number: ______

______)
Employer Withholder's Federal EIN Number

______)
Employer Withholder's Name

______)
Employer Withholder's Address

______)
Custodial Parent's Name (Last, First, MI)

______)
Custodial Parent's Mailing Address

______)
Child(ren)'s Mailing Address (if different from Custodial Parent's)

______)
______)
______)
Name, Mailing Address, and Telephone Number of a Representative of the Child(ren)

RE* ______
Employee's Name (Last, First, MI)

______
Employee's Social Security Number

______
Employee's Mailing Address

______
Substituted Official/Agency Name and Address

Child(ren)'s Name(s)	DOB	SSN	Child(ren)'s Name(s)	DOB	SSN
______	______	______	______	______	______
______	______	______	______	______	______
______	______	______	______	______	______

The order requires the child(ren) to be enrolled in [ ] any health coverages available; or [] only the following coverage(s): __Medical; __Dental; __Vision; __Prescription drug; __Mental health; __Other (specify): ______

THE PAPERWORK REDUCTION ACT OF 1995 (P.L. 104-13) Public reporting burden for this collection of information is estimated to average 10 minutes per response, including the time reviewing instructions, gathering and maintaining the data needed, and reviewing the collection of information. An agency may not conduct or sponsor and a person is not required to respond to, a collection of information unless it displays a currently valid OMB control number. OMB control number 0970-0222 Expiration Date 12/31/2003.

82168 Federal Register / Vol. 65, No. 249 / Wednesday, December 27, 2000 / Rules and Regulations

EMPLOYER RESPONSE

If either 1, 2, or 3 below applies, check the appropriate box and return this Part A to the Issuing Agency within 20 business days after the date of the Notice, or sooner if reasonable. NO OTHER ACTION IS NECESSARY. If neither 1, 2, nor 3 applies, forward Part B to the appropriate plan administrator(s) within 20 business days after the date of the Notice, or sooner if reasonable. Check number 4 and return this Part A to the Issuing Agency if the Plan Administrator informs you that the child(ren) is/are enrolled in an option under the plan for which you have determined that the employee contribution exceeds the amount that may be withheld from the employee's income due to State or Federal withholding limitations and/or prioritization.

☐ 1. Employer does not maintain or contribute to plans providing dependent or family health care coverage.

☐ 2. The employee is among a class of employees (for example, part-time or non-union) that are not eligible for family health coverage under any group health plan maintained by the employer or to which the employer contributes.

☐ 3. Health care coverage is not available because employee is no longer employed by the employer:

Date of termination: ______________________

Last known address: ______________________

Last known telephone number: ______________________

New employer (if known): ______________________

New employer address: ______________________

New employer telephone number: ______________________

☐ 4. State or Federal withholding limitations and/or prioritization prevent the withholding from the employee's income of the amount required to obtain coverage under the terms of the plan.

Employer Representative:

Name. ______________________ Telephone Number: ____________

Title: ______________________ Date: ____________

EIN (if not provided by Issuing Agency on Notice to Withhold for Health Care Coverage):______________

INSTRUCTIONS TO EMPLOYER

This document serves as notice that the employee identified on this National Medical Support Notice is obligated by a court or administrative child support order to provide health care coverage for the child(ren) identified on this Notice. This National Medical Support Notice replaces any Medical Support Notice that the Issuing Agency has previously served on you with respect to the employee and the children listed on this Notice.

The document consists of **Part A - Notice to Withhold for Health Care Coverage** for the employer to withhold any employee contributions required by the group health plan(s) in which the child(ren) is/are enrolled; and **Part B - Medical Support Notice to the Plan Administrator**, which must be forwarded to the administrator of each group health plan identified by the employer to enroll the eligible child(ren).

EMPLOYER RESPONSIBILITIES

1. If the individual named above is not your employee, or if family health care coverage is not available, please complete item 1, 2, or 3 of the Employer Response as appropriate, and return it to the Issuing Agency. NO FURTHER ACTION IS NECESSARY.

2. If family health care coverage is available for which the child(ren) identified above may be eligible, you are required to:

   a. Transfer, not later than 20 business days after the date of this Notice, a copy of **Part B - Medical Support Notice to the Plan Administrator** to the administrator of each appropriate group health plan for which the child(ren) may be eligible, and

   b. Upon notification from the plan administrator(s) that the child(ren) is/are enrolled, either

      1) withhold from the employee's income any employee contributions required under each group health plan, in accordance with the applicable law of the employee's principal place of employment and transfer employee contributions to the appropriate plan(s), or

      2) complete item 4 of the Employer Response to notify the Issuing Agency that enrollment cannot be completed because of prioritization or limitations on withholding.

   c. If the plan administrator notifies you that the employee is subject to a waiting period that expires more than 90 days from the date of its receipt of **Part B of** this Notice, or whose duration is determined by a measure other than the passage of time (for example, the completion of a certain number of hours worked), notify the plan administrator when the employee is eligible to enroll in the plan and that this

82170 Federal Register / Vol. 65, No. 249 / Wednesday, December 27, 2000 / Rules and Regulations

Notice requires the enrollment of the child(ren) named in the Notice in the plan.

LIMITATIONS ON WITHHOLDING

The total amount withheld for both cash and medical support cannot exceed ____% of the employee's aggregate disposable weekly earnings. The employer may not withhold more under this National Medical Support Notice than the lesser of:

1. The amounts allowed by the Federal Consumer Credit Protection Act (15 U.S.C., section 1673(b));

2. The amounts allowed by the State of the employee's principal place of employment; or

3. The amounts allowed for health insurance premiums by the child support order, as indicated here:______________________.

The Federal limit applies to the aggregate disposable weekly earnings (ADWE). ADWE is the net income left after making mandatory deductions such as State, Federal, local taxes; Social Security taxes; and Medicare taxes.

PRIORITY OF WITHHOLDING

If withholding is required for employee contributions to one or more plans under this notice and for a support obligation under a separate notice and available funds are insufficient for withholding for both cash and medical support contributions, the employer must withhold amounts for purposes of cash support and medical support contributions in accordance with the law, if any, of the State of the employee's principal place of employment requiring prioritization between cash and medical support, as described here:______________________
____.

DURATION OF WITHHOLDING

The child(ren) shall be treated as dependents under the terms of the plan. Coverage of a child as a dependent will end when similarly situated dependents are no longer eligible for coverage under the terms of the plan. However, the continuation coverage provisions of ERISA may entitle the child to continuation coverage under the plan. The employer must continue to withhold employee contributions and may not disenroll (or eliminate coverage for) the child(ren) unless:

1. The employer is provided satisfactory written evidence that:

    a. The court or administrative child support order referred to above is no longer in effect; or
    b. The child(ren) is or will be enrolled in comparable coverage which will take effect no later than the effective date of disenrollment from the plan; or

2. The employer eliminates family health coverage for all of its employees.

POSSIBLE SANCTIONS

An employer may be subject to sanctions or penalties imposed under State law and/or ERISA for discharging an employee from employment, refusing to employ, or taking disciplinary action against any employee because of medical child support withholding, or for failing to withhold income, or transmit such withheld amounts to the applicable plan(s) as the Notice directs.

NOTICE OF TERMINATION OF EMPLOYMENT

In any case in which the above employee's employment terminates, the employer must promptly notify the Issuing Agency listed above of such termination. This requirement may be satisfied by sending to the Issuing Agency a copy of any notice the employer is required to provide under the continuation coverage provisions of ERISA or the Health Insurance Portability and Accountability Act.

EMPLOYEE LIABILITY FOR CONTRIBUTION TO PLAN

The employee is liable for any employee contributions that are required under the plan(s) for enrollment of the child(ren) and is subject to appropriate enforcement. The employee may contest the withholding under this Notice based on a mistake of fact (such as the identity of the obligor). Should an employee contest the withholding under this Notice, the employer must proceed to comply with the employer responsibilities in this Notice until notified by the Issuing Agency to discontinue withholding. To contest the withholding under this Notice, the employee should contact the Issuing Agency at the address and telephone number listed on the Notice. With respect to plans subject to ERISA, it is the view of the Department of Labor that Federal Courts have jurisdiction if the employee challenges a determination that the Notice constitutes a Qualified Medical Child Support Order.

CONTACT FOR QUESTIONS

If you have any questions regarding this Notice, you may contact the Issuing Agency at the address and telephone number listed above.

Form **5500**

Department of the Treasury
Internal Revenue Service

Department of Labor
Pension and Welfare Benefits Administration

Pension Benefit Guaranty Corporation

Annual Return/Report of Employee Benefit Plan

This form is required to be filed under sections 104 and 4065 of the Employee Retirement Income Security Act of 1974 () and sections 6039D, 6047(e), 6057(b), and 6058(a) of the Internal Revenue Code (the Code).

▶ **Complete all entries in accordance with the instructions to the Form 5500.**

Official Use Only
OMB Nos 1210 – 0110
1210 – 0089

2000

This Form is Open to Public Inspection.

Part I Annual Report Identification Information

For the calendar plan year 2000 or fiscal plan year beginning ________ **and ending** ________,

A This return/report is for: **(1)** ☐ a multiemployer plan; **(2)** ☐ a single-employer plan (other than a multiple-employer plan); **(3)** ☐ a multiple-employer plan; or **(4)** ☐ a DFE (specify) ____

B This return/report is: **(1)** ☐ the first return/report filed for the plan; **(2)** ☐ an amended return/report; **(3)** ☐ the final return/report filed for the plan; **(4)** ☐ a short plan year return/report (less than 12 months).

C If the plan is a collectively-bargained plan, check here ▶ ☐

D If you filed for an extension of time to file, check the box and attach a copy of the extension application . . . . ▶ ☐

Part II Basic Plan Information — enter all requested information.

1a Name of plan

1b Three-digit plan number (PN) ▶

1c Effective date of plan (mo., day, yr.)

2a Plan sponsor's name and address (employer, if for a single-employer plan) (Address should include room or suite no.)

2b Employer Identification Number (EIN)

2c Sponsor's telephone number

2d Business code (see instructions)

Caution: A penalty for the late or incomplete filing of this return/report will be assessed unless reasonable cause is established.

Under penalties of perjury and other penalties set forth in the instructions, I declare that I have examined this return/report including accompanying schedules, statements, and attachments, and to the best of my knowledge and belief, it is true, correct, and complete.

Signature of plan administrator | Date | Typed or printed name of individual signing as plan administrator

Signature of employer/plan sponsor/DFE | Date | Typed or printed name of individual signing as employer, plan sponsor or DFE as applicable

For Paperwork Reduction Act Notice and OMB Control Numbers, see the instructions for Form 5500 v5.2 Form **5500** (2000)

0 2 0 0 0 0 0 1 0 3

Form 5500 (2000) Page **2**

Official Use Only

3a Plan administrator's name and address (If same as plan sponsor, enter "Same")

3b Administrator's EIN

3c Administrator's telephone number

4 If the name and/or EIN of the plan sponsor has changed since the last return/report filed for this plan, enter the name, EIN and the plan number from the last return/report below.

a Sponsor's name

b EIN

c PN

5 Preparer information (optional) **a** Name (including firm name, if applicable) and address

b EIN

c Telephone number

6	Total number of participants at the beginning of the plan year	**6**	
7	Number of participants as of the end of the plan year (welfare plans complete only lines **7a, 7b, 7c,** and **7d**)		
a	Active participants	**7a**	
b	Retired or separated participants receiving benefits	**7b**	
c	Other retired or separated participants entitled to future benefits	**7c**	
d	Subtotal. Add lines **7a, 7b,** and **7c**	**7d**	
e	Deceased participants whose beneficiaries are receiving or are entitled to receive benefits	**7e**	
f	Total. Add lines **7d** and **7e**	**7f**	
g	Number of participants with account balances as of the end of the plan year (only defined contribution plans complete this item)	**7g**	
h	Number of participants that terminated employment during the plan year with accrued benefits that were less than 100% vested	**7h**	
i	If any participant(s) separated from service with a deferred vested benefit, enter the number of separated participants required to be reported on a Schedule SSA (Form 5500)	**7i**	

8 Benefits provided under the plan (complete **8a** through **8c**, as applicable)

a ☐ Pension benefits (check this box if the plan provides pension benefits and enter the applicable pension feature codes from the List of Plan Characteristics Codes printed in the instructions): ☐ ☐ ☐ ☐ ☐ ☐ ☐ ☐ ☐ ☐

b ☐ Welfare benefits (check this box if the plan provides welfare benefits and enter the applicable welfare feature codes from the List of Plan Characteristics Codes printed in the instructions): ☐ ☐ ☐ ☐ ☐ ☐ ☐ ☐ ☐ ☐

c ☐ Fringe benefits (check this box if the plan provides fringe benefits)

9a Plan funding arrangement (check all that apply)

(1) ☐ Insurance

(2) ☐ Code section 412(i) insurance contracts

(3) ☐ Trust

(4) ☐ General assets of the sponsor

9b Plan benefit arrangement (check all that apply)

(1) ☐ Insurance

(2) ☐ Code section 412(i) insurance contracts

(3) ☐ Trust

(4) ☐ General assets of the sponsor

0 2 0 0 0 0 0 2 0 4

Form 5500 (2000) Page **3**

Official Use Only

10 Schedules attached (Check all applicable boxes and, where indicated, enter the number attached. See instructions.)

a Pension Benefit Schedules

- **(1)** ☐ **R** (Retirement Plan Information)
- **(2)** ☐ **T** (Qualified Pension Plan Coverage Information)

  If a Schedule T is not attached because the plan is relying on coverage testing information for a prior year, enter the year ▶ ______
- **(3)** ☐ **B** (Actuarial Information)
- **(4)** ☐ **E** (ESOP Annual Information)
- **(5)** ☐ **SSA** (Separated Vested Participant Information)

b Financial Schedules

- **(1)** ☐ **H** (Financial Information)
- **(2)** ☐ **I** (Financial Information -- Small Plan)
- **(3)** ☐ **A** (Insurance Information)
- **(4)** ☐ **C** (Service Provider Information)
- **(5)** ☐ **D** (DFE/Participating Plan Information)
- **(6)** ☐ **G** (Financial Transaction Schedules)
- **(7)** ☐ ___ **P** (Trust Fiduciary Information)

c Fringe Benefit Schedule

☐ **F** (Fringe Benefit Plan Annual Information)

0 2 0 0 0 0 0 3 0 5

Labor Condition Application for H-1B Nonimmigrants

U.S. Department of Labor
Employment and Training Administration

Form ETA 9035
OMB Approval: 1205-0310
Expiration Date: 19 JAN 2004

A. Employer's Information

! If you want the application returned by mail, leave the Return Fax Number blank.

1. Return Fax Number ( ) -

2. Employer's Full Legal Name

3. Employer's Address (Number and Street)

4. Employer's City State Zip/Postal Code

5. Employer's EIN Number -

6. Employer's Phone Number ( ) - Extension

B. Rate of Pay

1. Wage Rate (or Rate From) (Required): $ .0 0

2. Rate Up To (Optional): $ .0 0

3. Rate is Per:
○ Year ○ Week
○ Month ○ Hour
○ 2 Weeks

4. Is this position part-time?
○ Yes
○ No

! **Please Note: Part-time hours worked by nonimmigrant(s) will be in the range of hours stated on the INS Form(s) I-129.**

C. Period Of Employment and Occupation Information

! **Please Note: The Date Information MUST be in MM/DD/YYYY format**

1. Begin Date / /

2. End Date / /

3. Occupational Code

4. Number of H-1B Nonimmigrants

5. Job Title

D. Information relating to Work Location for the H-1B Nonimmigrants

! **This section is REQUIRED**

1. City State

! **Do NOT write "Same As Above". This section MUST be filled out.**

2. Prevailing Wage $ .0 0

3. Wage is Per:
○ Year ○ Week
○ Month ○ Hour
○ 2 Weeks

4. Wage Source
○ SESA
○ Collective Bargaining Agreement
○ Other

If OTHER is chosen as the Wage Source, Numbers 5 and 6 in this section MUST be filled out.

5. Year Source Published

6. Other Wage Source

Page Link

3	1	3	7	7	5

! **If filing the form electronically, the Page Link field will be automatically created for you upon printing. If filing the form manually, please ensure that the Page Link field contains a 6 digit number that is repeated on all 3 pages.**

26277

Form ETA 9035 - Page 1 of 3

Labor Condition Application for H-1B Nonimmigrants

U.S. Department of Labor
Employment and Training Administration

Form ETA 9035
OMB Approval: 1205-0310
Expiration Date: 19 JAN 2004

D. Subsection A Information For Additional or Subsequent Work Location

! This Section should be completed only if filing for more than 1 work location.

1. City ______ , State ______

2. Prevailing Wage $ ______ . 0 0

3. Wage is Per: ○ Year ○ Week ○ Month ○ Hour ○ 2 Weeks

4. Wage Source: ○ SESA ○ Collective Bargaining Agreement ○ Other

If OTHER is chosen as the Wage Source, Numbers 5 and 6 in this section MUST be filled out.

5. Year Source Published ______

6. Other Wage Source ______

E. Employer Labor Condition Statements

! **Please Note: In order for your application to be processed, you MUST read section E of the Labor Condition Application cover pages under the heading "Employer Labor Condition Statements" and agree to all 4 labor condition statements summarized below:**

(1) Wages: Pay nonimmigrants at least the local prevailing wage or the employer's actual wage, whichever is higher, and pay for non-productive time. Offer nonimmigrants benefits on the same basis as U.S. workers.

(2) Working Conditions: Provide working conditions for nonimmigrants which will not adversely affect the working conditions of workers similarly employed.

(3) Strike, Lockout, or Work Stoppage: No strike or lockout in the occupational classification at the place of employment.

(4) Notice: Notice to union or to workers at the place of employment. A copy of this form to H-1B workers.

I have read and agree to Employer Labor Condition Statements 1, 2, 3, and 4 as set forth in Section E of the Labor Condition Application Cover Pages. ○ Yes ○ No

F. Additional Employer Labor Condition Statments

! **Please Note: In order for your application to be processed, you MUST read Section F - Subsections 1 and 2 of the Labor Condition Application cover pages under the heading "Additional Employer Labor Condition Statements" and choose one of the 3 alternatives (A, B, or C) listed below in Subsection 1. If you mark Alternative B, you MUST read Section F - Subsection 2 of the cover pages under the heading "Additional Employer Labor Condition Statements" and indicate your agreement to all 3 additional statements summarized below in Subsection 2.**

1. Subsection 1
Choose ONE of the following 3 alternatives:

A ○ **Employer is not H-1B dependent and is not a willful violator.**

B ○ **Employer is H-1B dependent and/or a willful violator.**

C ○ **Employer is H-1B dependent and/or a willful violator BUT will use this application ONLY to support H-1B petitions for exempt nonimmigrants.**

2. Subsection 2
If Alternative B in Subsection 1 is marked, the following Additional Labor Condition Statements are applicable:

A. **Displacement: Non-displacement of the U.S. workers in employer's work force;**

B. **Secondary Displacement: Non-displacement of U.S. workers in another employer's work force; and**

C. **Recruitment and Hiring: Recruitment of U.S. workers and hiring of U.S. worker applicant(s) who are equally or better qualified than the H-1B nonimmigrant(s).**

I have read and agree to Additional Labor Conditional Statements 2 A, B, and C. ○ Yes ○ No

Page Link: 3 1 3 7 7 5

! **If filing the form electronically, the Page Link field will be automatically created for you upon printing. If filing the form manually, please ensure that the Page Link field contains a 6 digit number that is repeated on all 3 pages.**

26277

Labor Condition Application for H-1B Nonimmigrants

U.S. Department of Labor
Employment and Training Administration

Form ETA 9035
OMB Approval: 1205-0310
Expiration Date: 19 JAN 2004

G. Public Disclosure Information

Public disclosure information will be kept at:

! You must choose one of the two options listed in this Section.

○ Employer's principal place of business

○ Place of employment

H. Declaration of Employer

! **By signing this form, I, on behalf of the employer, attest that the information and labor condition statements provided are true and accurate; that I have read the sections E and F of the cover pages (Form ETA 9035CP), and that I agree to comply with the Labor Condition Statements as set forth in the cover pages and with the Department of Labor regulations (20 CFR part 655, Subparts H and I). I agree to make this applicaton, supporting documentation, and other records, available to officials of the Department of Labor upon request during any investigation under the Immigration and Nationality Act.**

1. First Name of Hiring or Other Designated Official ______ MI __

2. Last Name of Hiring or Other Designated Official ______

3. Hiring or Other Designated Official Title ______

4. Signature - Do NOT let signature extend beyond the box

5. Date __ / __ / ____

I. Contact Information

1. Contact First Name ______ MI __

2. Contact Last Name ______

3. Contact Phone Number (___) ___ - ____ Extension ____

J. U.S. Government Agency Use Only

By virtue of my signature below, I hereby acknowledge this application certified for

Date Starting ______ and Date Ending ______

Signature and Title of Authorized DOL Official ______ ETA Case Number ______ Date ______

The Department of Labor is not the guarantor of the accuracy, truthfulness, or adequacy of a certified labor condition application.

K. Complaints

Complaints alleging misrepresentation of material facts in the labor condition application and/or failure to comply with the terms of the labor condition application may be filed with any office of the Wage and Hour Division of the United States Department of Labor. Complaints alleging failure to offer employment to an equally or better qualified U.S. worker, or an employer's misrepresentation regarding such offer(s) of employment, may be filed with: U.S Department of Justice * 10th Street and Constitution Avenue, NW * Washington, DC * 20530.

Page Link: 3 1 3 7 7 5

! **If filing the form electronically, the Page Link field will be automatically created for you upon printing. If filing the form manually, please ensure that the Page Link field contains a 6 digit number that is repeated on all 3 pages.**

26277

INDEX

L

M

N

O

P

Q

R

S

T

U

V

W